To:
ALL THE HOFERS:

Thankyou very much
for having me I had a
great time. You were all fantastic
to meet I hope to see you all

♡ Marie

Steve Parish

CELEBRATING AUSTRALIA

THE WEST

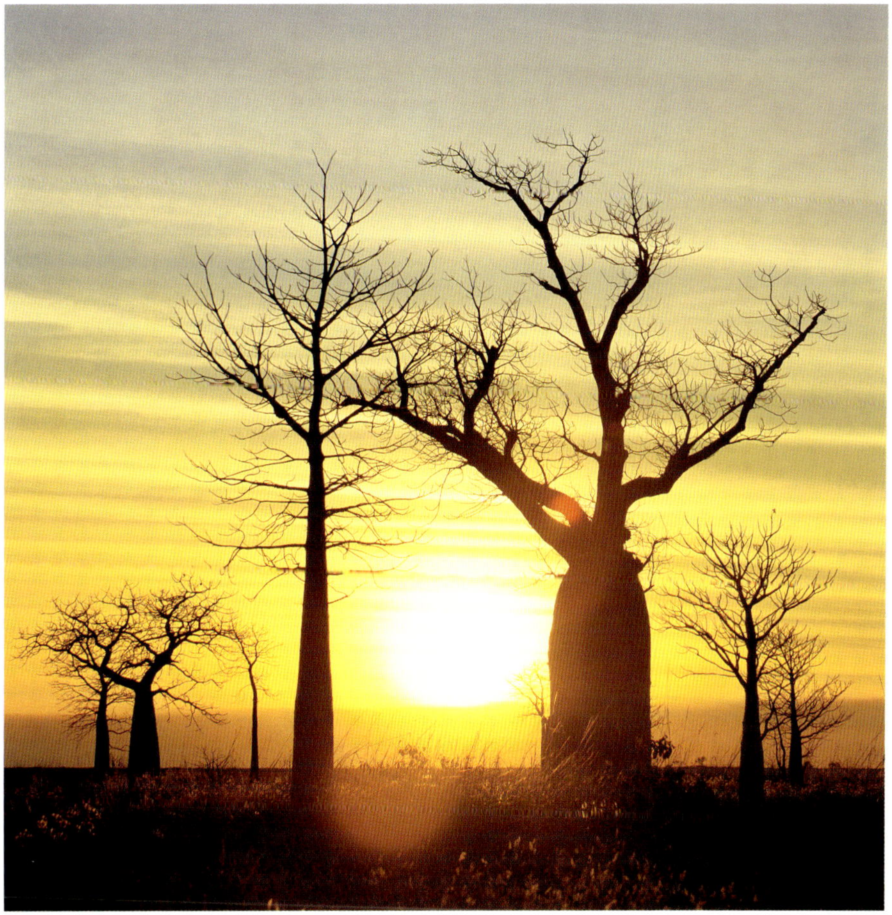

Steve Parish
PUBLISHING

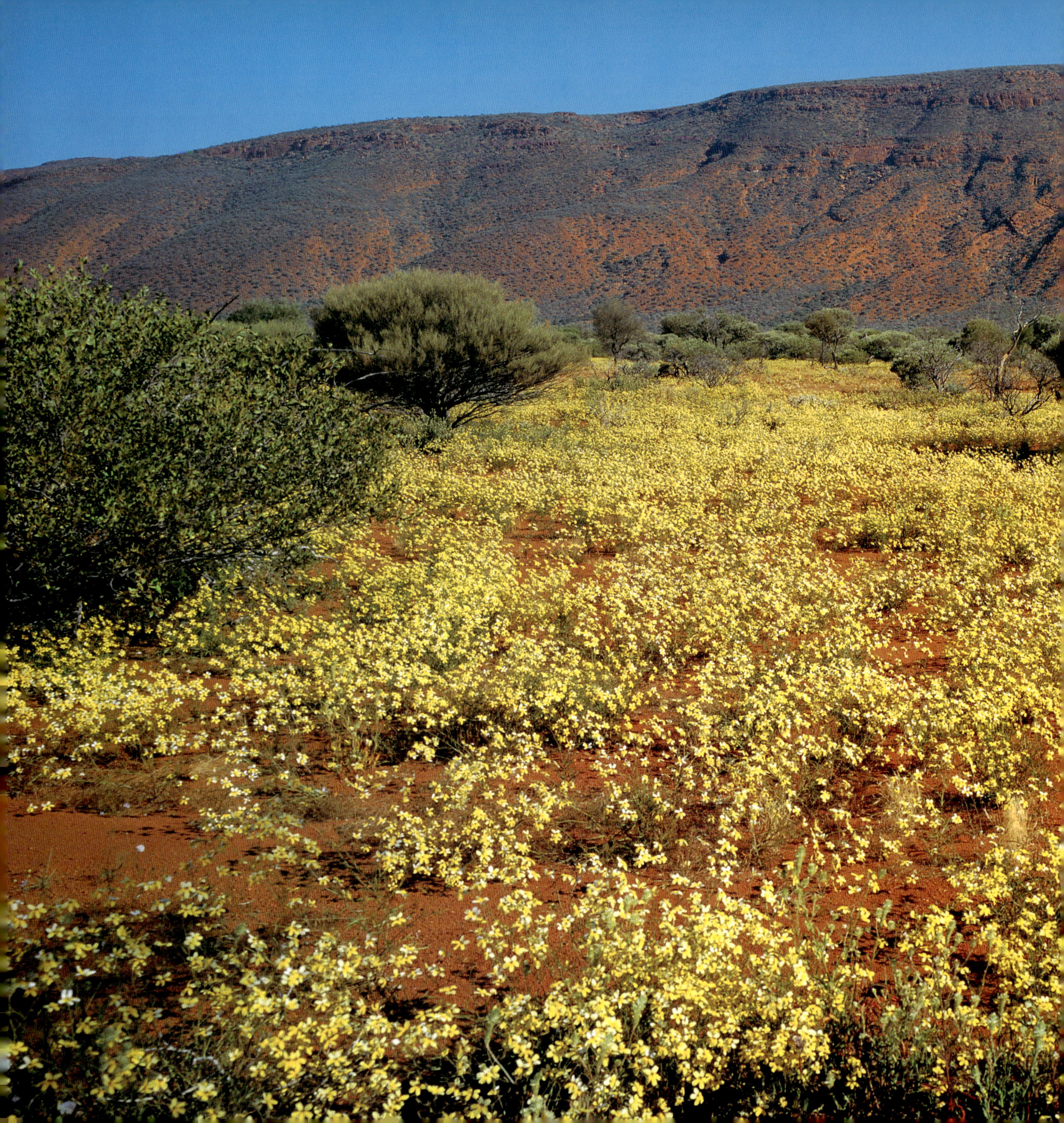

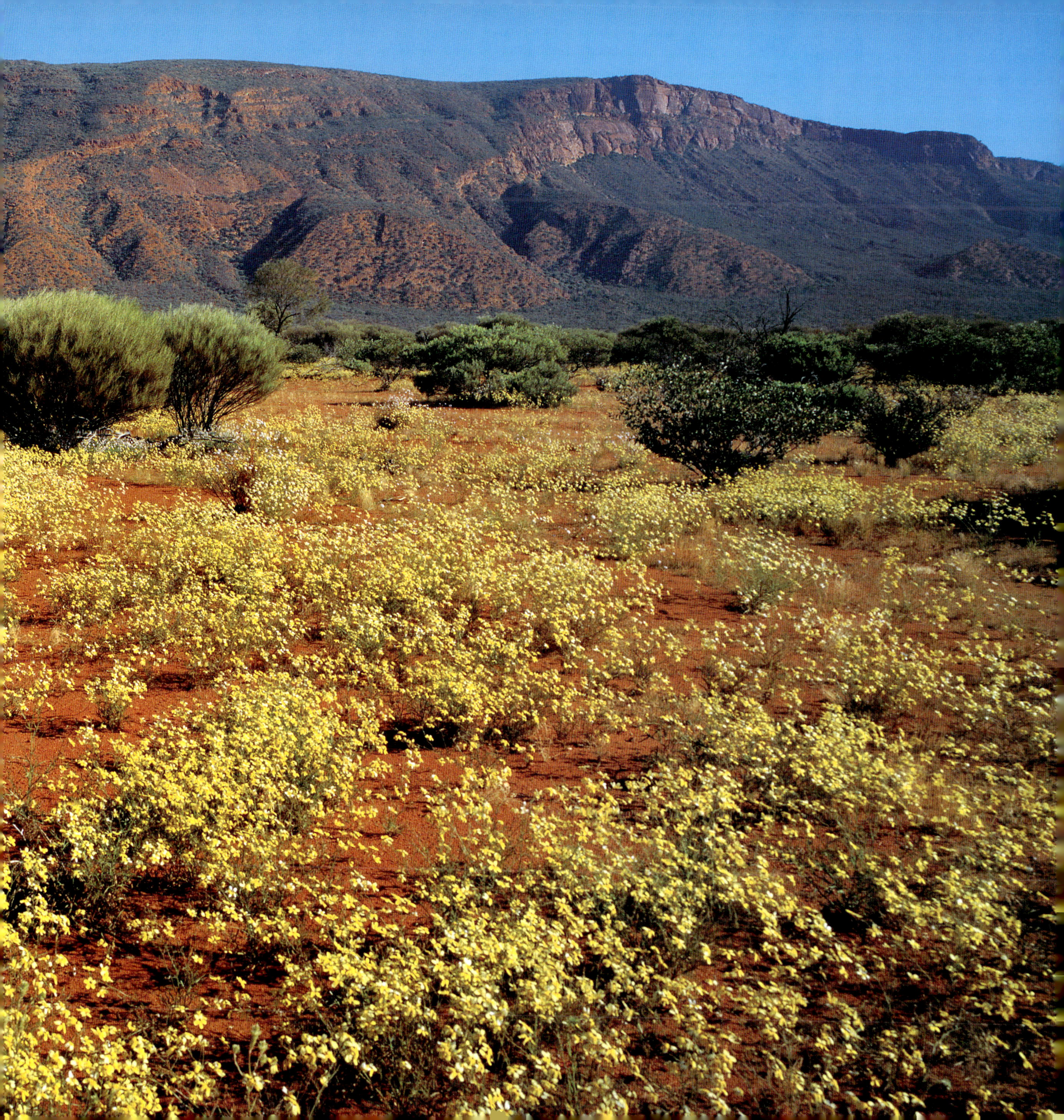

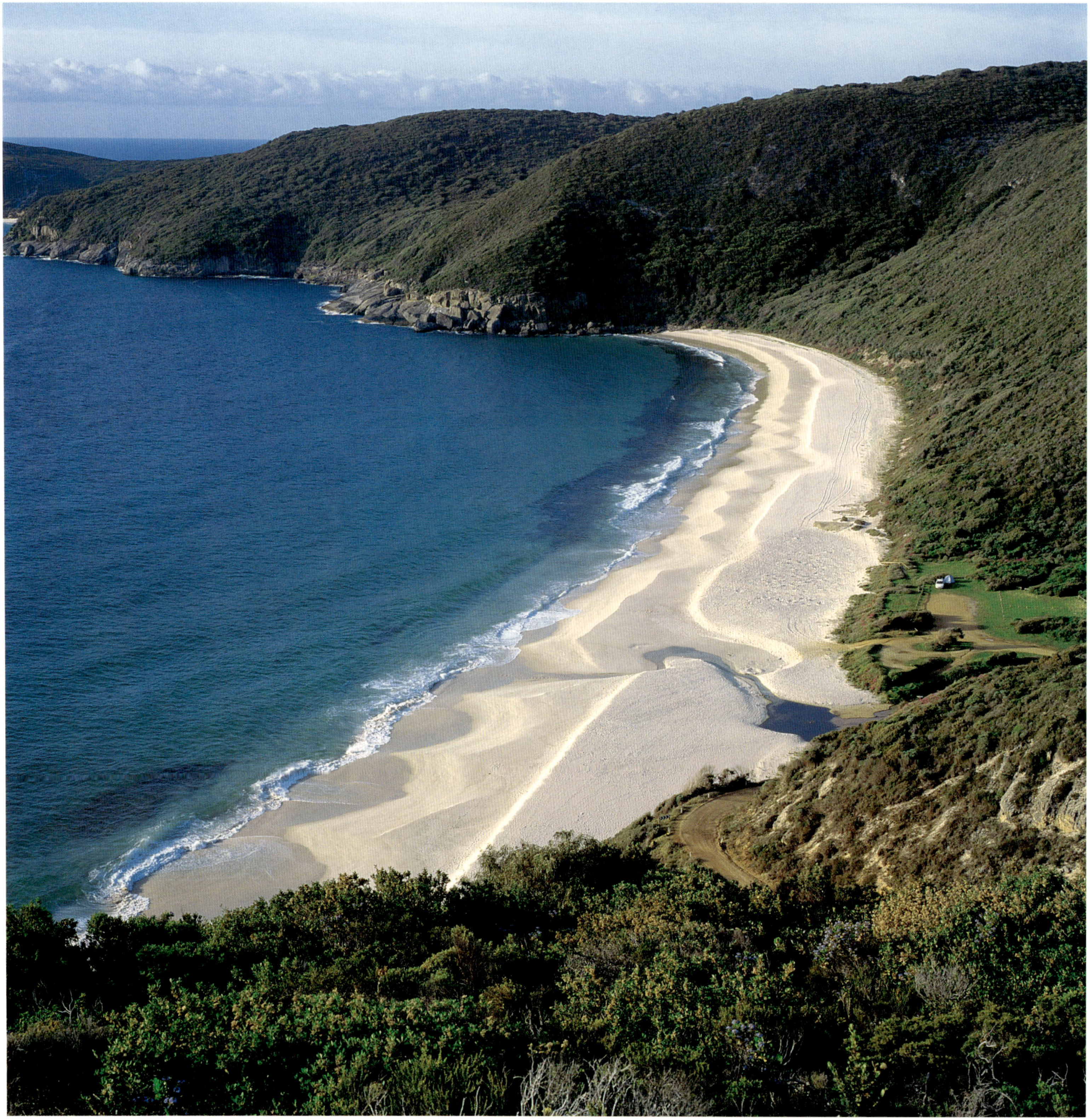

Previous page: Wildflowers in Mt Augustus National Park.

Above: The southern coast of Western Australia is noted for its magnificent beaches.

Introduction

There is a journey through Western Australia which every nature lover should make at least once in a lifetime. This journey has its start in the Kimberley, the remote northern part of the State, in June and July, when dry winter conditions allow access to rugged ranges, monsoon woodlands and plains. The adventure continues with a leisurely drive down the coast, past Broome and along Eighty Mile Beach, so that early August is spent in the Pilbara amidst magnificent scenery and fascinating wildlife. Then the explorer should move south in stages, with stopovers at attractions ranging from fields of wildflowers to friendly wild dolphins and the fantastic Pinnacles of Nambung National Park. At the end of this journey are the delights of the State capital, Perth and the nearby port of Fremantle, with a voyage to Rottnest Island as the crowning touch.

Another wonderful expedition takes the traveller through the green south-west of the State, with its tall Karri trees, vineyards, orchards and scenic coastline. This route turns eastwards from Cape Leeuwin and eventually allows the wanderer to revel in the splendour of some of the finest unspoiled coastline remaining in the world today.

The historically-minded should follow the long, straight highway that runs east from Perth to the Goldfields area, where, since the late nineteenth century, fortunes have been made and lost. This arid country, with its picturesque relics of the mining days, is best tackled during the cooler months of the year.

It's a huge State, and I for one never grow tired of exploring its vastness and marvelling at the beauty of the panoramas which confront me at every turn of the road. The images in this book pay tribute to some of the aspects of Western Australia I love best.

Steve Parish

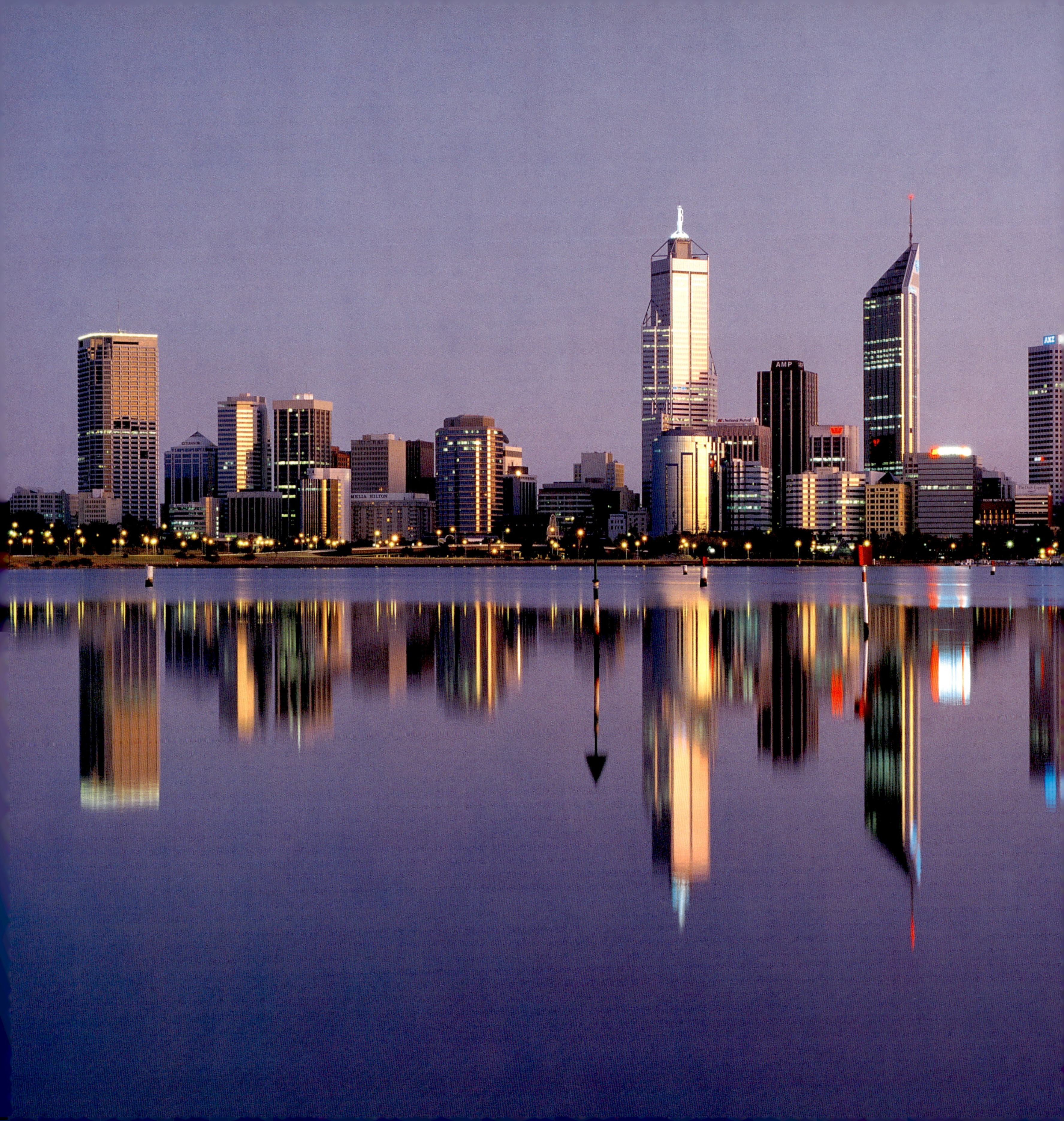
AMP
ANZ

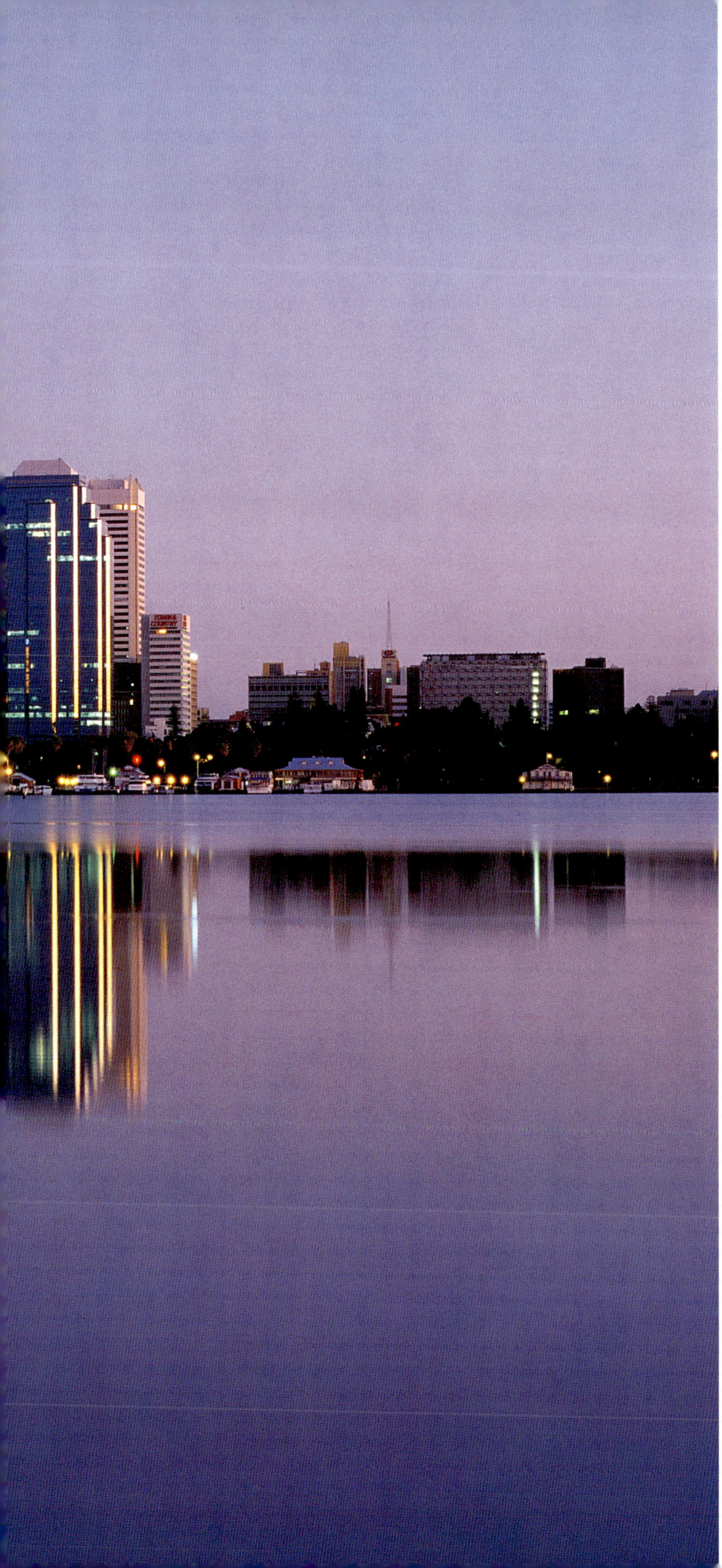

Perth, the riverside city

The Swan River winds through the heart of Perth, bordered by green parks and cycling tracks, dividing the glittering towers of the city's business heart from the prosperous suburbs which grace its southern bank. It provides Western Australia's capital with a focus, a playground and a vista which changes from placid navy-blue to ruffled silver-grey as weather fronts roll in from the Indian Ocean to the west.

Perth is divided by more than 2000 kilometres from the nearest State capital. Its population of more than 1.2 million people treasures the relaxed Perth lifestyle. While many of Perth's people journey far from the city on the Swan River, the majority of them return to make their homes in this spacious, gracious city with its magnificent Mediterranean climate and hospitable atmosphere.

Perth city centre, viewed across the Swan River.

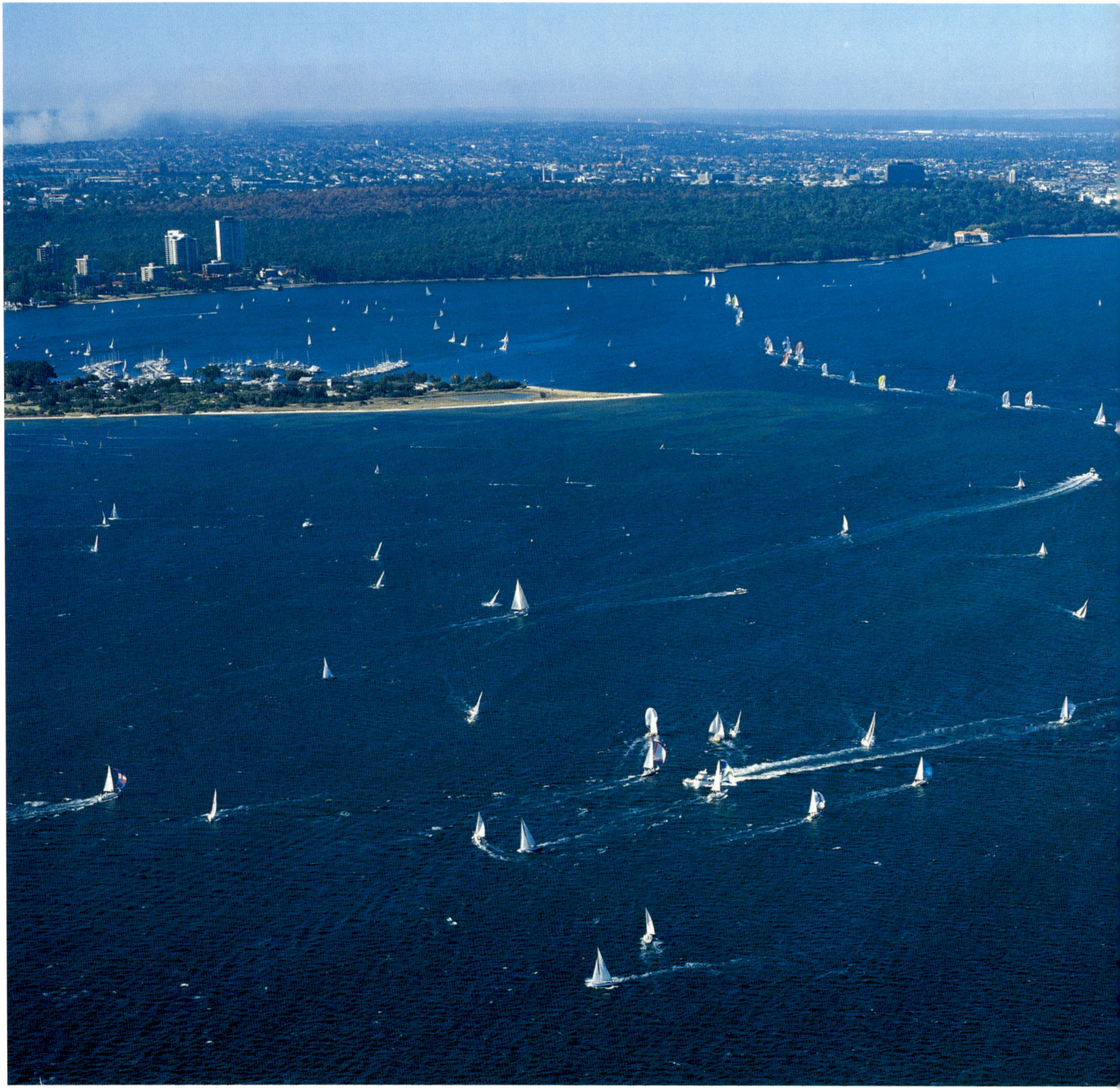

A view across the Swan River and Point Currie to Kings Park, Mill Point, the Narrows Bridge, Perth Water and the Perth central business district.

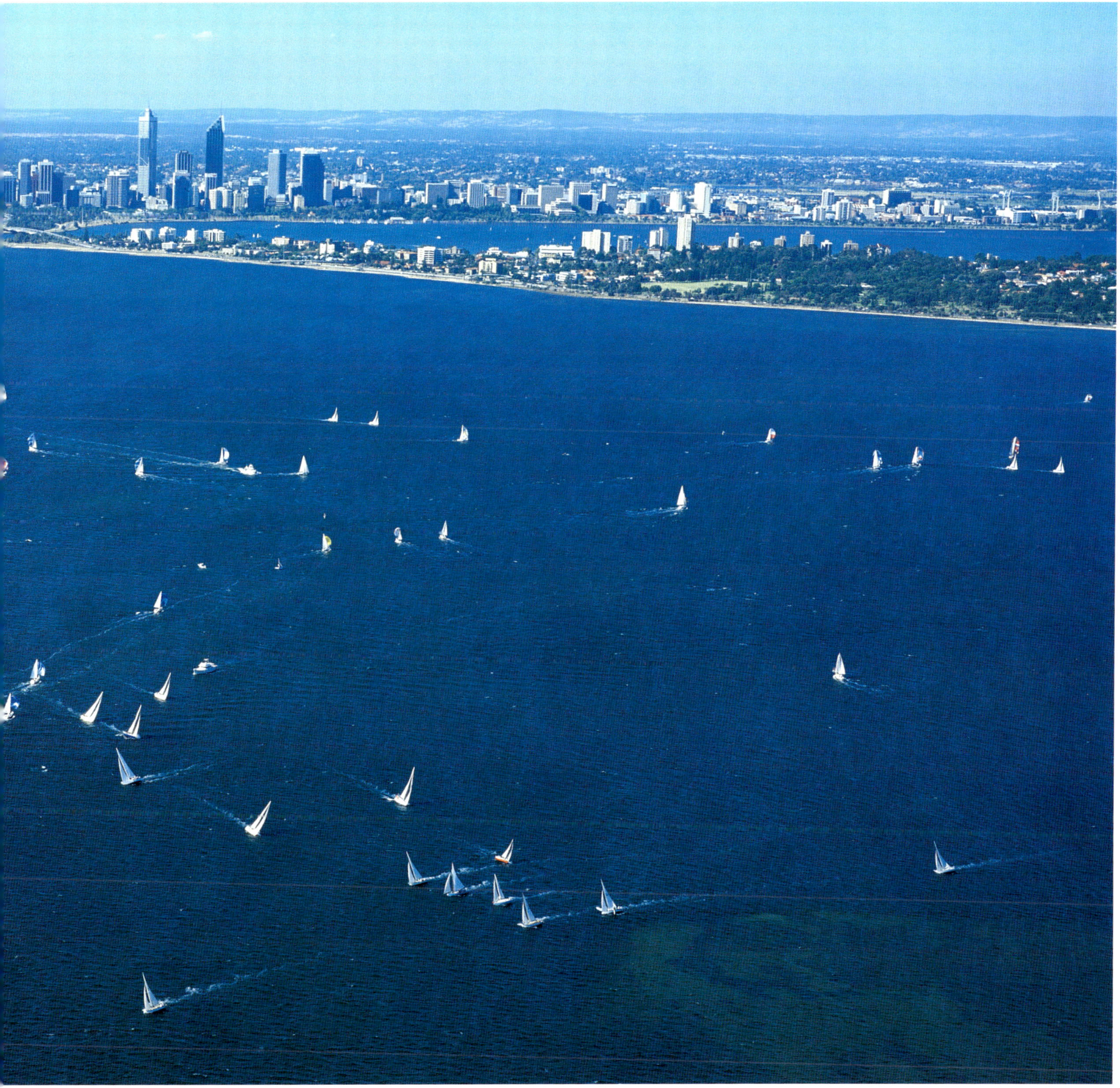

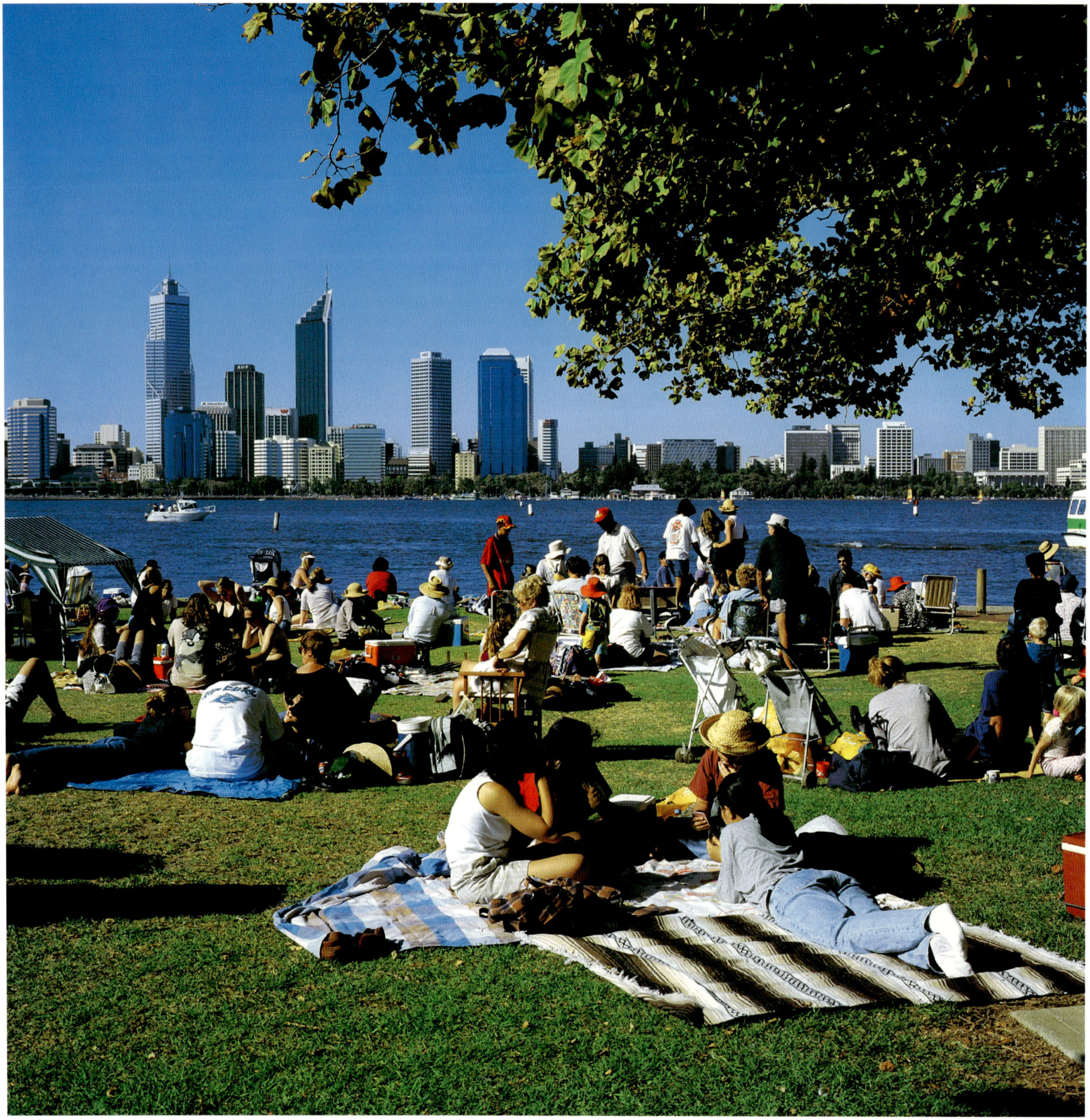

Picnicking by the Swan River.

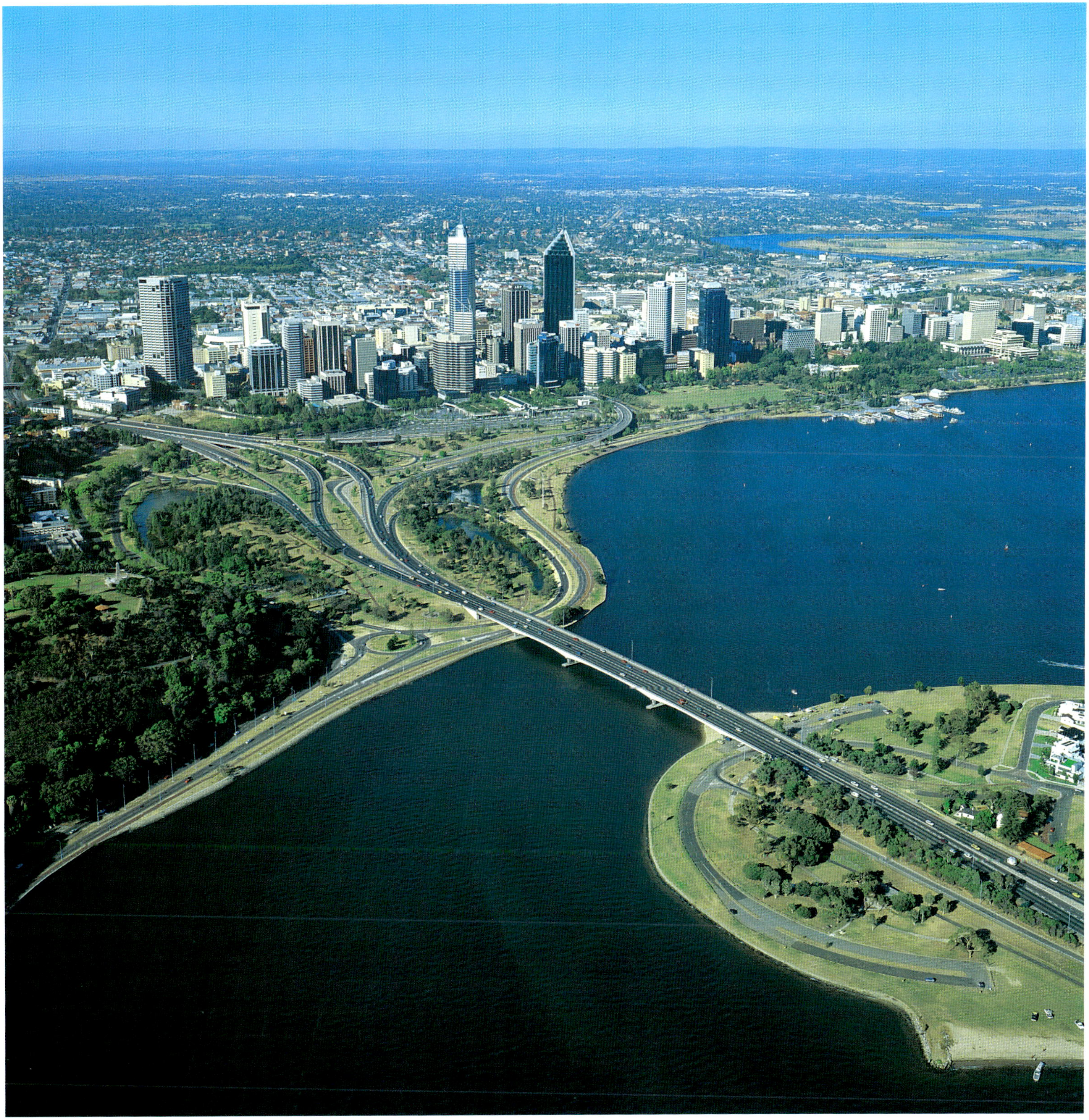

Above: The Narrows Bridge, in the foreground, leads to Perth's central business district.

Following pages: Catamarans on Perth Water, against the city skyline.

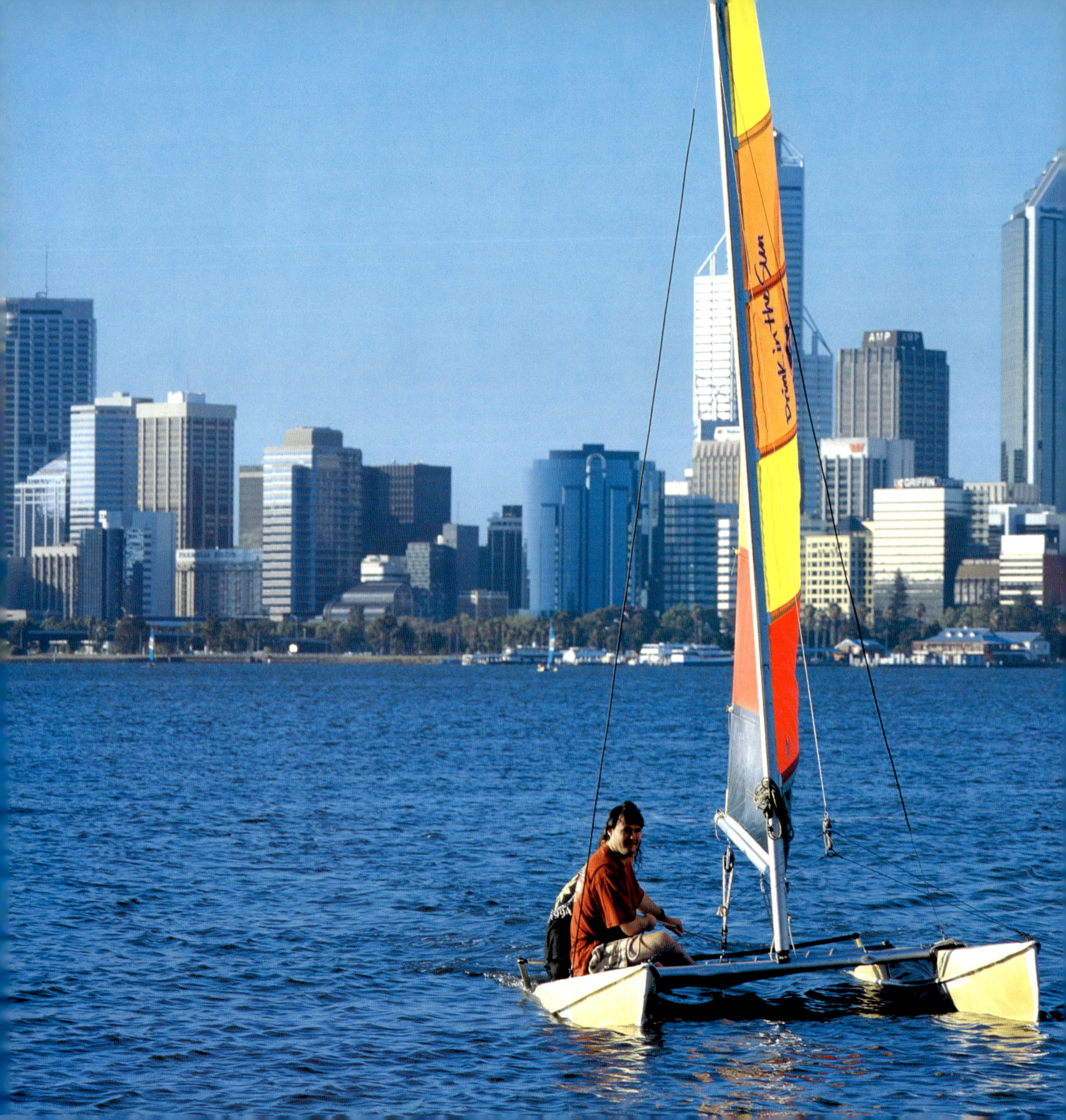
Drink in the Sun
AMP
GRIFFIN

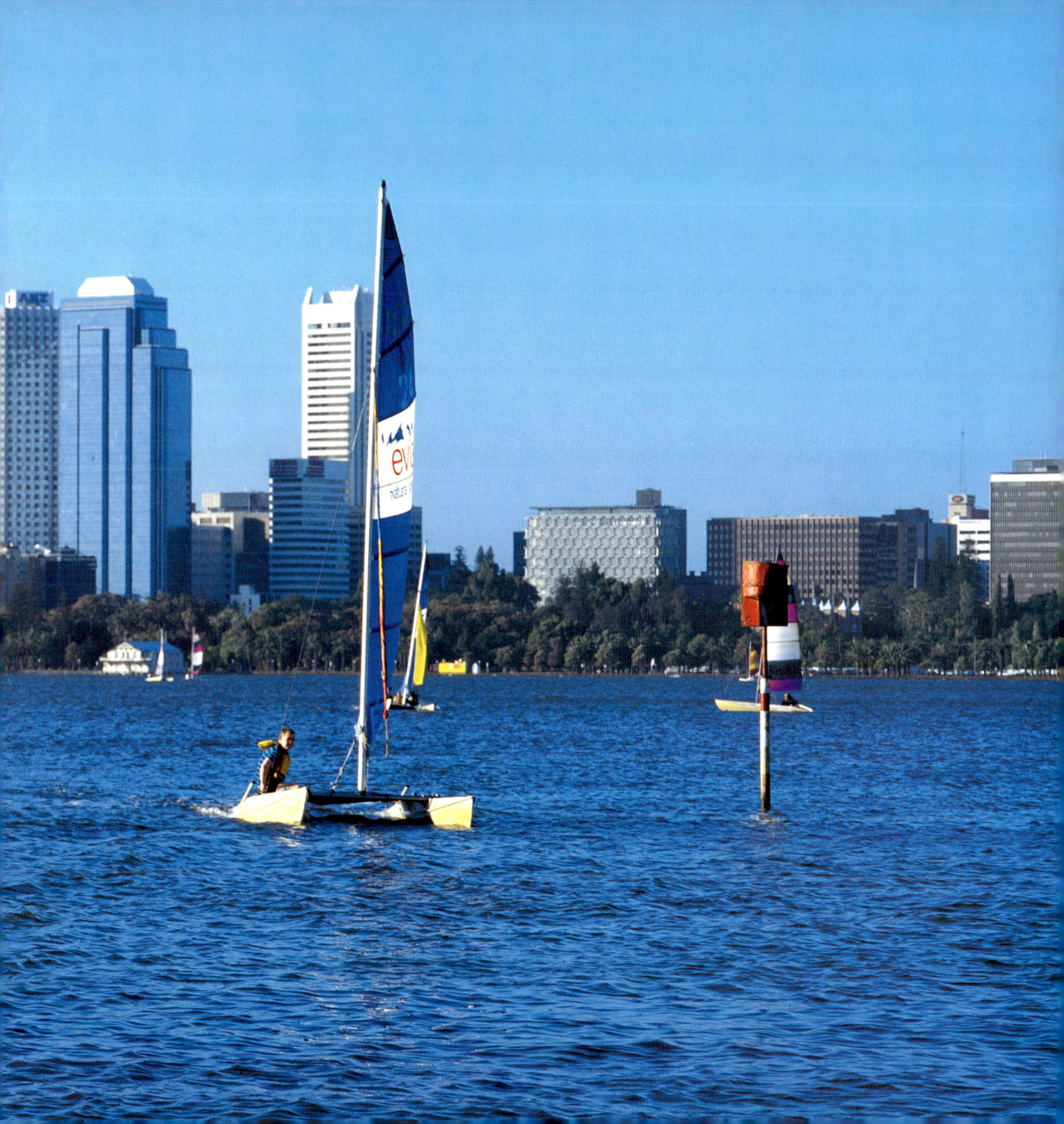

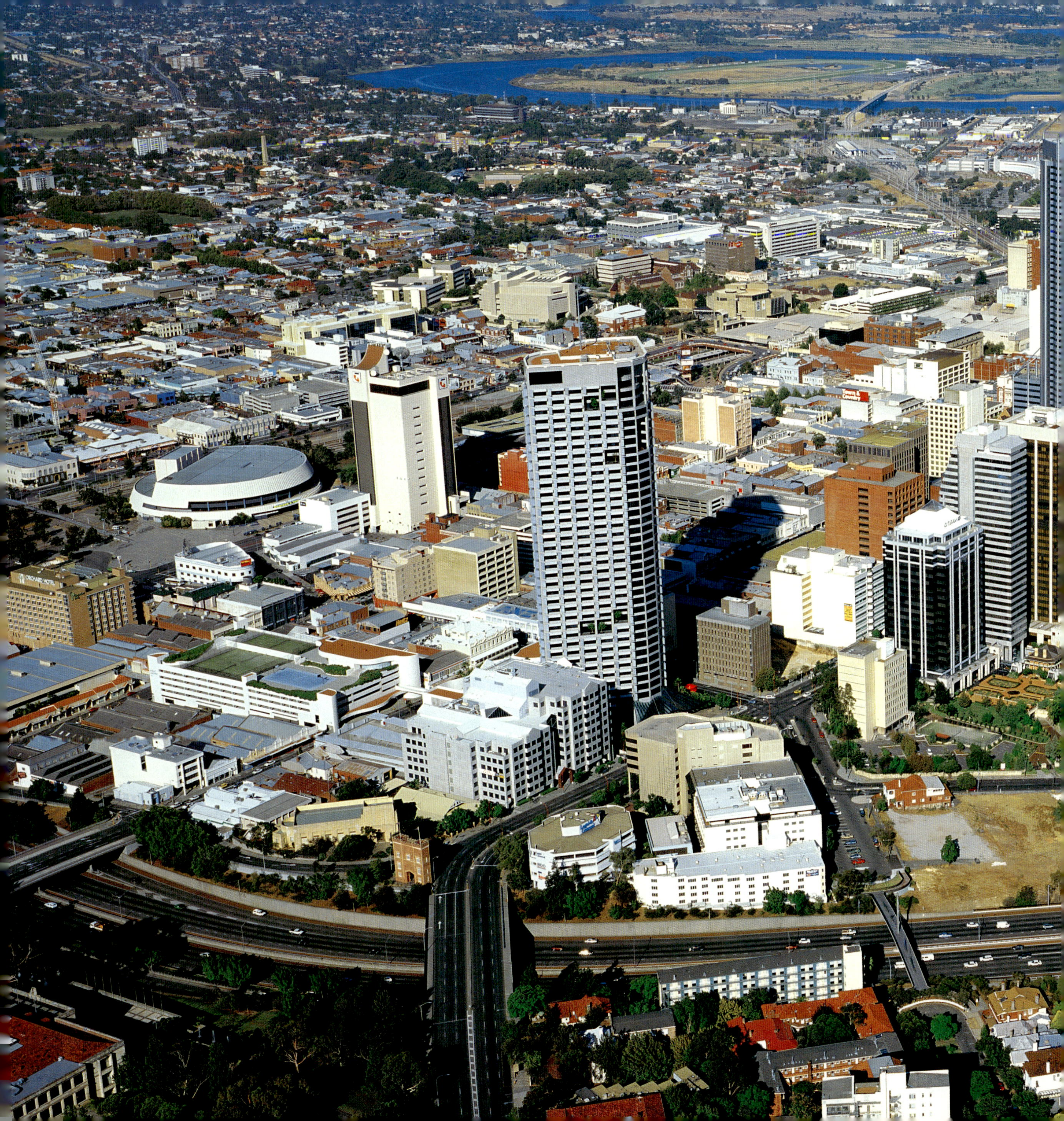

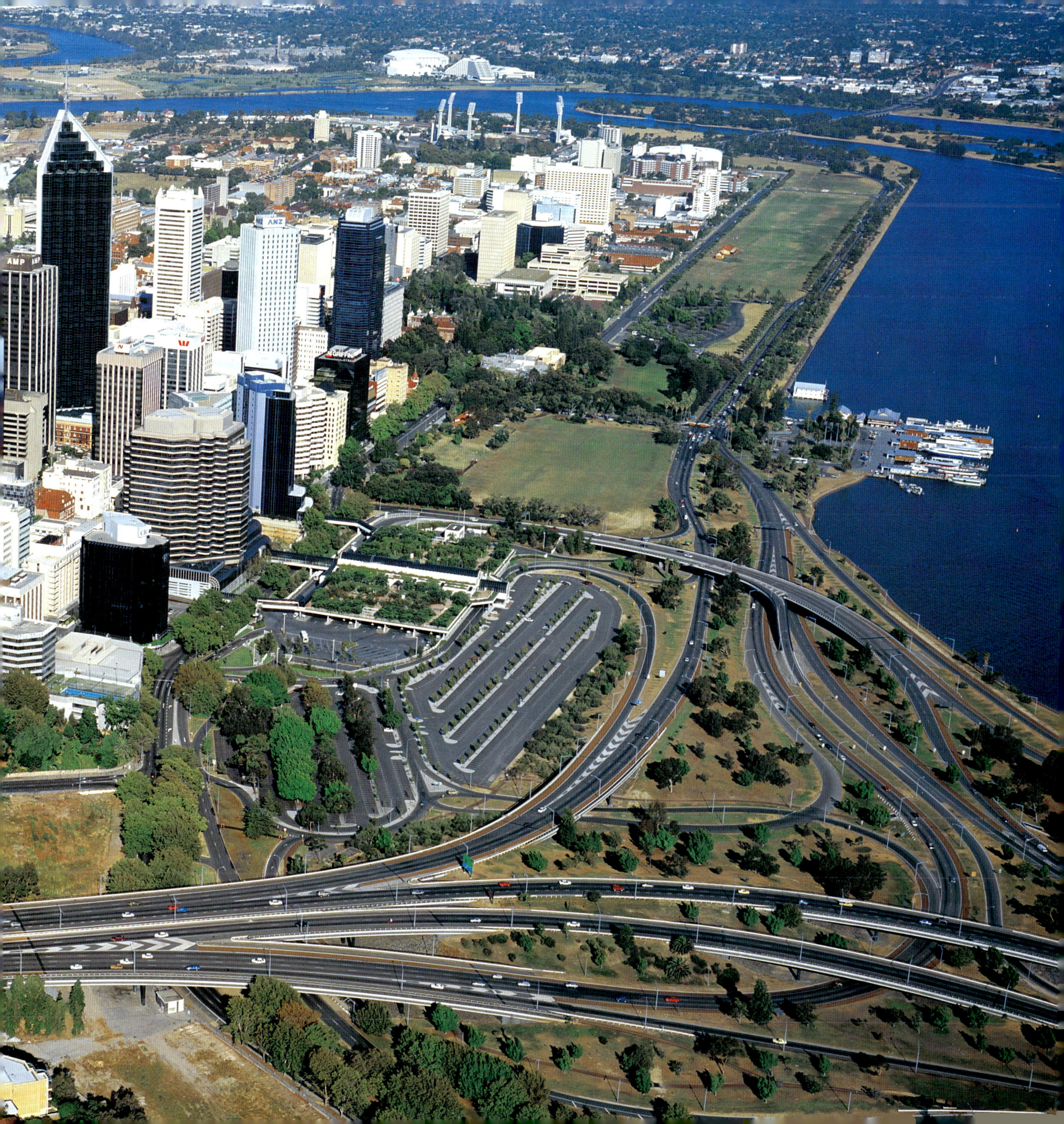

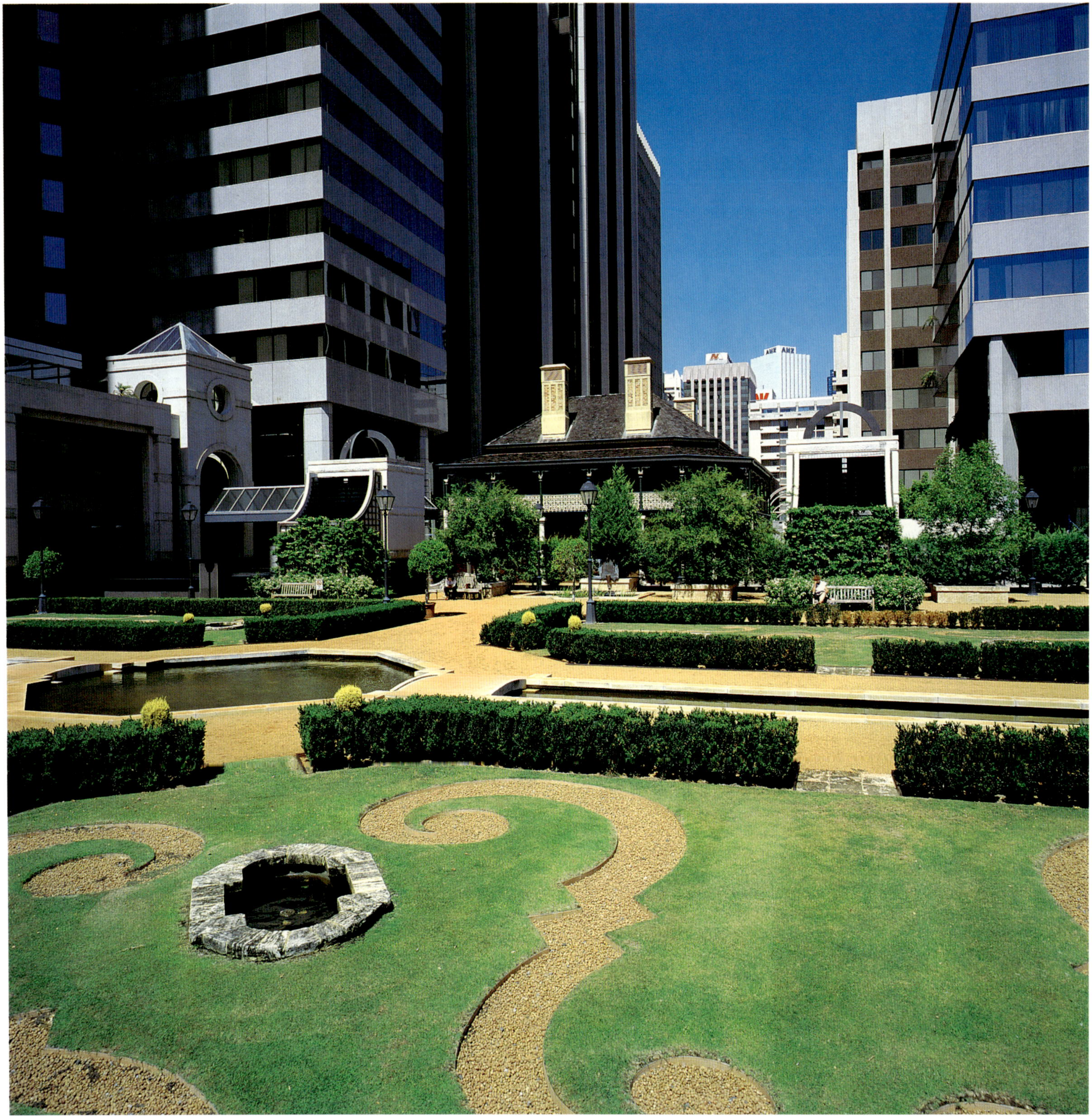

Previous pages: Perth city centre with, at right, the Swan River and Barrack Street Jetty.

Above: A restored heritage building stands amongst the high-rise offices of Perth's city centre.

The heart of the city

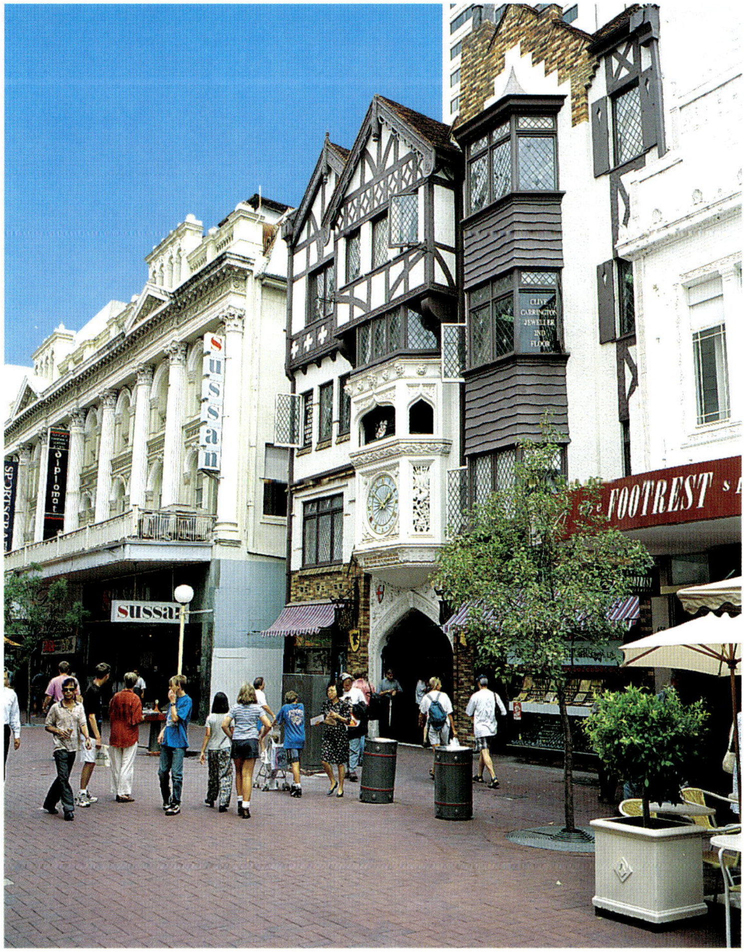

The Hay Street Mall entrance to London Court.

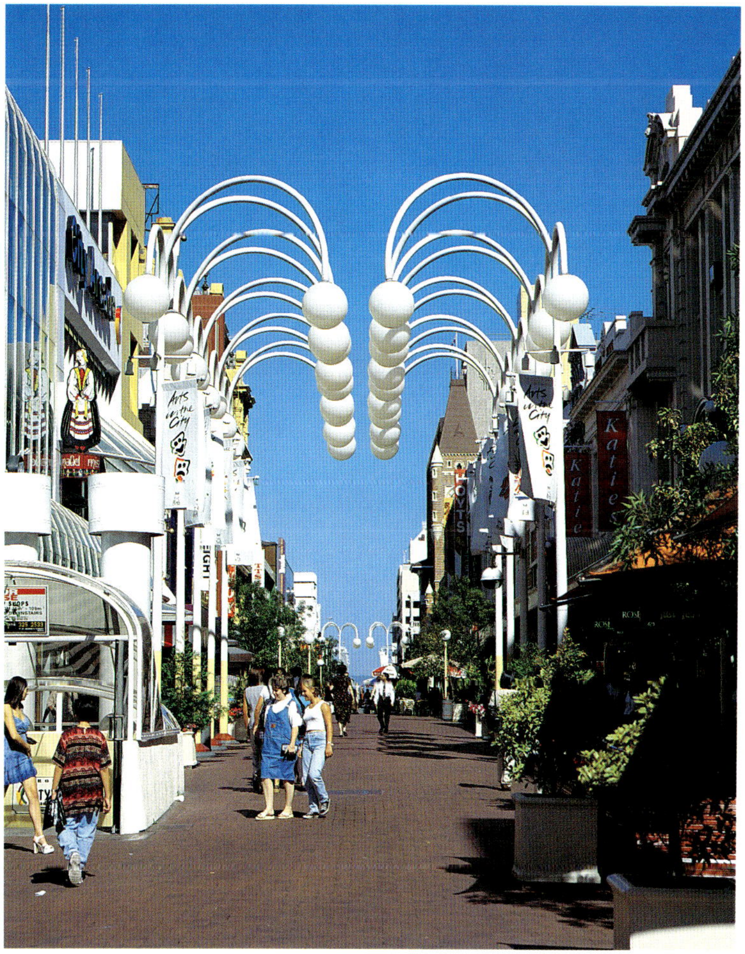

Hay Street Mall.

In Perth, the historical and the modern blend in charming and orderly fashion. Heritage buildings have been lovingly restored and provide fascinating accents amongst the big-city towers which have appeared following Western Australia's leap in prosperity over the past few decades. Modernisation has been well thought out. Hay Street, in the heart of Perth, was once a narrow thoroughfare, cluttered with motor vehicles, but is now a busy and popular mall. London Court, which leads from the mall to St Georges Terrace, is a mock-Tudor landmark. It was opened in 1937 and its boutiques attract interested shoppers.

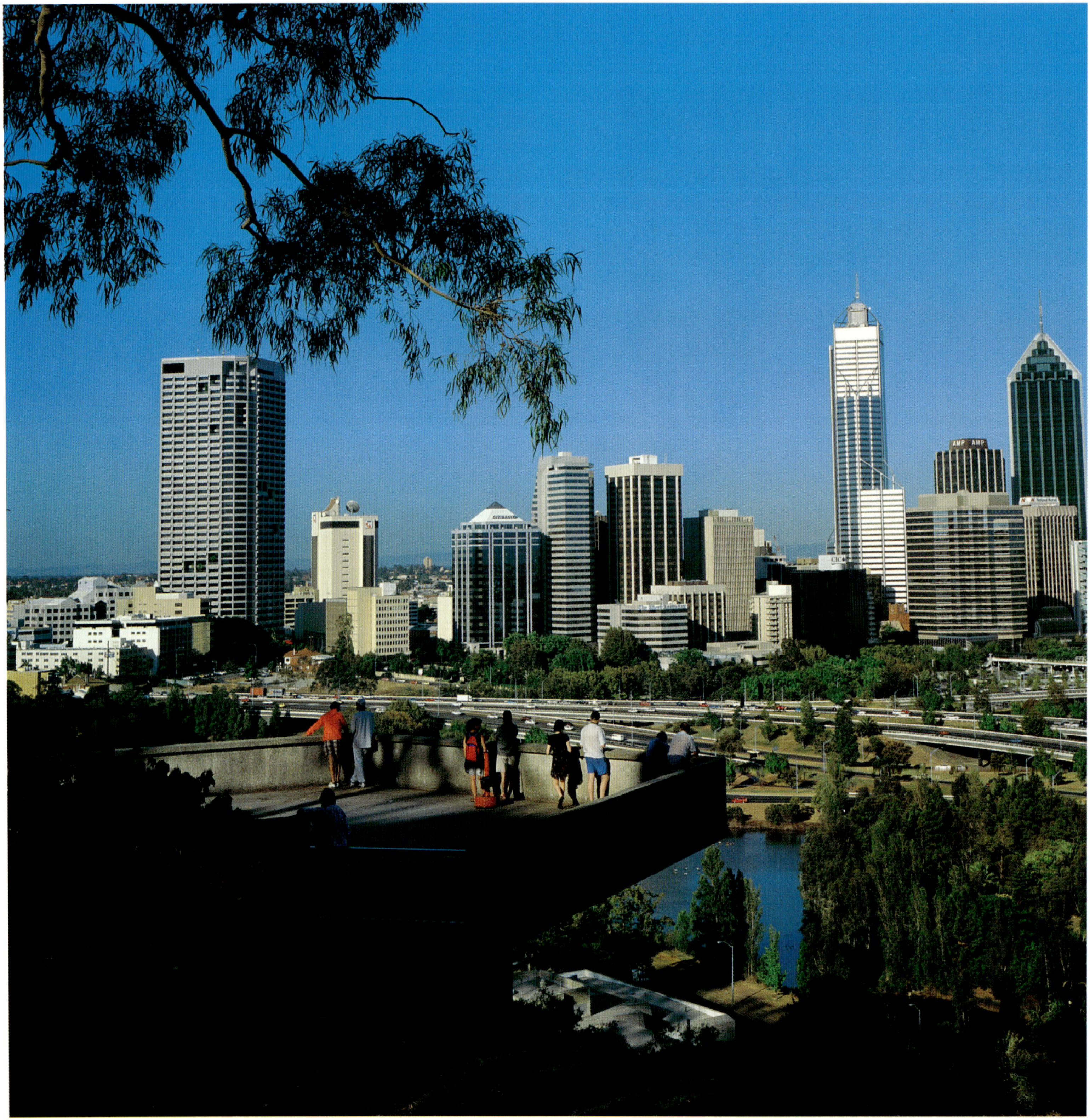

The city centre and Swan River can be viewed from Kings Park's many vantage points.

Kings Park

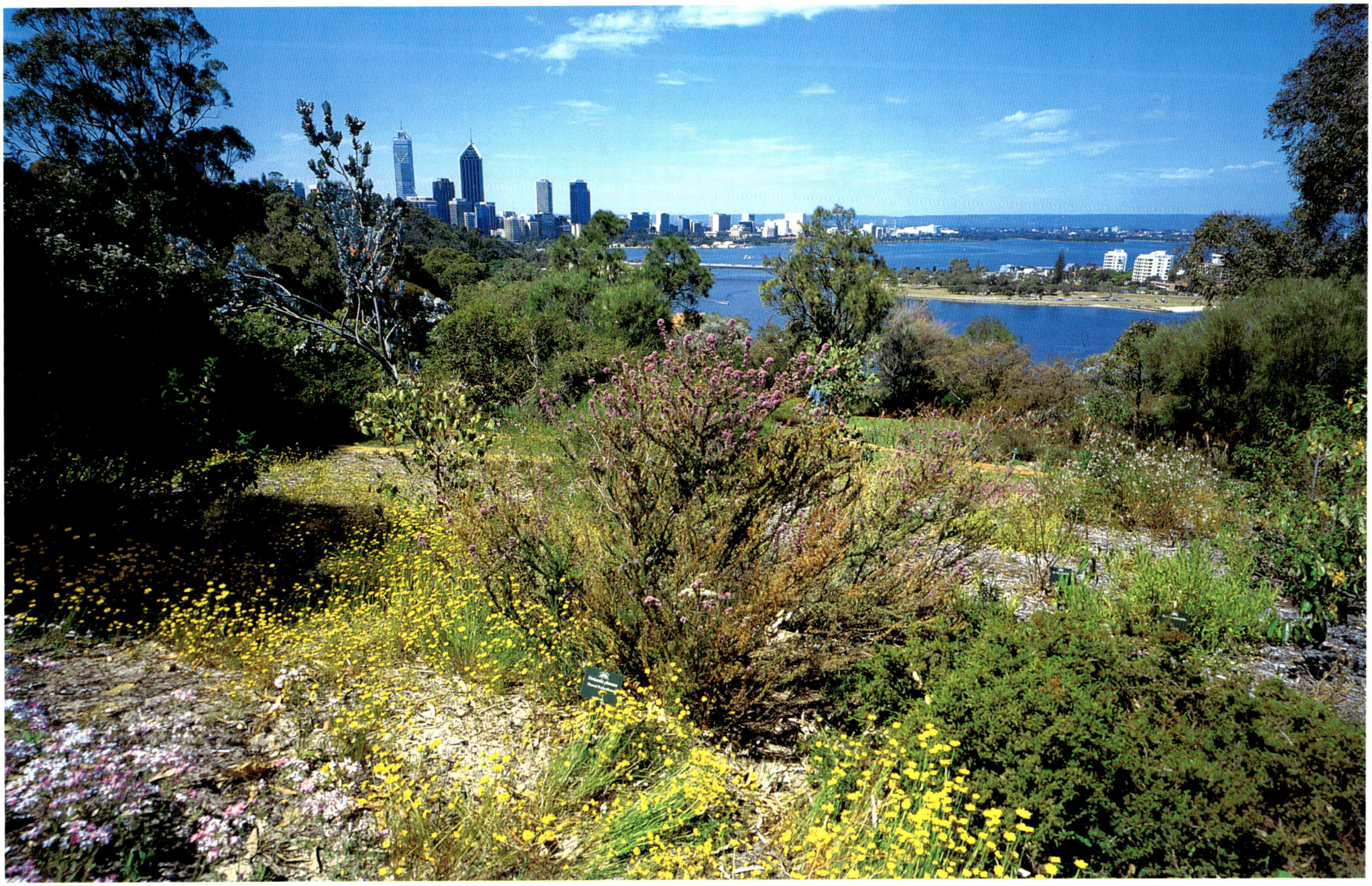

Kings Park has extensive gardens of native wildflowers and feature displays of other countries' flora.

The wonderful eucalypt and banksia woodlands and magnificent wildflower gardens of Kings Park form a 400-hectare oasis on the slopes and summit of Mt Eliza, overlooking the Swan River and Perth city centre. The park features an excellent restaurant and cafe and a number of picnicking and barbecue areas. The statue of Lord Forrest of Bunbury stands near the park's two War Memorials: other attractions are the trunk of a giant Karri tree, the DNA Tower and the Pioneer Womens Memorial Fountain.

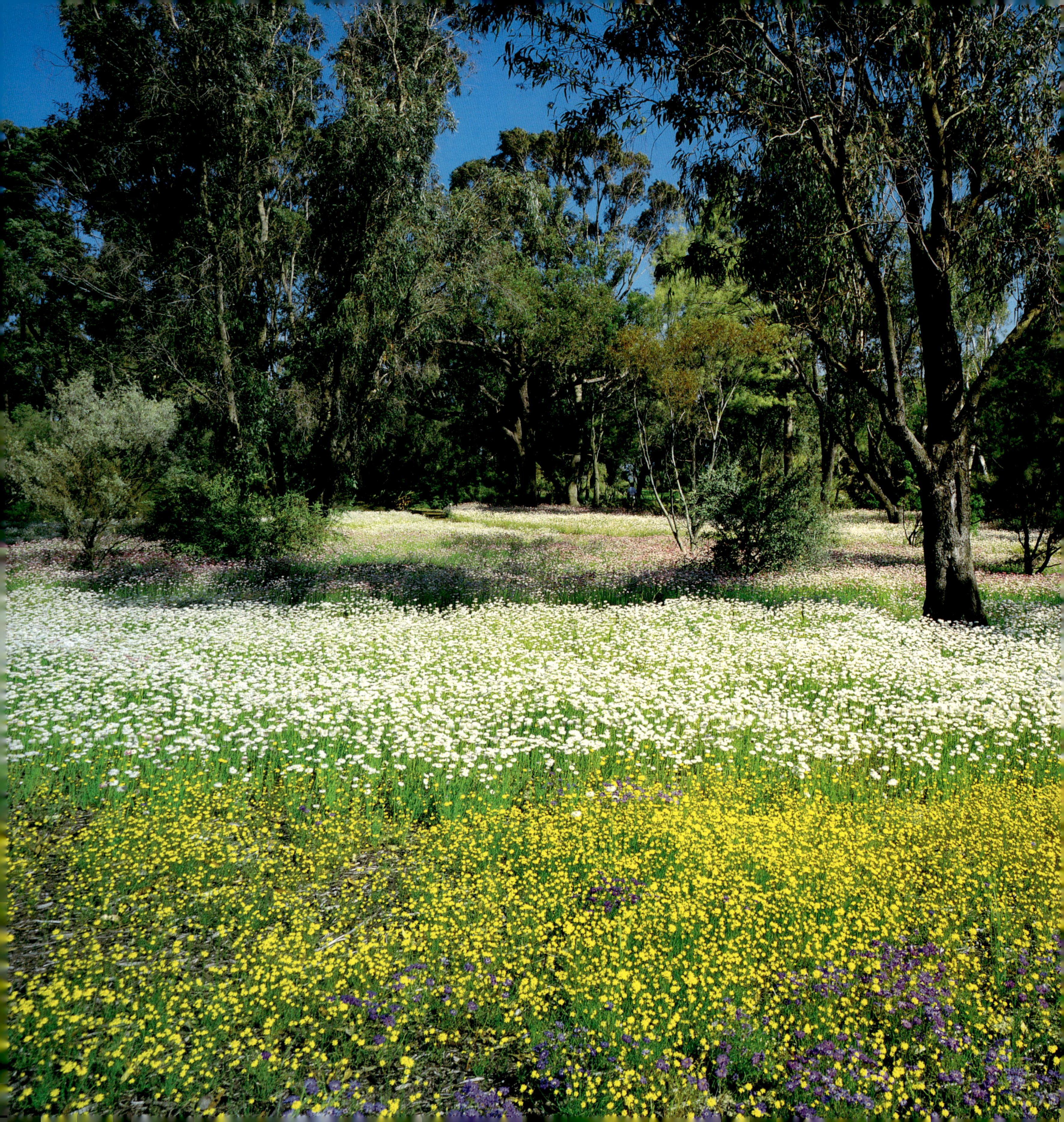

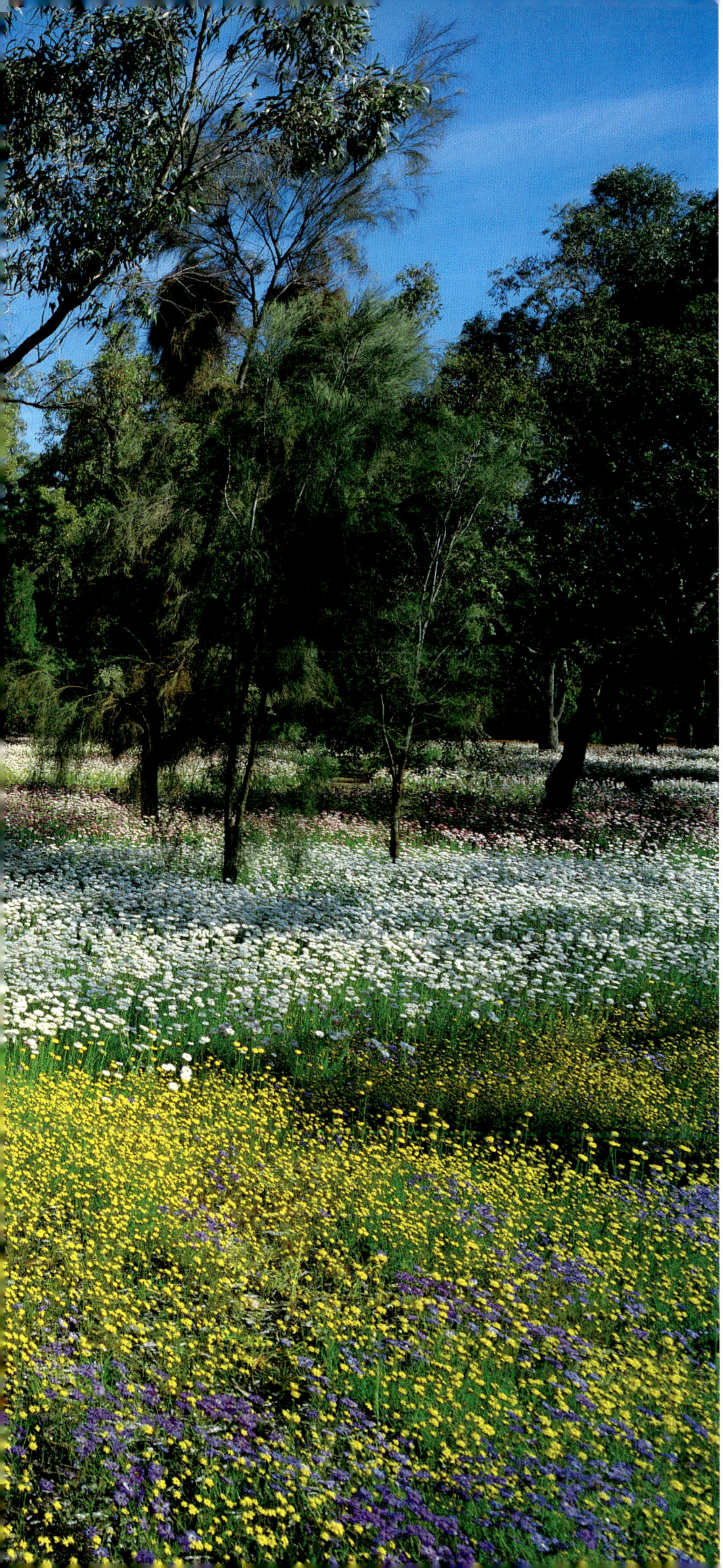

Wildflower heaven

The area on Mt Eliza now occupied by Kings Park was called by the Aboriginal Nyoongah people *Mooro Katta*, an all-sit-down-place, or friendly ground.

Since the park's formal establishment in 1895, it has survived attempts to allocate land for other uses and defied the ravages of bushfires. Dedicated volunteers and hard-working staff have successfully implemented ambitious plans which include a marvellous Botanic Garden, botanical research facilities, and the popular Wildflower Festival which sees thousands visit the park each September. As the picture at left shows, this is truly a wild place in the heart of a city.

Wildflowers carpet the ground in Kings Park.

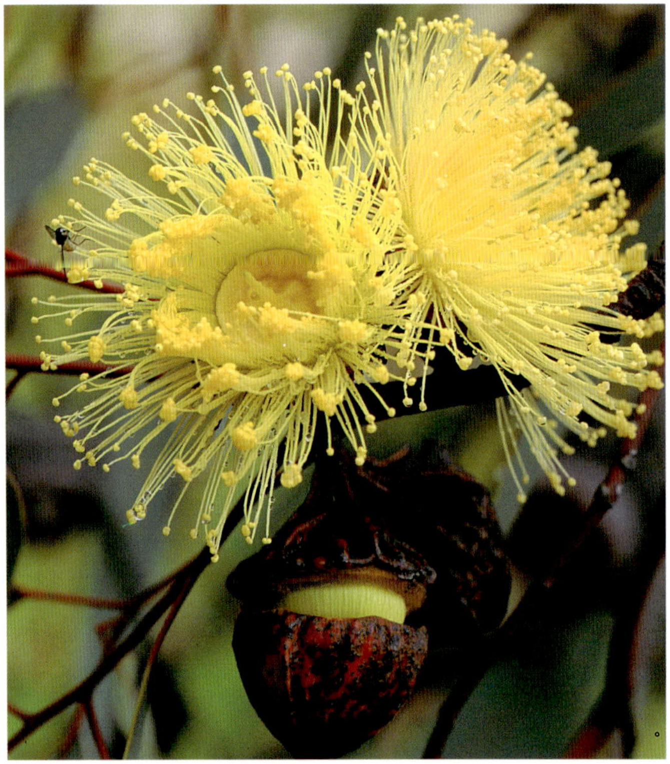

Mallee blossoms and buds.

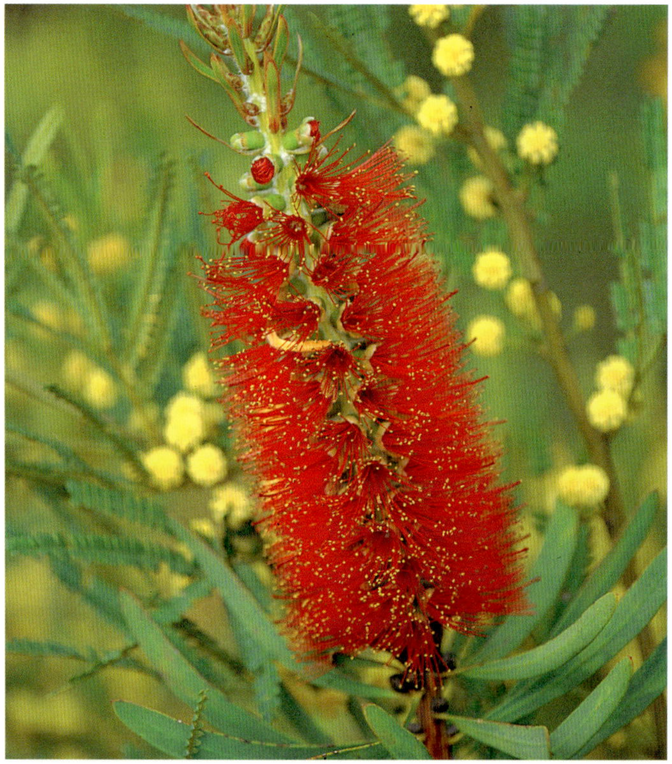

Scarlet Bottlebrush.

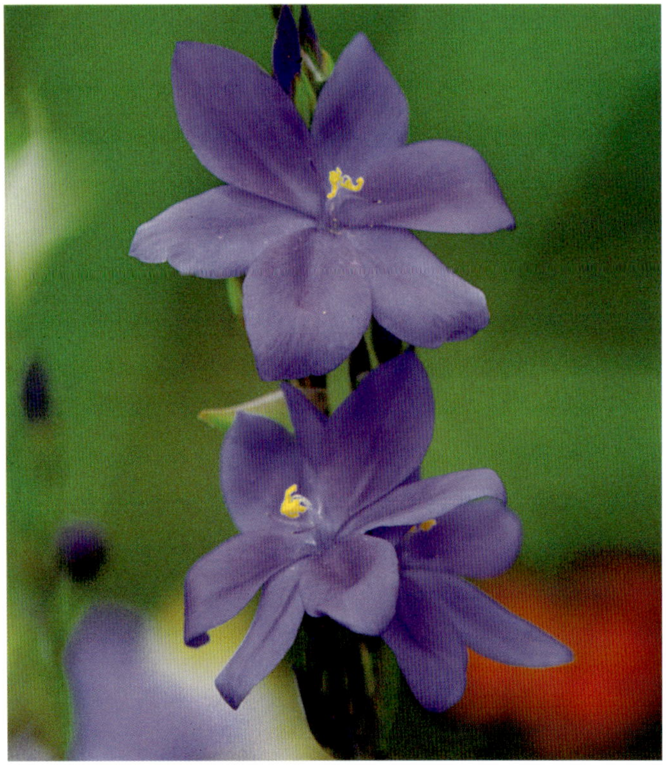

Morning Iris.

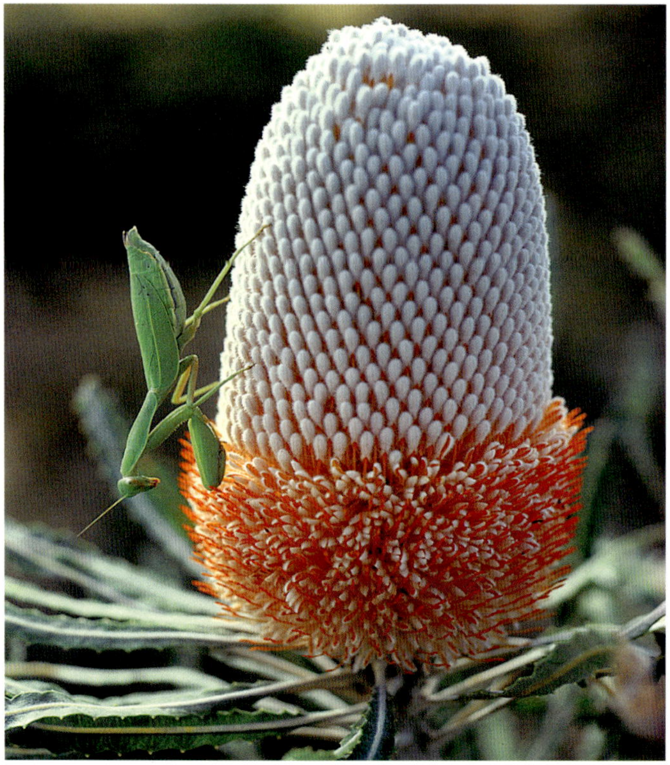

Orange Banksia.

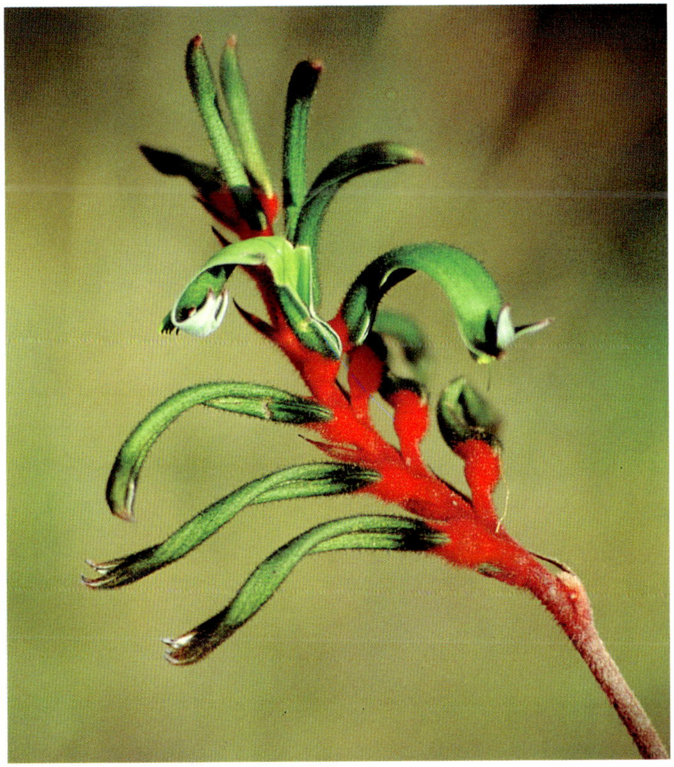

Mangles' Kangaroo Paw.

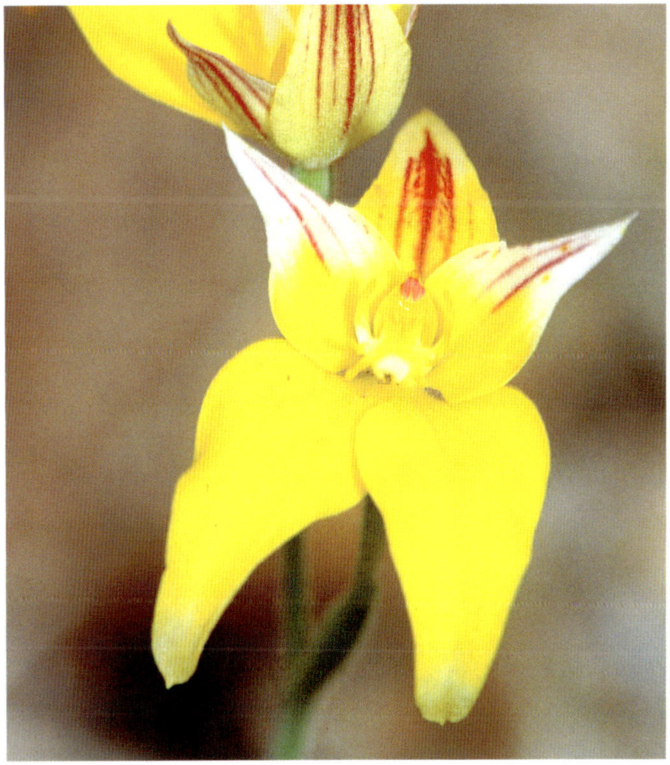

Cowslip Orchid.

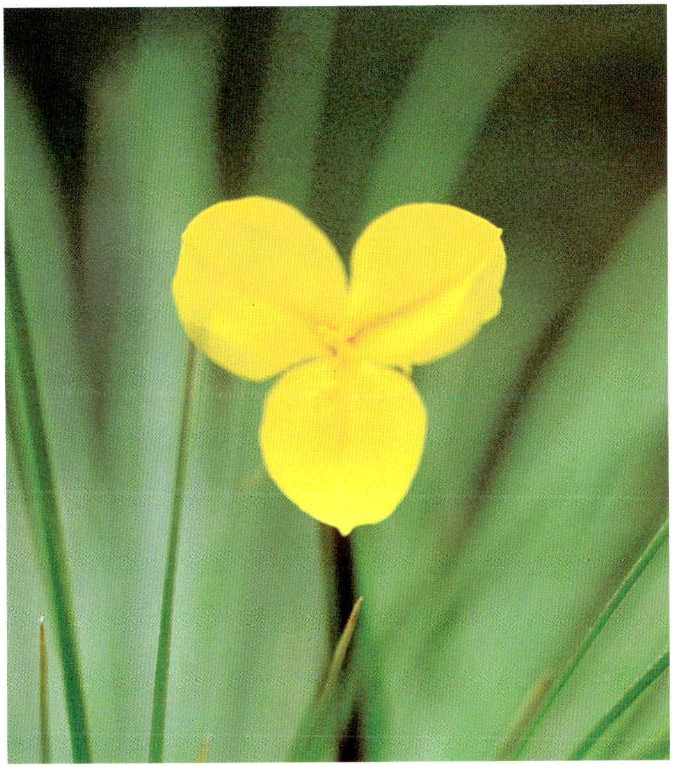

Yellow Flag.

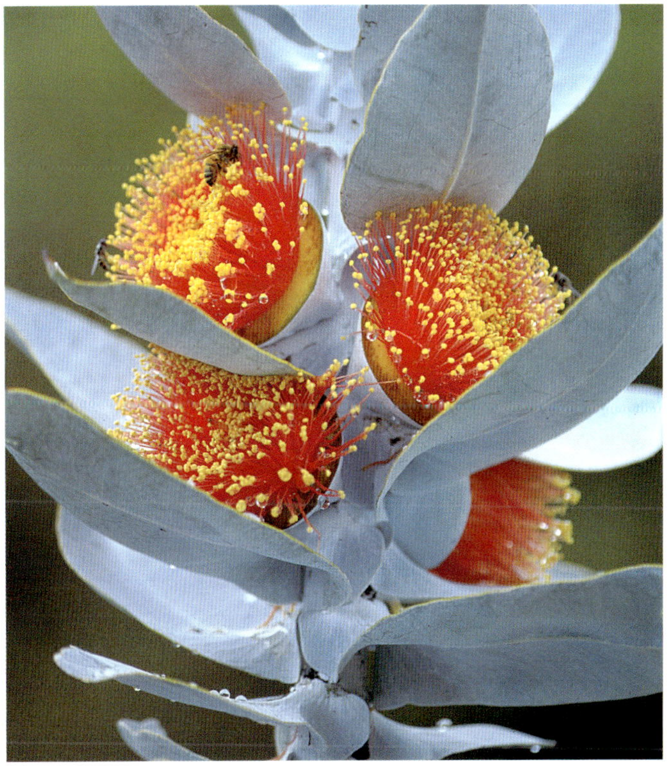

Mottlecah.

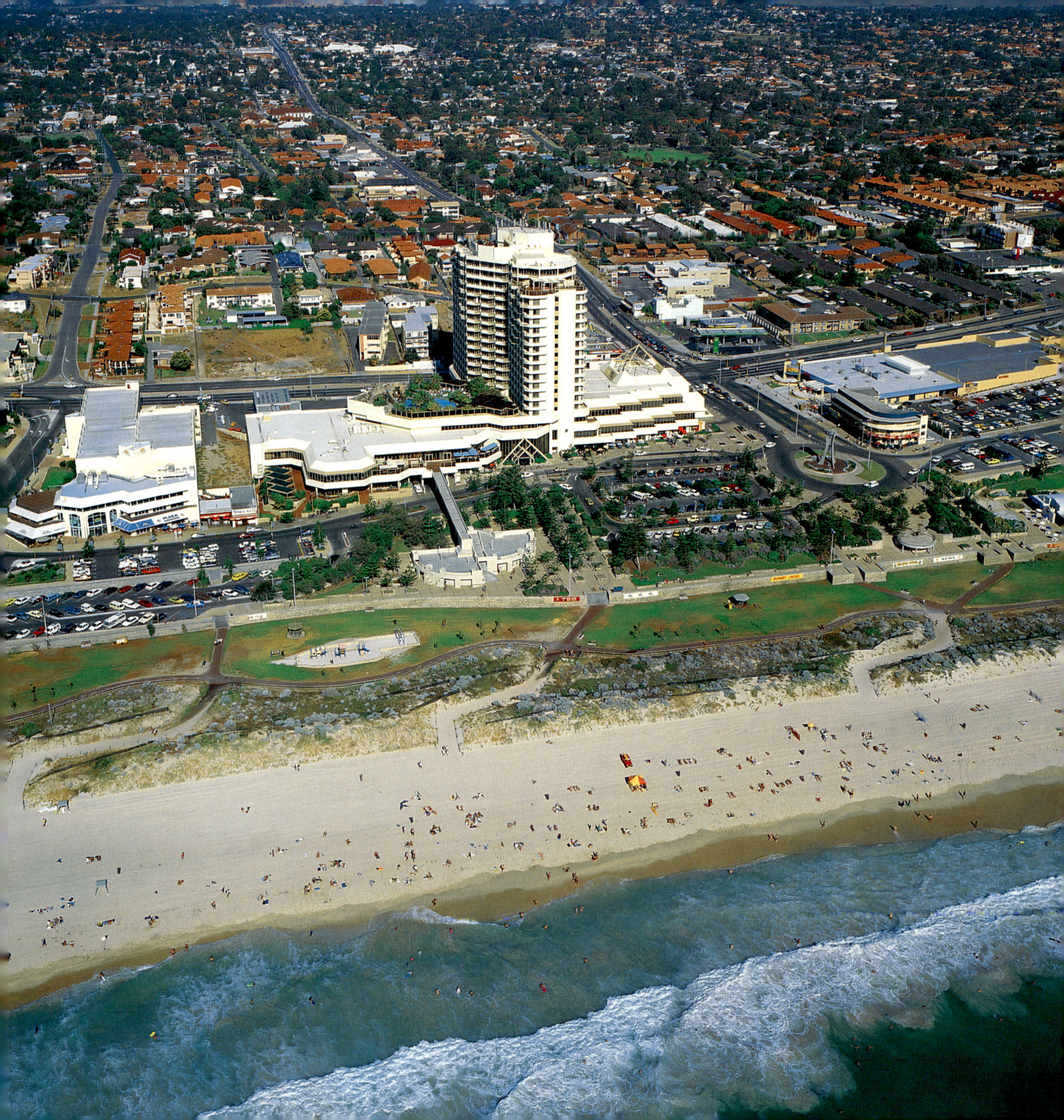

Perth's beaches

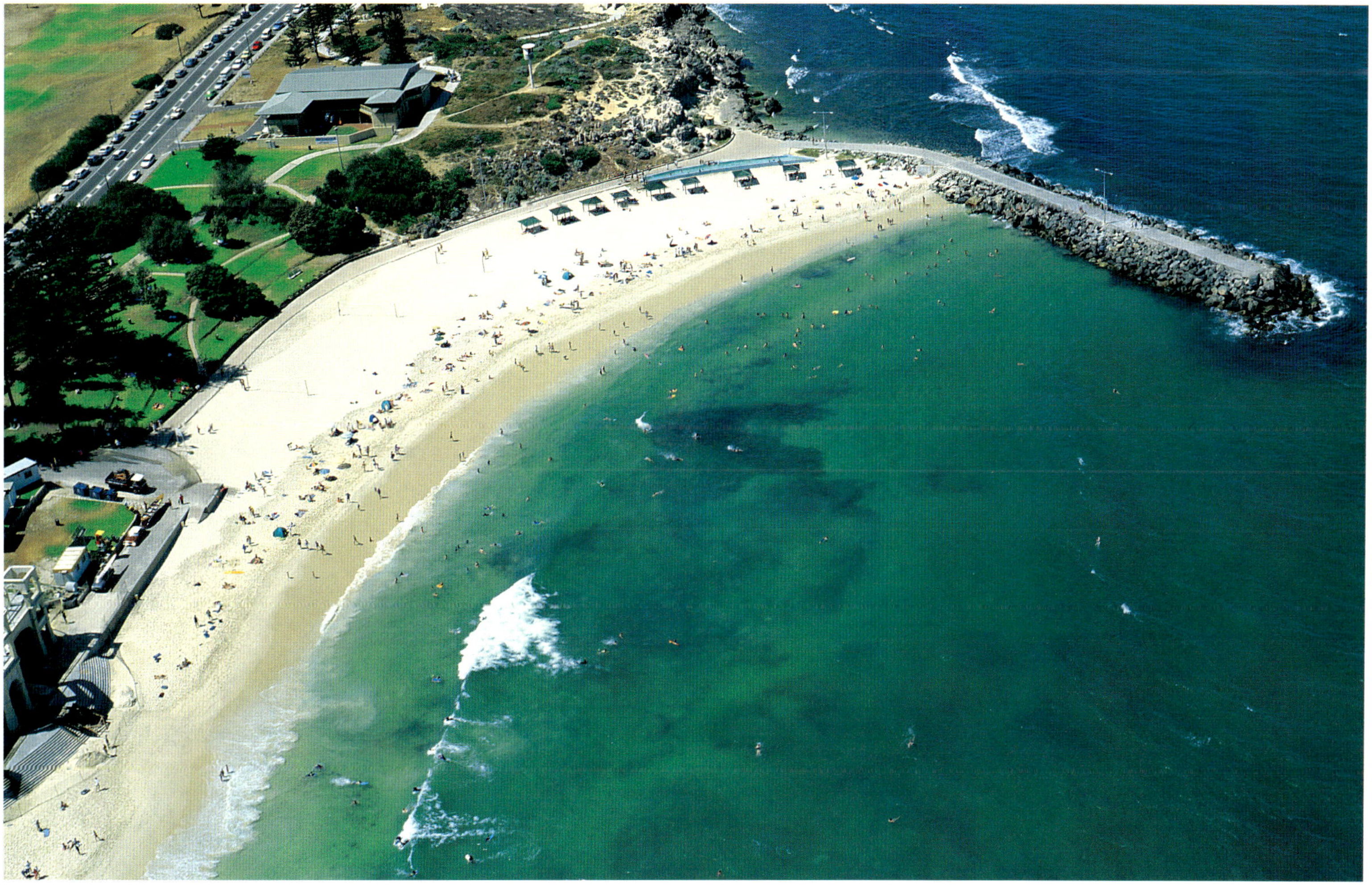

Above: Cottesloe Beach, a popular family recreation area.

Opposite: At Scarborough Beach, the tower of Radisson Observation City Hotel overlooks the Indian Ocean.

Perth's Mediterranean climate guarantees a warm, dry summer and a delightful, usually rainless spring and autumn. For most months of the year, the glorious beaches which stretch from Port Beach, north of Fremantle, to Burns Beach, at the end of the Mitchell Freeway, are popular places to swim, surf, fish, walk and picnic. In winter, when swimming is less popular, strolling along the beaches in the crisp, cold weather, looking for shells and other flotsam, is a great way to spend weekend hours.

Rottnest Island

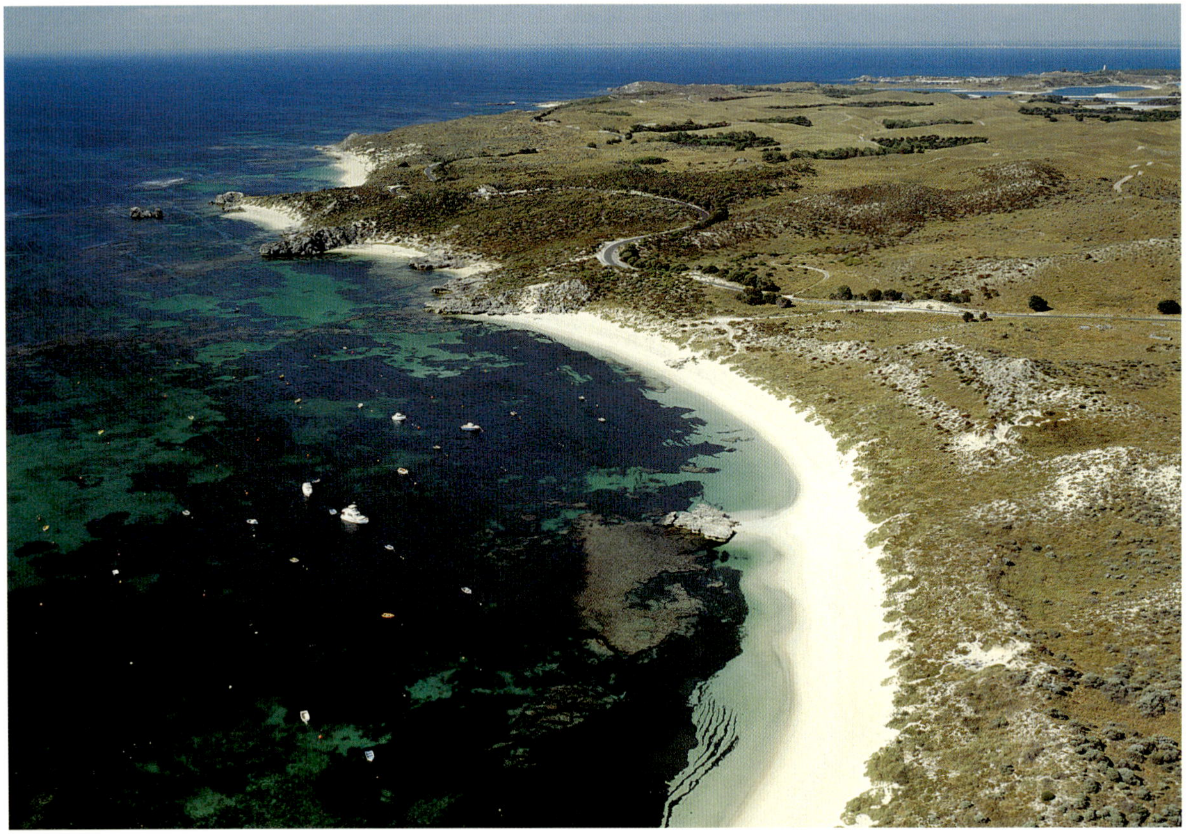

Above: The island of Rottnest was explored by Dutch seamen in 1658.

Rottnest is an island 19 kilometres from the coast of Western Australia, 11 kilometres in length and 4.5 kilometres at its widest point. It features five salt lakes which have their own unique wildlife. A short journey by sea and an even briefer one by air, this holiday-makers' paradise is made all the more attractive by a ban on private vehicles, which brings the silent, non-polluting bicycle into its own. For many West Australians, a trip to "Rotto" is the reward for a year's hard work. For visitors to the State, it is a highlight in a journey full of wonderful experiences.

Opposite: The flash of the lighthouse (left) can be seen on the mainland.
Following pages: An aerial view of Fremantle's Success Harbour and, above, Fishing Boat Harbour.

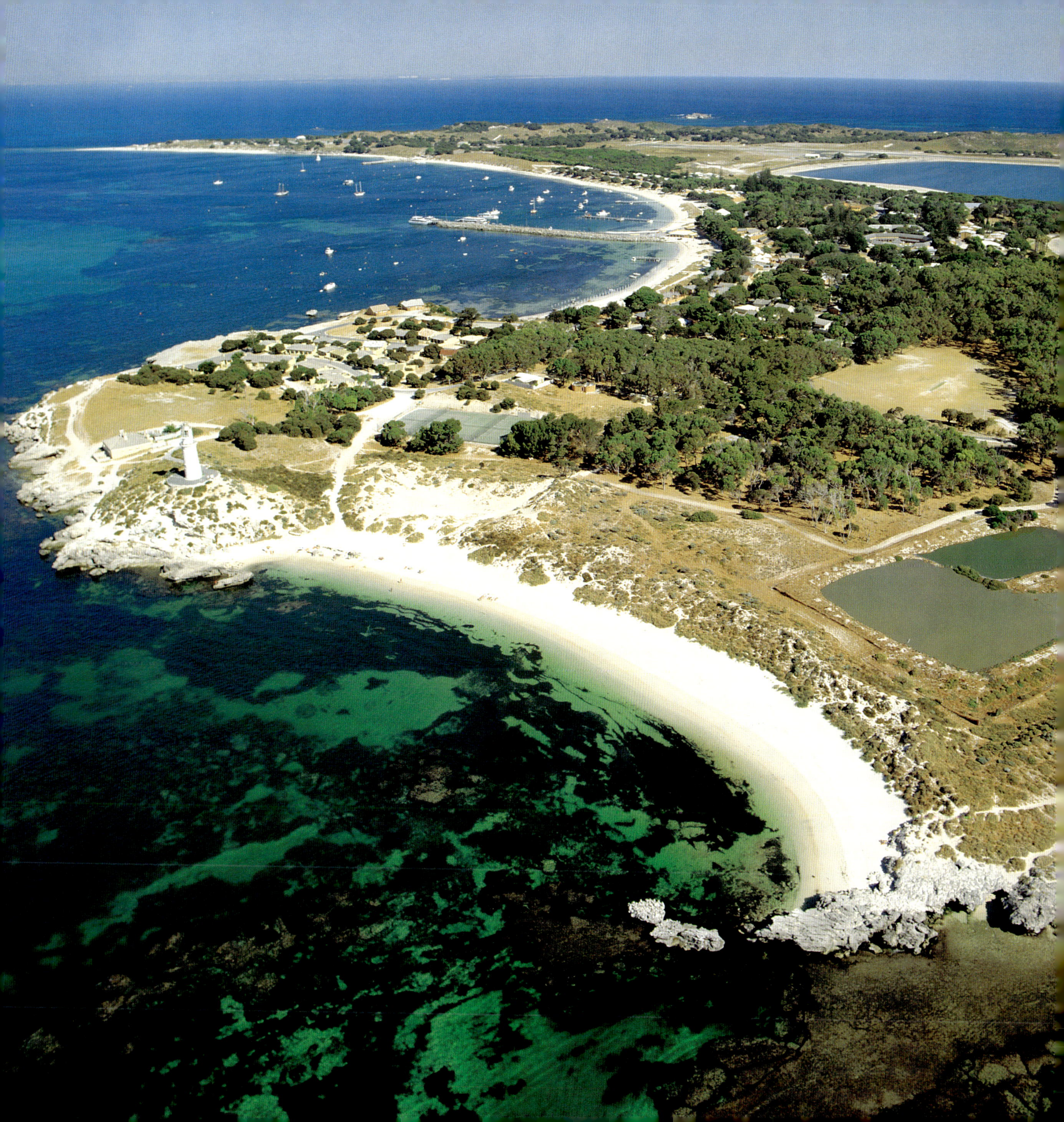

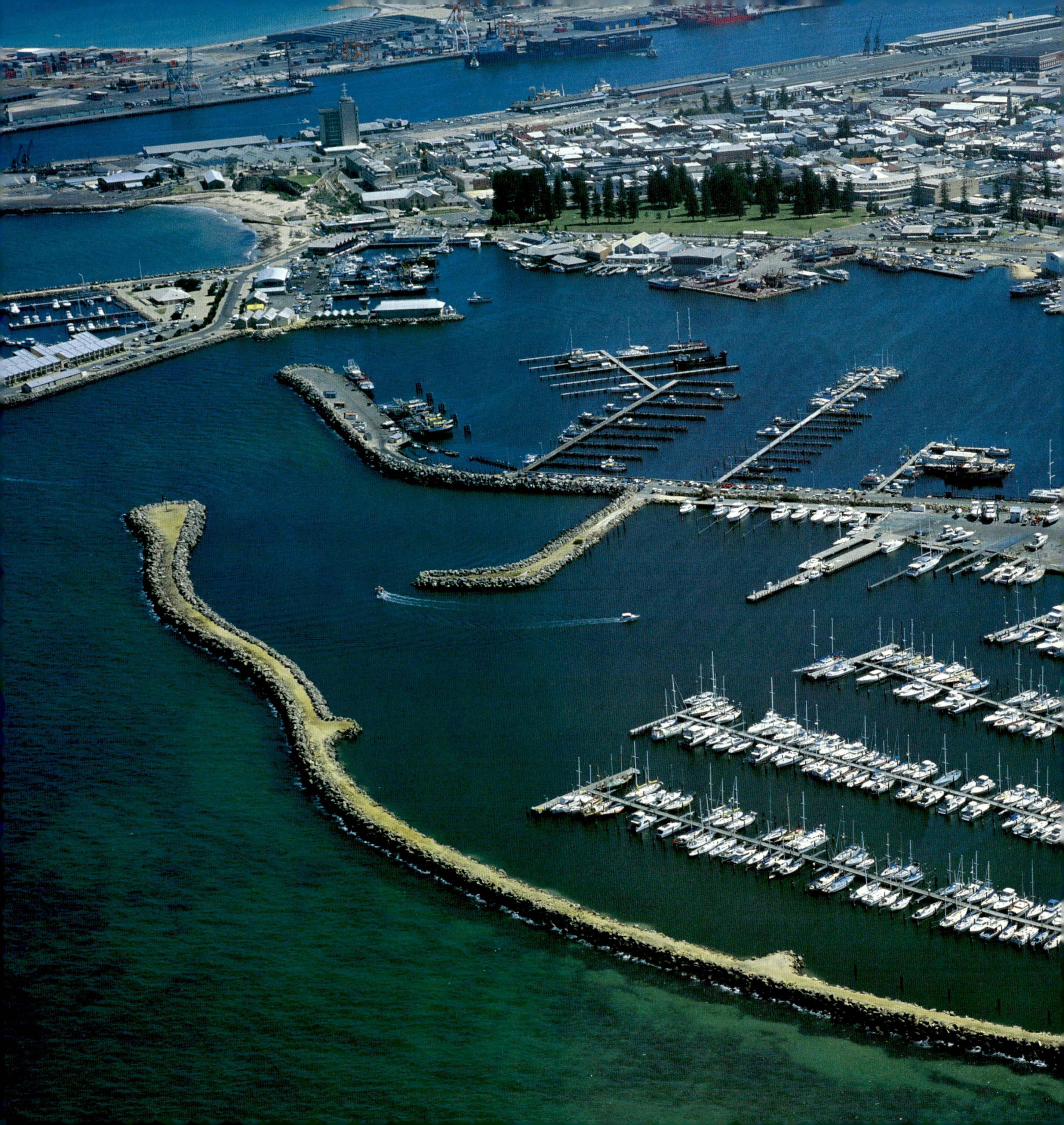

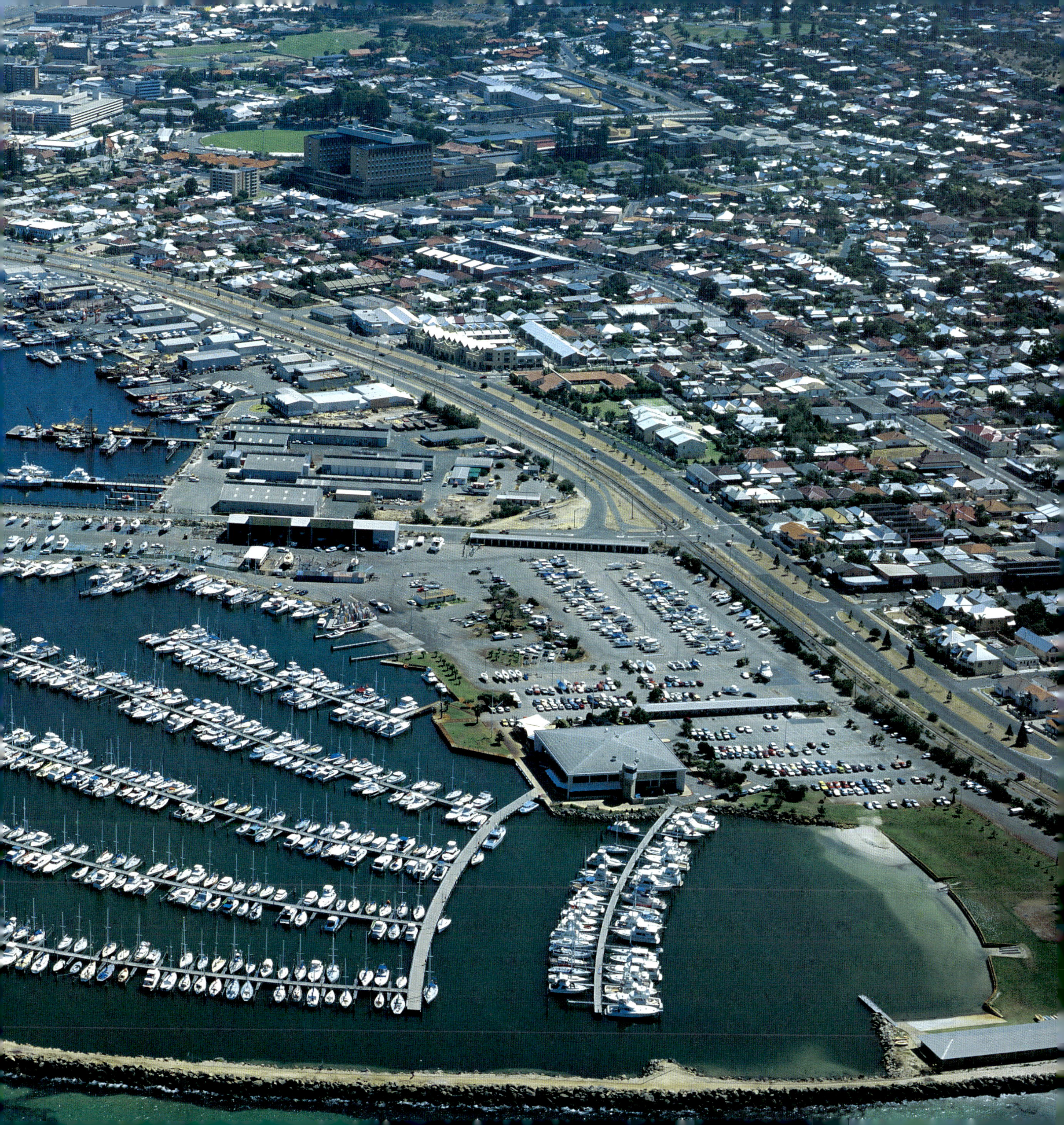

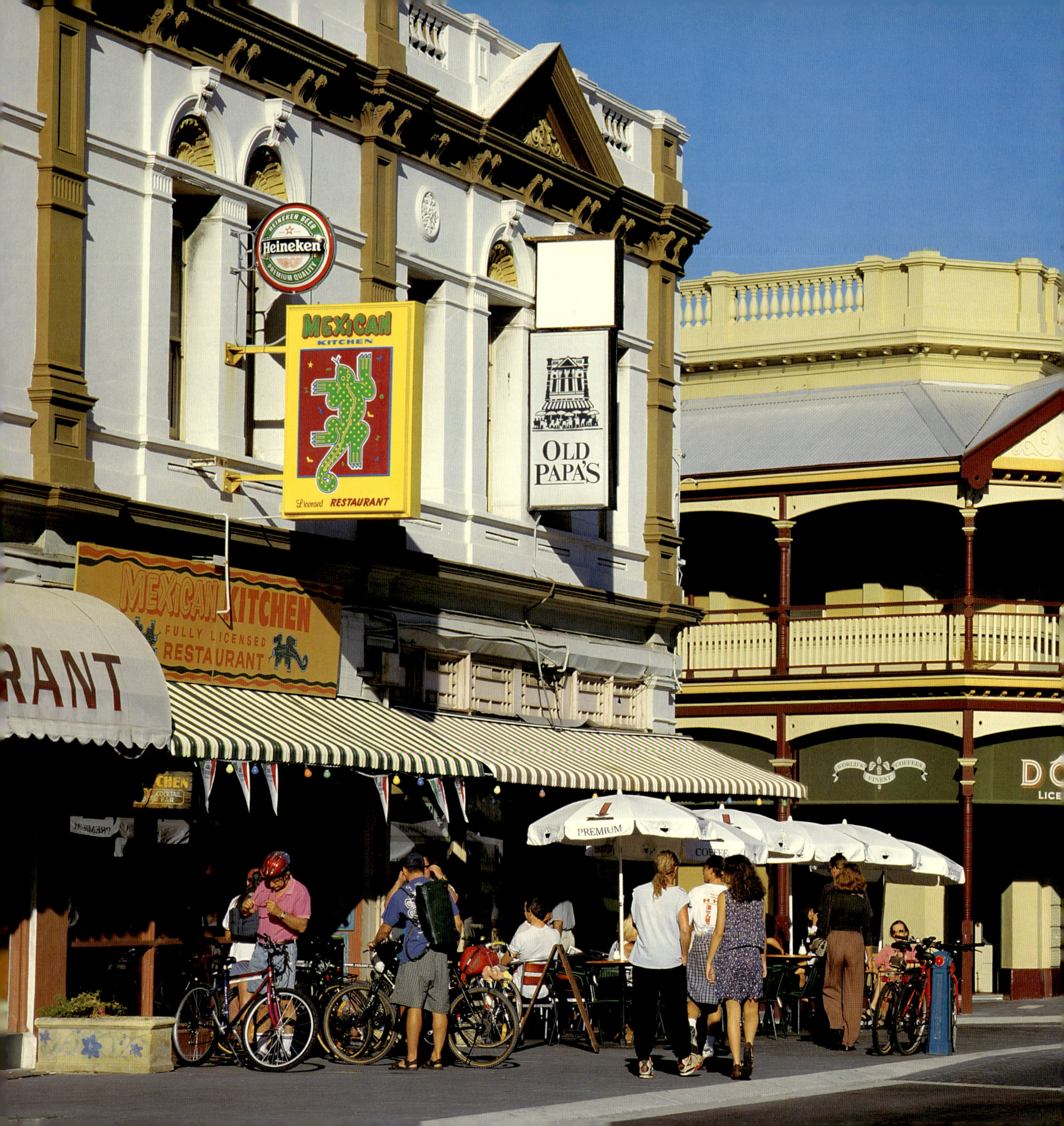
Heineken
MEXICAN KITCHEN
Licensed RESTAURANT
OLD PAPA'S
MEXICAN KITCHEN
FULLY LICENSED
RESTAURANT
RANT
PREMIUM

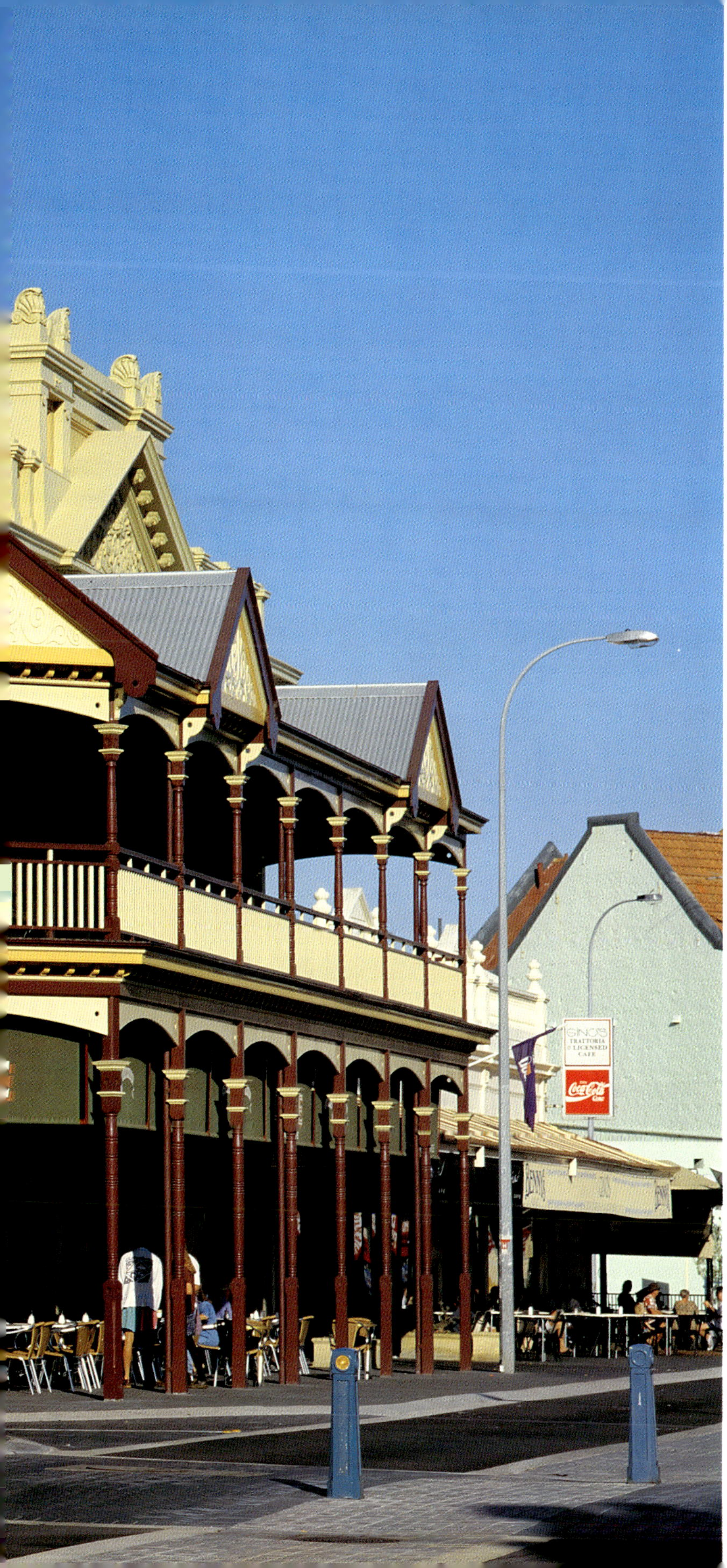

Fremantle

A visitor to the capital of the Golden West gets two cities instead of one. Only 19 kilometres from the centre of Perth, where the Swan River meets the sea, stands the port of Fremantle. The America's Cup competition of 1987 brought new fame and renewed vigour to a place whose historic public and commercial buildings and workaday port facilities had long been taken for granted. Suddenly Fremantle was scrubbed up and rejuvenated for its international media coverage. Once the Cup frenzy was over, many people remembered the city's charm and multicultural vitality. Today, Fremantle is a working port and harbours a large fishing fleet, but it is also home to countless arts and crafts practitioners, has a magnificent Maritime Museum and splendid Arts Centre. Dining and cafe-visiting in Fremantle have outlasted fashion's whim, and the solid limestone and brick cottages which once housed dock workers and factory workers have become sought-after dwellings for those who enjoy the ambience of this fascinating and historic port.

Fremantle's famous Cappuccino Strip on South Terrace.

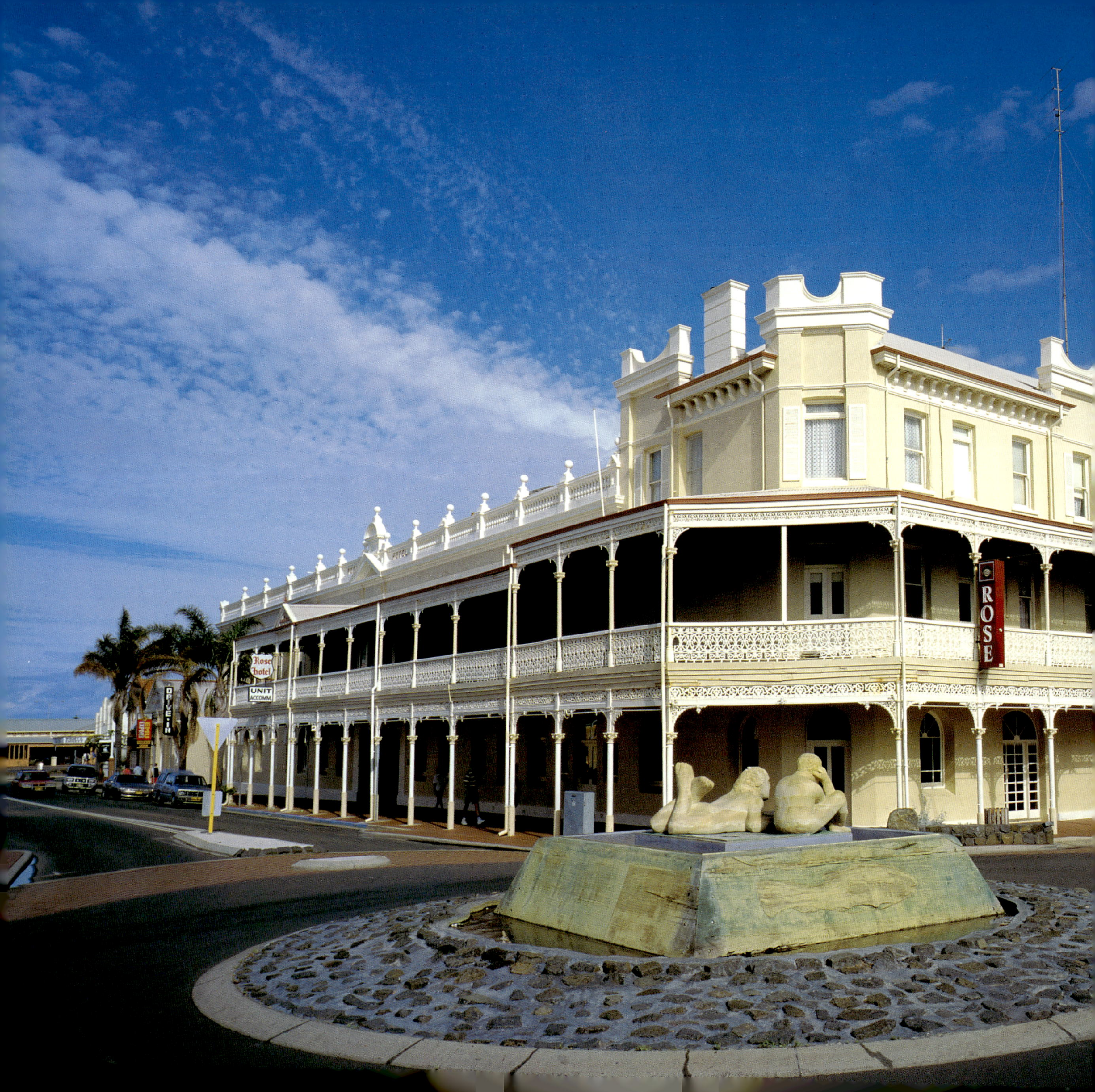
ROSE
Rose Hotel
UNIT ACCOMM
DRIVE-IN

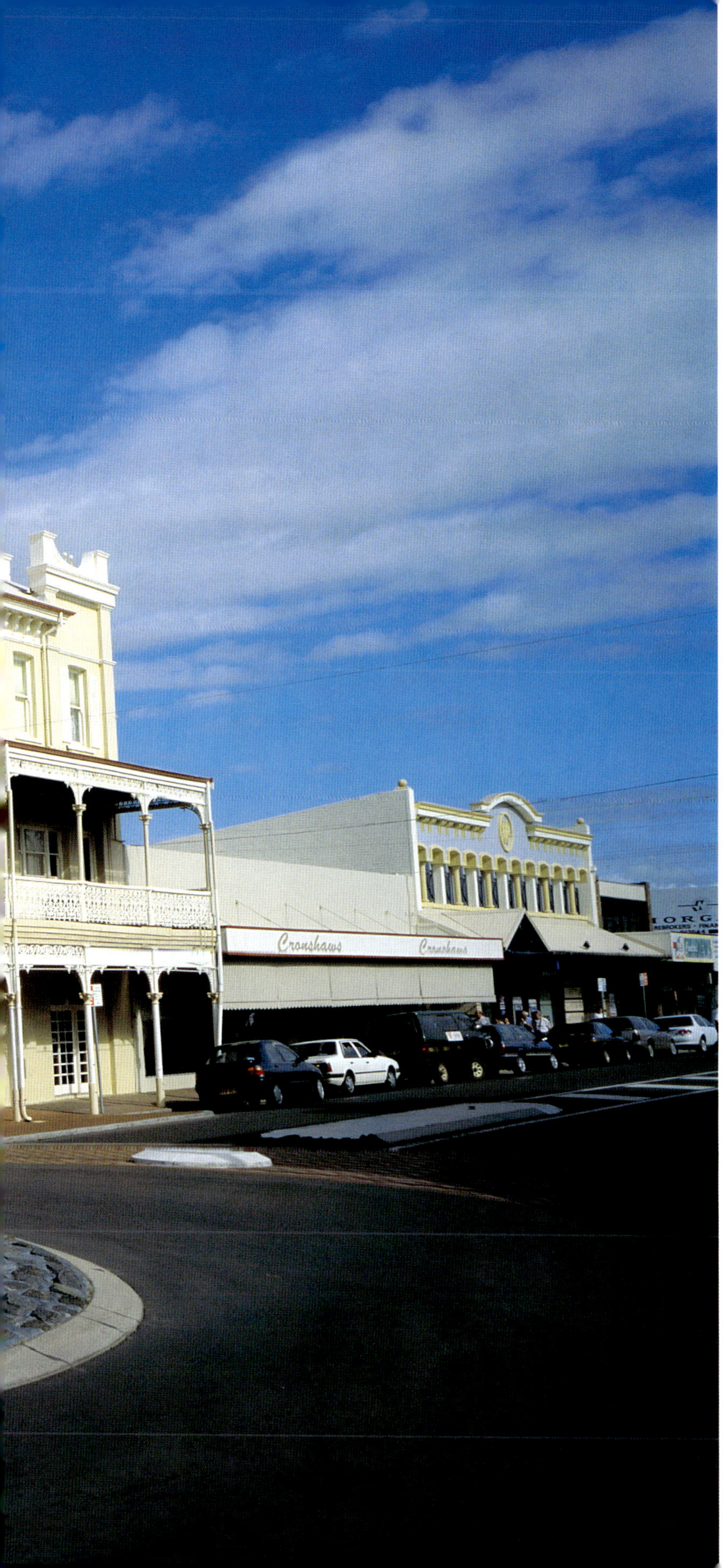

Western Australia's heritage

The first European towns in Western Australia were Albany and Perth, both established in the late 1820s. Farmers and graziers rapidly extended the boundaries of settlement through the south-western corner of the State and northwards from Perth. Nearly every town had some convenient source of stone, and civic buildings, schools, churches and hostelries quickly graced the streets. These amenities were built to last and today towns such as Bunbury, Busselton, York, Geraldton, Kalgoorlie and Albany proudly display their heritage. Increasingly, visitors from interstate and overseas are exploring the towns of the south-west, the Wheatbelt, Goldfields and Batavia Coast north of Perth, admiring fine examples of nineteenth century architecture which, in many cases, have been restored to their former glory.

Figures on a traffic roundabout contemplate the splendid facade of the Rose Hotel, Bunbury.

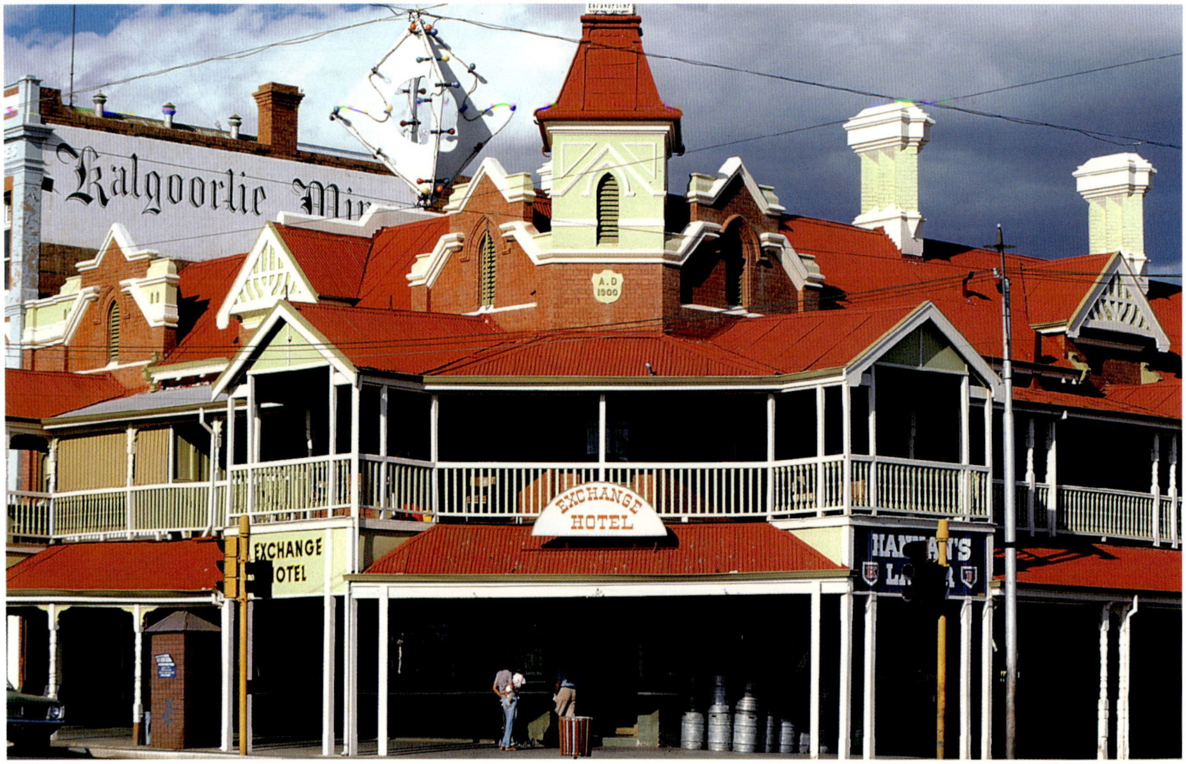

The Exchange, one of Kalgoorlie's many hotels, stands near the offices of the famous Goldfields newspaper, the *Kalgoorlie Miner*.

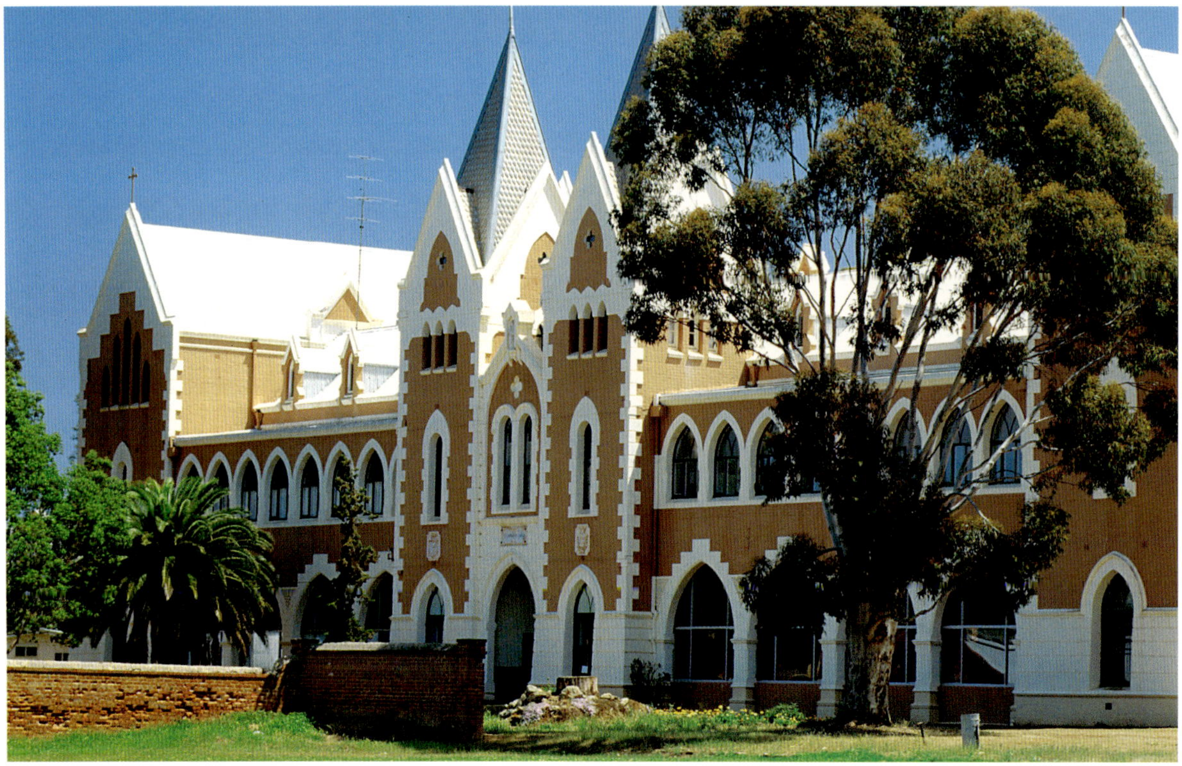

New Norcia was founded in 1846 by the Benedictine order of monks as an Aboriginal mission. Today it is noted for its art gallery and museum.

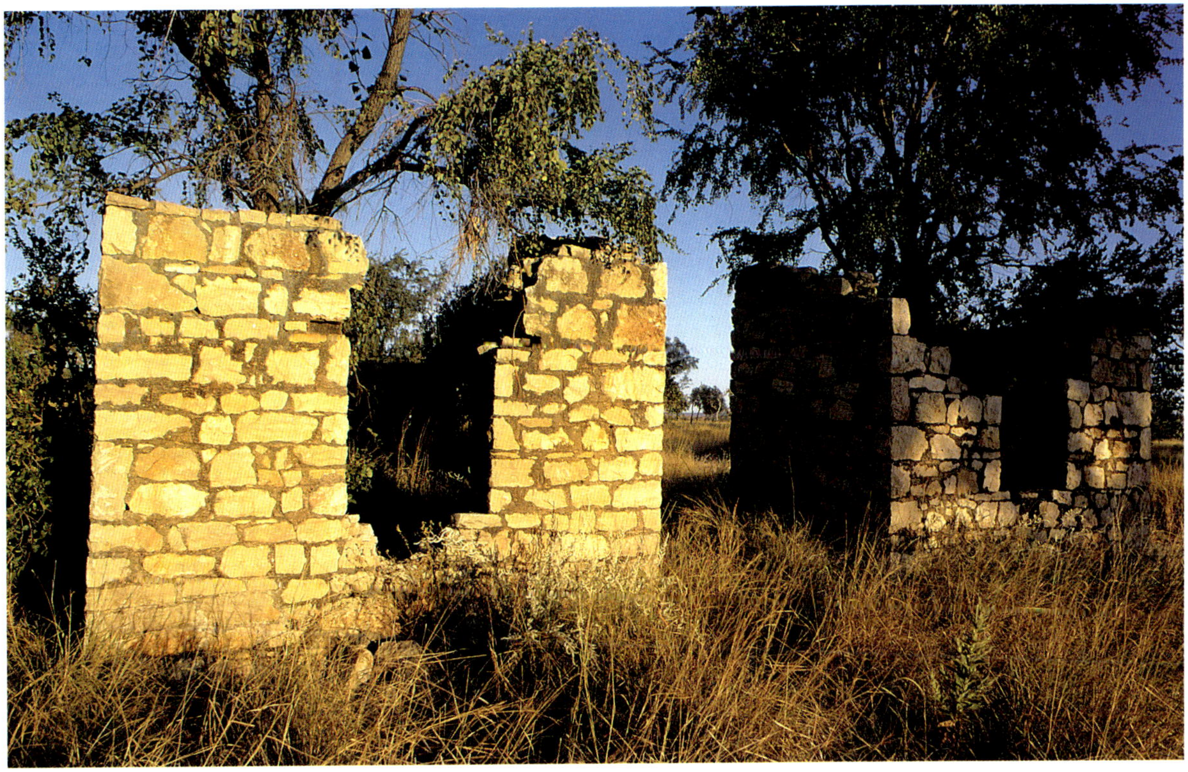

The ruins of historic Lillimilura Police Station, located within Windjana Gorge National Park.

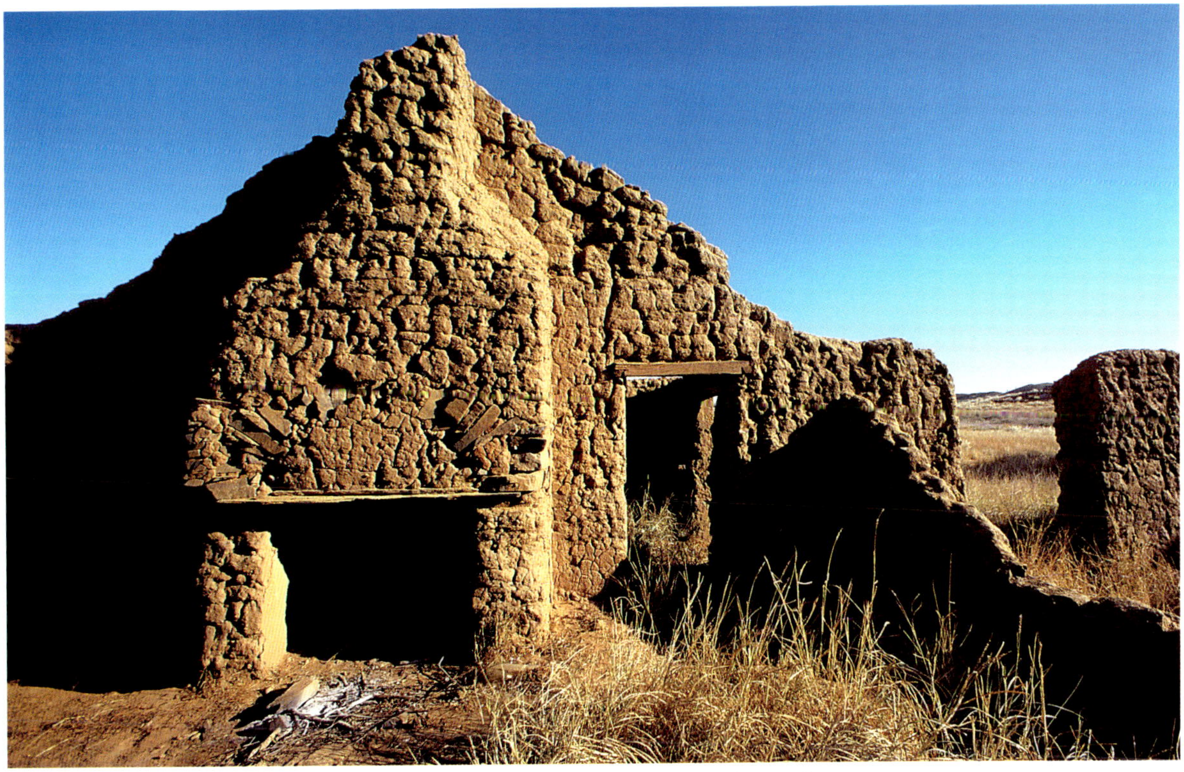

The remains of the mudbrick post office at Halls Creek, a Kimberley outpost where gold was discovered in 1885.

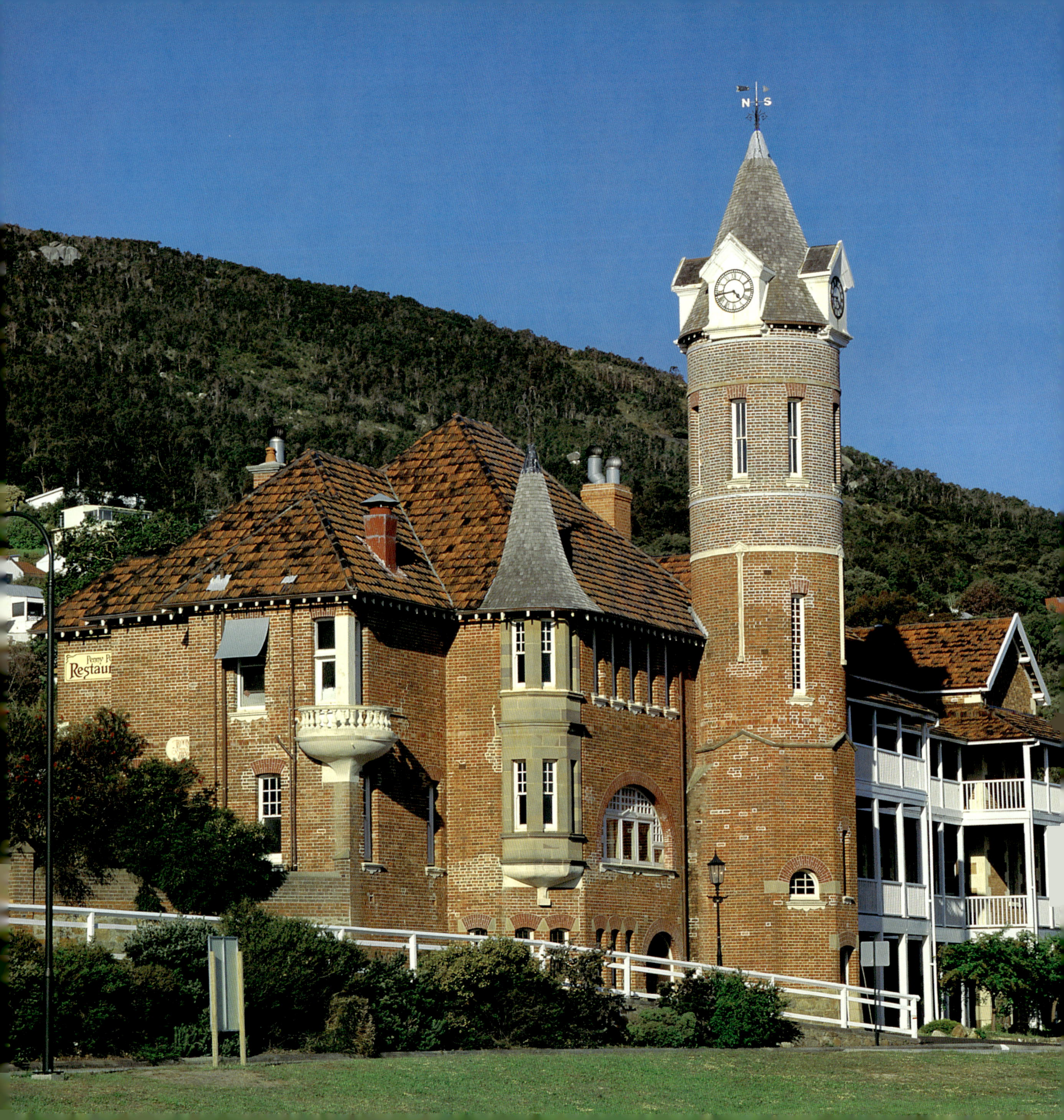
N S
Restaur

Albany

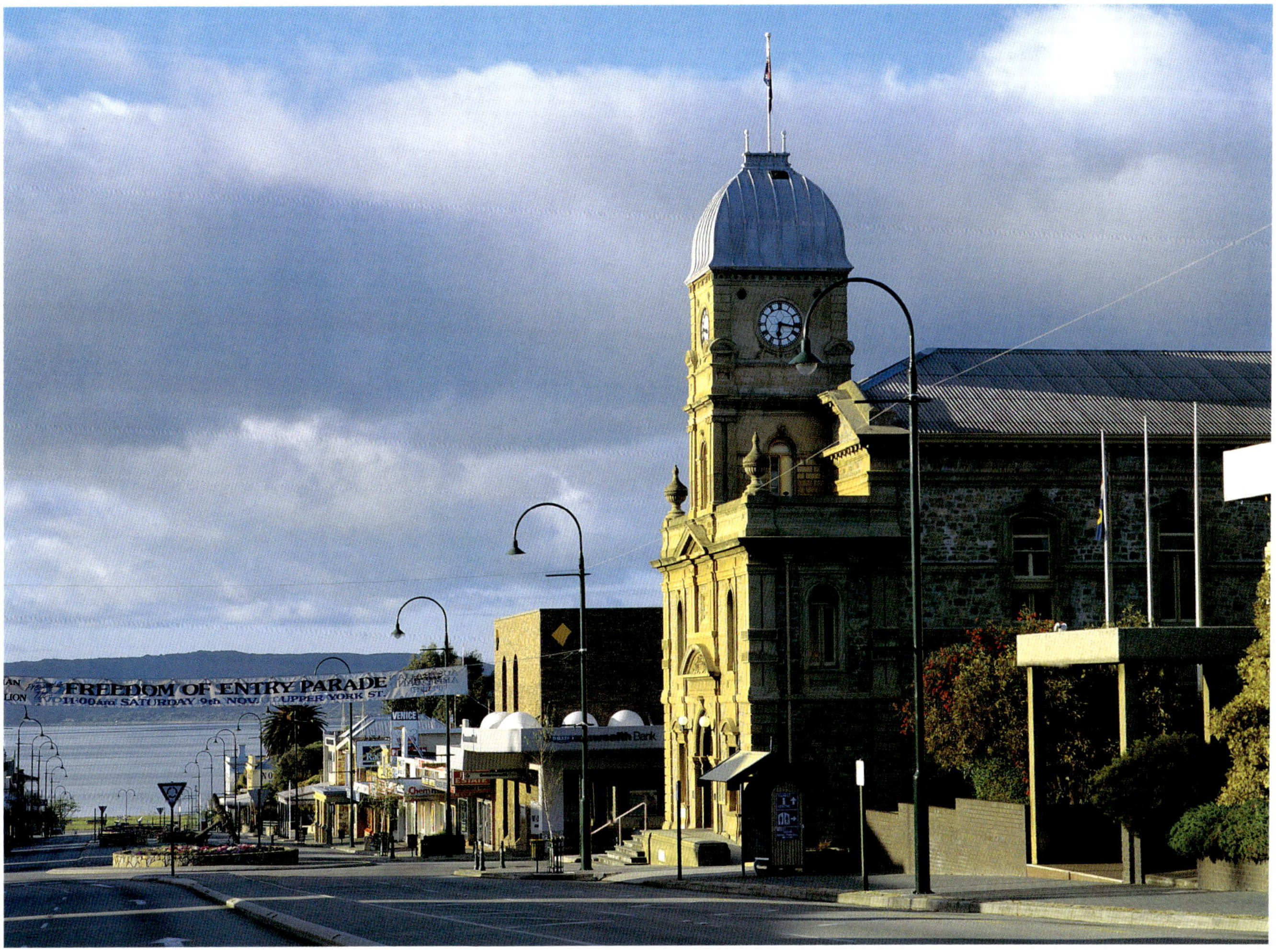

Above: A view down Albany's York Street to Princess Royal Harbour. On the right is the Town Hall.

The charming town of Albany, on the south-east coast of Western Australia, was settled by the British in 1826. Its fine harbour meant that it became a thriving whaling port and coaling station. Today, this historic town is an excellent base for exploration of some of Australia's most rugged and spectacular coastal scenery, and for scenic and wildflower tours of Porongurup and the Stirling Range.

Opposite: Albany's old Post Office now houses the Inter-Colonial Museum. In the background is Mt Clarence.

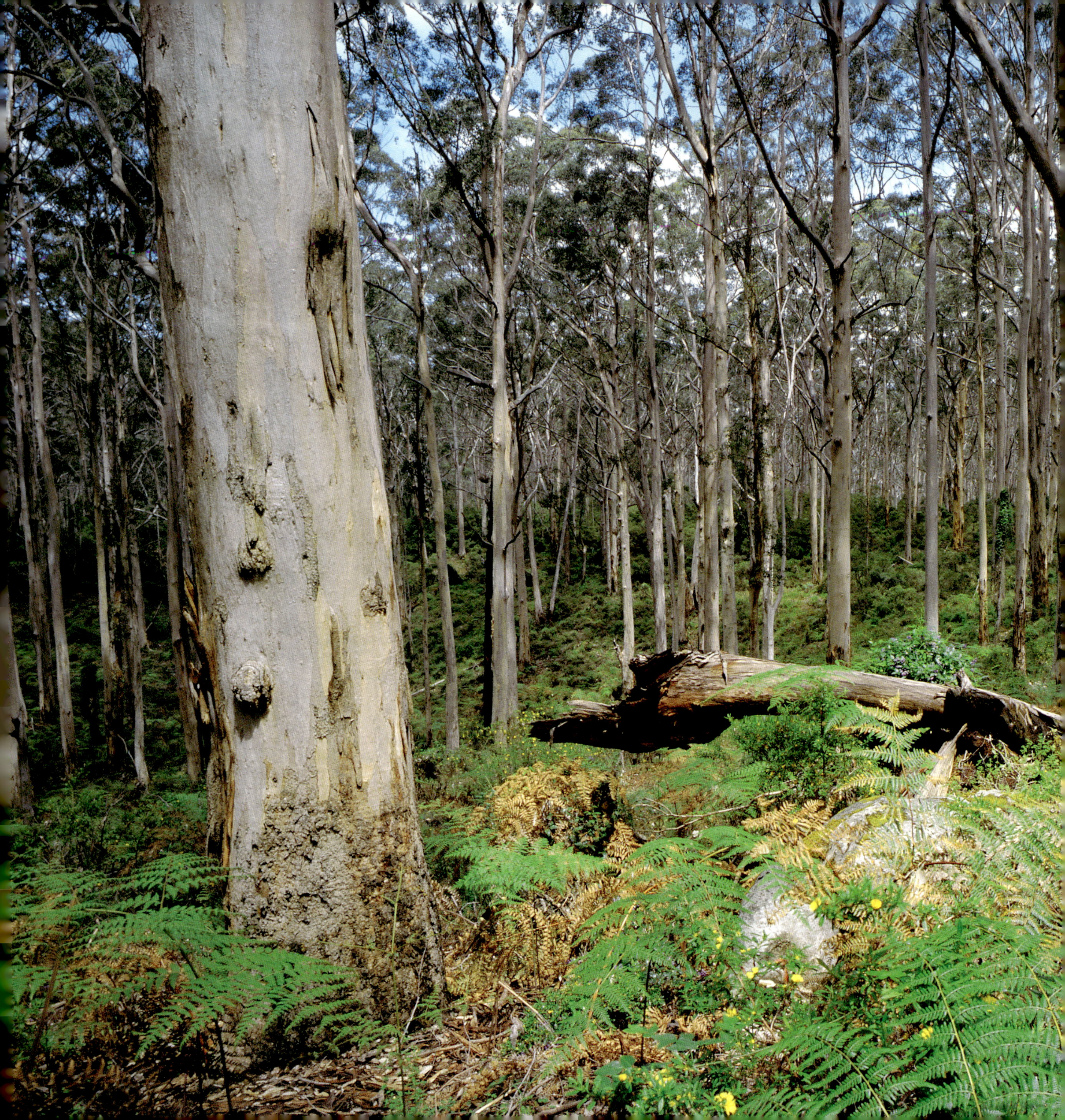

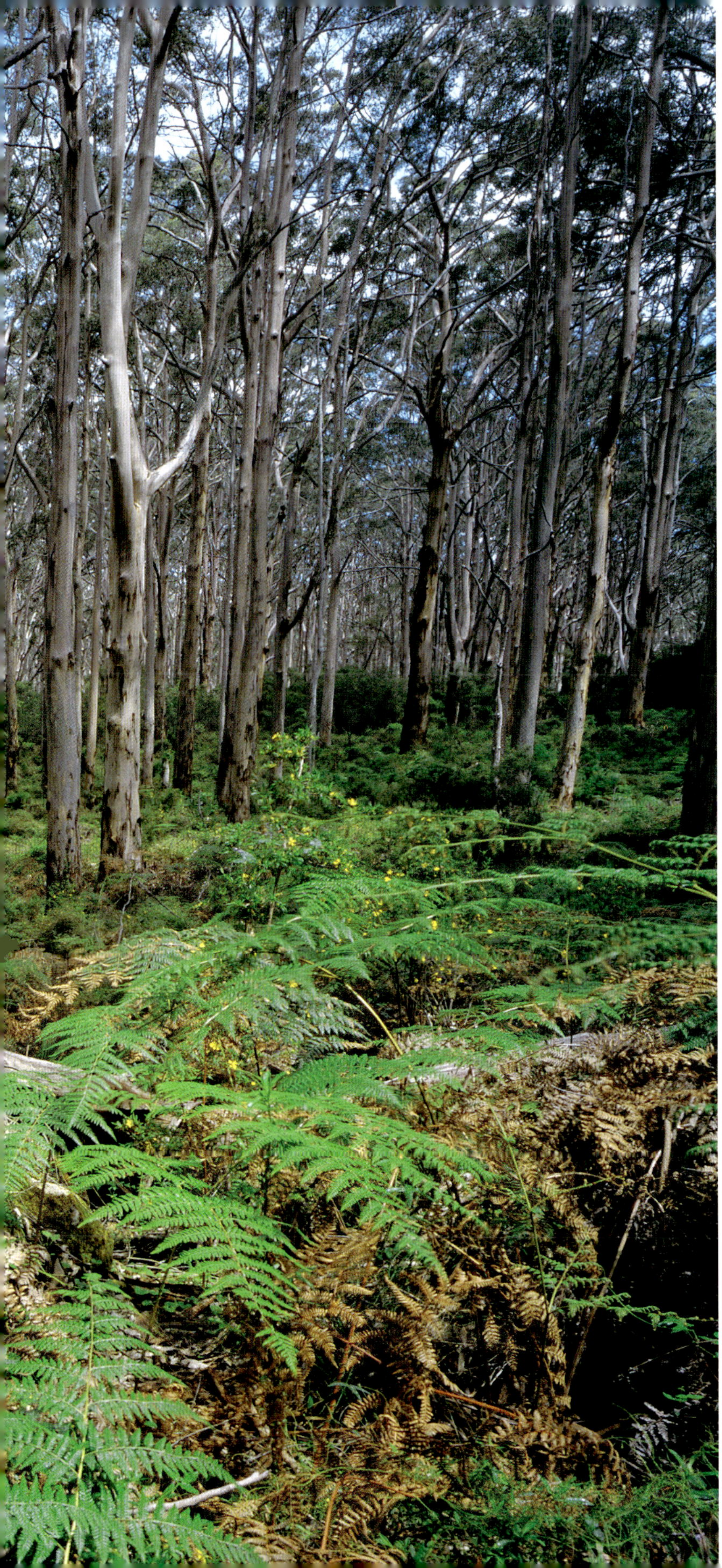

Leeuwin–Naturaliste National Park

Leeuwin–Naturaliste National Park, which runs around the coast in a narrow strip from Bunker Bay to Augusta, protects 120 kilometres of scenic grandeur.

The names of the features of this area are steeped in history. In 1622, the Dutch ship *Leeuwin (Lioness)*, gave her name to the cape at the south-west corner of the great southern continent. On 30 May, 1801, the French mariner Nicholas Baudin arrived at Géographe Bay with the ships *Le Géographe* and *Le Naturaliste* on a voyage of scientific discovery.

The shoreline of the park includes rugged cliffs, stark headlands and sheltered, sandy coves. Inland are coastal heathlands, woodlands and forests. In amongst the Jarrah and Marri trees, small patches of Karri, one of the world's tallest trees, can be seen. The Boranup Karri Forest, which was logged extensively in the late nineteenth century, contains regrowth trees up to 60 metres tall. This is the "limestone coast", and the area is famed for its cave systems, with spectacular stalactites and stalagmites.

Regrowth Karri trees and bracken fern, Leeuwin–Naturaliste National Park.

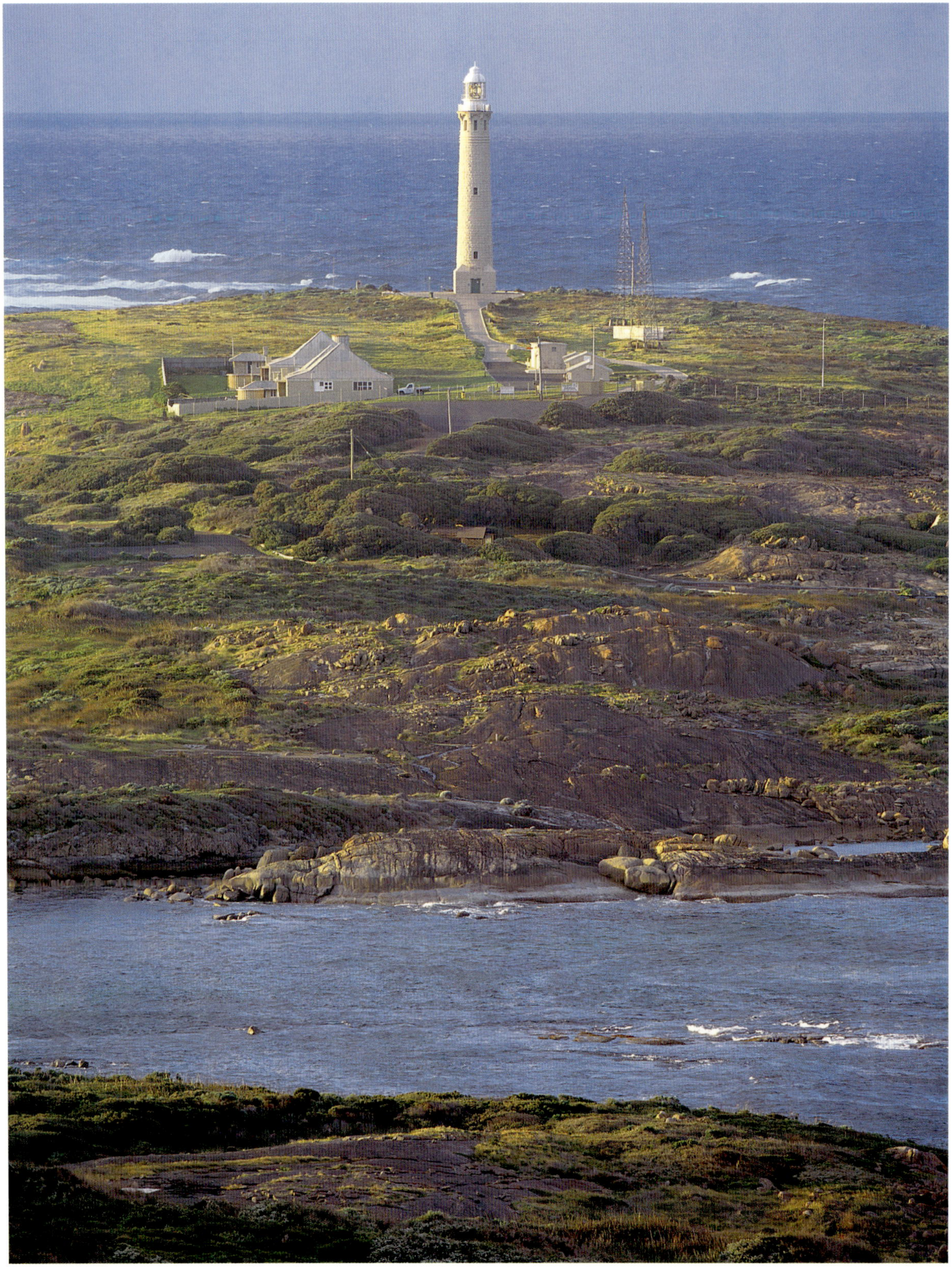

Cape Leeuwin lighthouse stands on the southernmost prominence of Leeuwin–Naturaliste National Park.

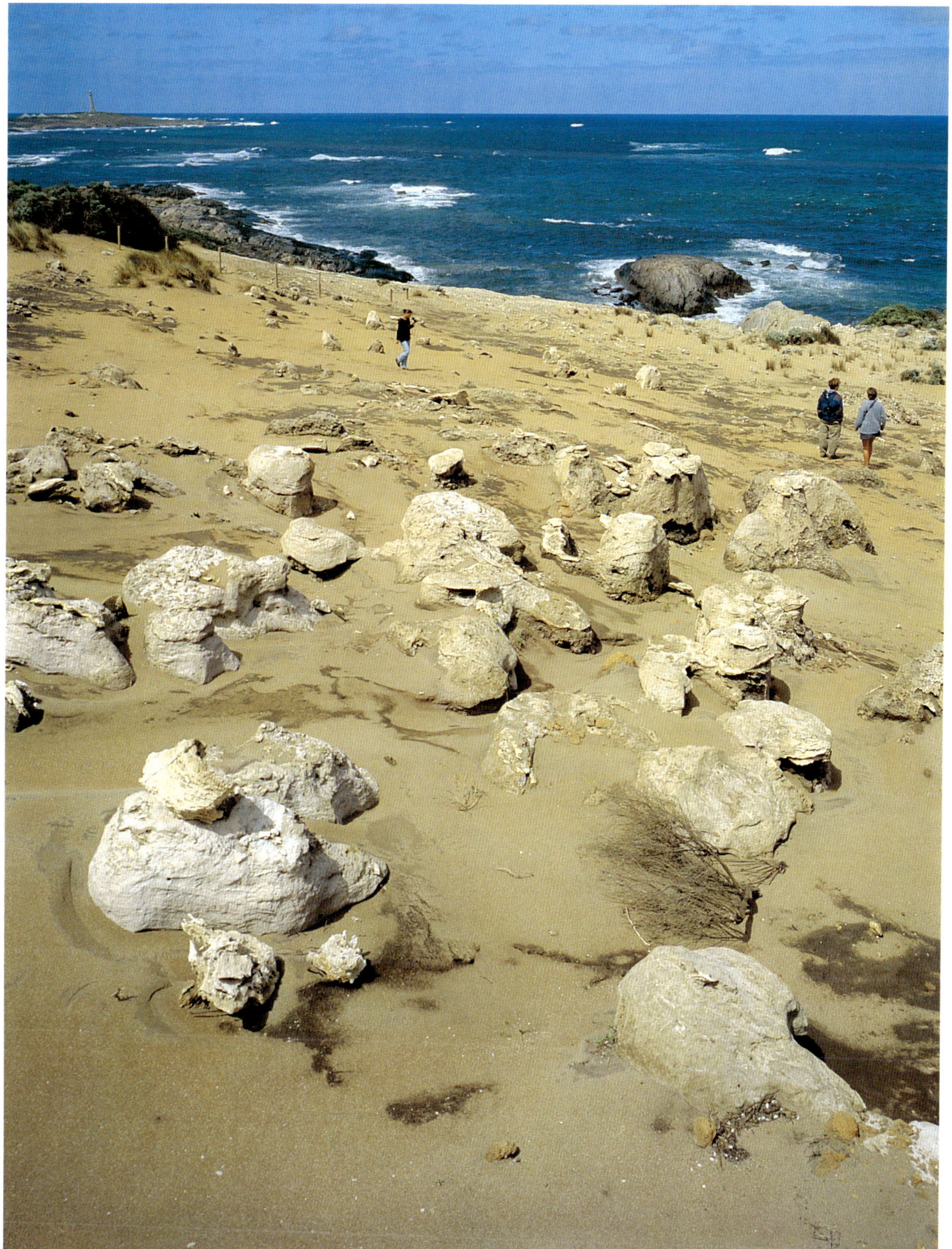

Above: Coastal limestone formations, Leeuwin–Naturaliste National Park.

Following pages: Sugarloaf Rock, just south of Cape Naturaliste.

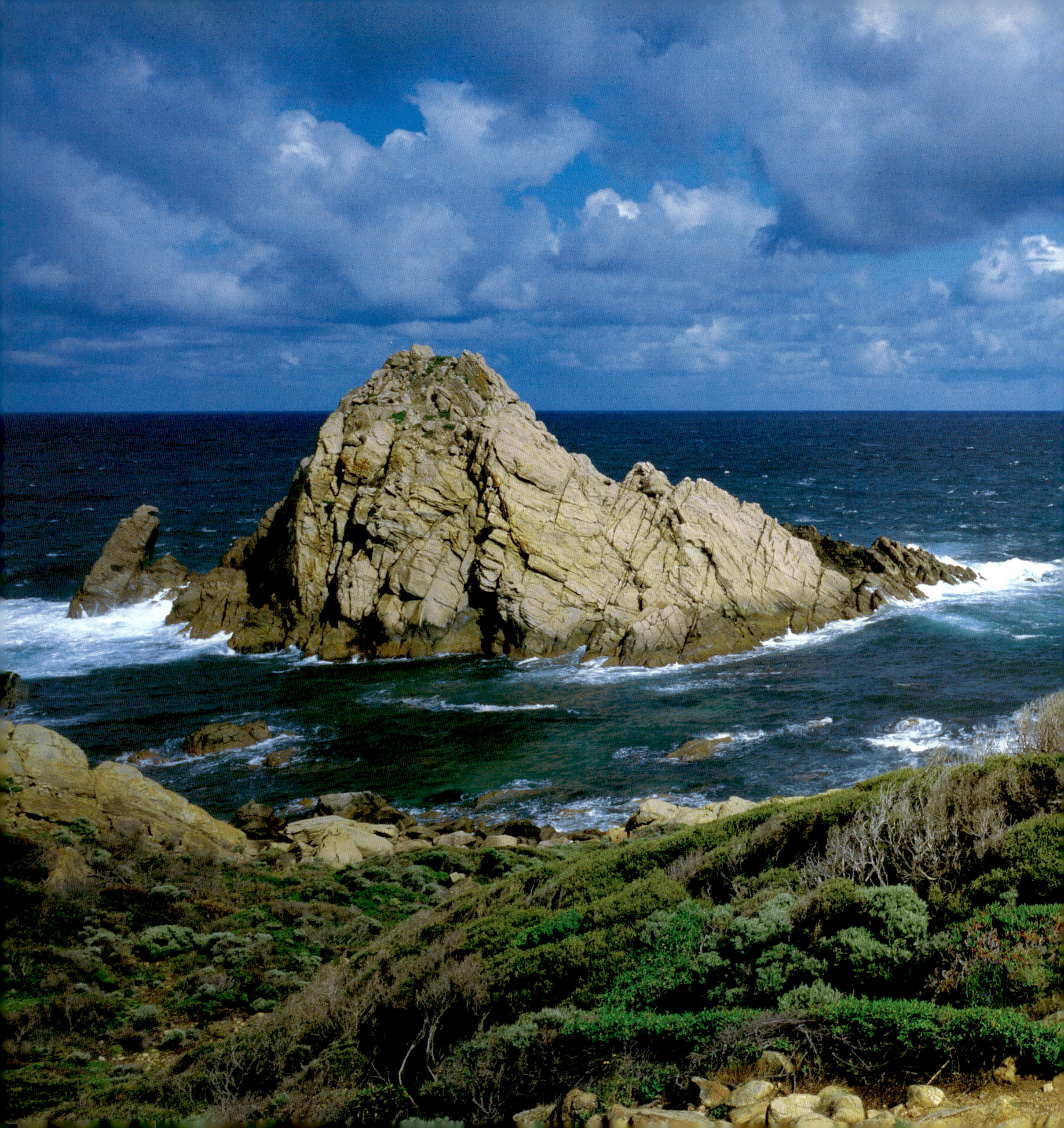

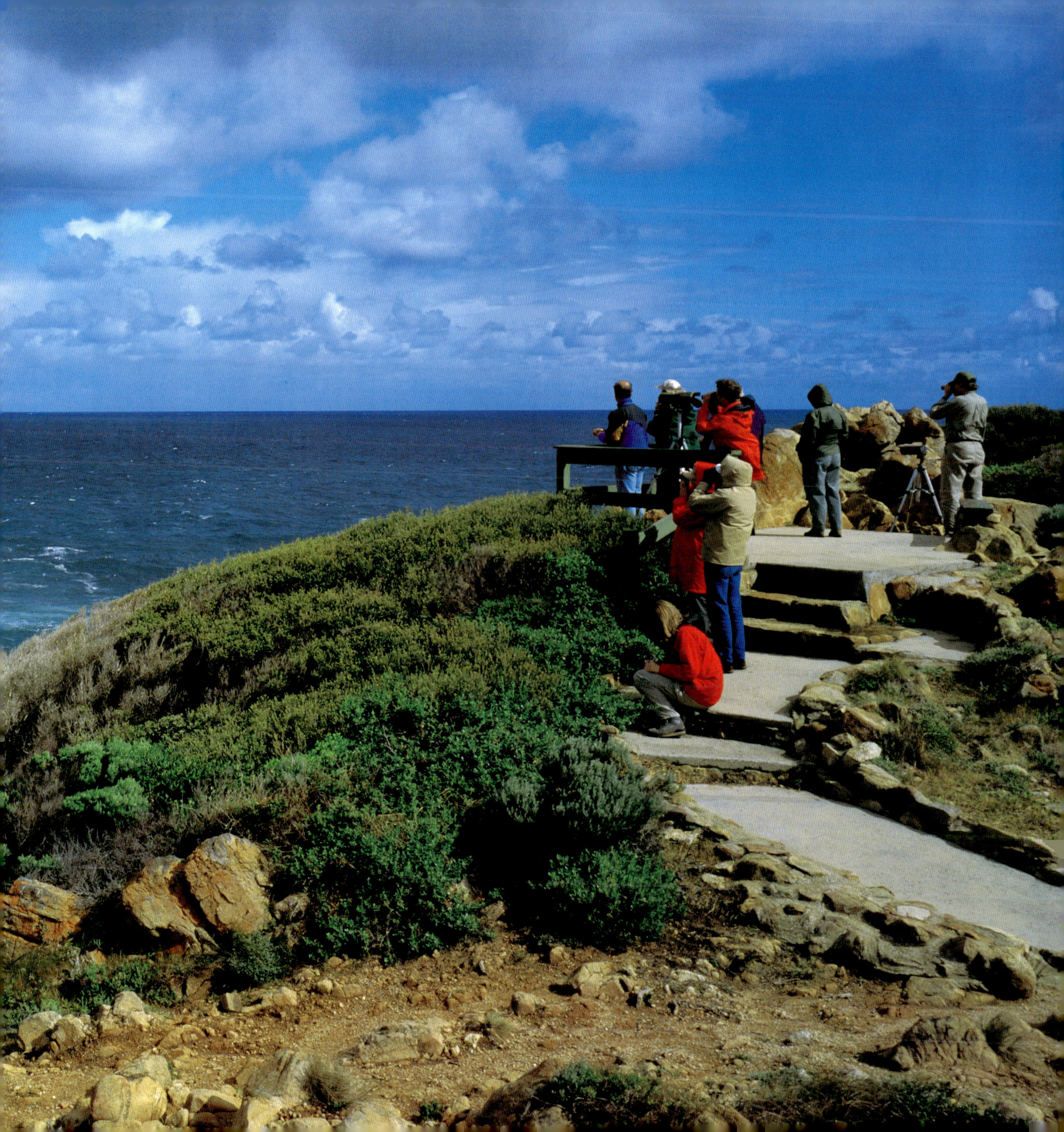

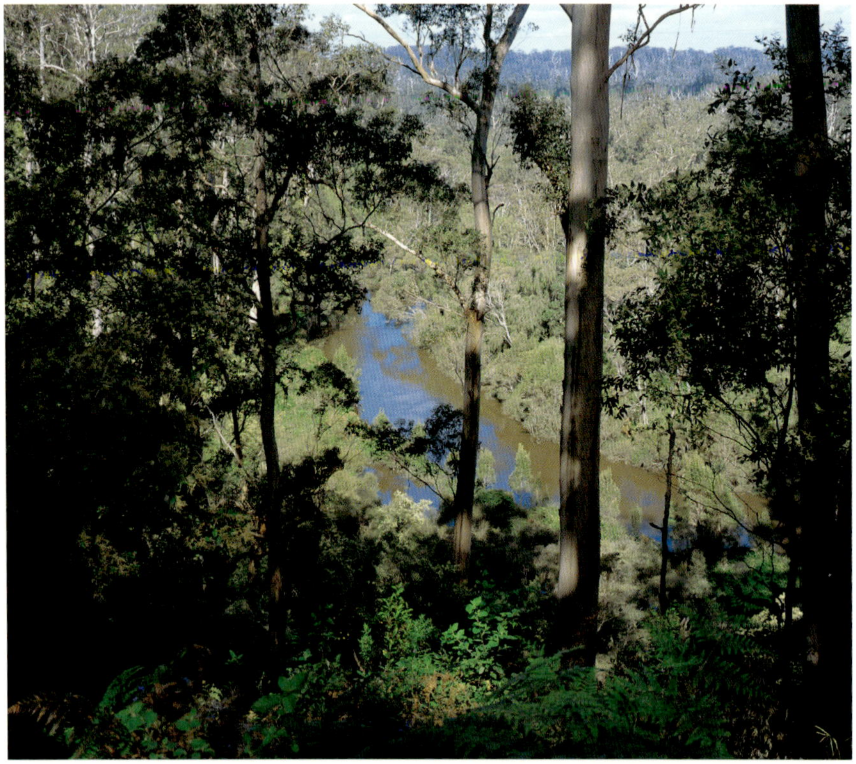

Above: A peaceful view of the Warren River, Warren National Park.

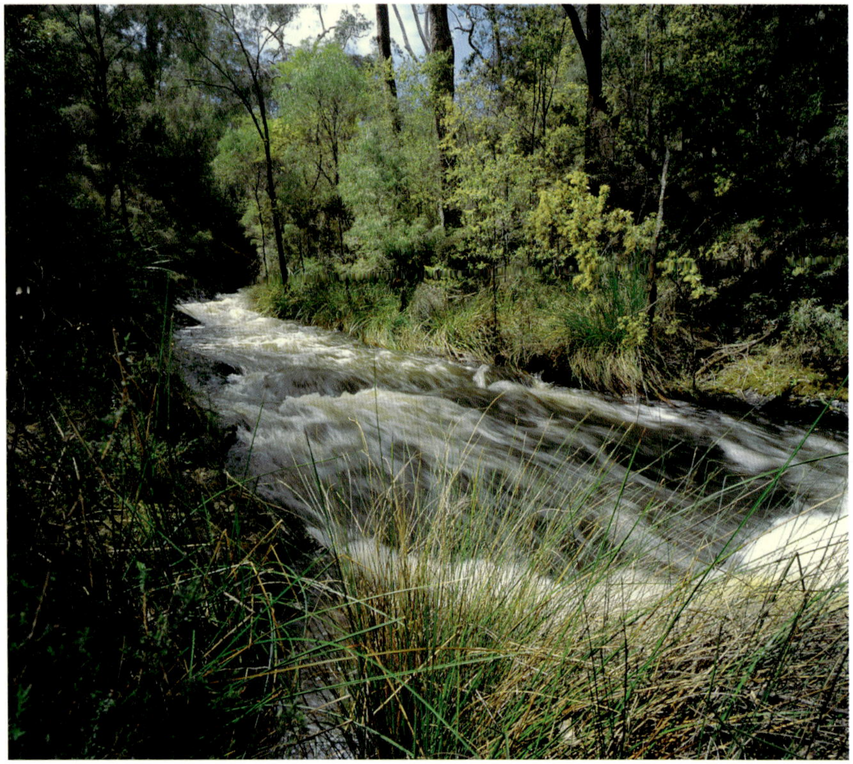

Above: Rapids on Beedelup Brook, Beedelup National Park.

Warren, Beedelup and Shannon National Parks

Uncut stands of Karri are a highlight of Warren National Park, near Pemberton, in the tall timber country. Much of this 1400-hectare area can be accessed only on foot by those dedicated to experiencing south-western wilderness. One of the two major routes through this magnificent area is called the Heartbreak Trail, while the other, not noticeably less rugged, has the milder title of the Maidenbush Trail.

Beedelup Brook and Beedelup Falls are attractions of Beedelup National Park, 15 kilometres west of Pemberton. Besides dense Karri forest, this lovely park contains pure stands of Marri, a rough-barked eucalypt whose white flowers provide plentiful nectar for insects and birds.

Shannon National Park is 30 minutes' drive from Pemberton. It covers the basin of the Shannon River and is an ideal place to learn the secrets of Western Australia's famed forests. Look for wildflowers in these parks from October to December.

Opposite: On the road to discoveries in Shannon National Park.

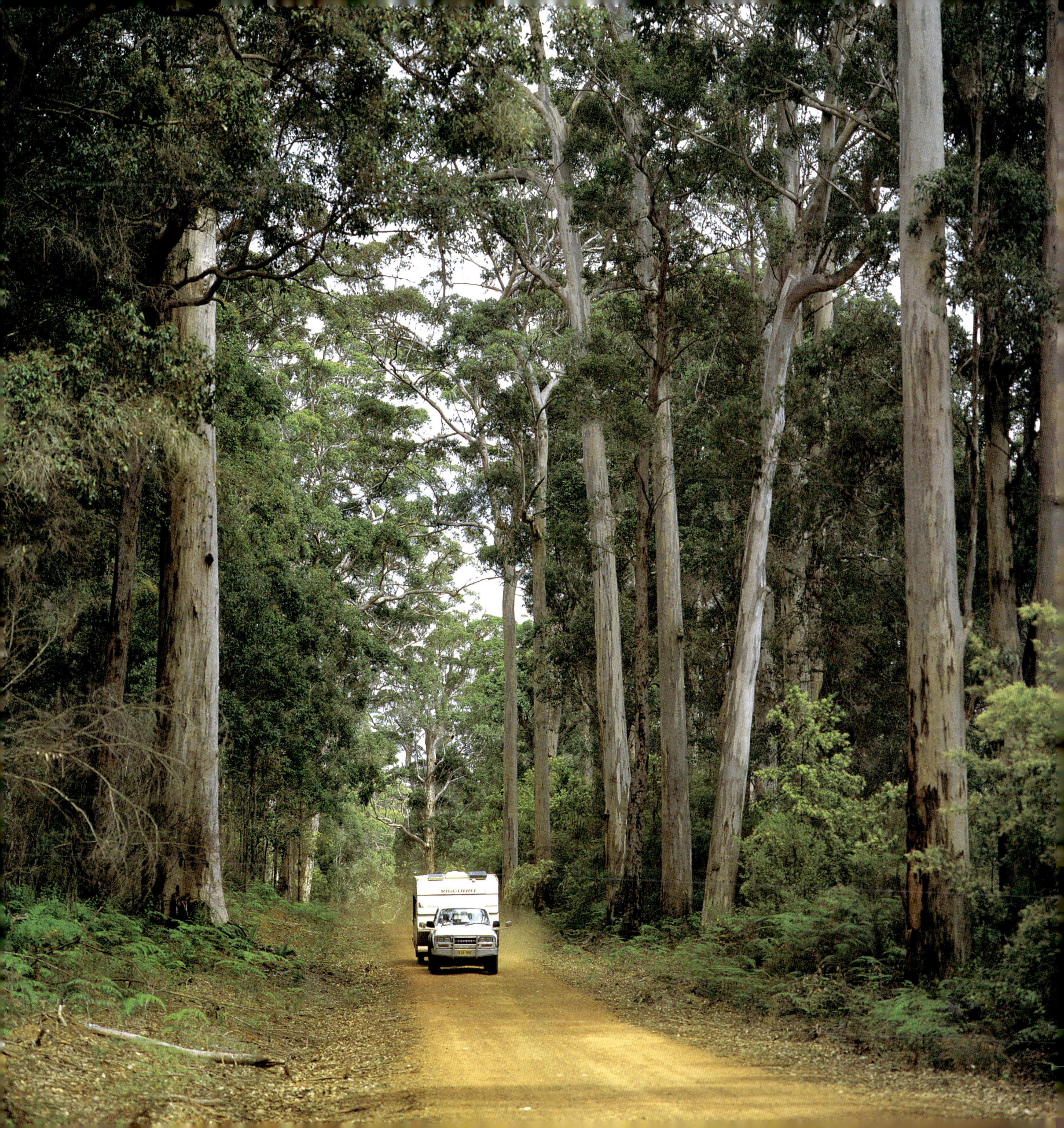

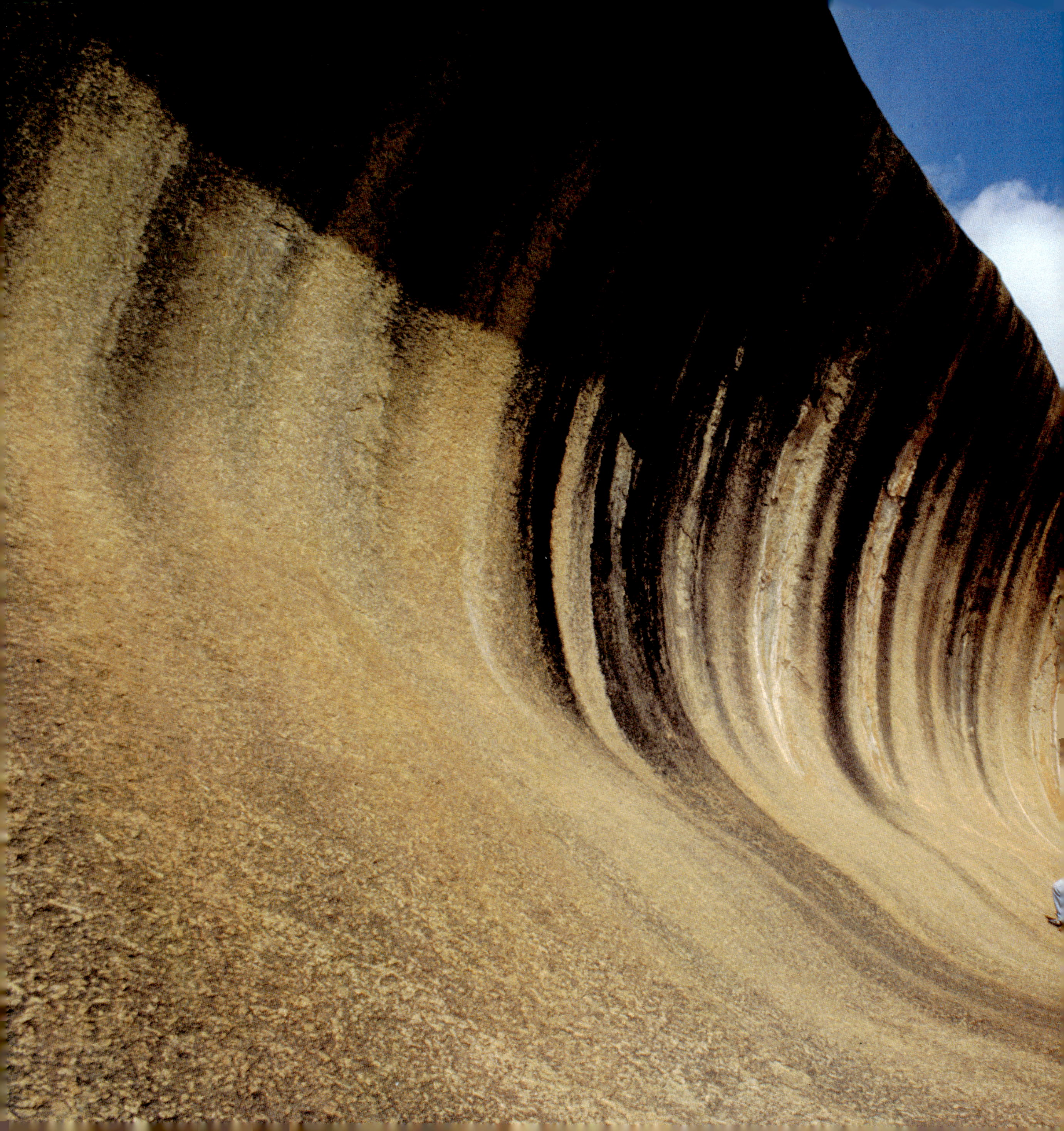

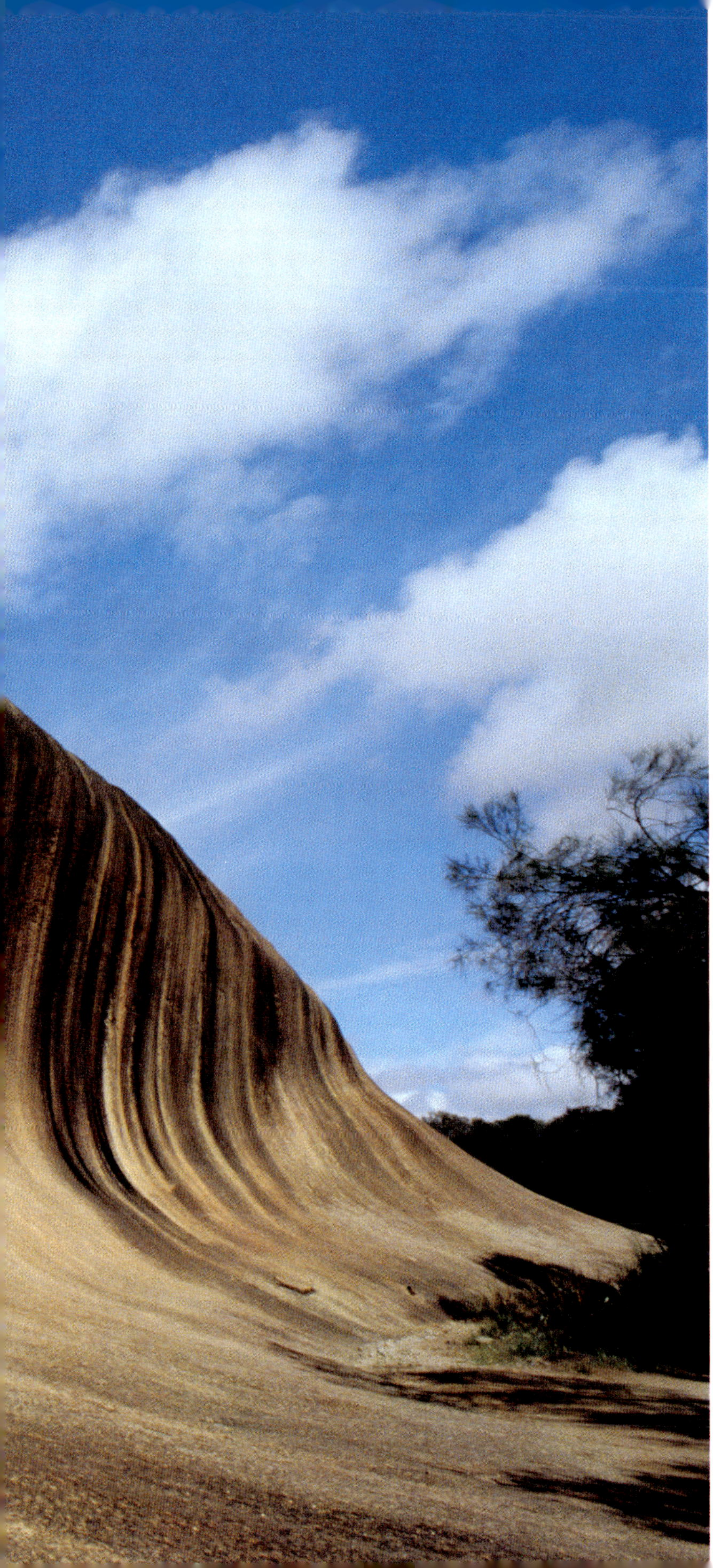

Wave Rock, Hyden

The inland plains to the east and south-east of Perth, first explored by timber-cutters seeking aromatic sandalwood, are now the source of wheat and wool. Isolated outcrops of granite called tors are characteristic of the Wheatbelt, and the little town of Hyden stands near a number of these. The end of one tor, Hyden Rock, forms the remarkable Wave Rock, whose lip hangs 15 metres above the ground.

It has taken around 300 million years of weathering to scour out the area under the overhang. The bands which run up and down the face are caused by dark-coloured algae which grow on streaks of minerals washed down the rock.

Wave Rock is the north wall of Hyden Rock, a huge mass of granite.

The Stirling Range

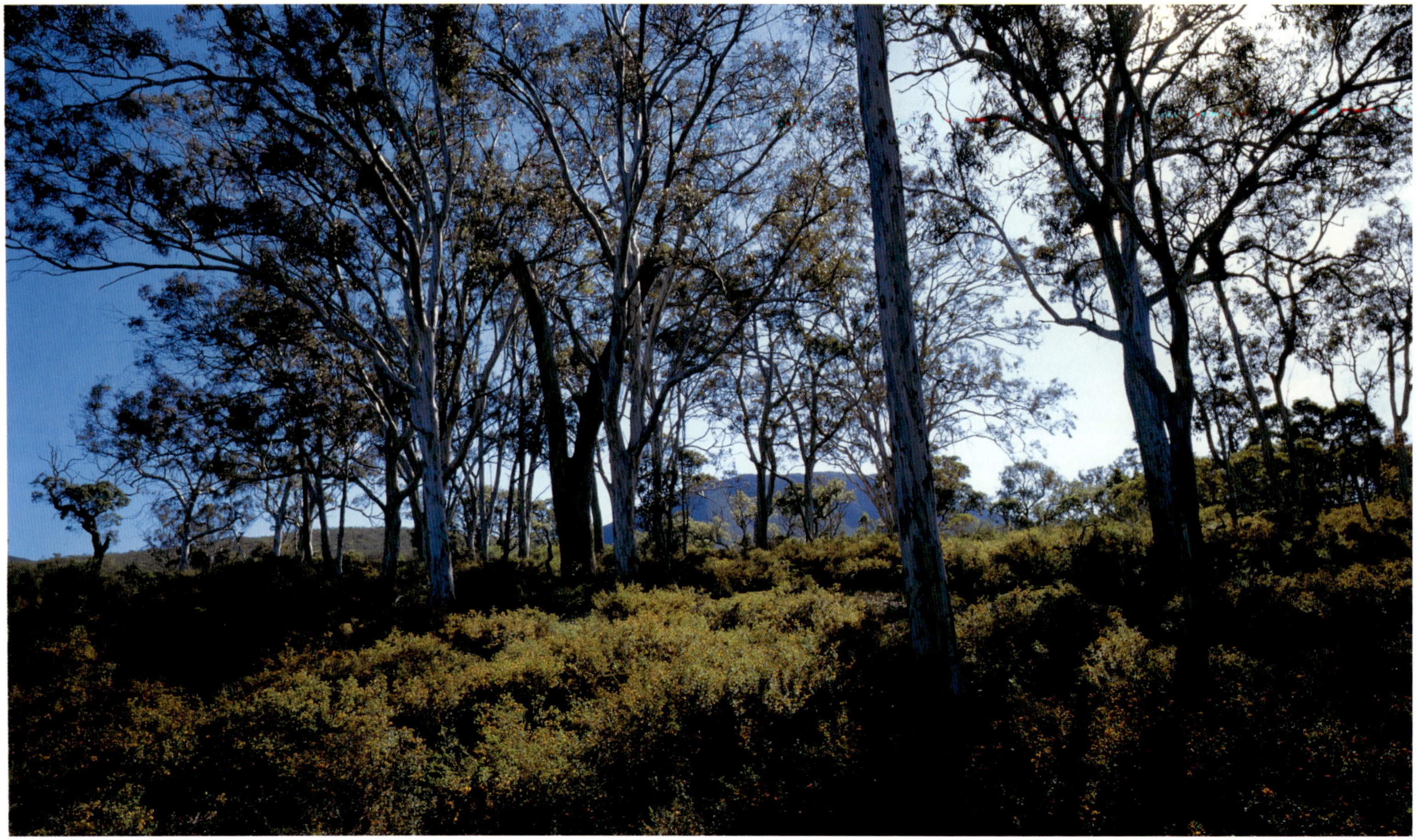

Above: Springtime in Stirling Range National Park.

The south-west of Western Australia is famous world wide for its wildflowers, which have developed in great variety on comparatively poor soils. Many of these flowers rely on birds, insects and mammals for pollination, so they are rich in nectar. The rugged Stirling Range, which rises to more than 1000 metres above sea level some 80 kilometres north of Albany, and stretches for around 65 kilometres from east to west, is a well known wildflower area. Over 1000 species grow on the various peaks of the range, and at least 60 of these plants are found nowhere else in the world.

Opposite: Wildflowers in Stirling Range National Park.

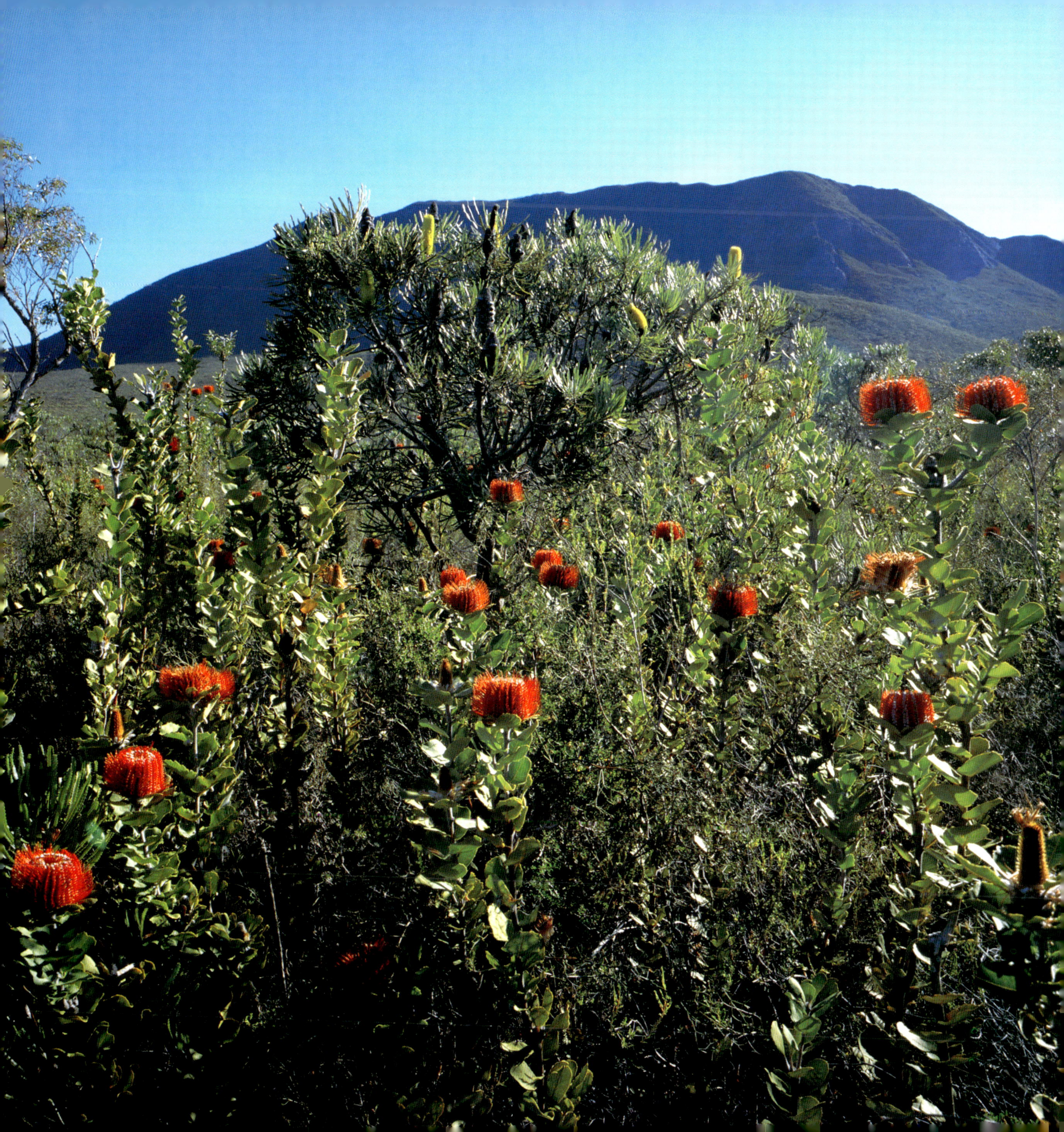

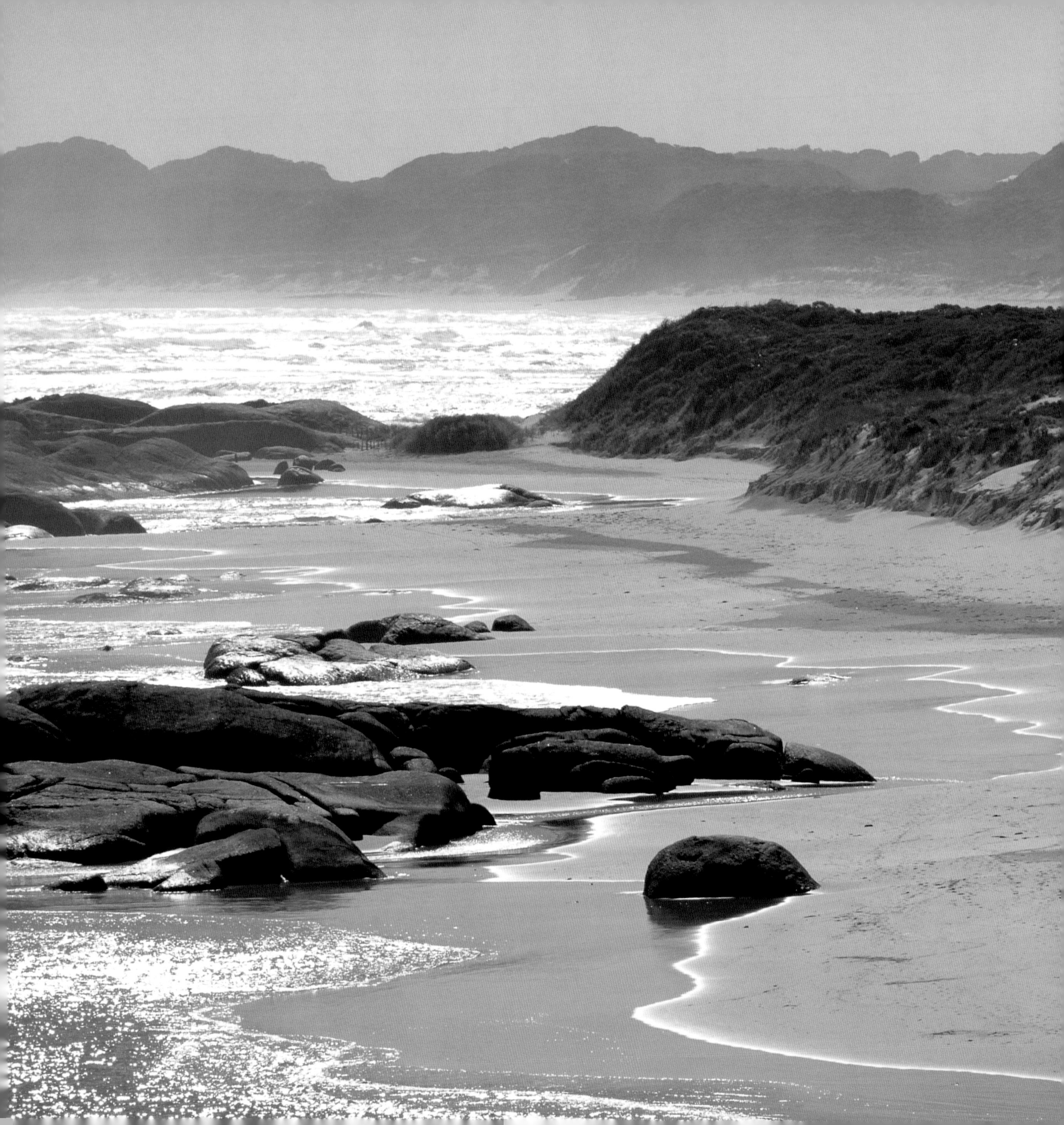

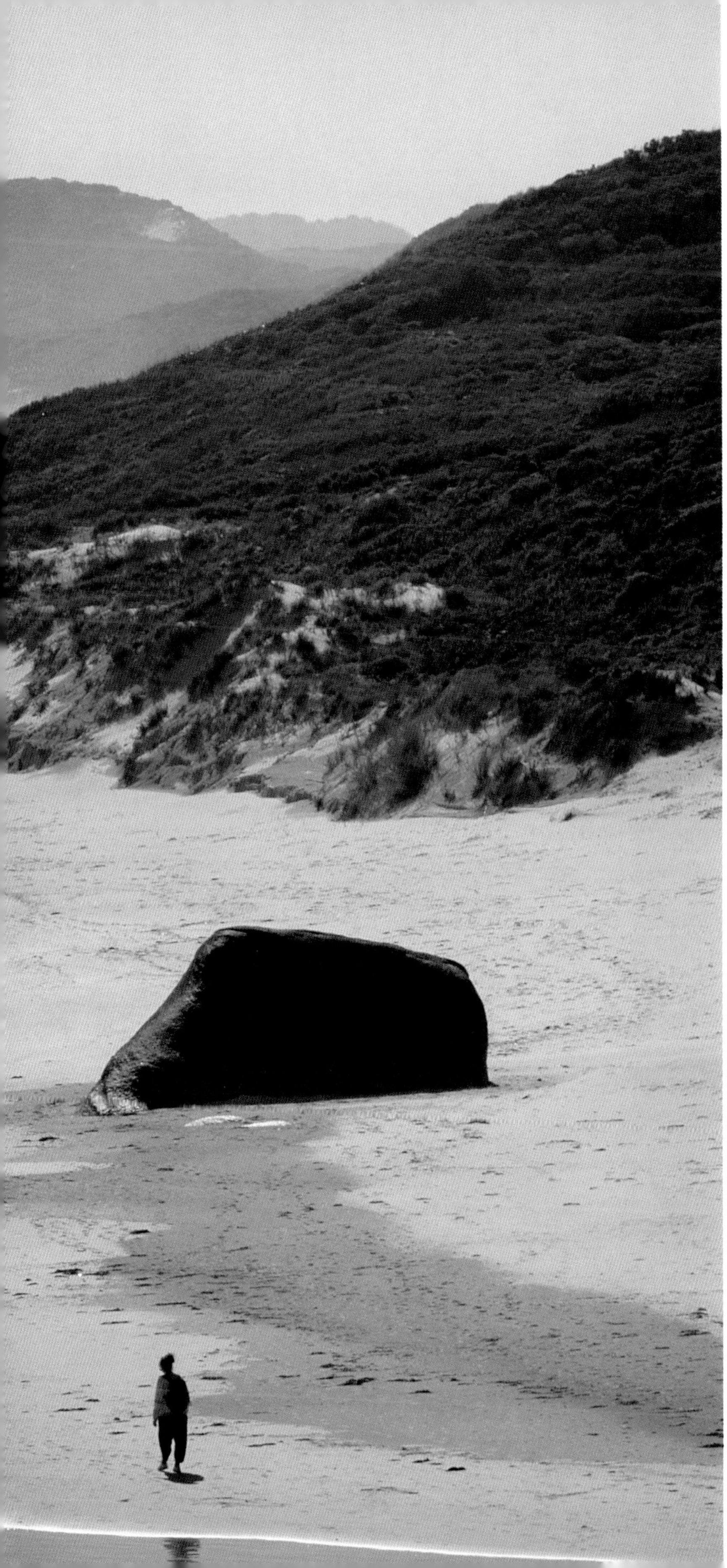

The spectacular south coast

The south-western corner and southern coast of Western Australia offer scenes of beauty which invite the traveller to stay awhile, explore and forget the stresses of civilisation.

Along the south coast, the edge of the continental shelf (the shallow submerged ledge which normally breaks the force of waves before they reach the coast) lies close inshore. With no undersea ledge to break their force, the surging waves of the Southern Ocean have carved inlets and coves into the coastline and continue to worry away at the massive granite headlands which defy their power.

Getting away from it all in William Bay National Park, a scenic gem between Walpole and Denmark.

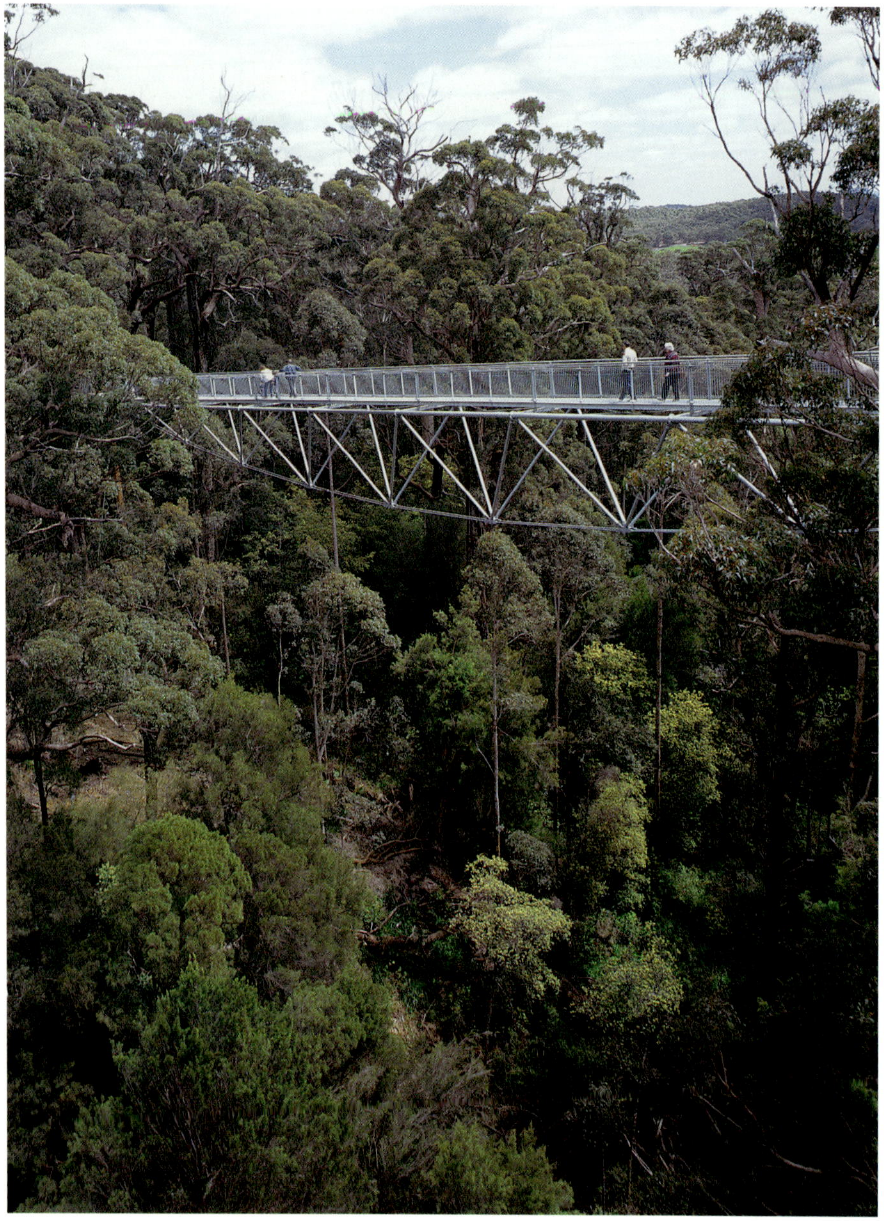

Above: This treetop walk allows close viewing of a Karri forest canopy. *Opposite:* Amongst the Tingle tree giants.

Walpole–Nornalup National Park

Waterfalls, massive granite domes and majestic forests are features of this park which surrounds Walpole and Nornalup inlets. A wonderful place for bushwalkers, birdwatchers and photographers, it is also ideal for those who love fishing or just sitting by the sea. Nearby, the impressive Valley of the Giants contains a forest of rare Red Tingle trees, towering above distinctive buttressed roots.

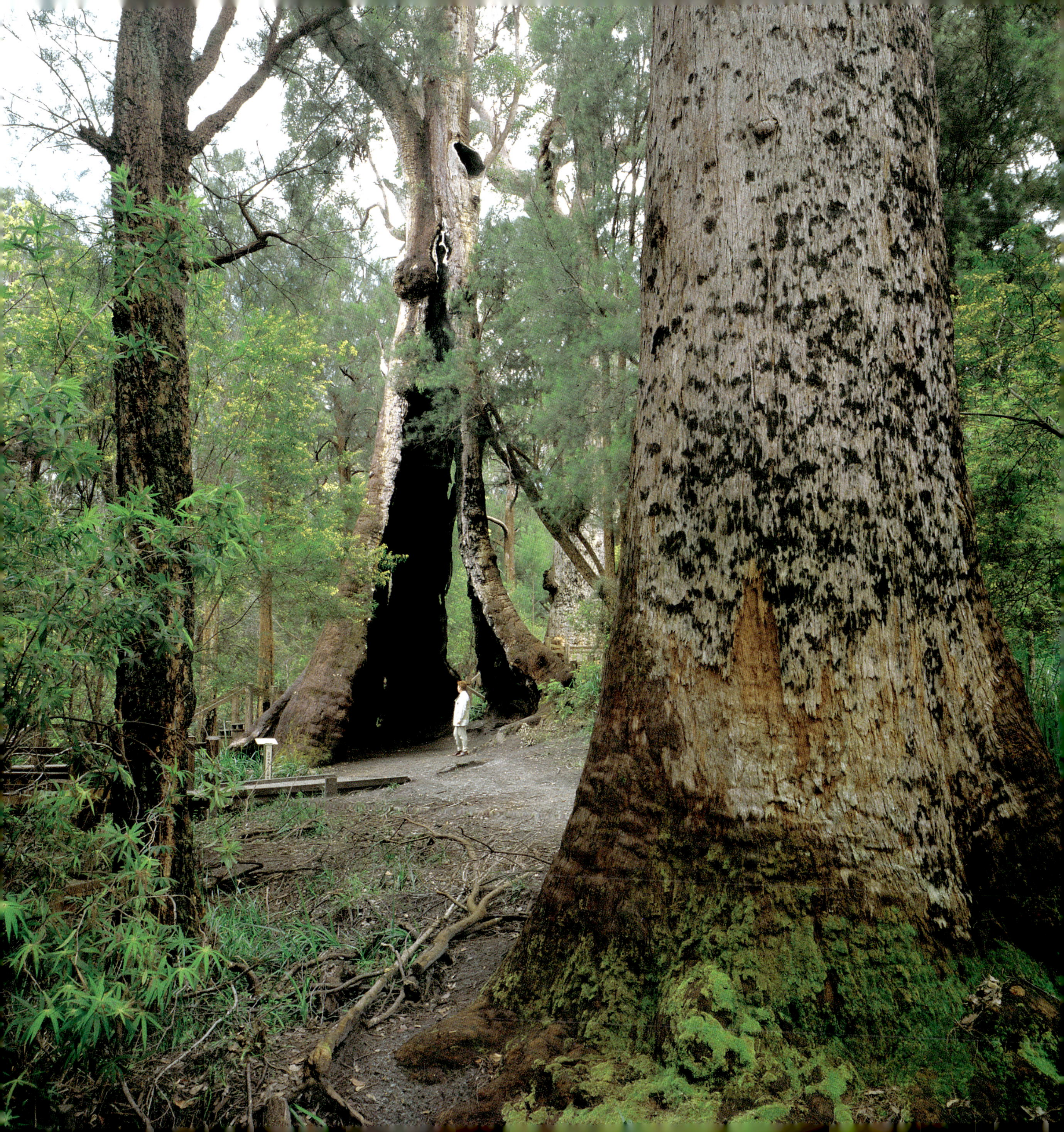

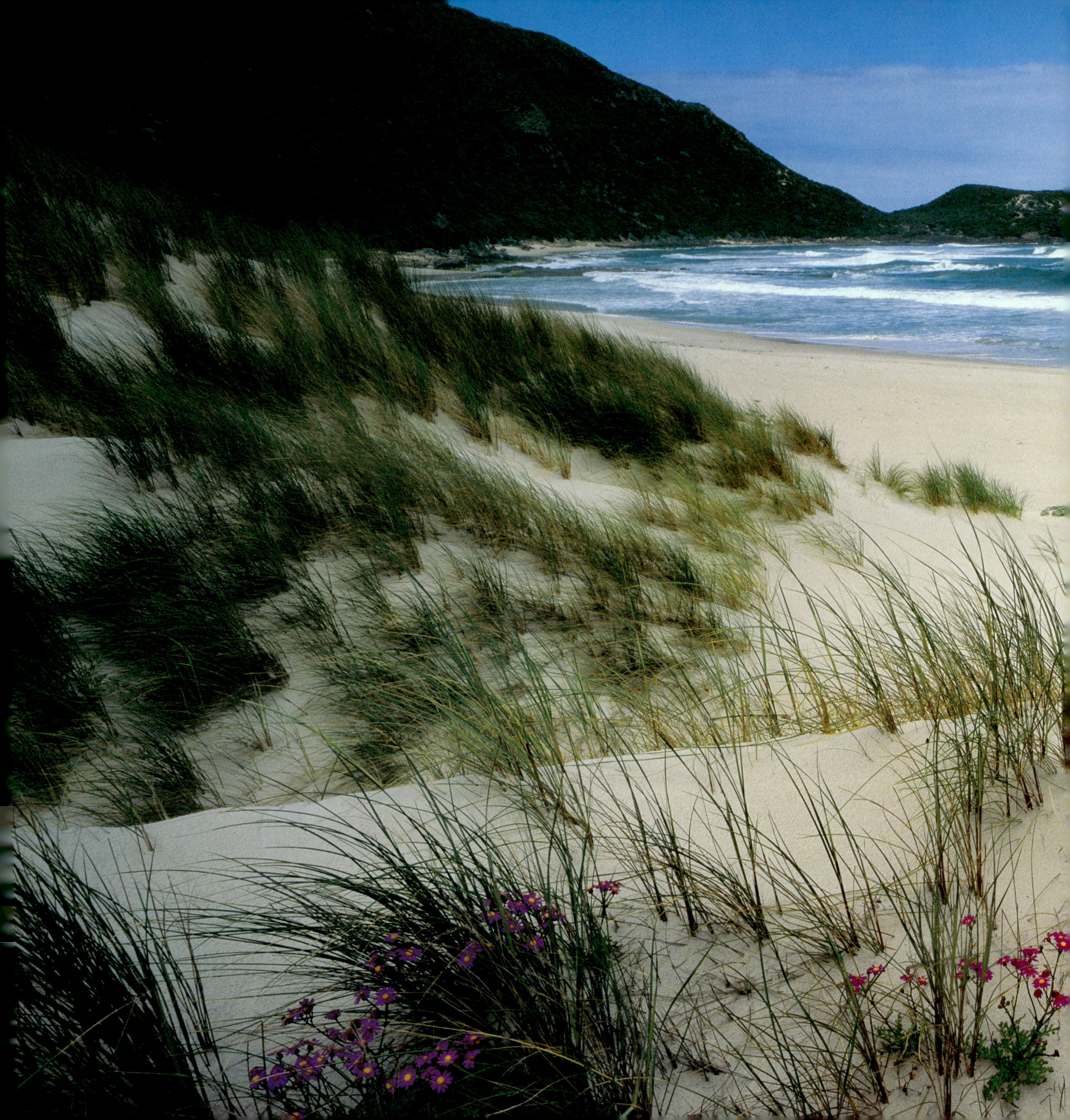

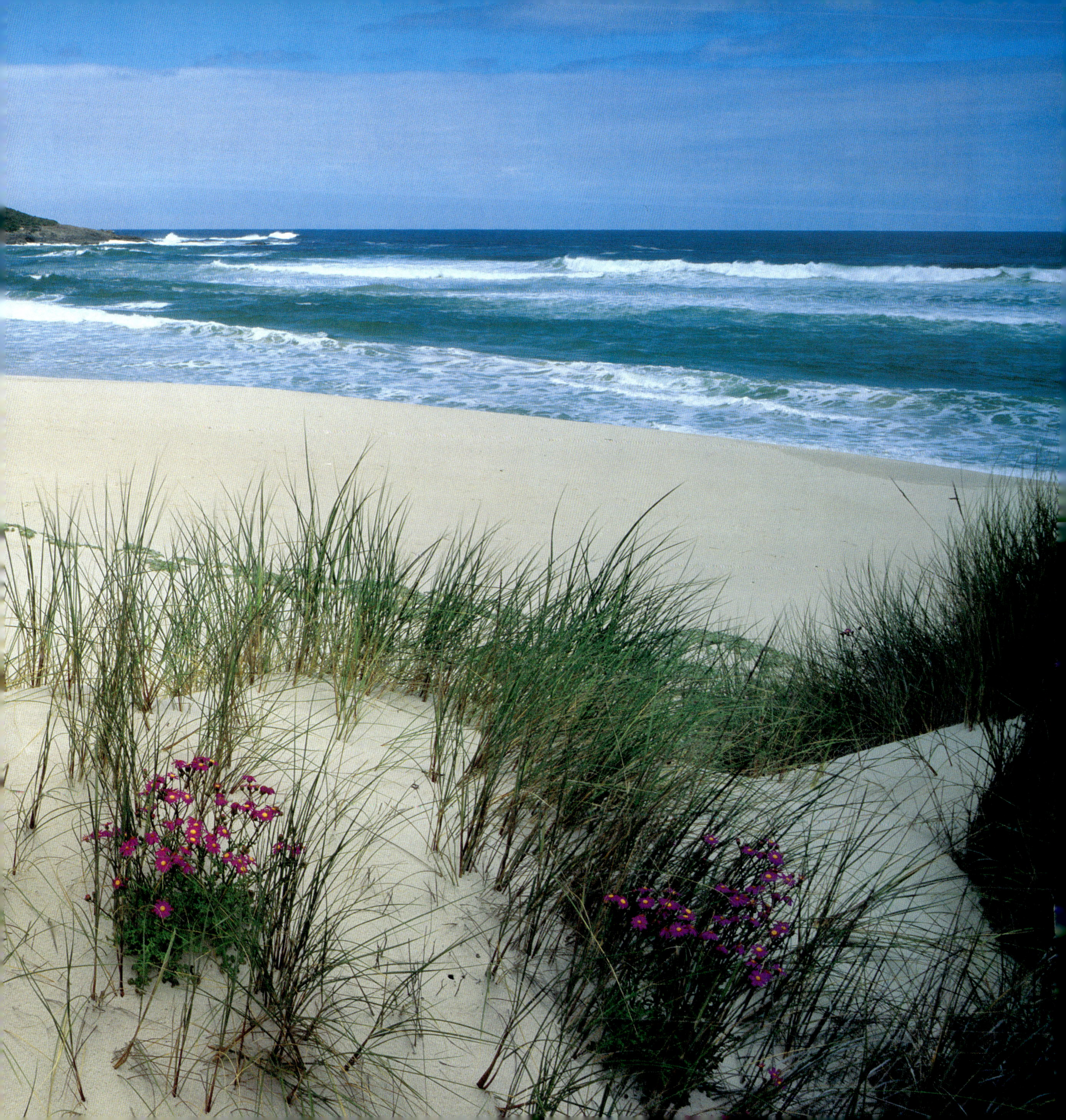

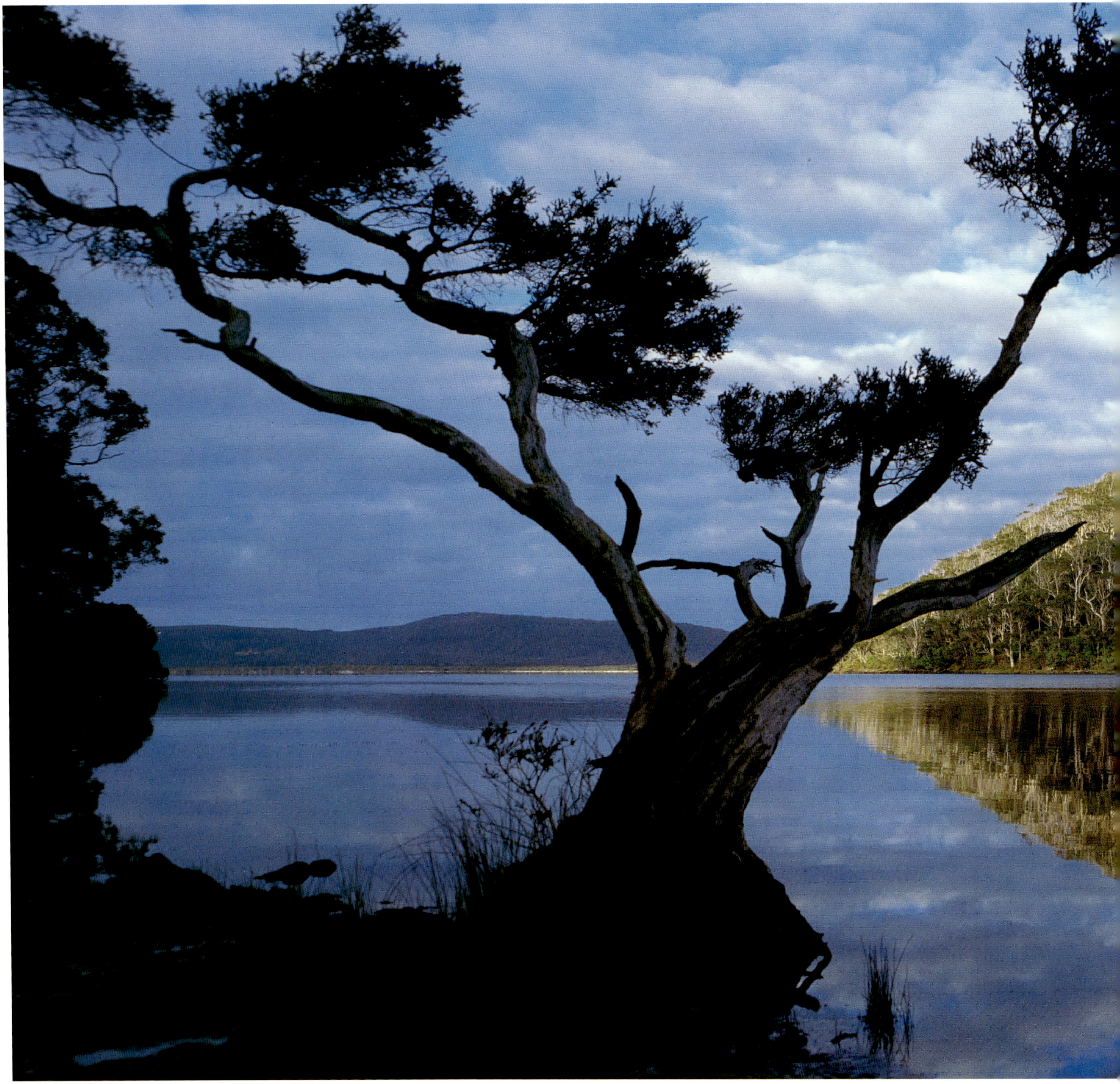

Previous pages: Coastal dunes, Walpole–Nornalup National Park.

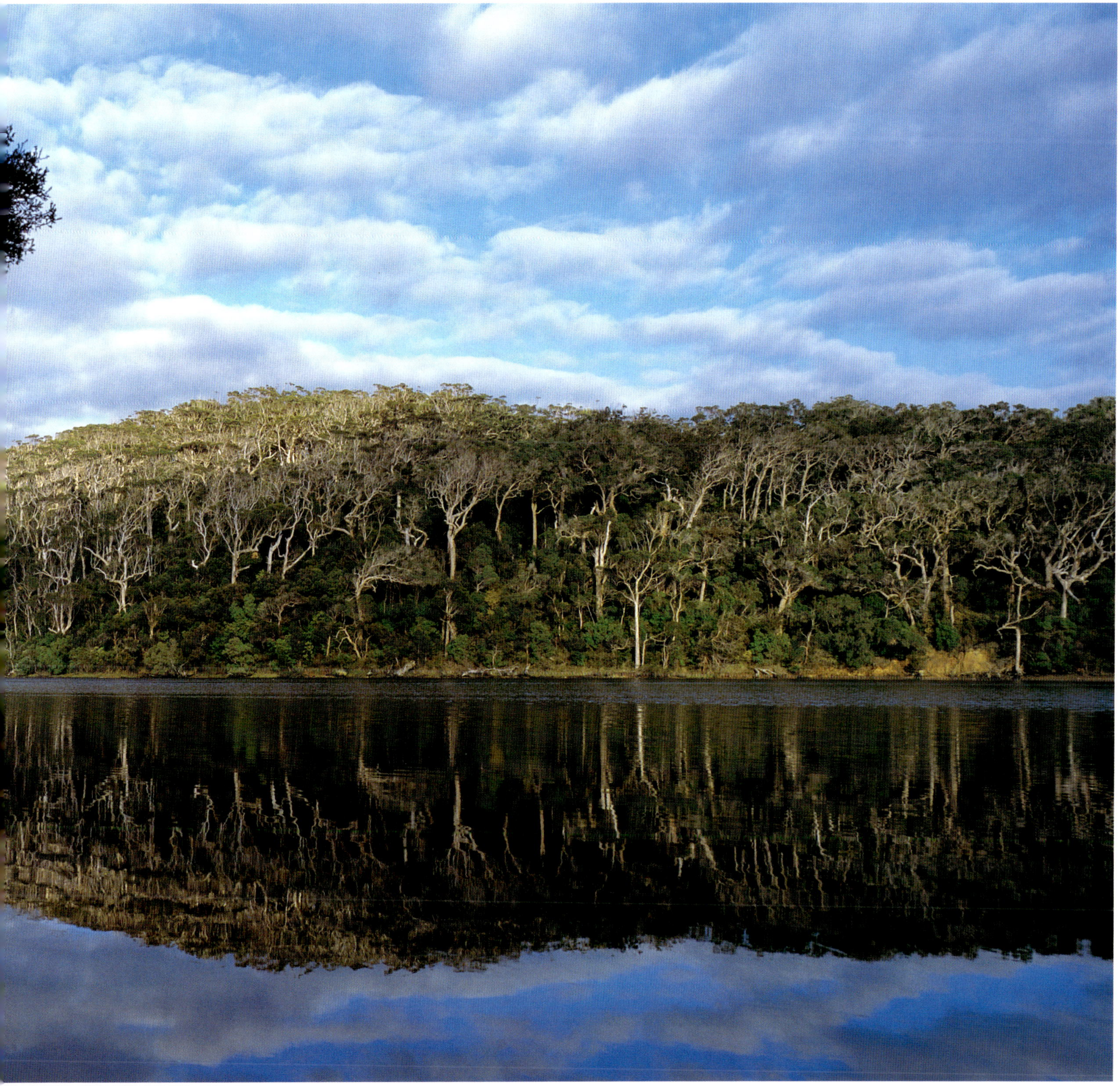

Above: Walpole–Nornalup National Park.

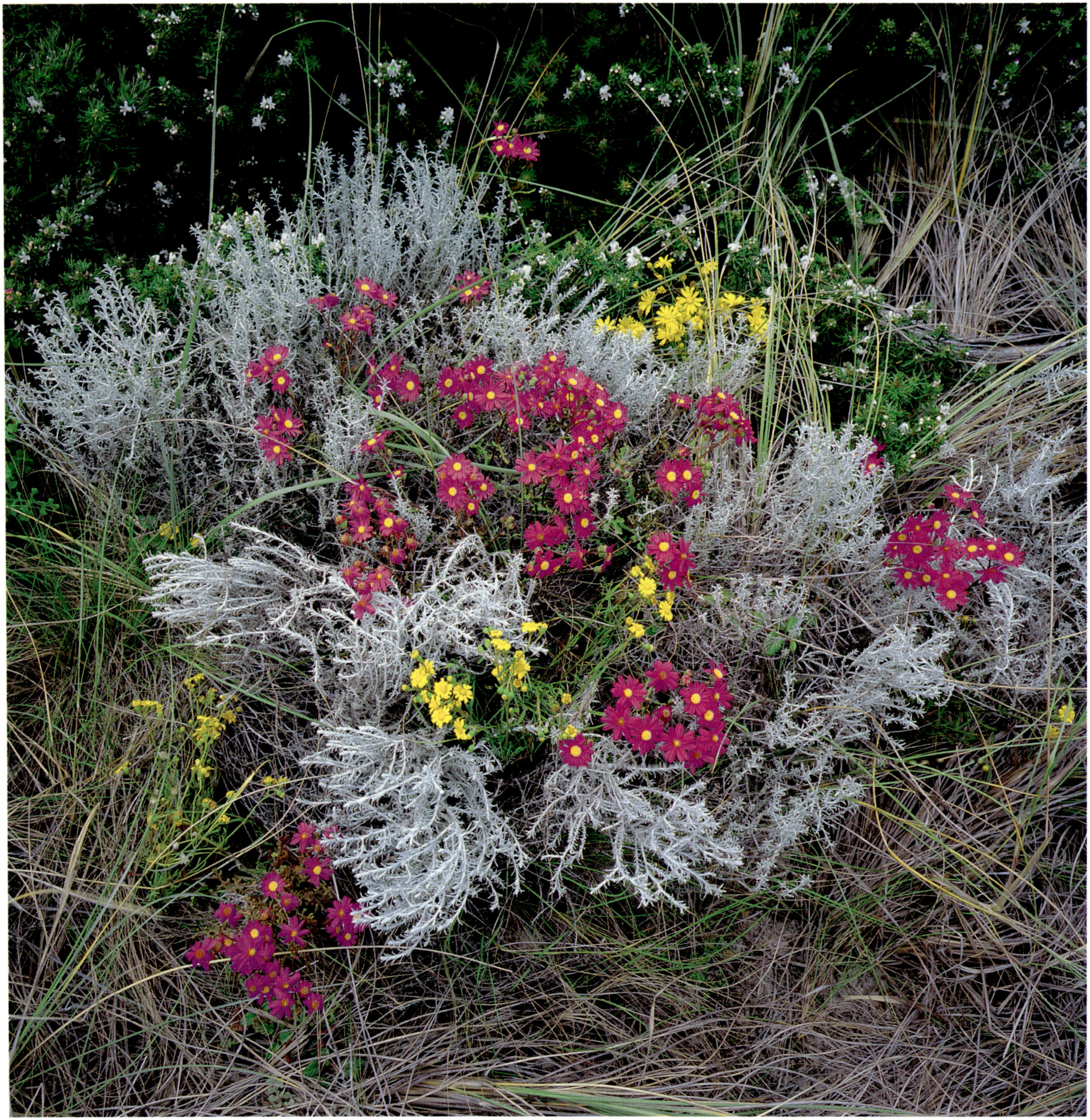

Flowers in the sand dunes, Walpole–Nornalup National Park.

Fragile flowers on a rugged coast

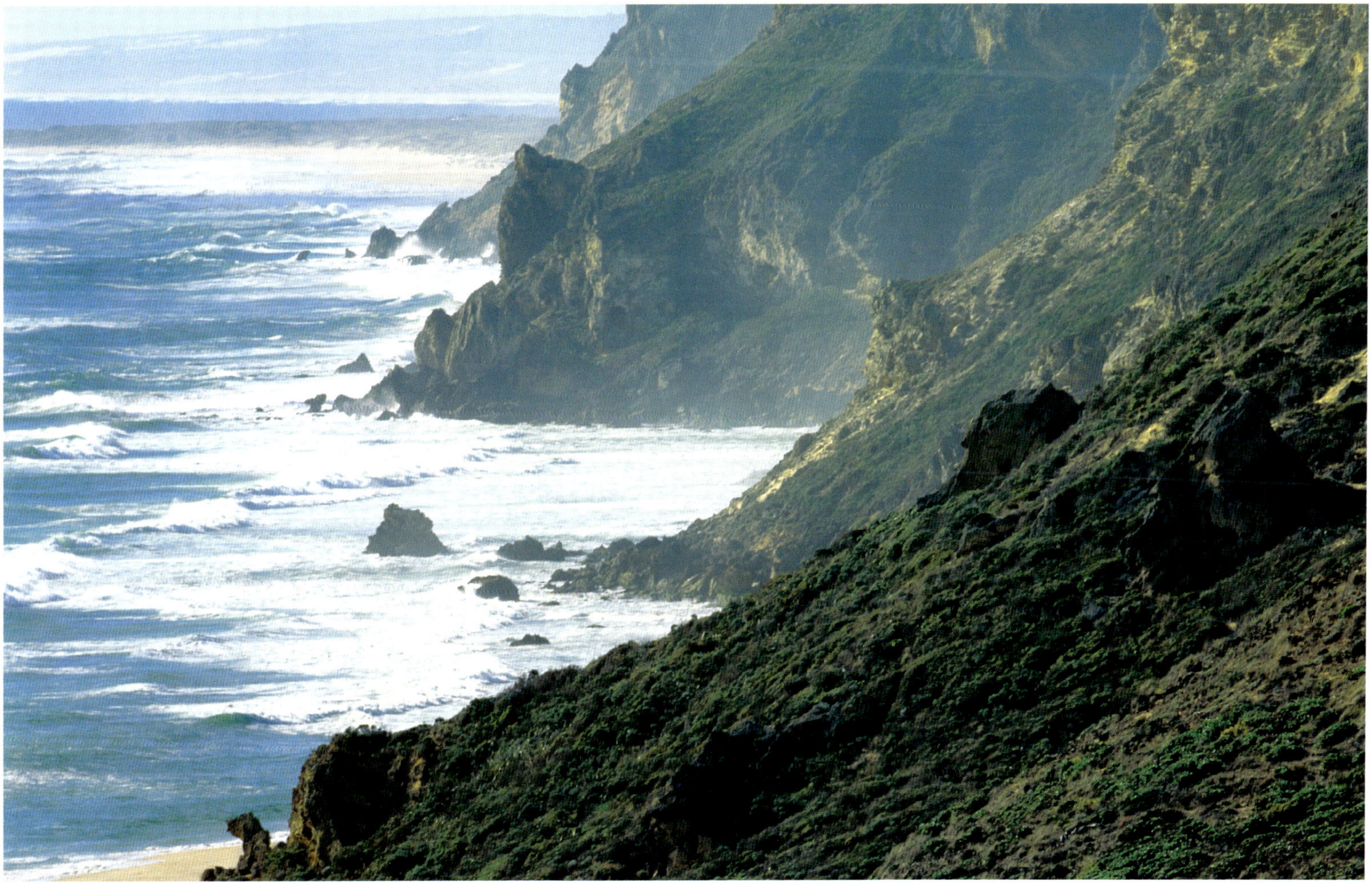

Coastal heaths cling to these rugged cliffs at Salmon Beach, D'Entrecasteaux National Park.

The sea constantly wears away the cliffs, headlands and silver-sand beaches of Western Australia's southern shores. It fails to daunt the coastal plants, which defy salt-laden winds and root themselves in sand dunes, on almost sheer faces and in cracks in the limestone. The leaves of these tough survivors colour the coast in silver-grey and blue-green, and in springtime they bloom in fragile splendour.

Torndirrup National Park

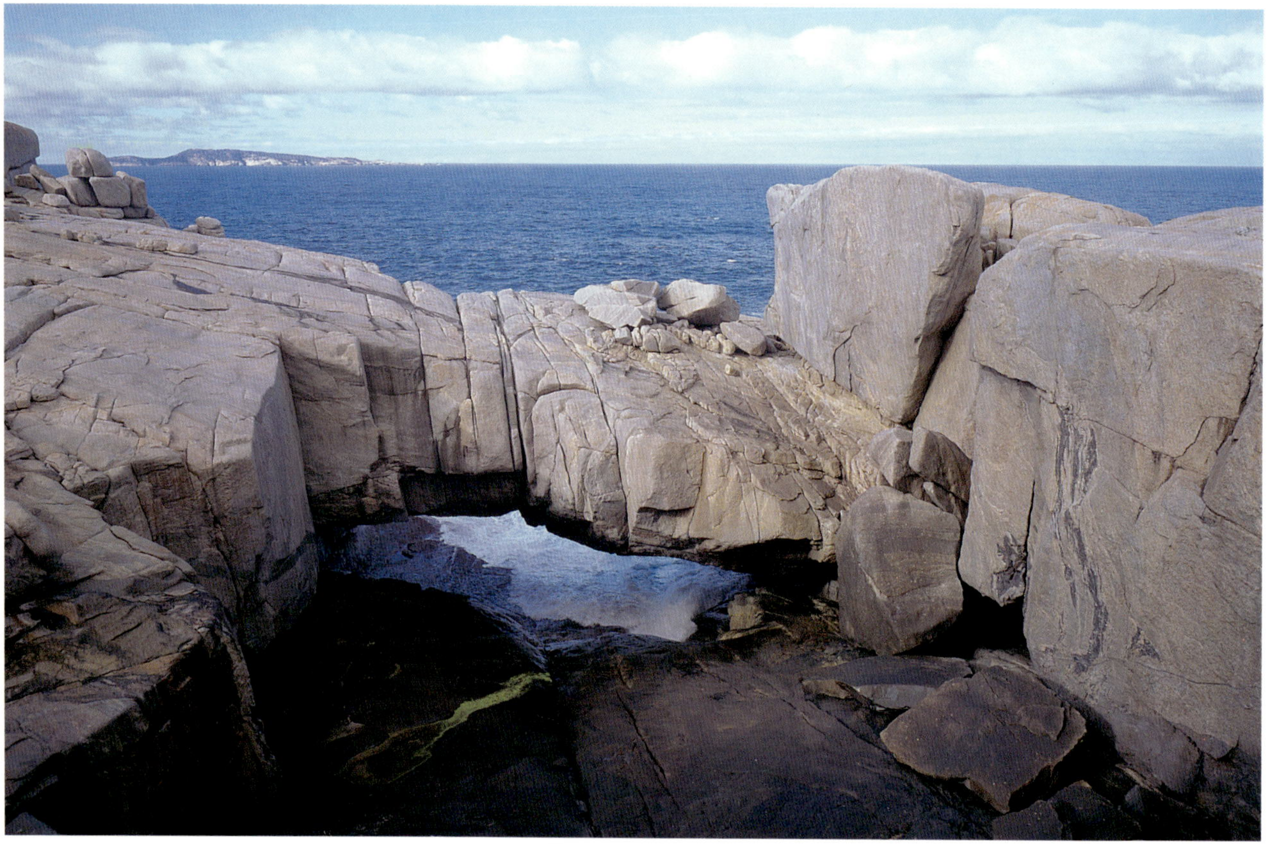

Natural Bridge, Torndirrup National Park.

The dramatic coastal scenery of Torndirrup National Park, only 10 kilometres south of Albany across Princess Royal Harbour, is due to the granite rocks which have been battered by the sea into cliffs such as The Gap, headlands such as Bald Head, and phenomena such as Natural Bridge. Whales swim past these coasts in winter, the fishing is superb and rock climbers and bushwalkers find special joys in the challenging terrain.

Those who fish from the headlands of this awesome coast must guard against the freak giant waves which occasionally surge without warning from a calm sea.

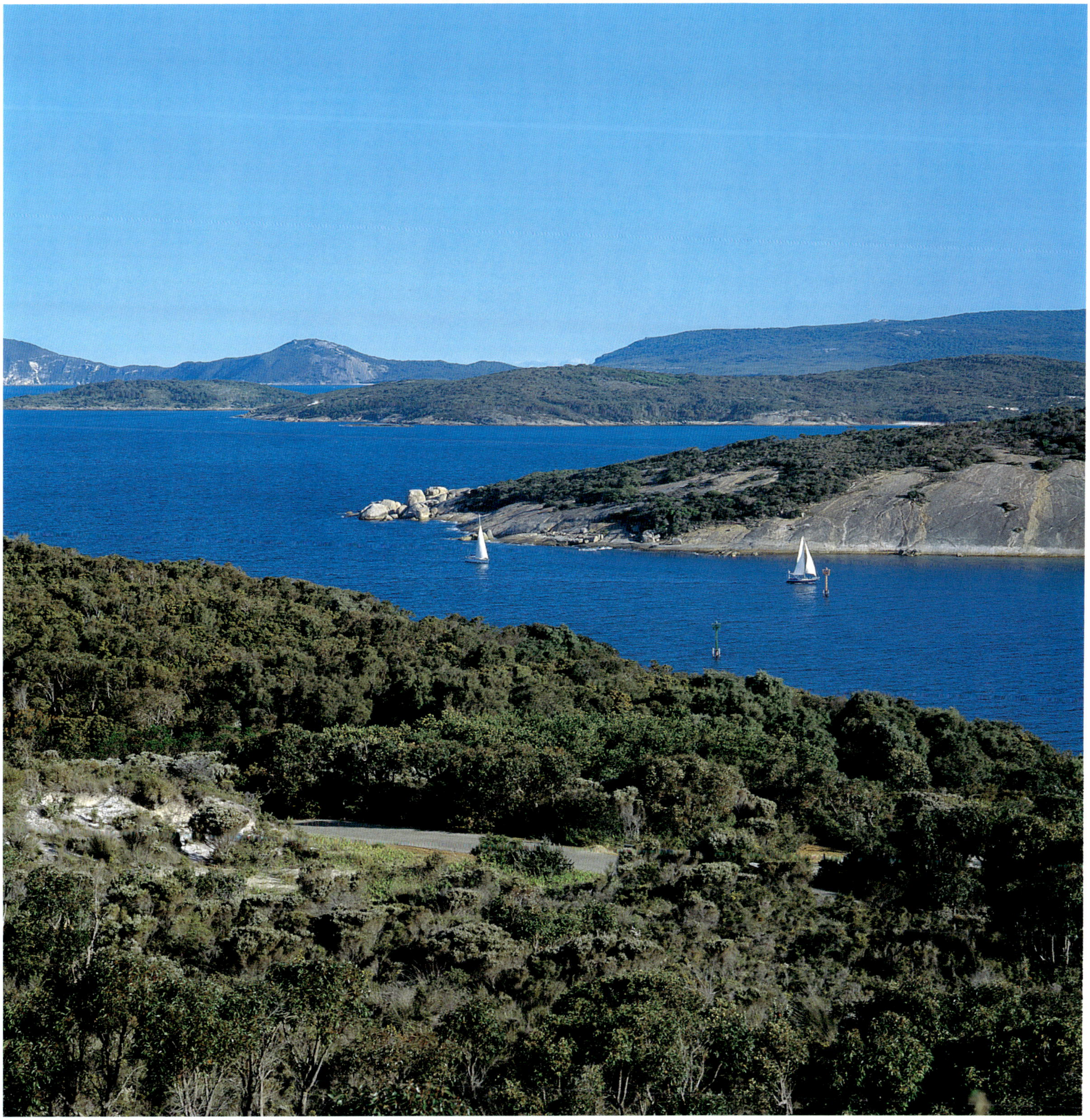

Above: The entrance to Princess Royal Harbour.

Following pages: The Salmon Holes, Torndirrup National Park.

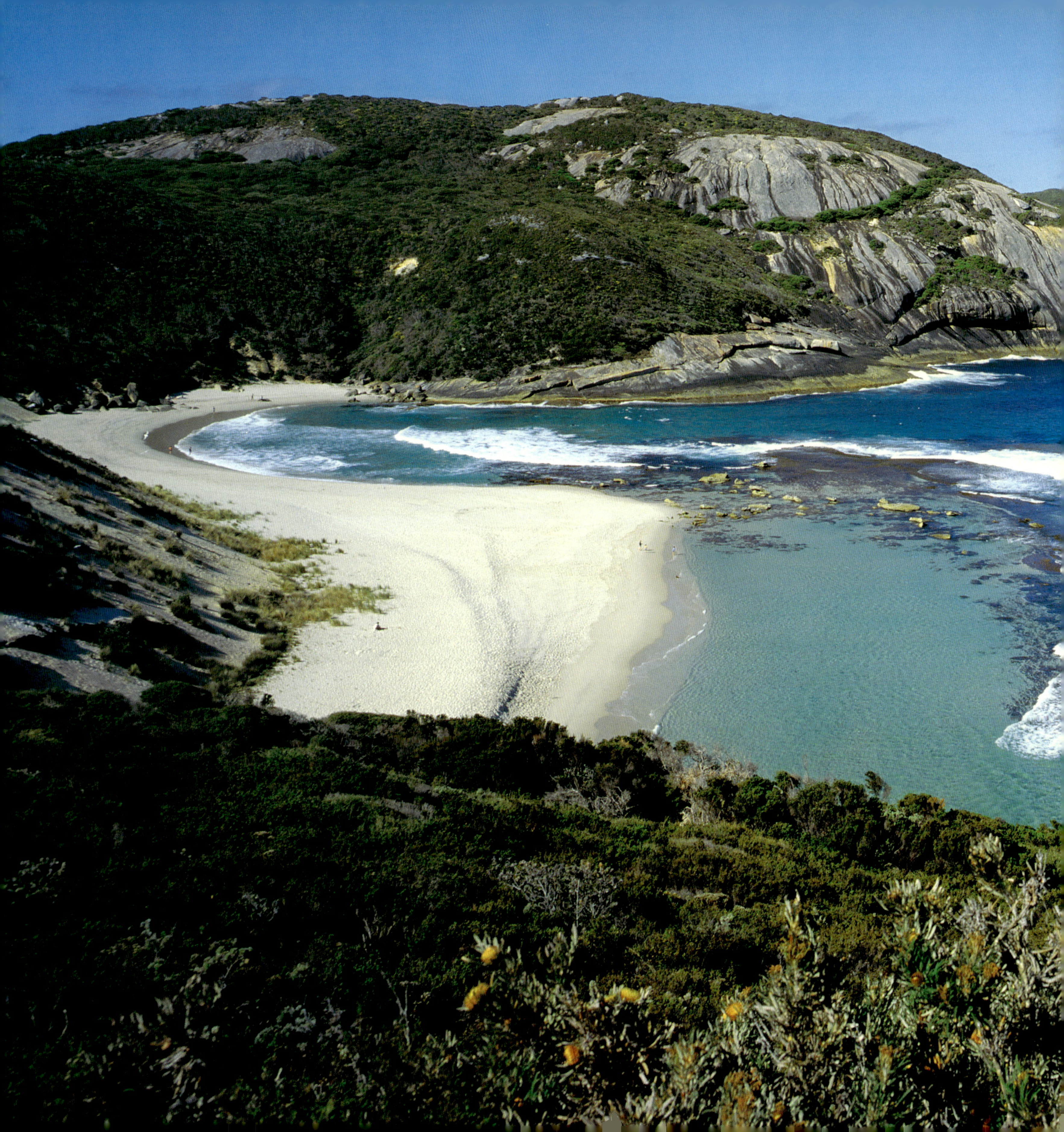

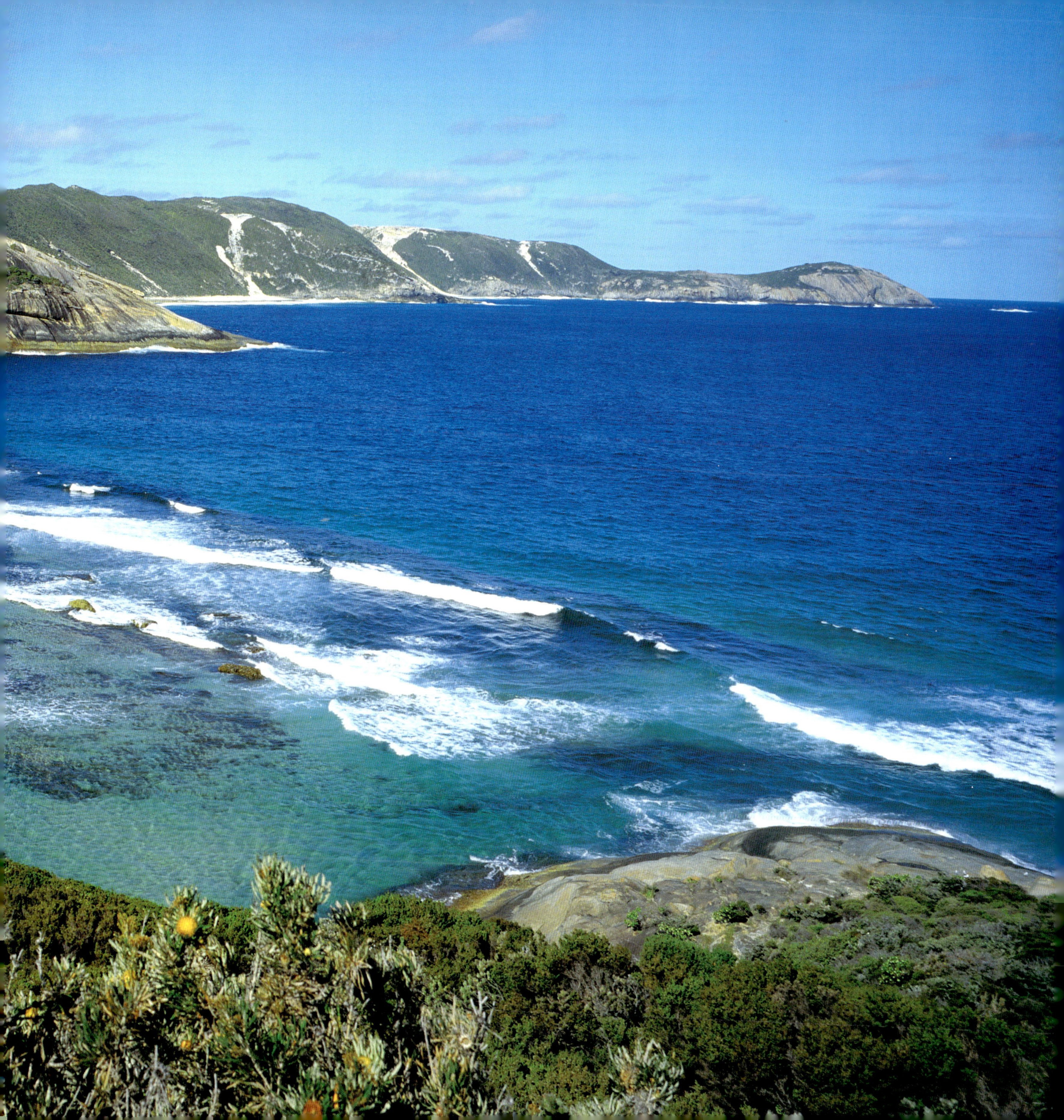

Two Peoples Bay

The nature reserve which extends into the heathland and wooded gullies behind Two Peoples Bay, 20 kilometres east of Albany, is a very important place for nature lovers. Several very rare bird and mammal species, including the endangered Noisy Scrub-bird and Long-footed Potoroo, survive here.

One of the world's remaining great wilderness areas lies around 180 kilometres east of Albany. Fitzgerald River National Park is a haven for wildflower species, including the extraordinary Royal Hakea. It also harbours rare mammals, and is classed as a World Biosphere Reserve.

Two Peoples Bay, named to commemorate peaceful contact between French and English ships on this coast two centuries ago.

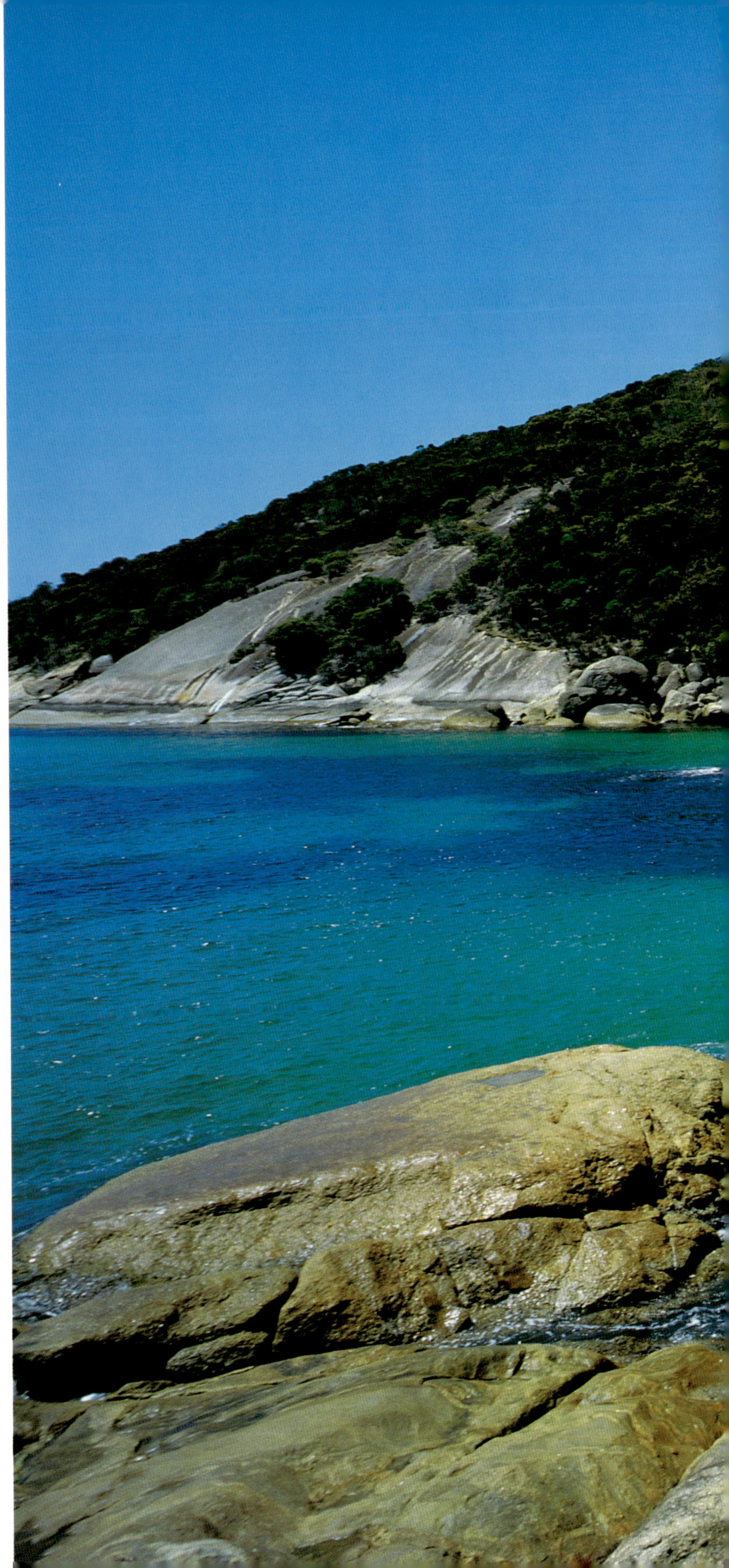

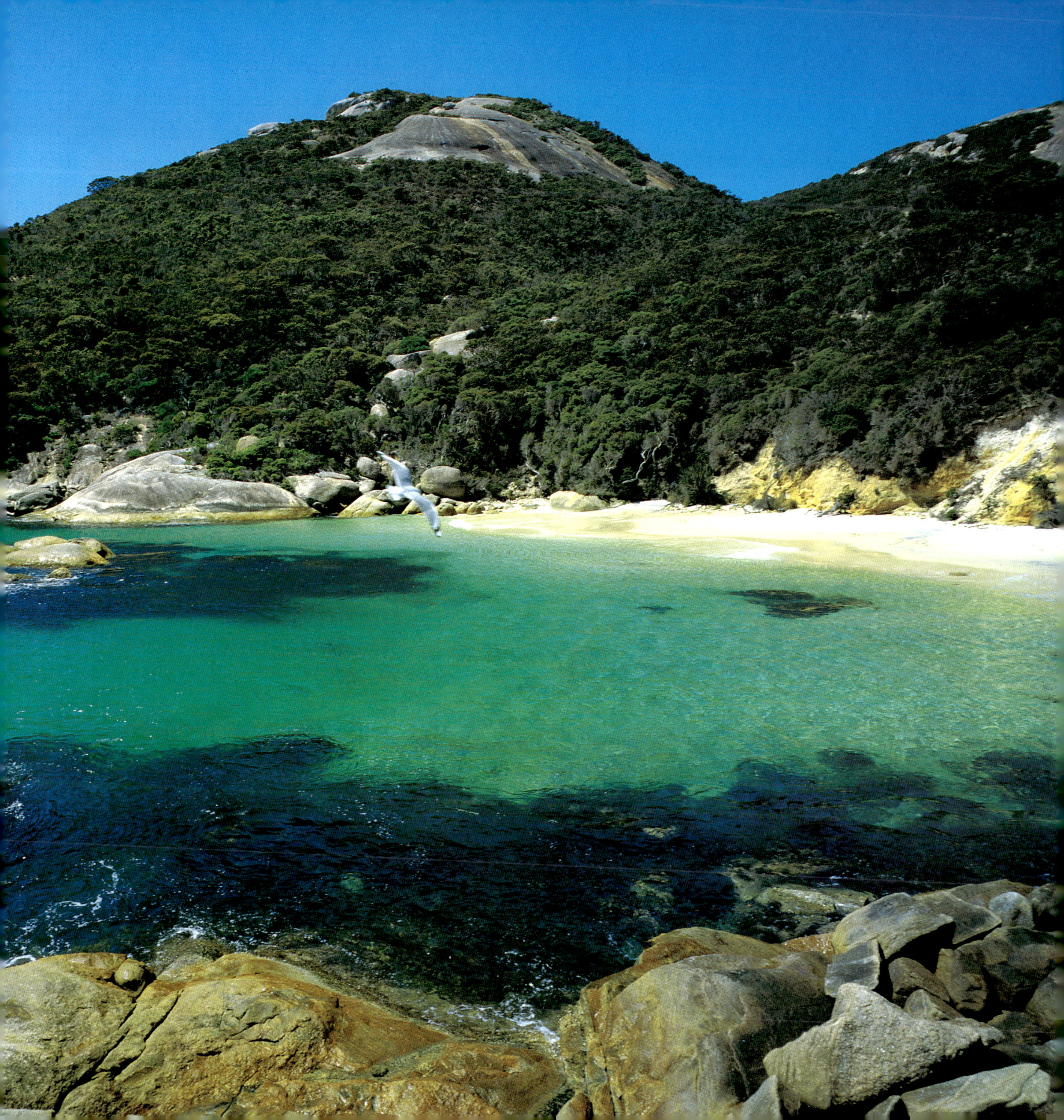

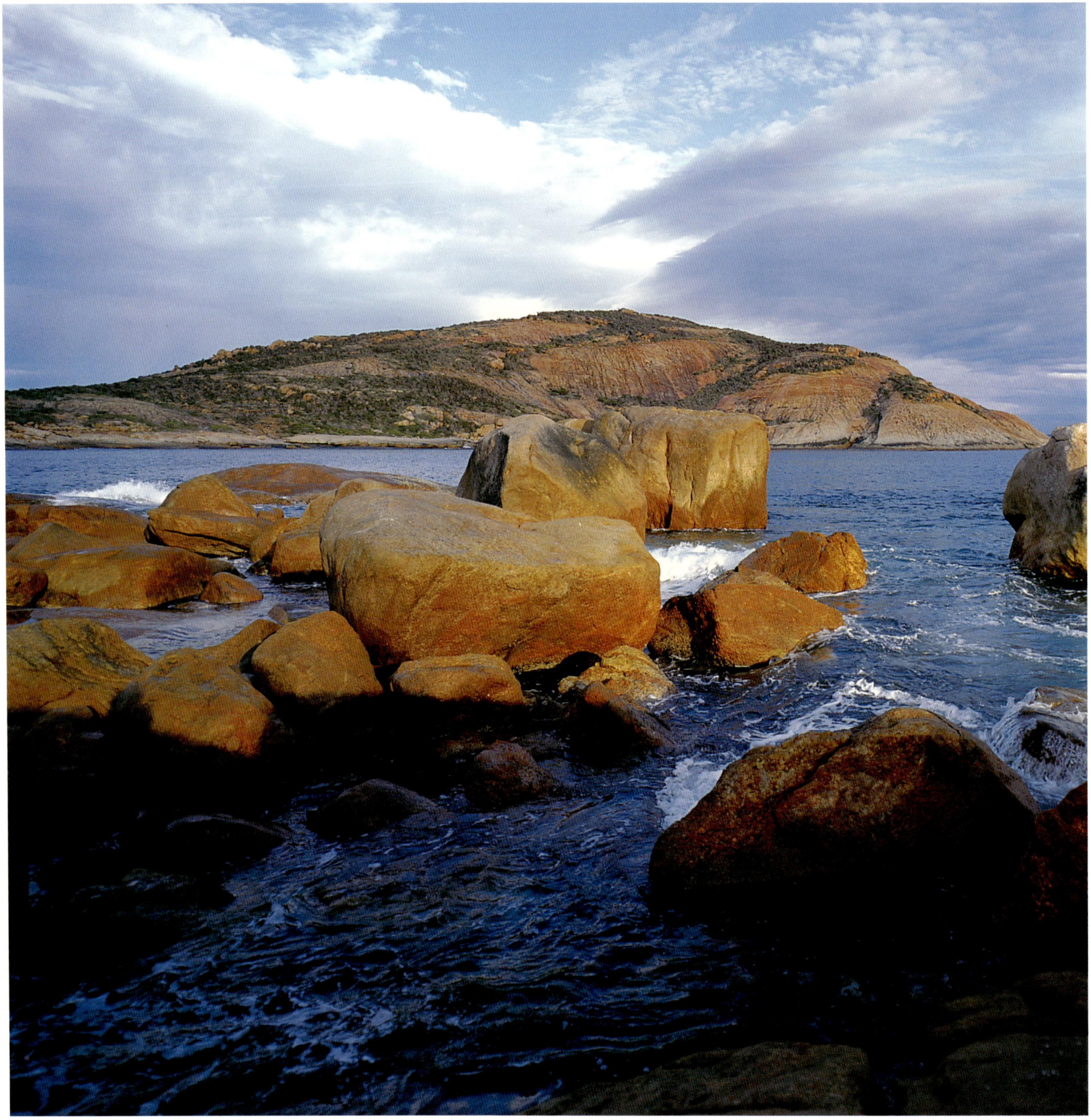

Cape Le Grand National Park, near the port of Esperance.

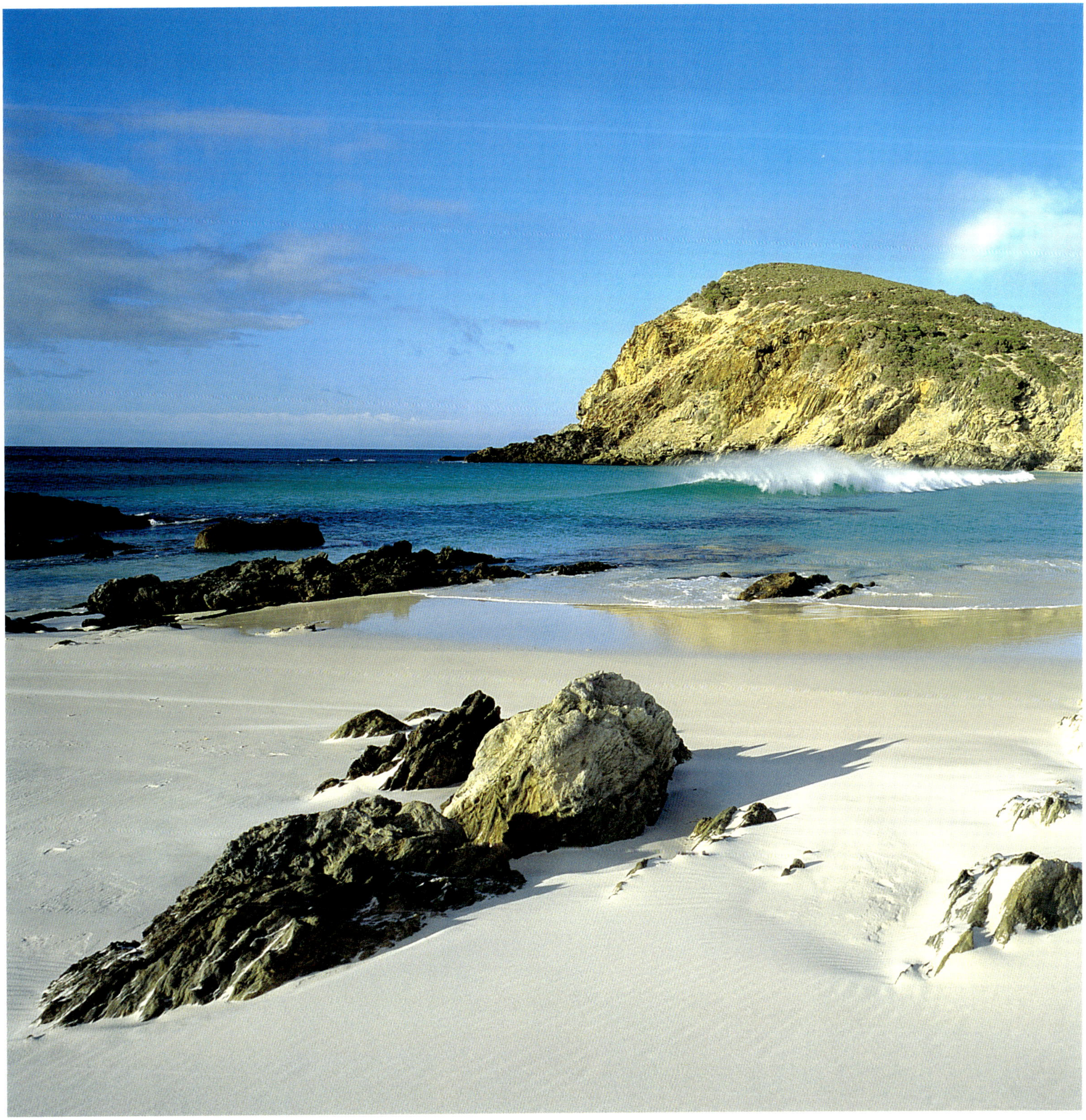

An unspoiled beach in Fitzgerald River National Park.

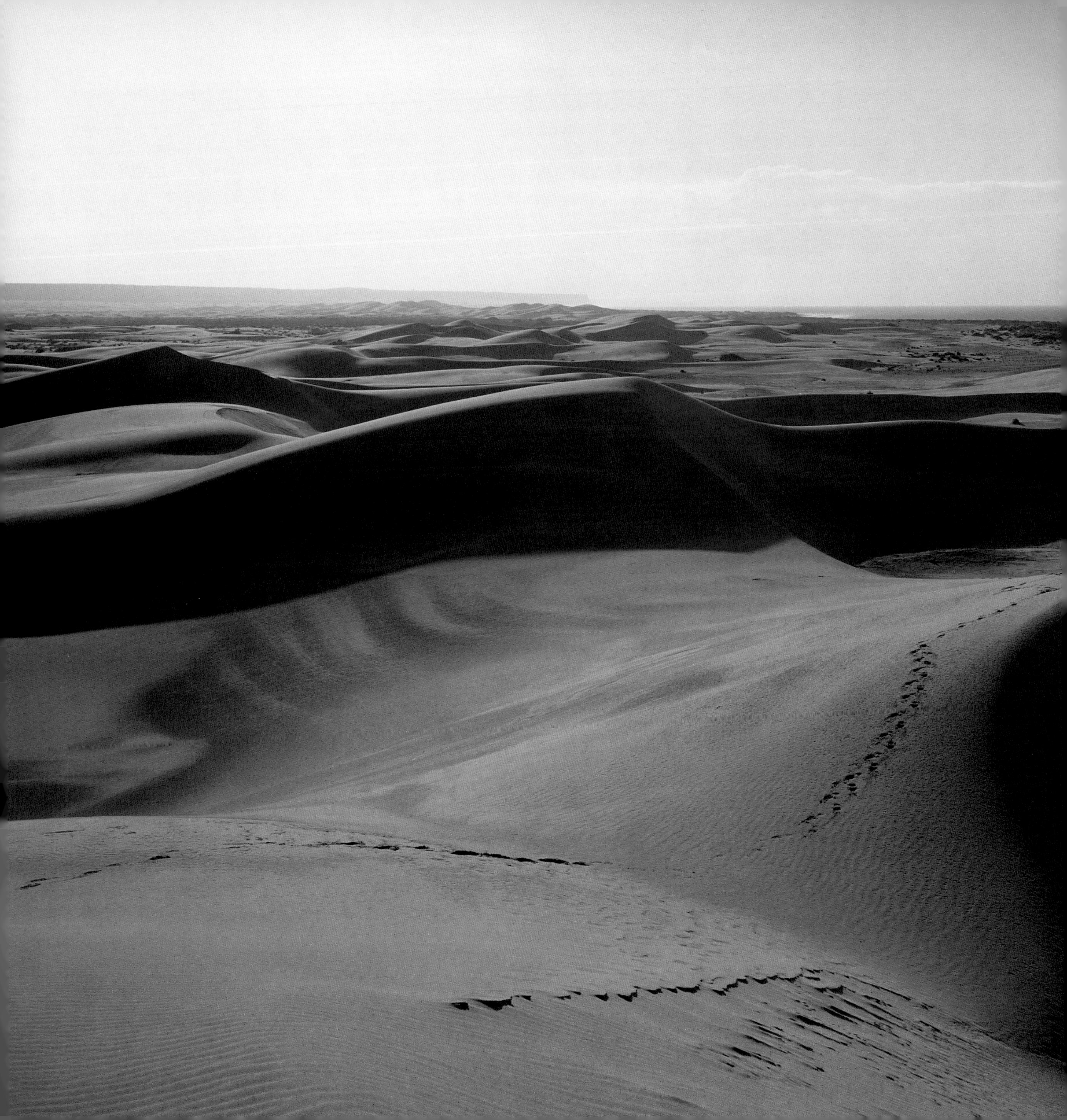

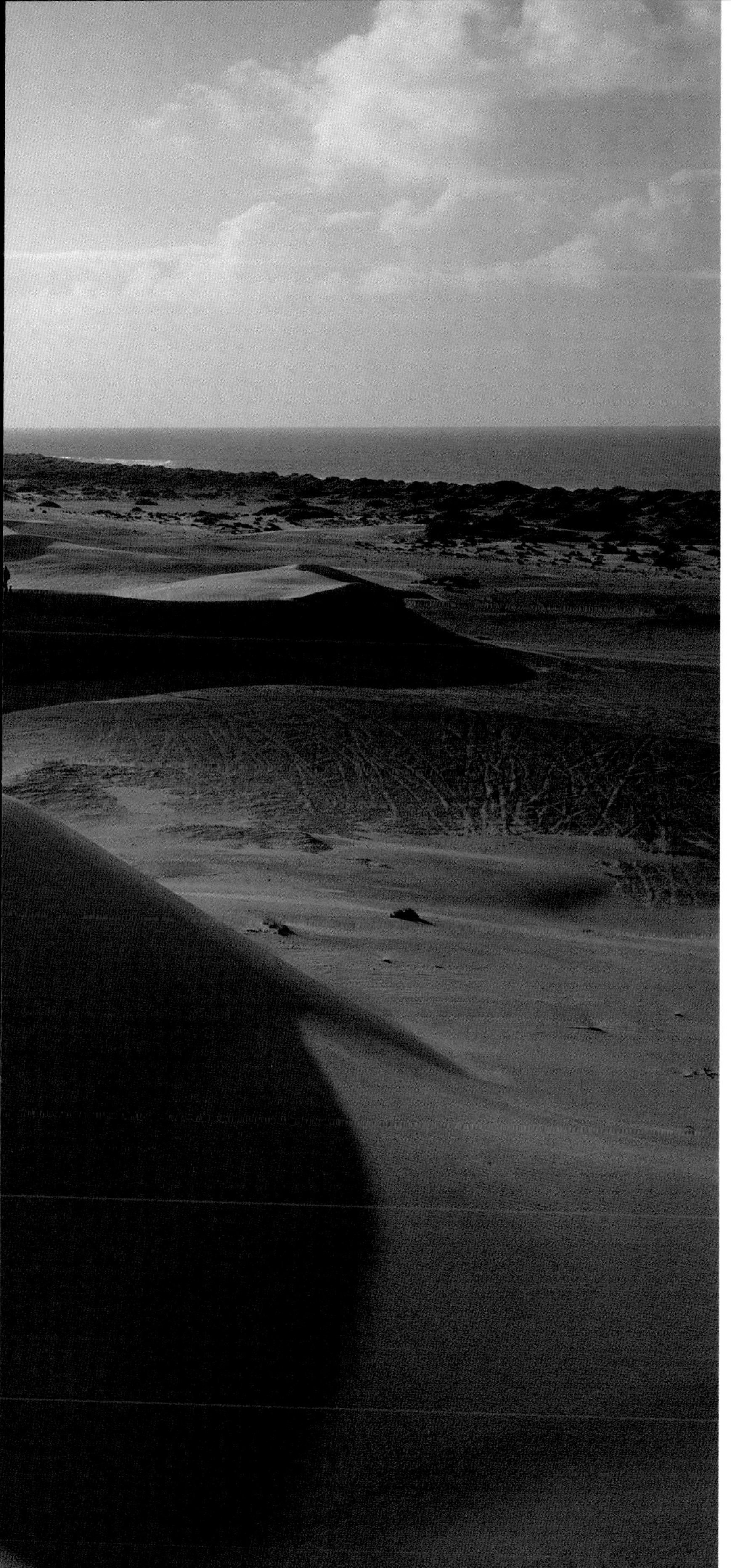

Eucla National Park

The sand dunes, heathlands and mallee which comprise Eucla National Park are near the border dividing Western Australia from South Australia. The lover of nature, who appreciates the impressive sand dunes, with their subtle tints and sensuous shapes, will find the view of the spectacular sea cliffs which border the Great Australian Bight worth the lack of normal tourist amenities. The traveller who wishes to experience Australia's ancient landscapes, or observe first-hand the ever-changing face of Nature, will find Eucla National Park, where shifting sands slowly but surely engulf anything in their path, both beautiful and inspiring.

Footsteps across the sand dunes at Eucla.

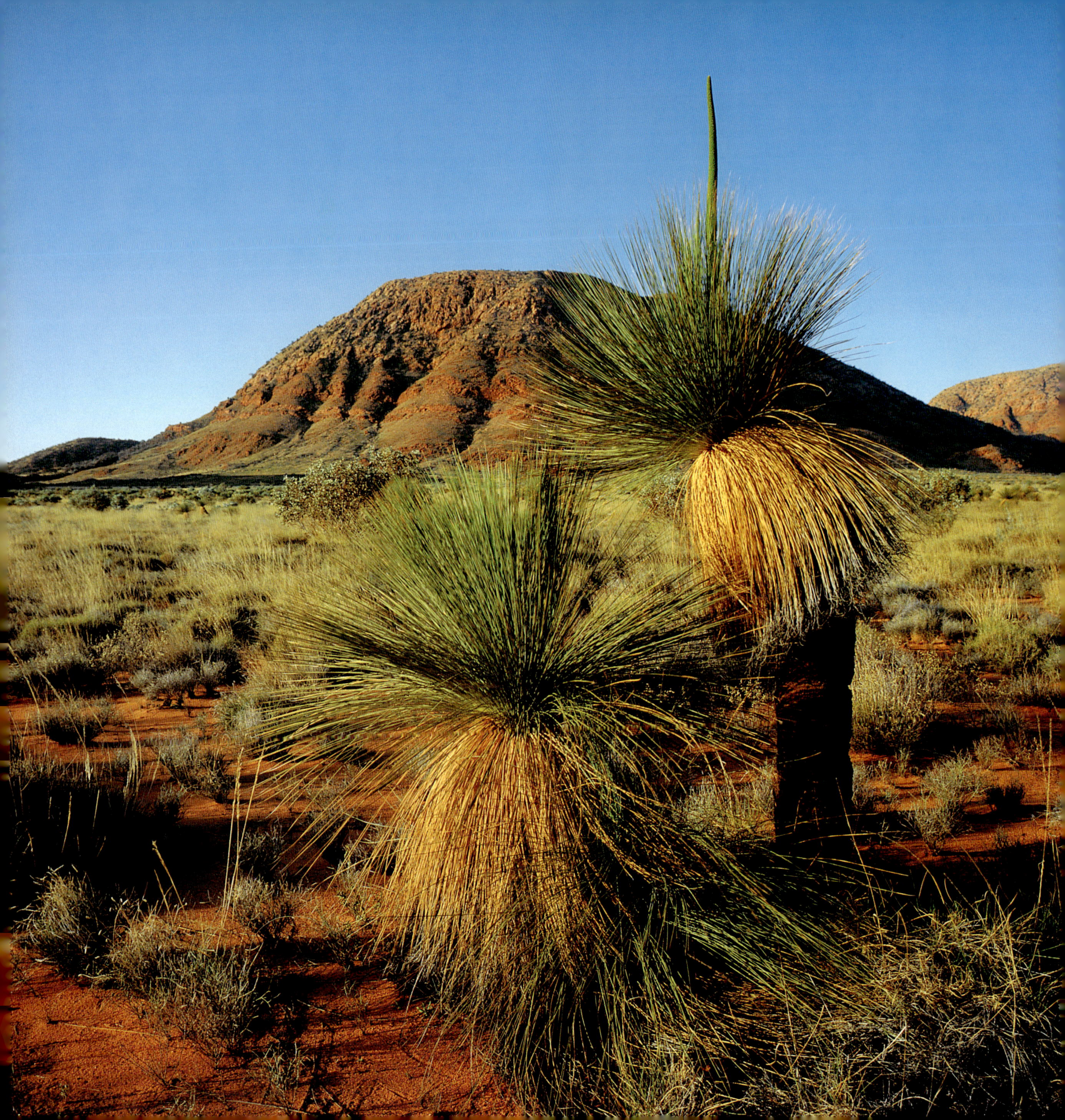

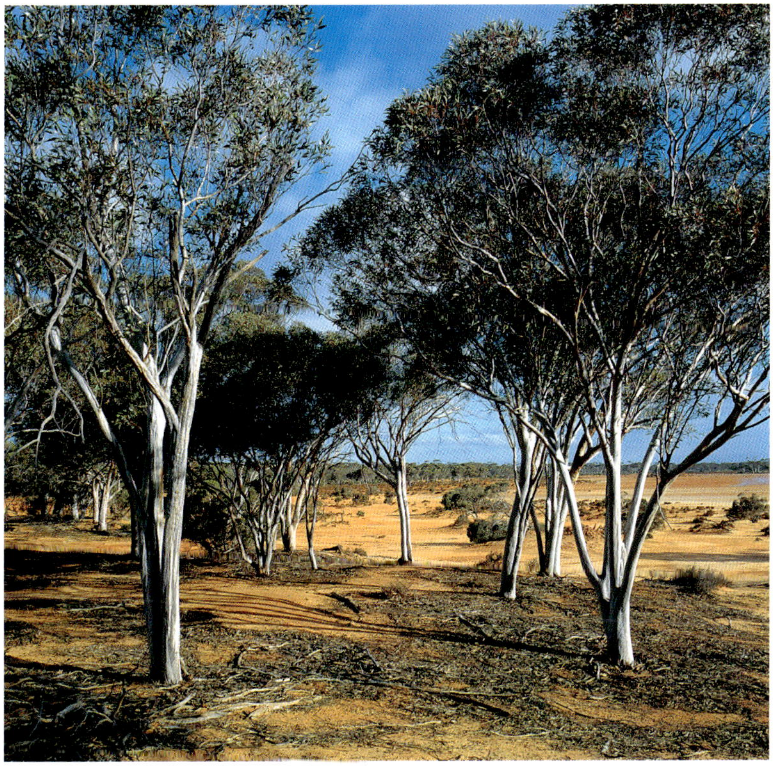

Above: Dry woodlands border the salt lakes in the south-east of the State.

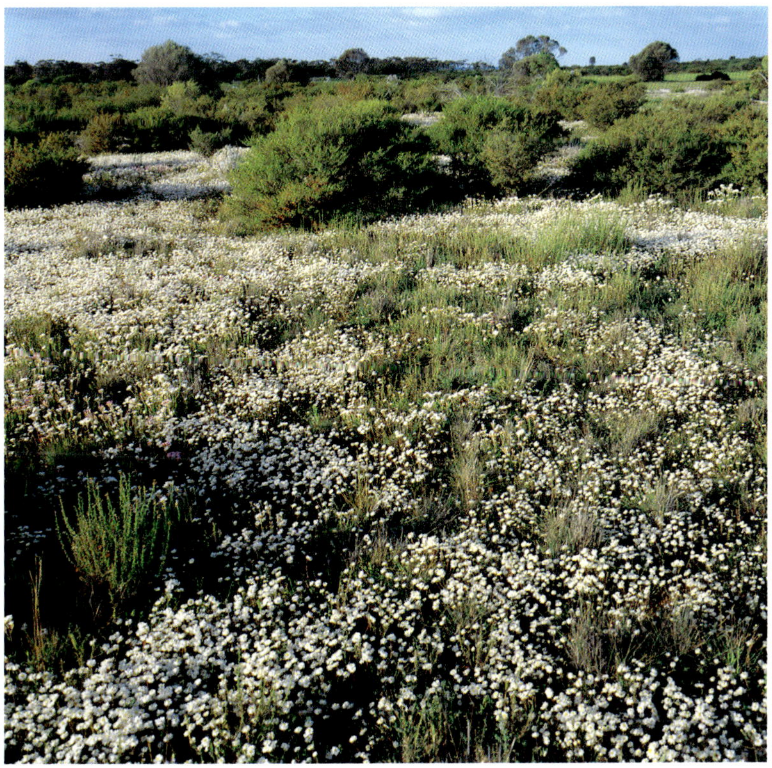

Above: The Nullarbor, the flat coastal plain north of the Great Australian Bight, becomes bright with flowers after rainfall.

The Nullarbor

A number of reserves protect the flora and fauna of Western Australia's arid south-eastern corner. Nature reserves surround the Nullarbor Plain which stretches across the land, and preserve the rugged coastline of the Great Australian Bight.

Because of its low rainfall, much of this country could be classed as desert. However, it is home to unique animals, and to a fascinating range of plants which survive the dry seasons in comfort then flower and seed in abundance once rain falls.

Opposite: Grass-trees, spinifex and a flat-topped hill, typical of aridland.

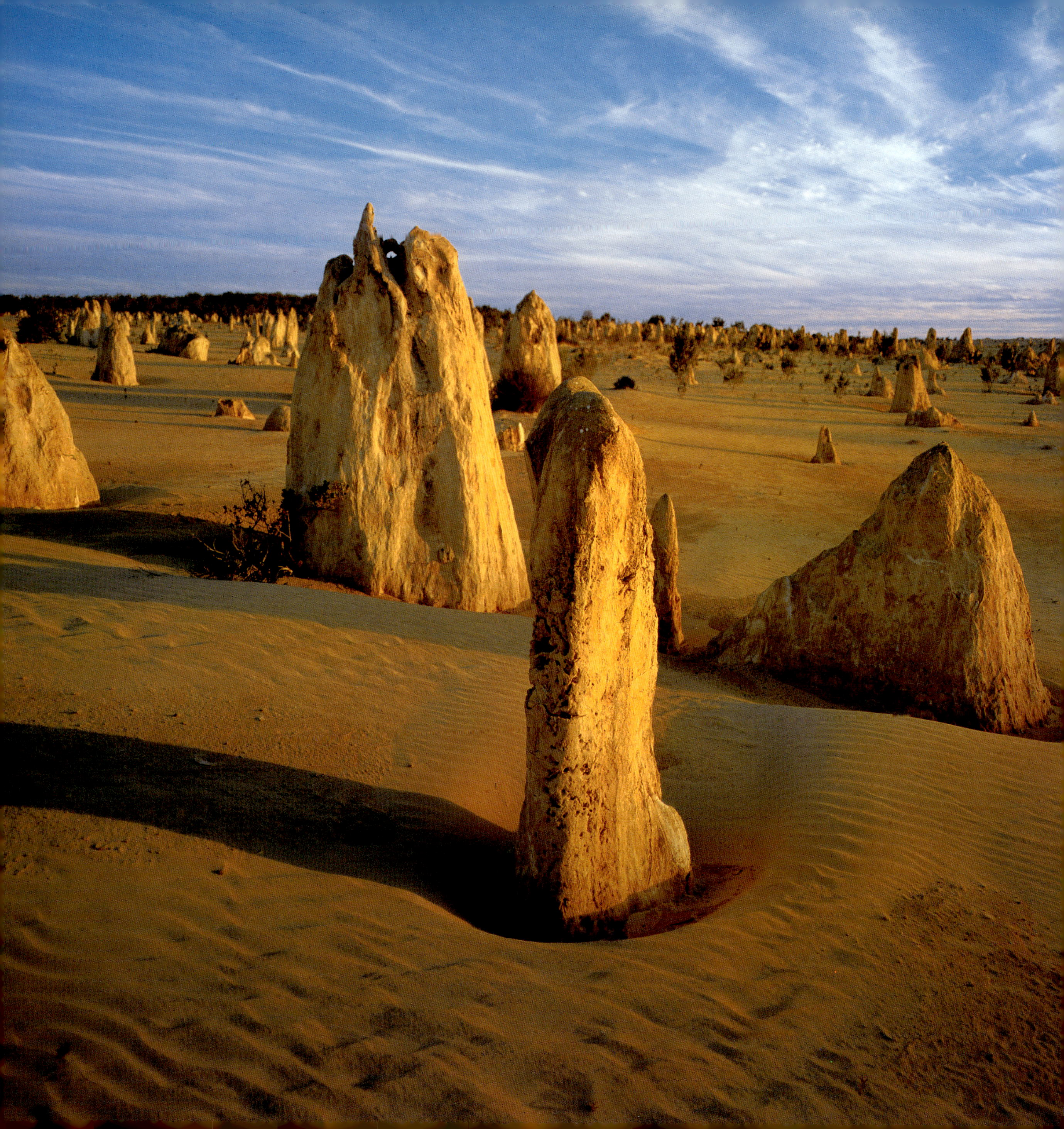

Nambung National Park

Nambung National Park, famous for its Pinnacles and Painted Desert, is an area of coastal dunes, heathlands and sandplains near the crayfishing town of Cervantes, 245 kilometres north of Perth.

The fantastic Pinnacles were formed many thousands of years ago, as rainwater seeped through the sand dunes and dissolved out lime. This cemented sand together to form pillars and columns, which were later exposed as the dunes were shifted by the sea wind.

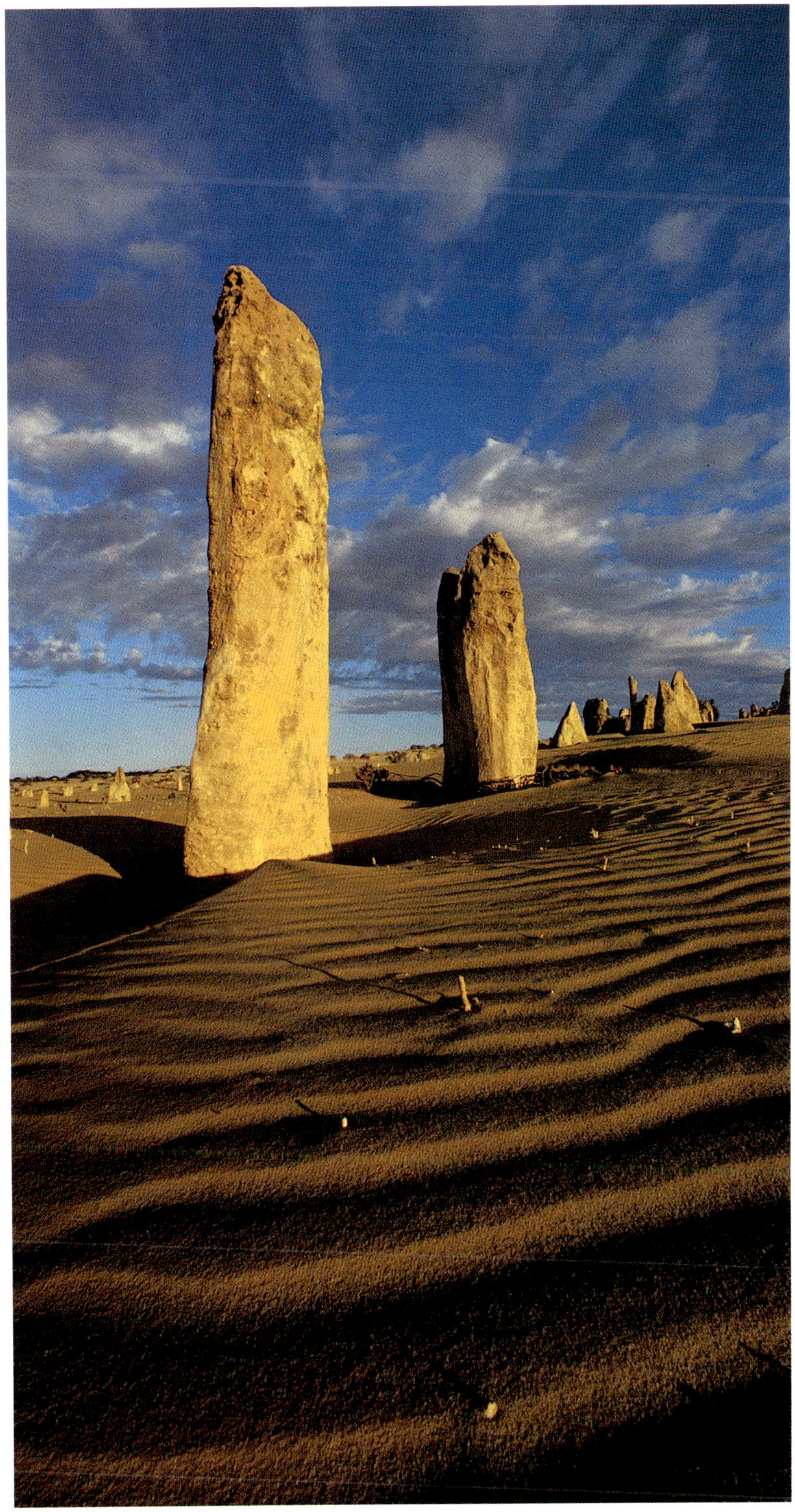

Opposite and right: The Pinnacles, Nambung National Park.

Kalbarri National Park

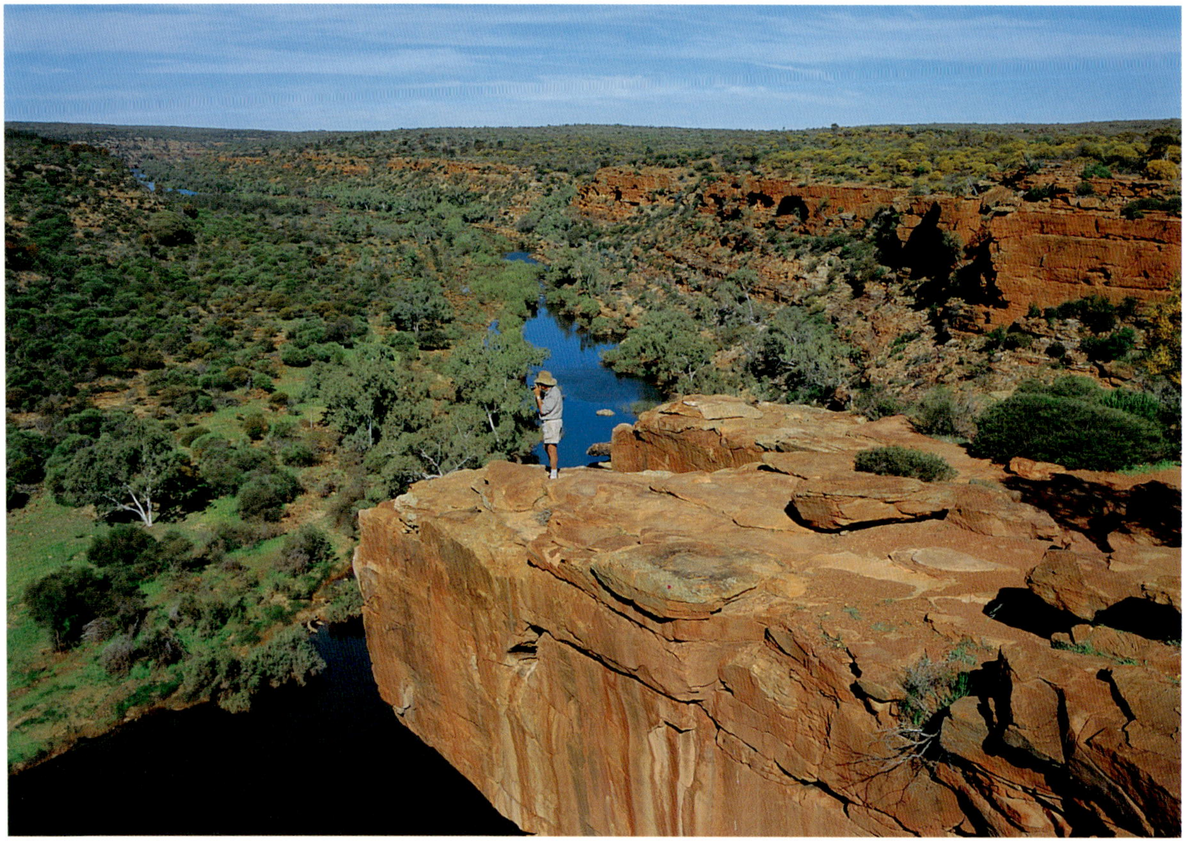

Above: Kalbarri National Park offers spectacular scenes for the photographer.

Kalbarri National Park, around 530 kilometres north of Perth, is noted for its scenic splendours, its wildflowers, which blossom from August into early summer, and its wildlife. The multicoloured rock for which the area is famous, the Tumblegooda Sandstone, was laid down under the sea around 400 million years ago. When upheavals within the earth raised the sea bed, the Murchison River, with wind-blown sand and rain, carved the rocks into gorges, cliffs, ledges and lookouts.

Opposite: Nature's Window, Kalbarri National Park.
Following pages: Zuytdorp Cliffs rise up to 170 metres above the Indian Ocean between Kalbarri and Steep Point, Shark Bay.

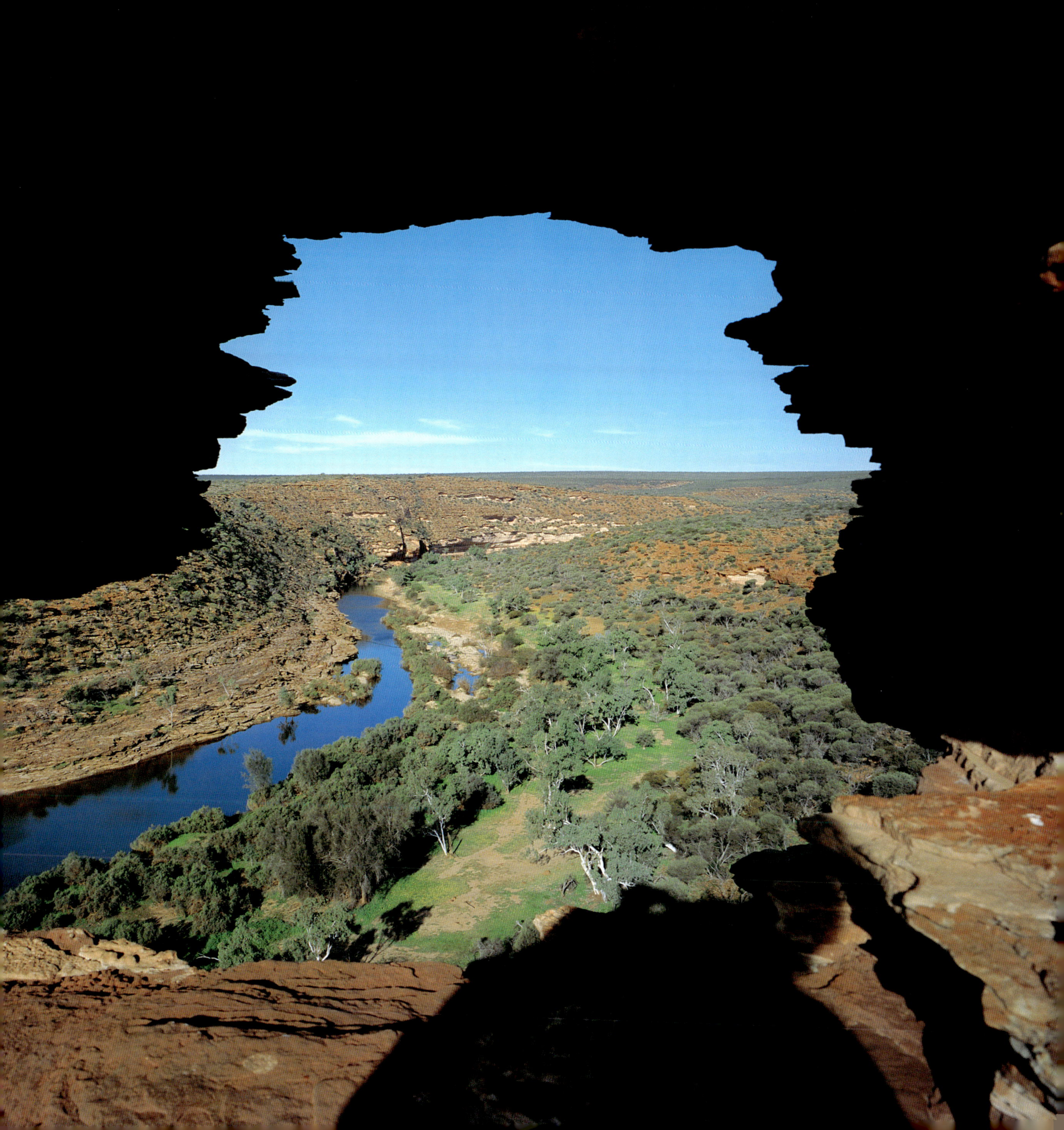

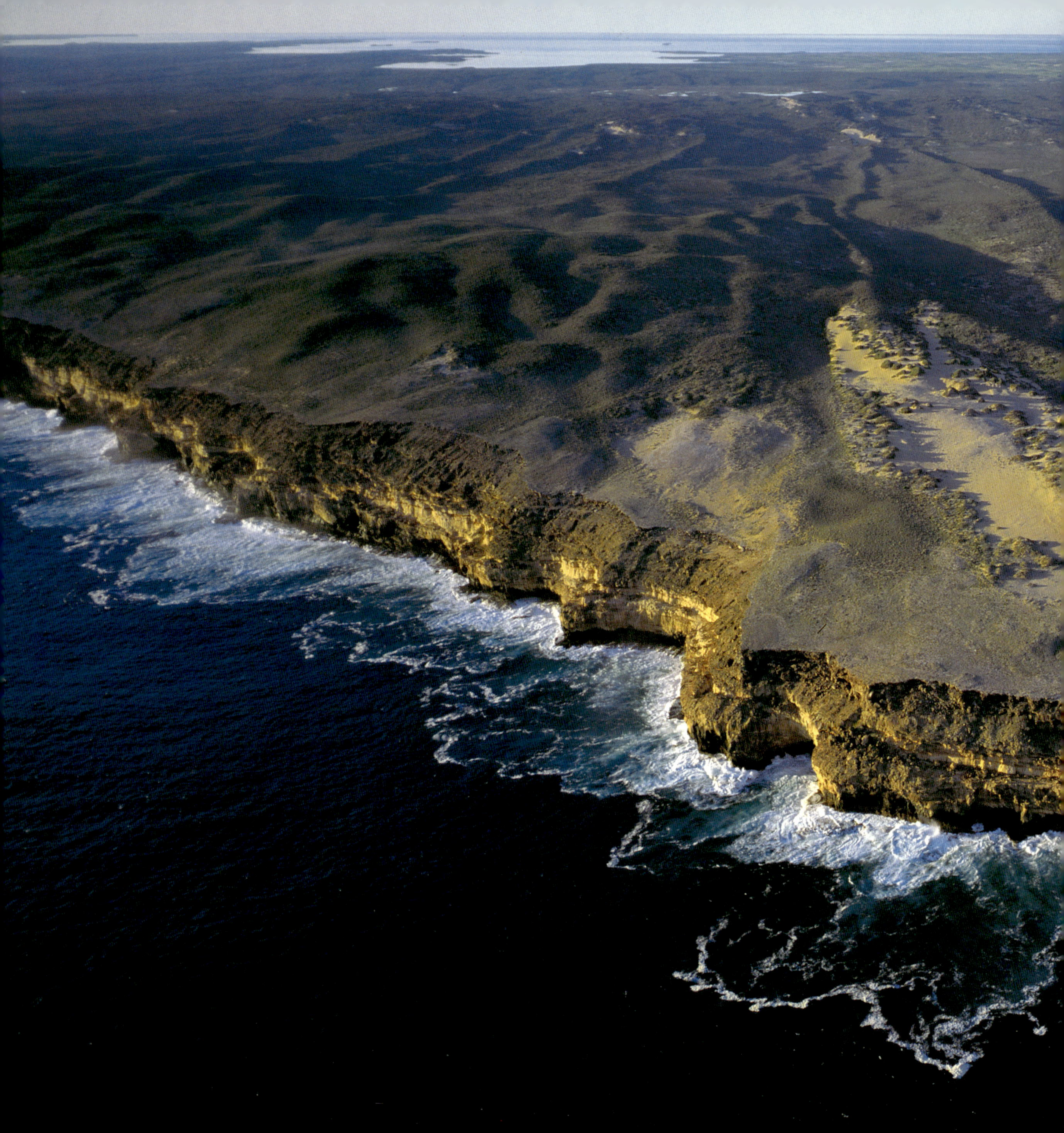

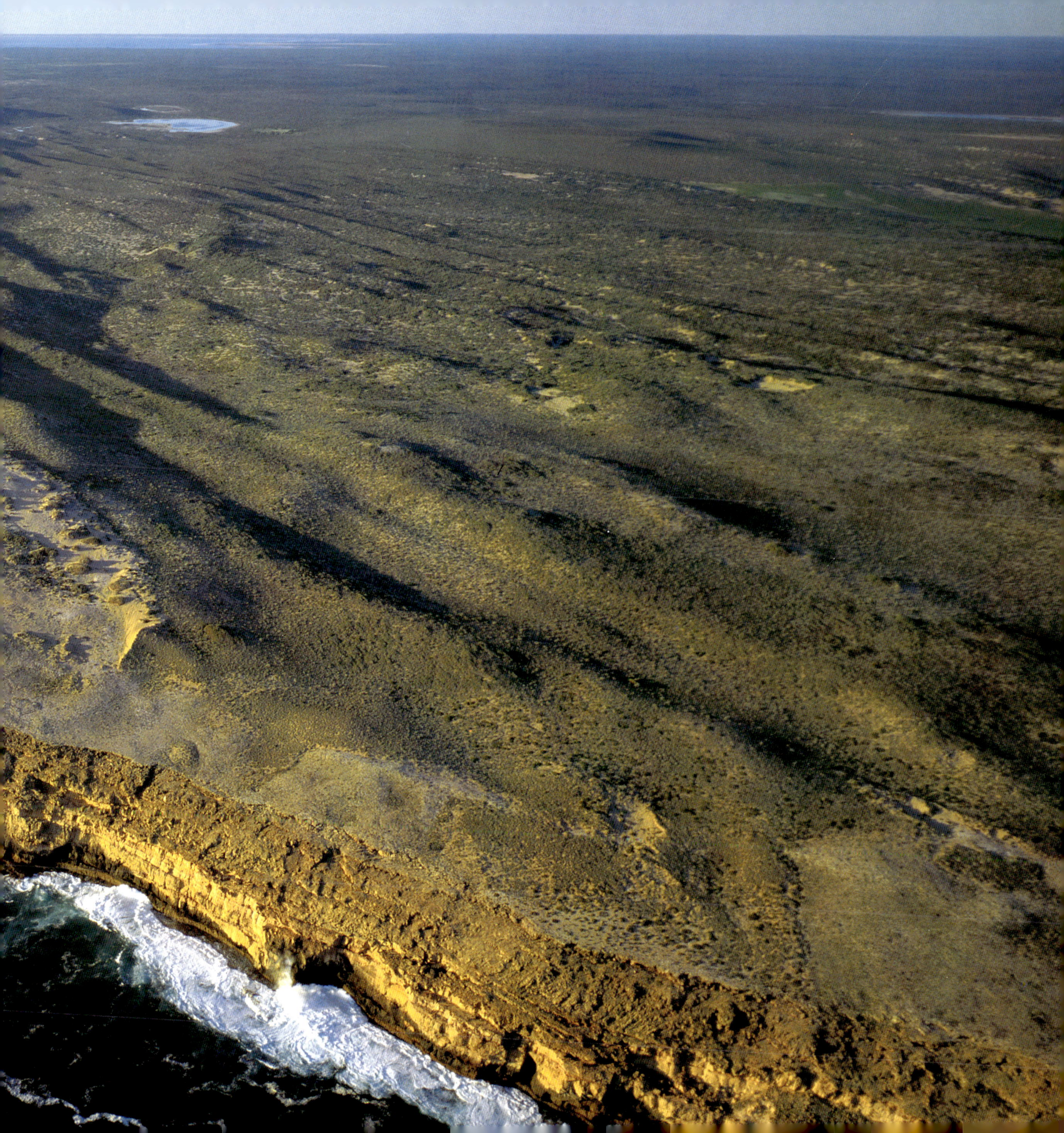

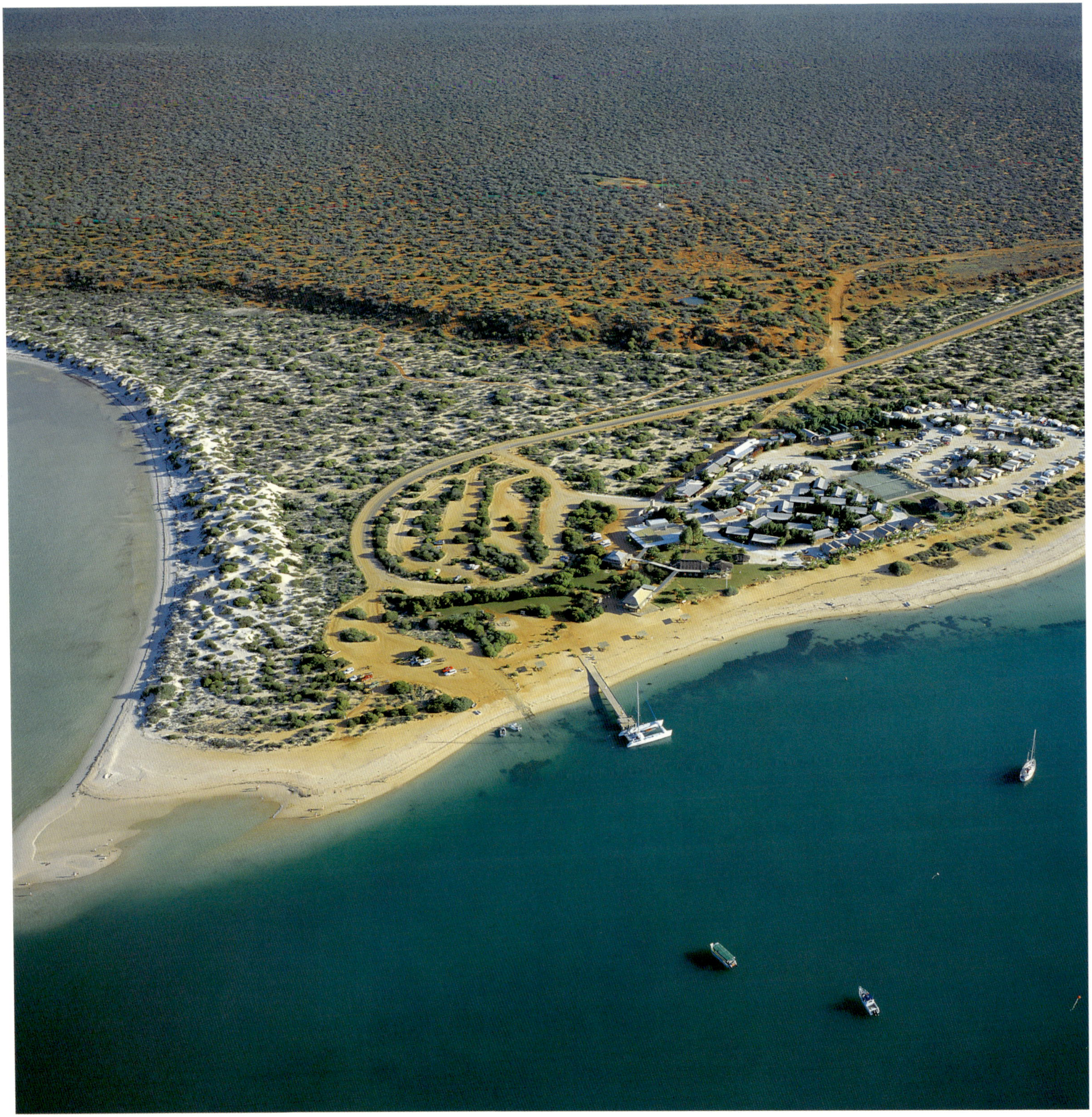

Monkey Mia, Peron Peninsula.

Monkey Mia

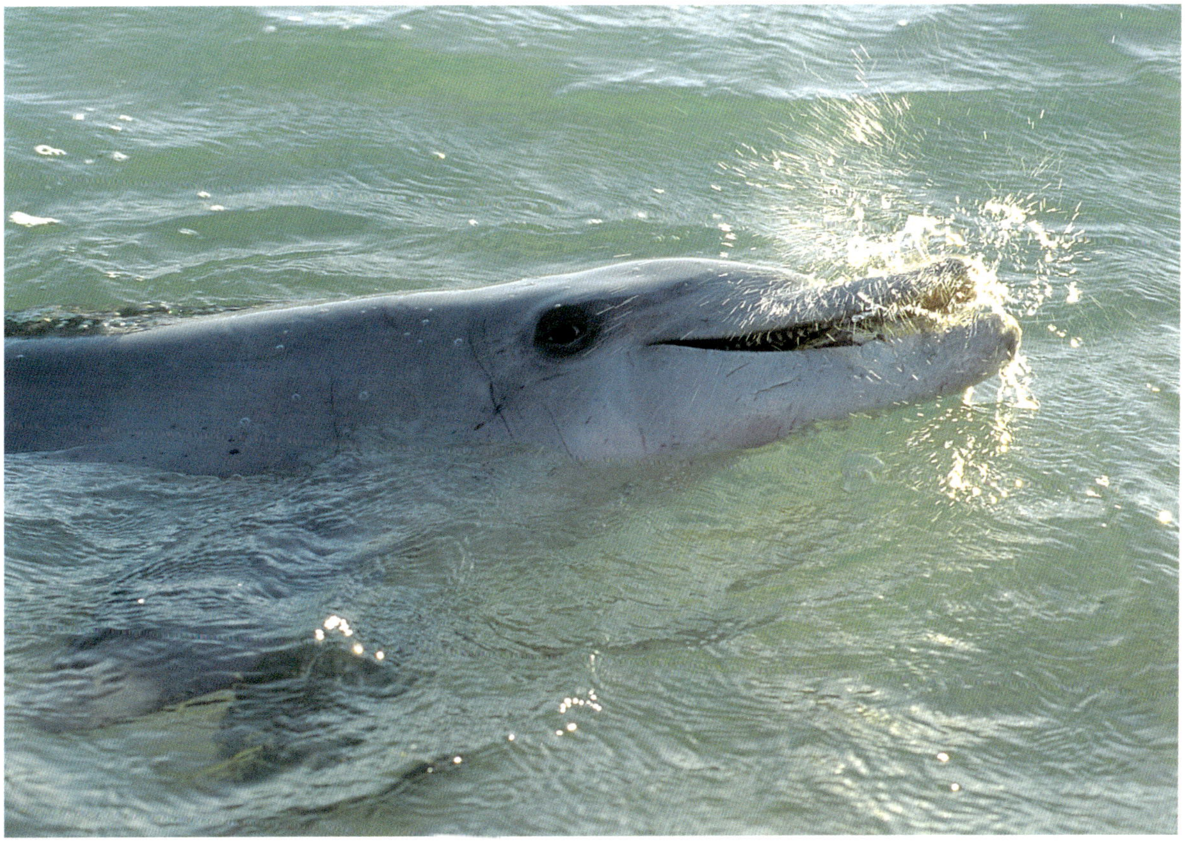

A Bottlenose Dolphin invites contact with humans.

François Peron National Park is named after a naturalist who visited the area on *Le Géographe* in 1801 and 1803. The park occupies much of the Peron Peninsula which juts into the Indian Ocean 400 kilometres north of the port of Geraldton, and helps enclose the waters of Shark Bay.

A pod of around 300 Bottlenose Dolphins feed on fish and other marine life in the bay. A number of these dolphins regularly come to the shallow waters off Monkey Mia, 26 kilometres from the town of Denham, to interact with humans. These dolphins are not trained, rather, they have chosen to participate of their own free will. For the dolphins' protection, feeding is supervised by the local park rangers.

Shark Bay

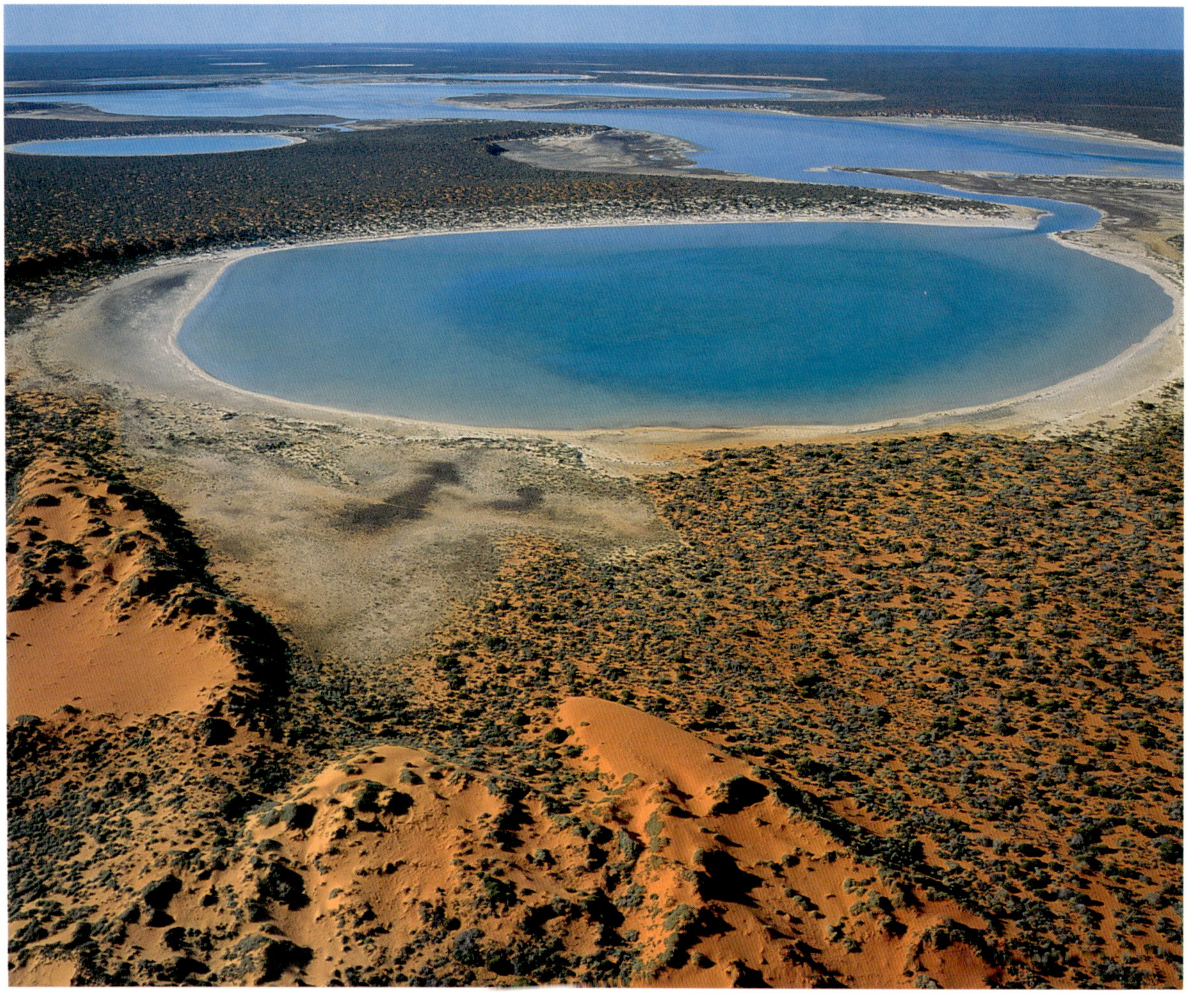

Above: Water evaporates from Shark Bay's lagoons, leaving crusts of salt crystals. *Opposite:* The soil of the Peron Peninsula is a dramatic red in colour.

Shark Bay is a World Heritage Area, protecting examples of the world's oldest surviving lifeform, the mounds of blue-green algae called stromatolites, which live in Hamelin Pool.

A number of rare and endangered animals live in the area, both on land and in the waters of Shark Bay. In the bay, vast banks of seagrass sustain groups of Dugongs, shy sea mammals which shun human attention.

Following pages: Kennedy Range National Park, 160 kilmetres east of Carnarvon.

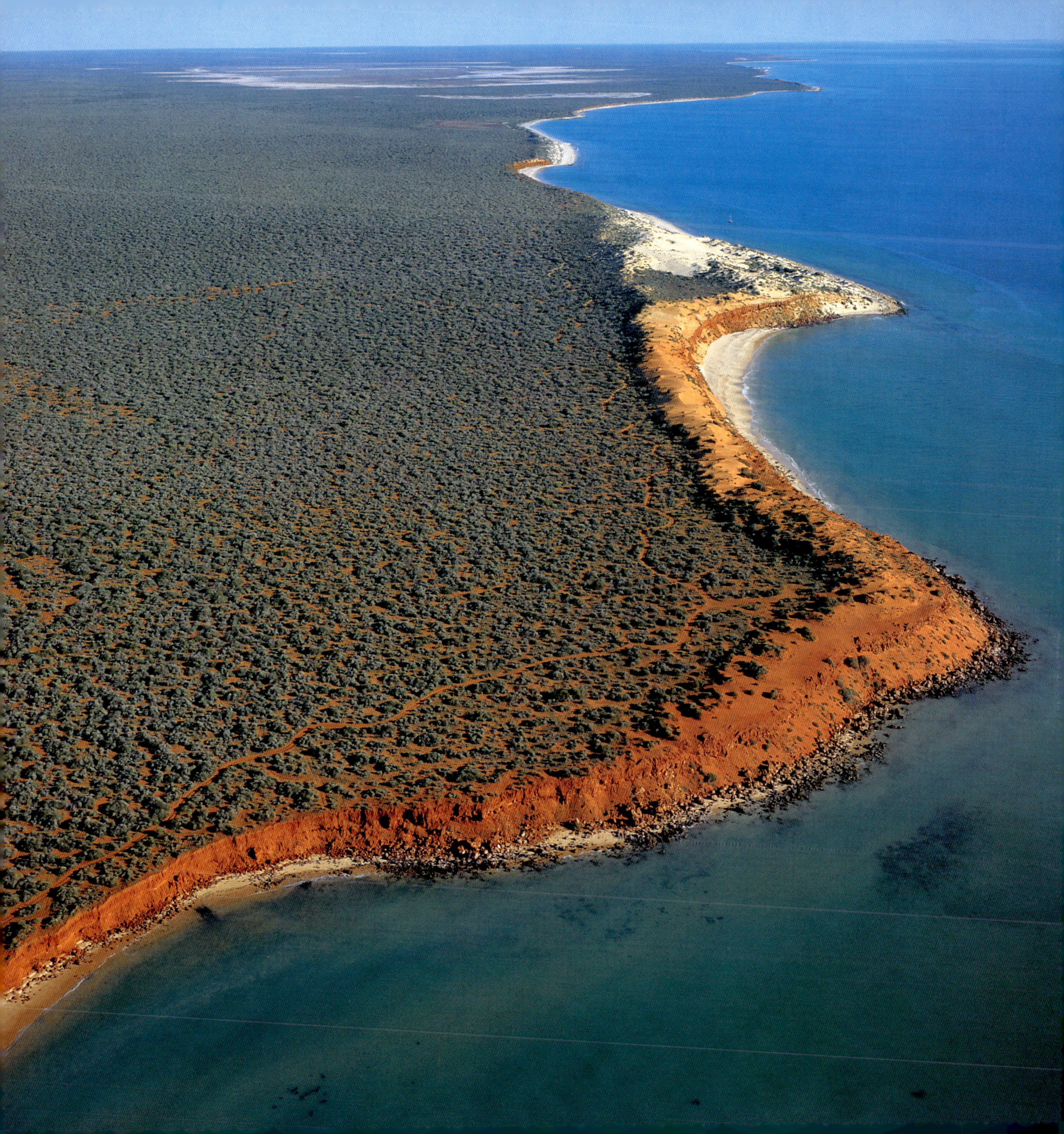

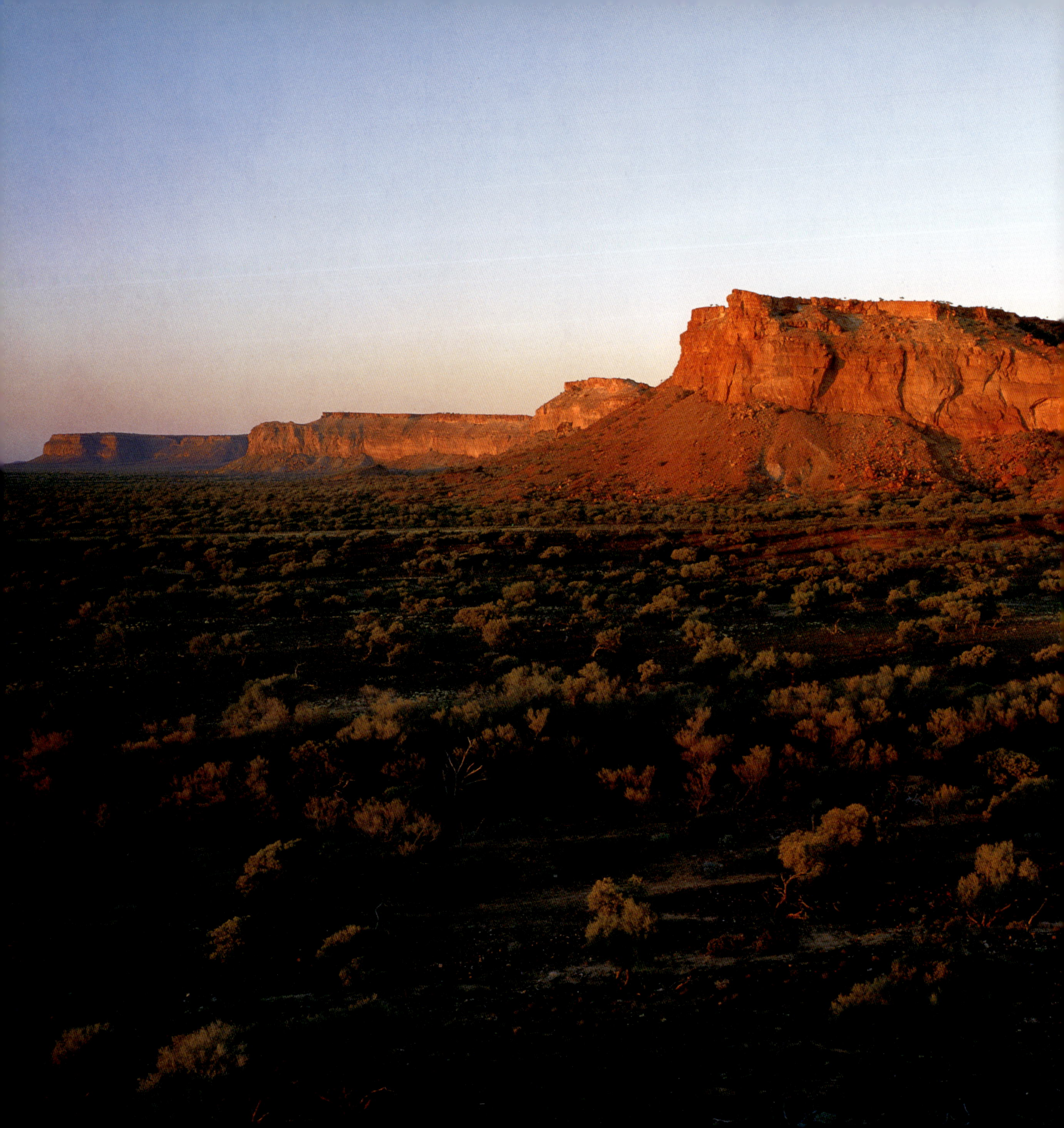

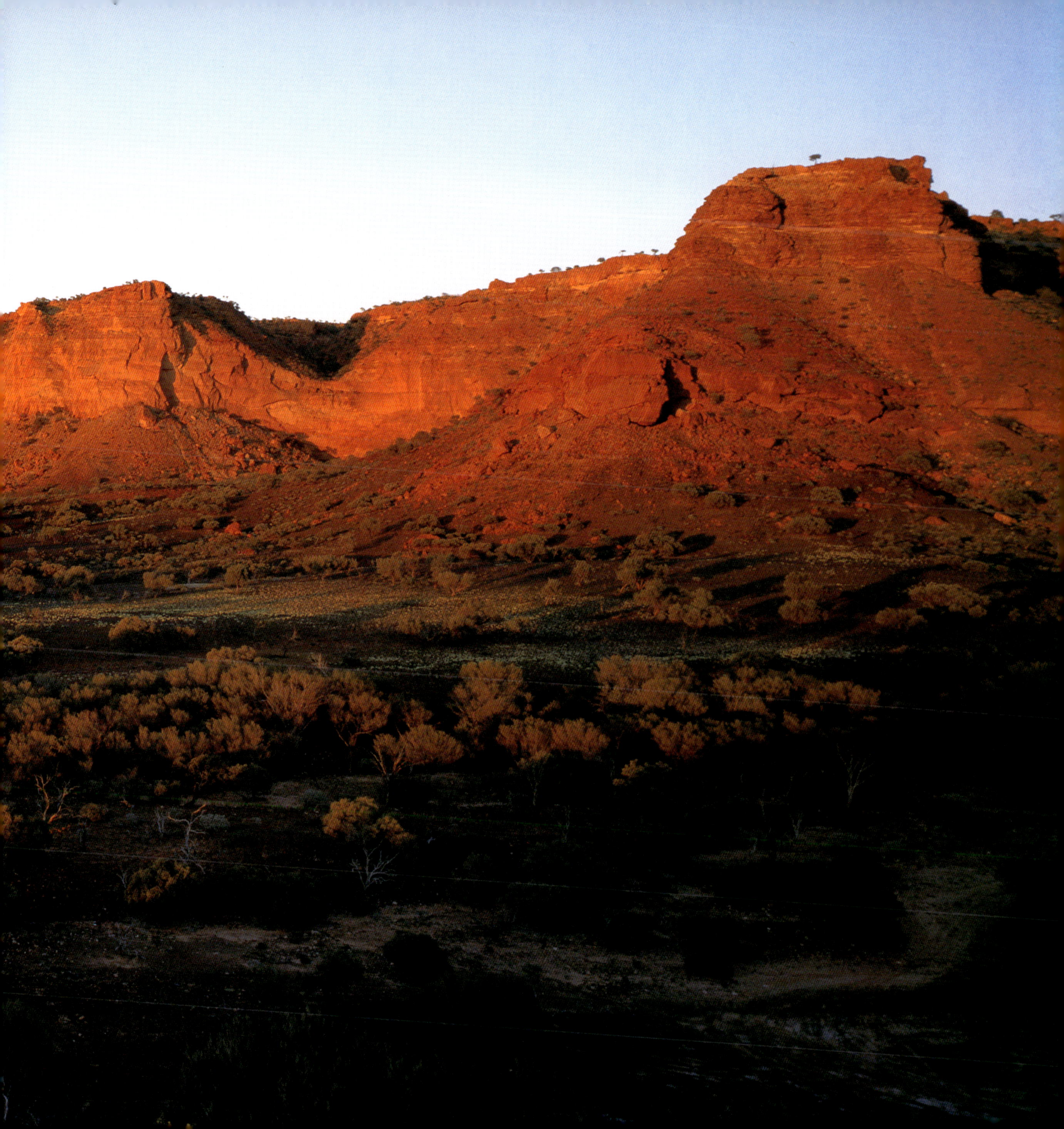

The Gascoyne River

The Gascoyne River flows to the Indian Ocean at Carnarvon through some of Australia's driest country. Its steep red banks are lined with tall eucalypts and where billabongs have been cut off by the river breaking through a bend, the still waters attract birds of all kinds, kangaroos, emus and other creatures.

Gascoyne Junction, where the Lyons River joins the Gascoyne, is 177 kilometres east of Carnarvon. The adventurous traveller will journey another 315 kilometres and experience the stunning sight of Mt Augustus, the world's greatest rock.

Waterhole at Gascoyne Junction. The massive trees provide nesting sites for parrots and many other birds.

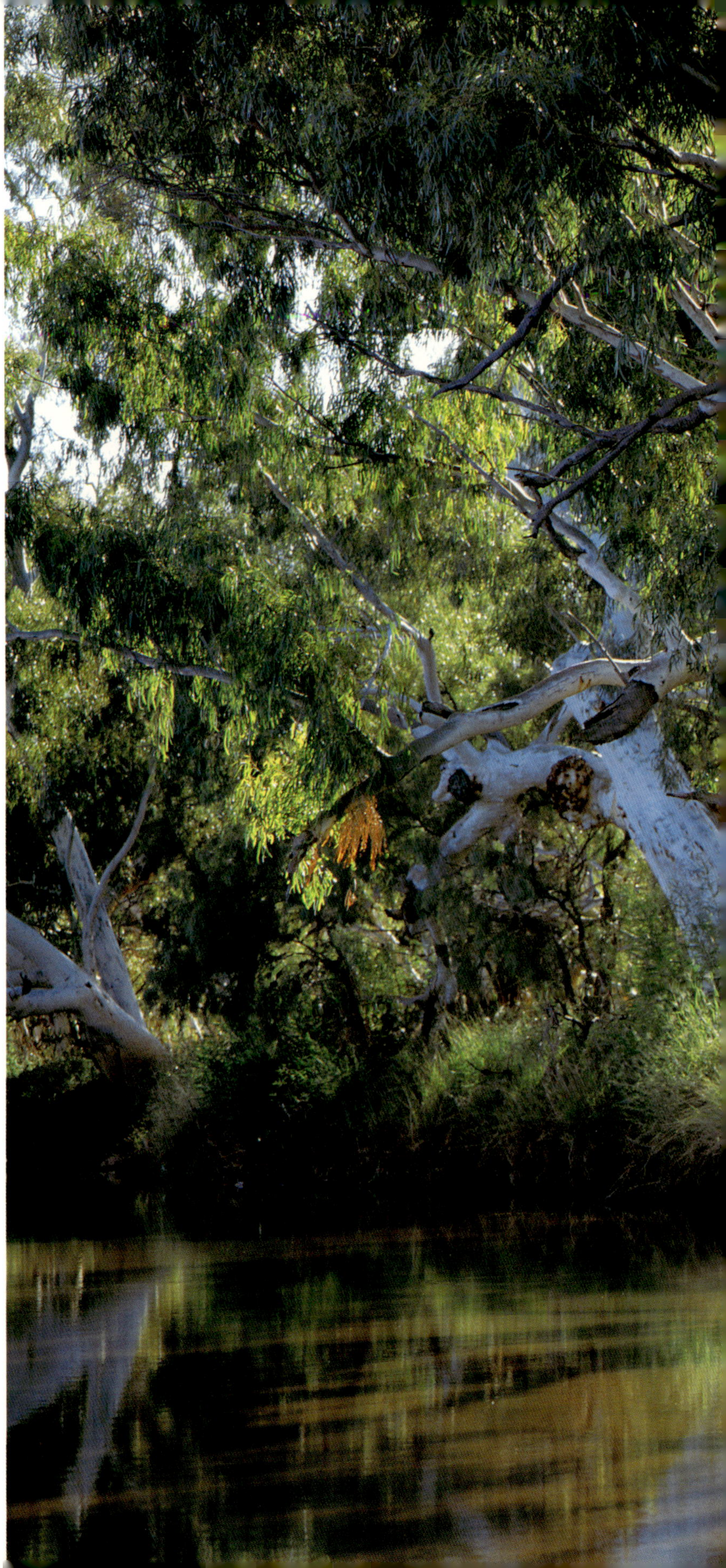

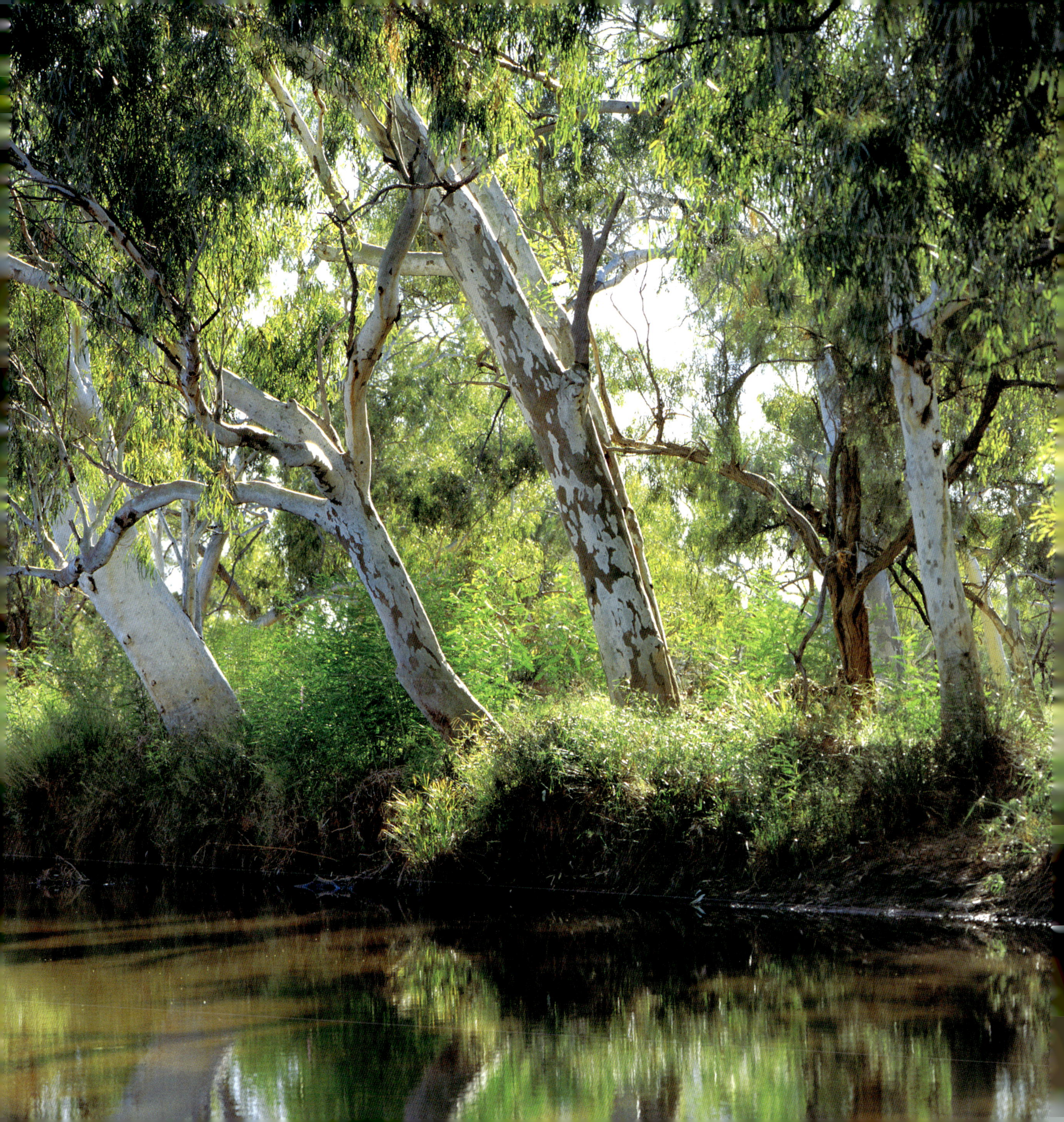

Mt Augustus National Park

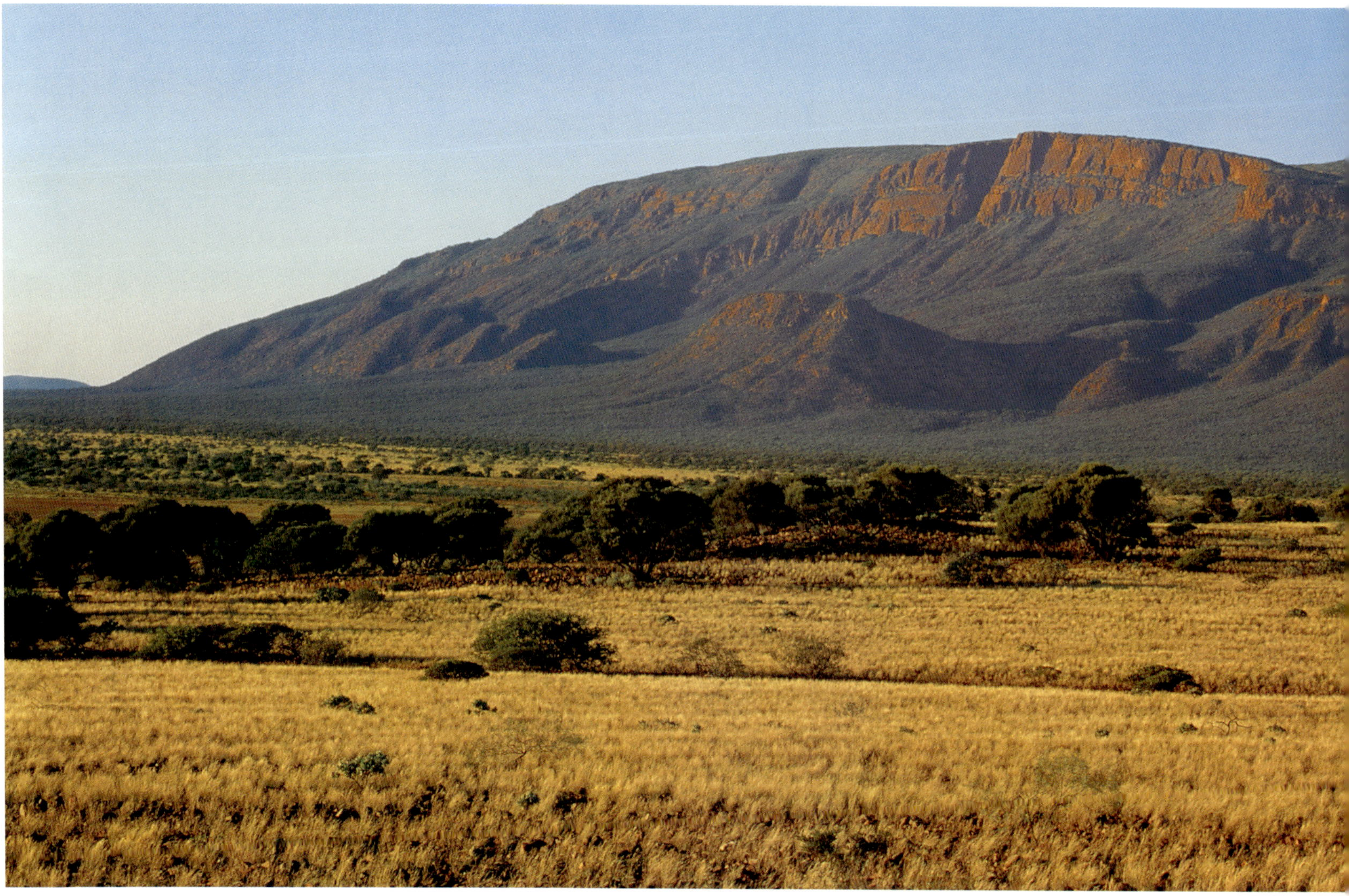

Mt Augustus, the biggest rock in the world, stands in its own National Park.

Although Mt Augustus, 492 kilometres from Carnarvon, rises 1106 metres above sea level and is twice the size of Uluru, it appears far less spectacular because of its stepped formation and the sparse vegetation growing on its flanks. Its core is granite, estimated to be around 1750 million years old. To the Aboriginal people of the area, this immense rock represented the body of a traveller called Burringurrah, speared as he travelled through the area.

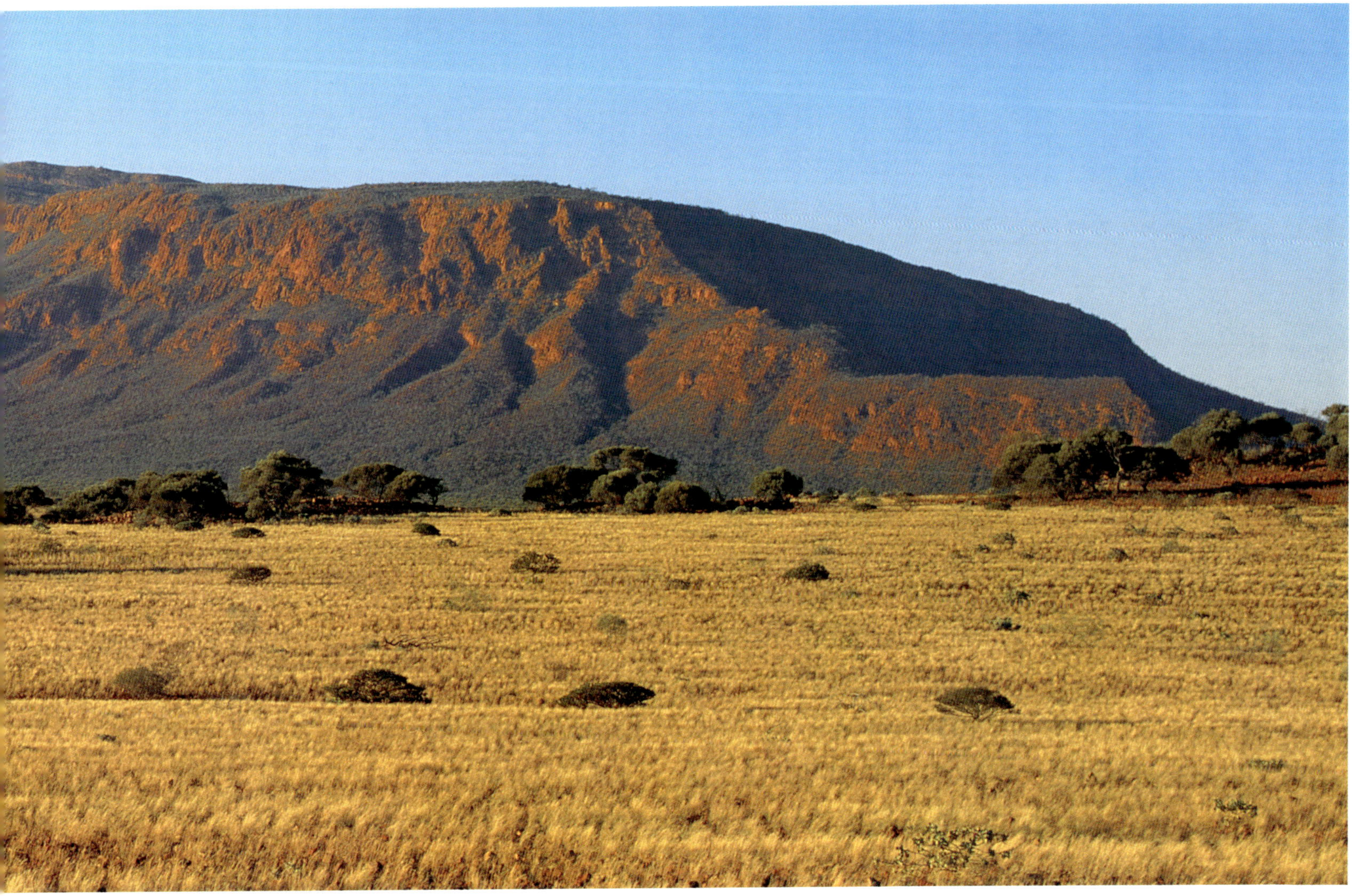

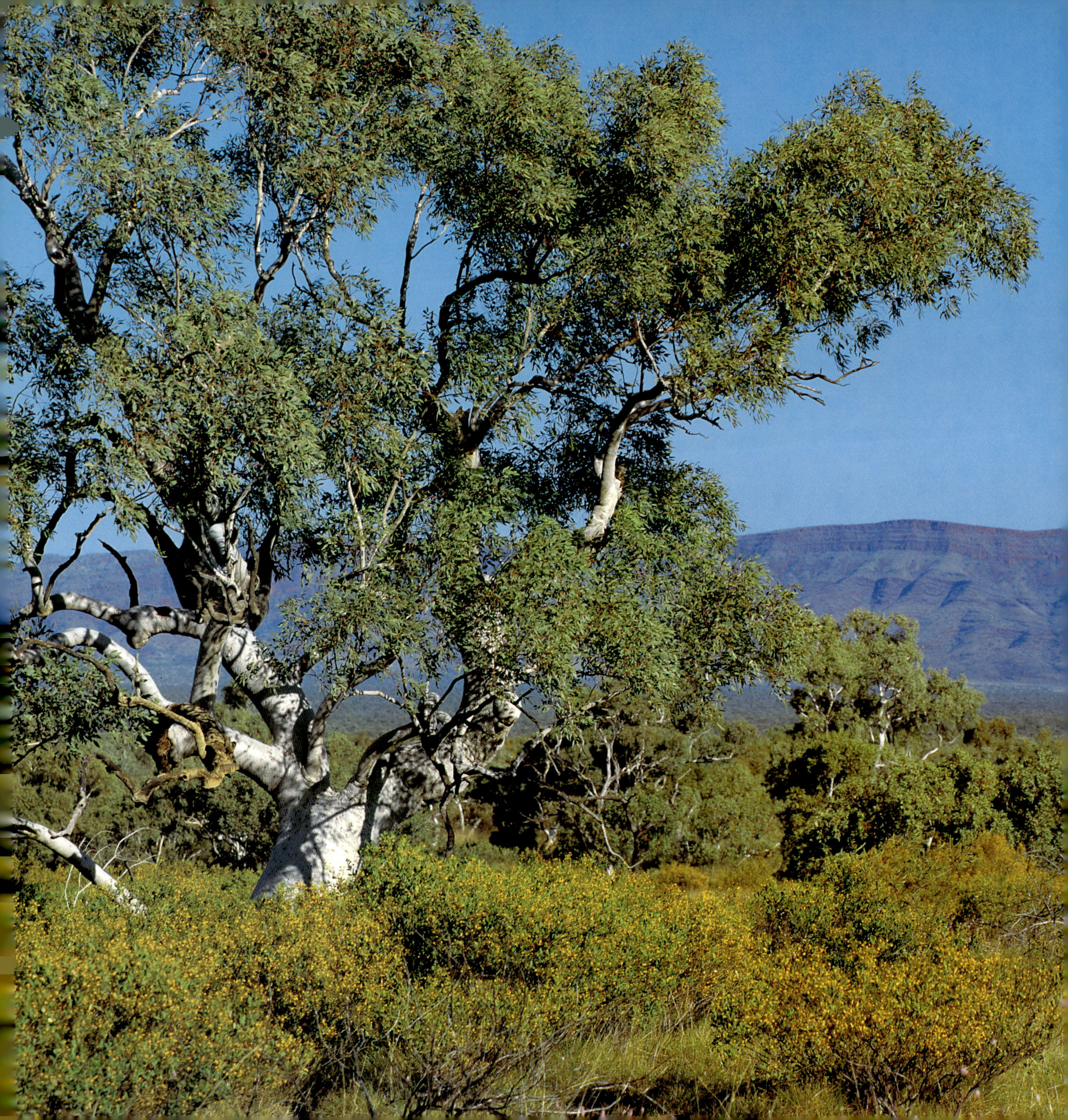

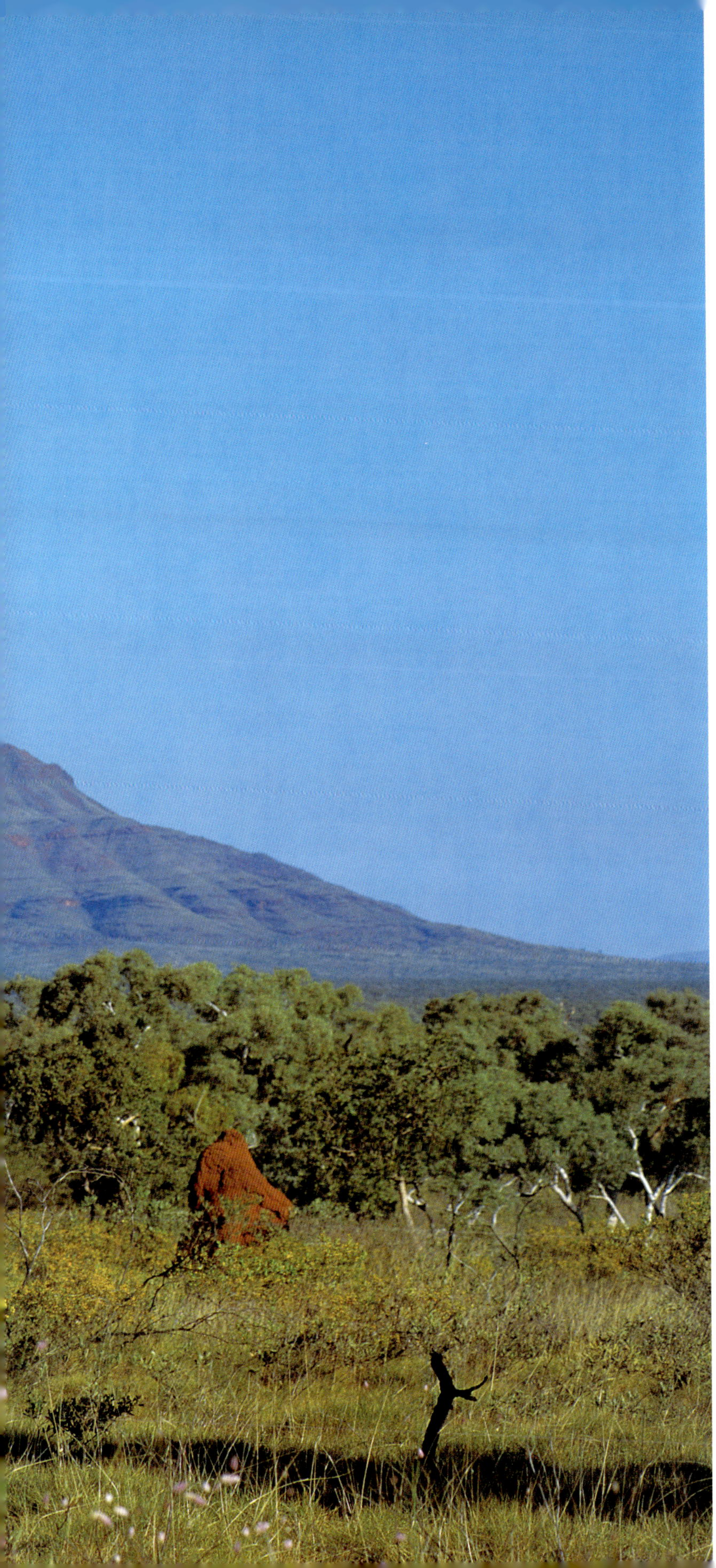

Karijini National Park

Karijini National Park, in the Pilbara of north-western Western Australia, is the State's second largest national park. Its landscapes are dominated by iron-ore-rich rock which forms one of the State's most notable natural resources, and gives the country its distinctive red colour. This magnificent area is brutally hot in summer, but its ranges, gorges, wildlife and wildflowers make visiting it a compelling experience. A visit between May and August will find warm, sunny days and crisp, clear nights, perfect weather for the exploration of landmarks such as Dales Gorge, Joffre Falls, Weano Gorge and Mt Bruce, Western Australia's second highest peak.

A distant view of the Hamersley Range, Karijini National Park.

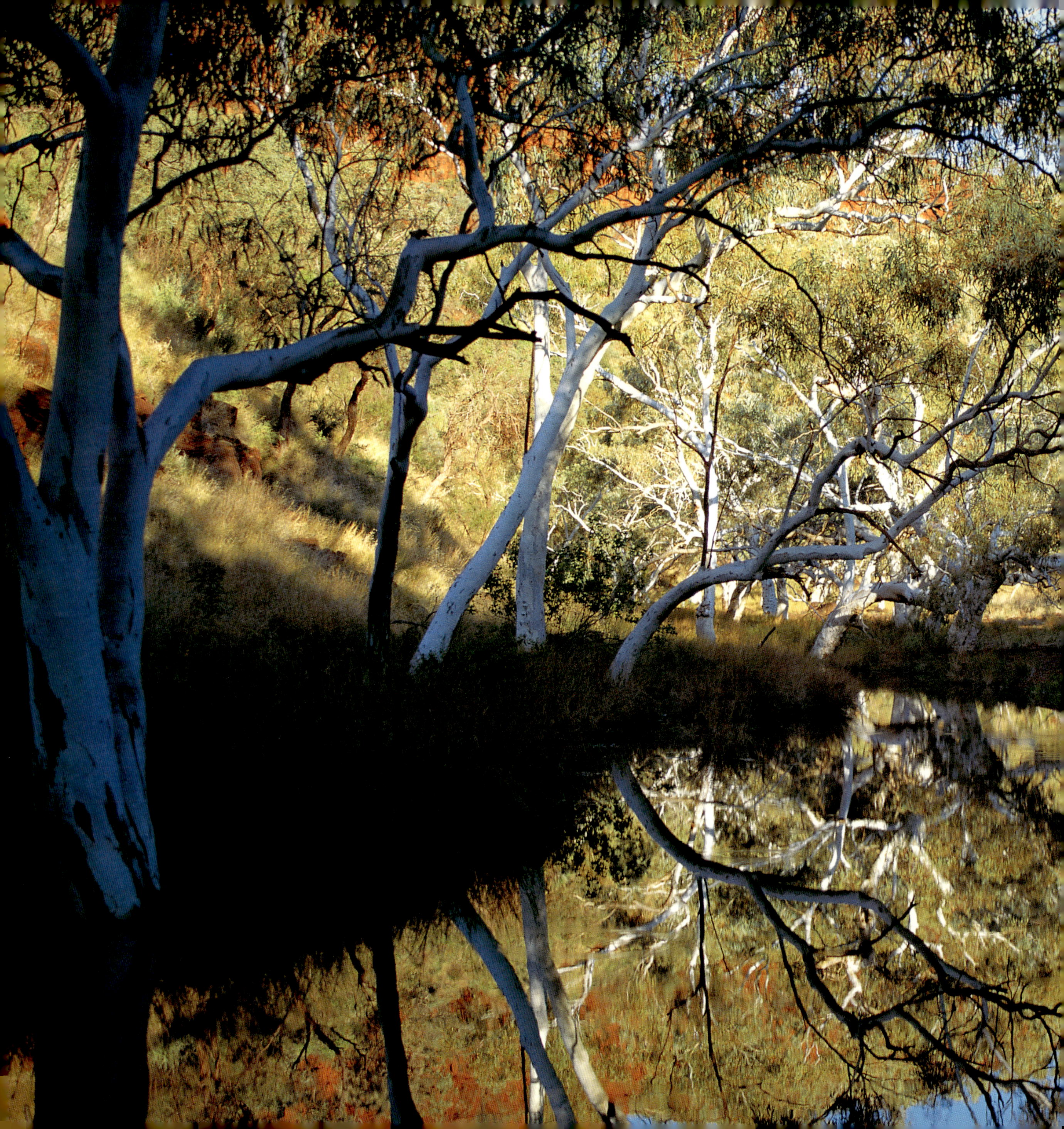

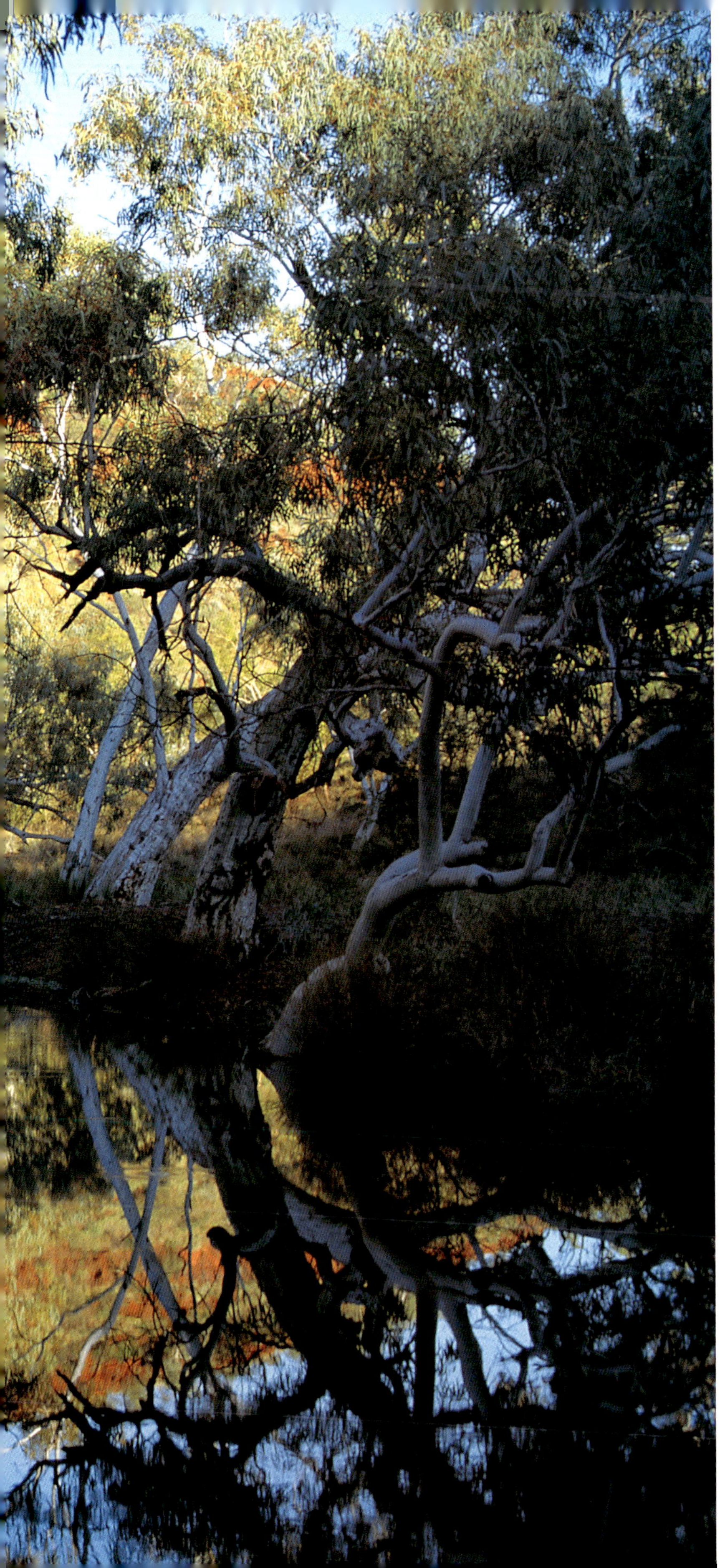

Hamersley Range

Few living things can survive without water. Australia's aridland plants and animals are adapted to going for long periods on a minimum of moisture, but a waterhole such as that shown here, nestled in a gorge in the Hamersley Range, becomes a focus for wildlife. At noon, such an oasis is quiet and still. Visit just before dawn, or sit quietly on a fallen log for an hour or so before and after sunset, and you will be amazed at the number of creatures which warily make their way to the water to drink.

Left: Waterhole in a gorge in the Hamersley Range.
Following pages: Landscape with clumps of spinifex and Ghost Gums, Karijini National Park.

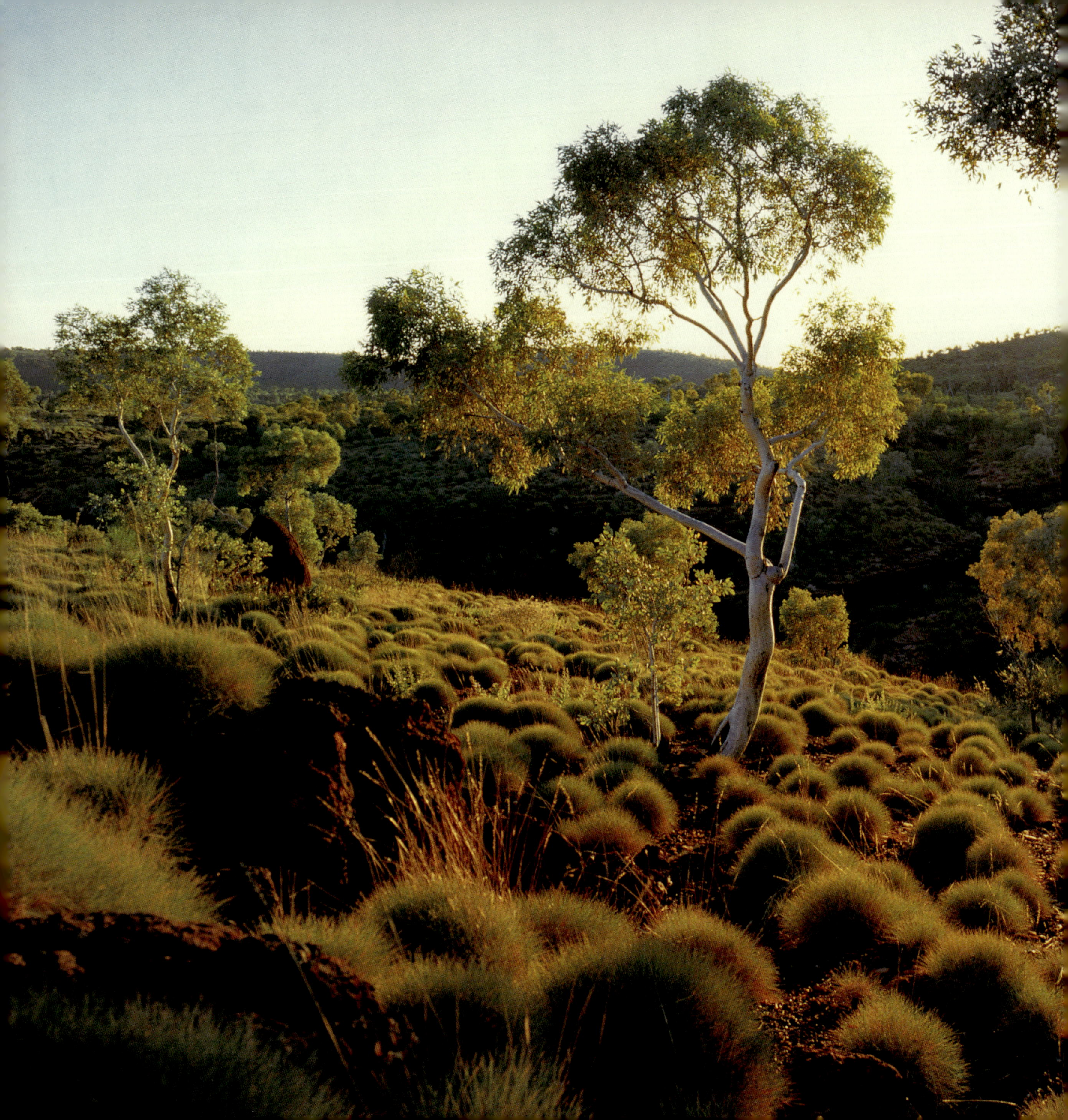

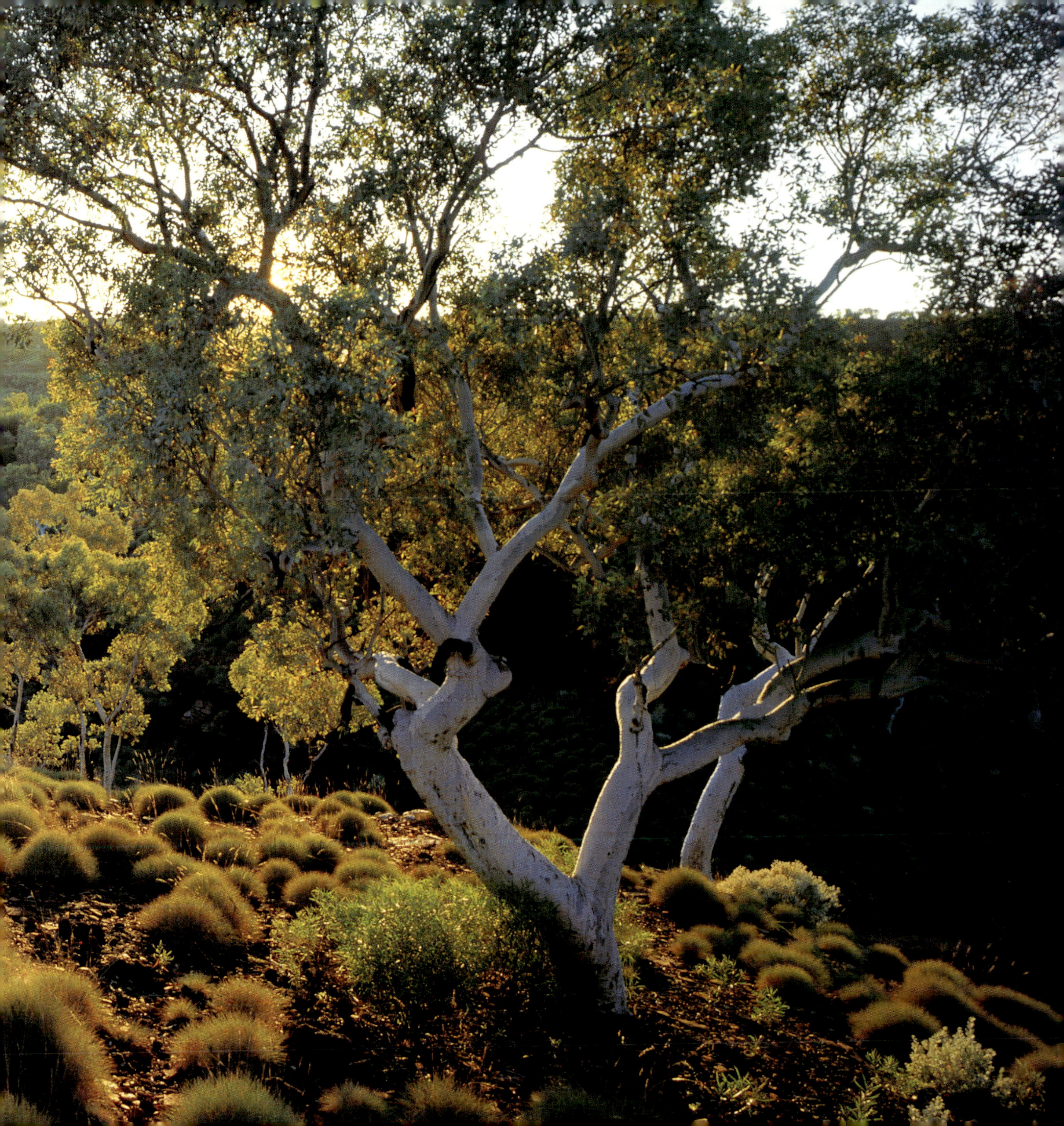

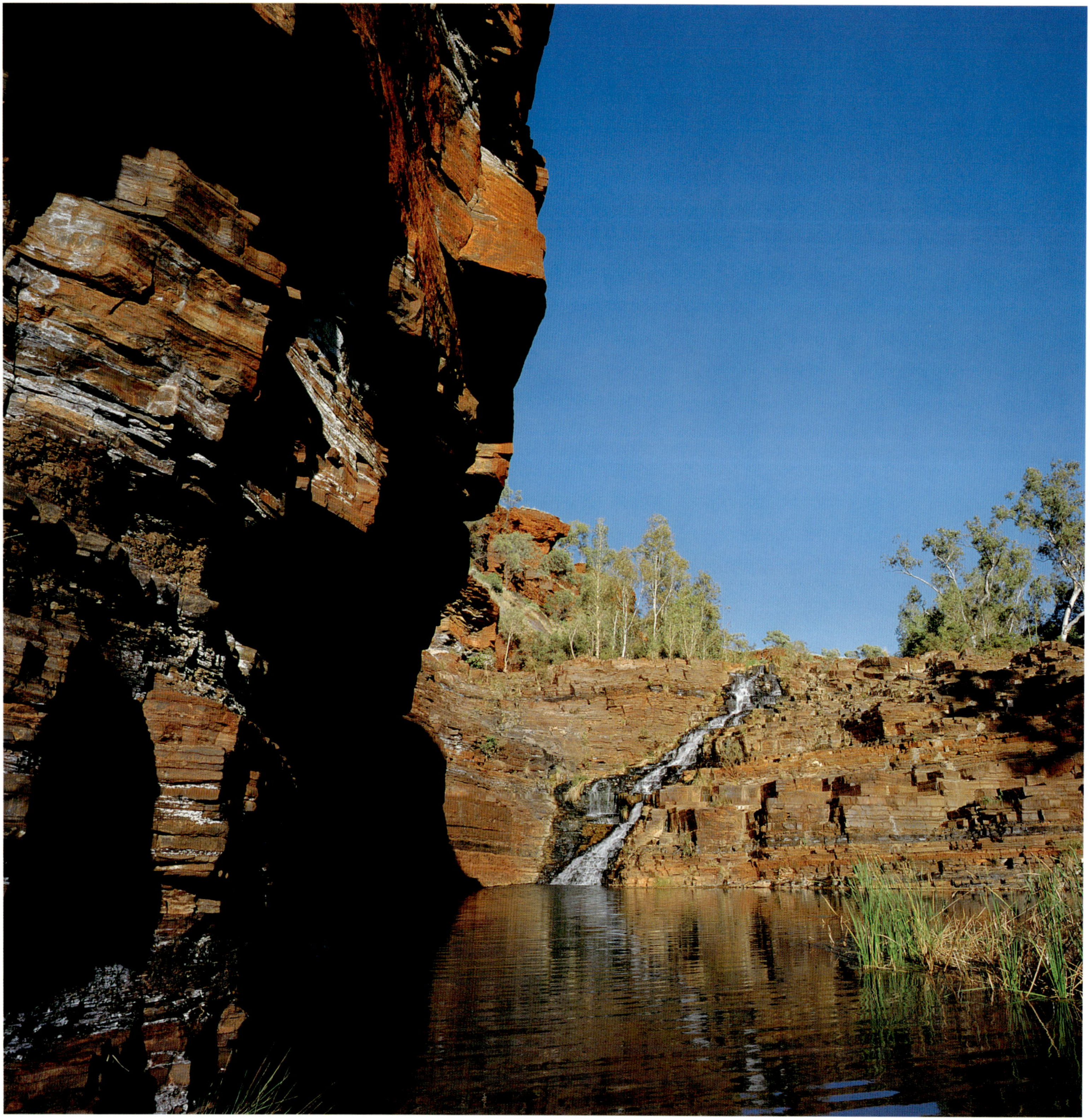

Gorge wall, pool and waterfall, Karijini National Park.

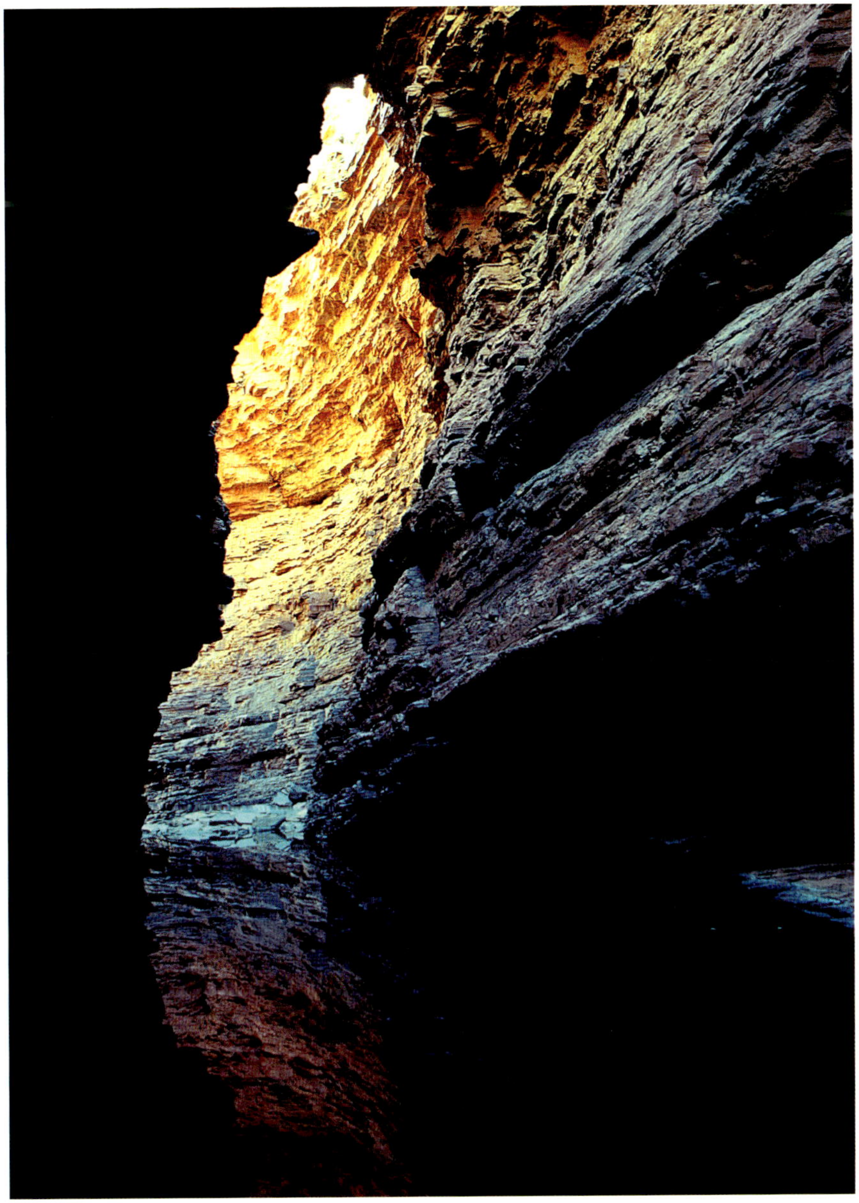

Weano Gorge, Karijini National Park.

The Pilbara

The rocks of the Hamersley Range were laid down on the sea floor 2500 million years ago. Today, this ancient stone has been carved by seasonal streams into spectacular gorges such as Weano, Dales and Hancock. Many can be appreciated fully only by energetic climbing, or by exploring at water level. The deepest, permanent pools harbour aquatic creatures of all kinds. The Aboriginal word for this region, "Pilbara", means "freshwater fish", which pays tribute to the inhabitants of these remarkable bodies of water.

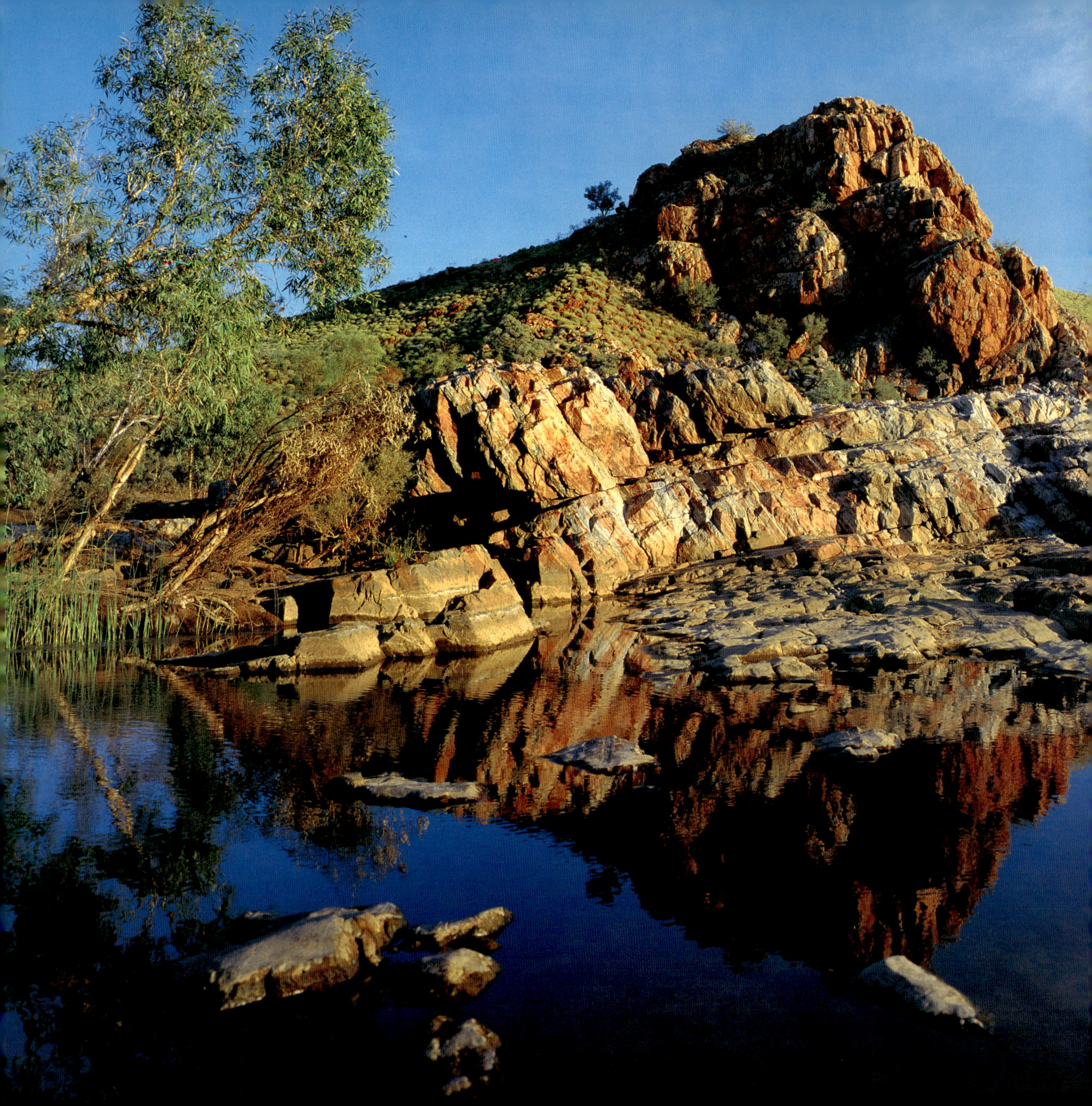

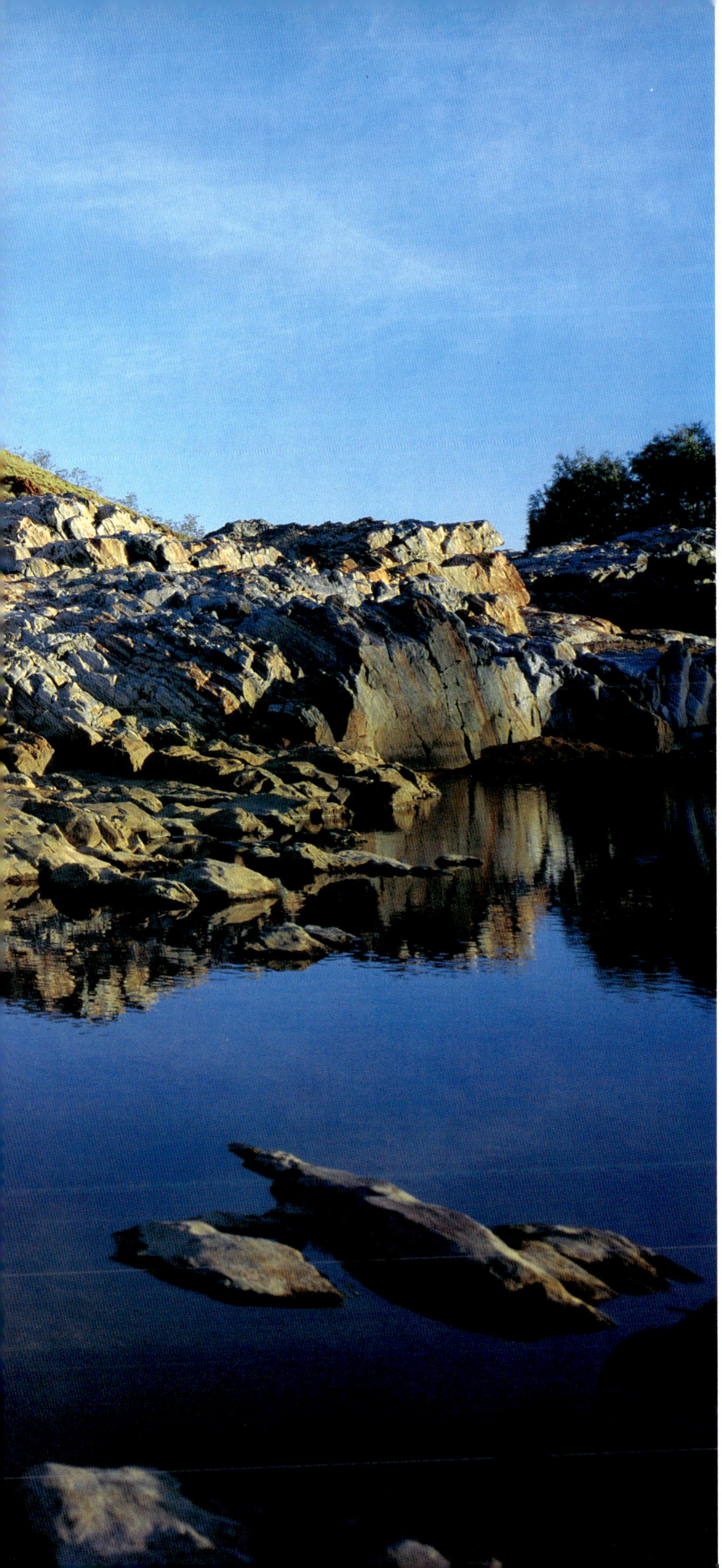

Marble Bar

Gold was discovered near the town of Marble Bar in 1890 and thousands flocked to search for the precious metal.

Today the town, which takes its name from the impressive ribboned bar of jasper on the Coongan River, 5 kilometres away, is connected with tin and manganese mining. Marble Bar in summertime has the reputation of being the hottest place on Earth. In winter, the weather is delightful and a visit to the famous "marble bar" is a memorable experience.

Banded jasper gives Marble Bar its name.

Broome

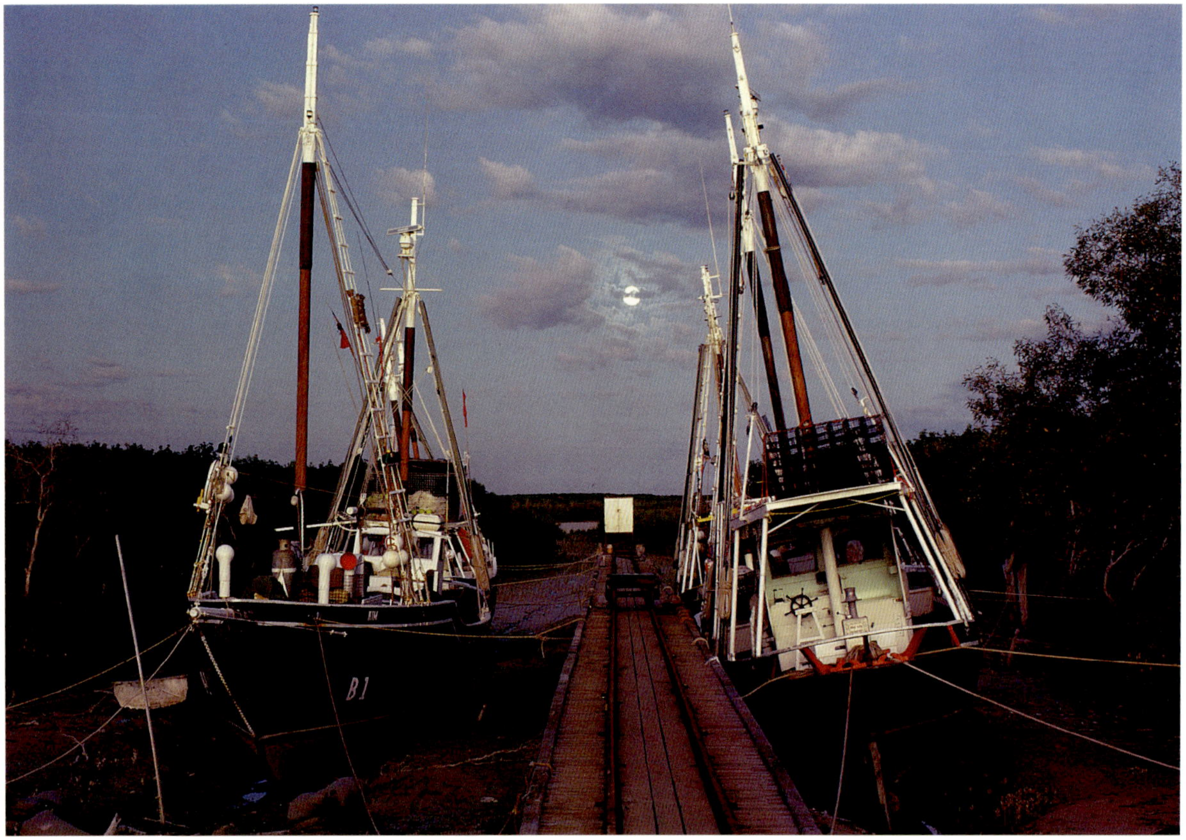

Above: Luggers stranded at low tide, Broome.

North of Eighty Mile Beach, at the southern edge of the Kimberley, lies Broome. From this port, luggers carried divers who harvested oysters for their mother-of-pearl shells and, they hoped, fabulous pearls. Today, the world wears cultivated pearls, plastics have replaced pearl buttons, and divers are spared the perils of the sea. Broome's multicultural population, a legacy of the pearling days, together with its historic interest and the beauty of its setting, make the town a rewarding stopover on any journey of exploration. Cable Beach and Gantheaume Point are of particular interest.

Opposite: The rocks of Gantheaume Point, near Broome.

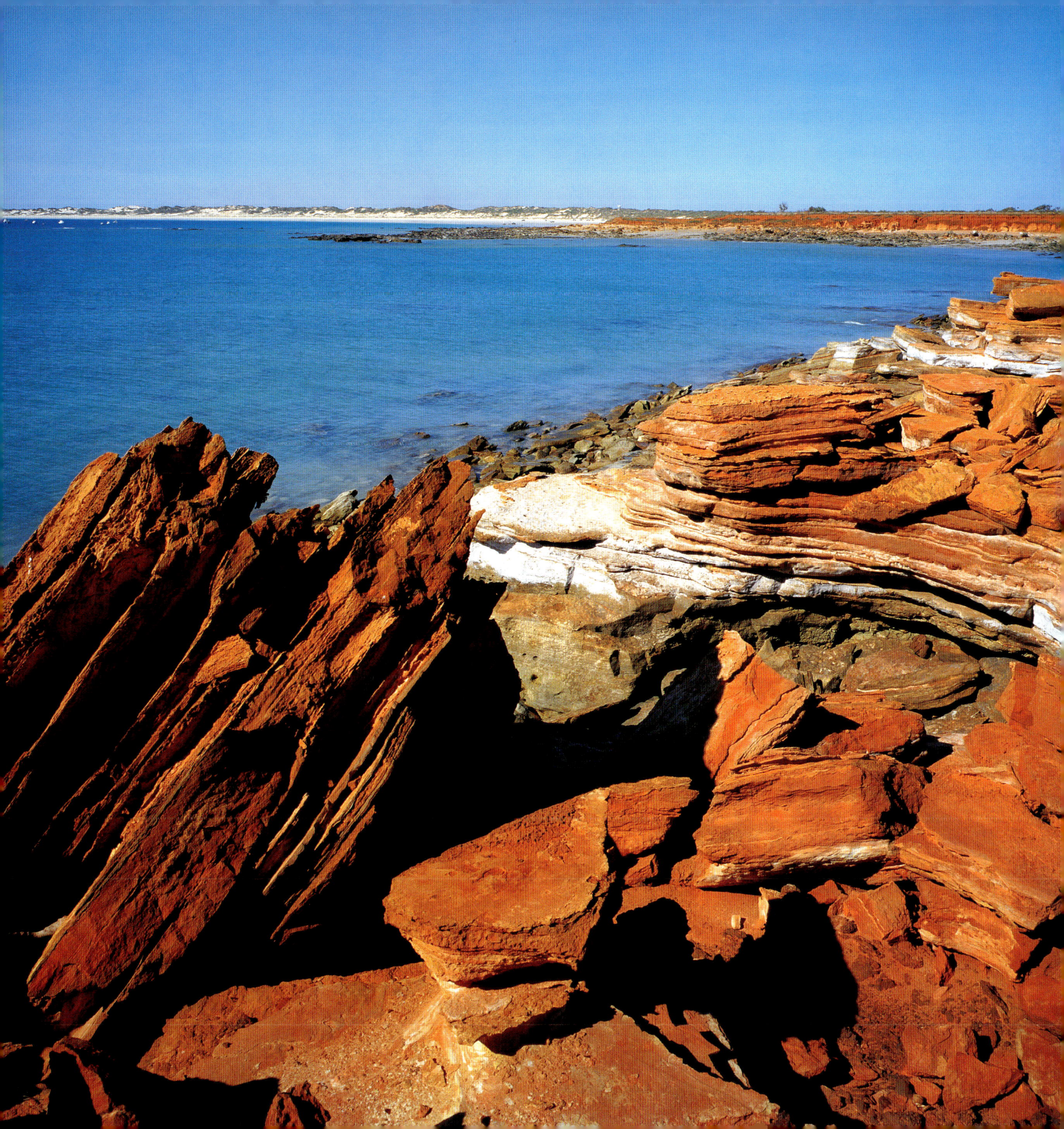

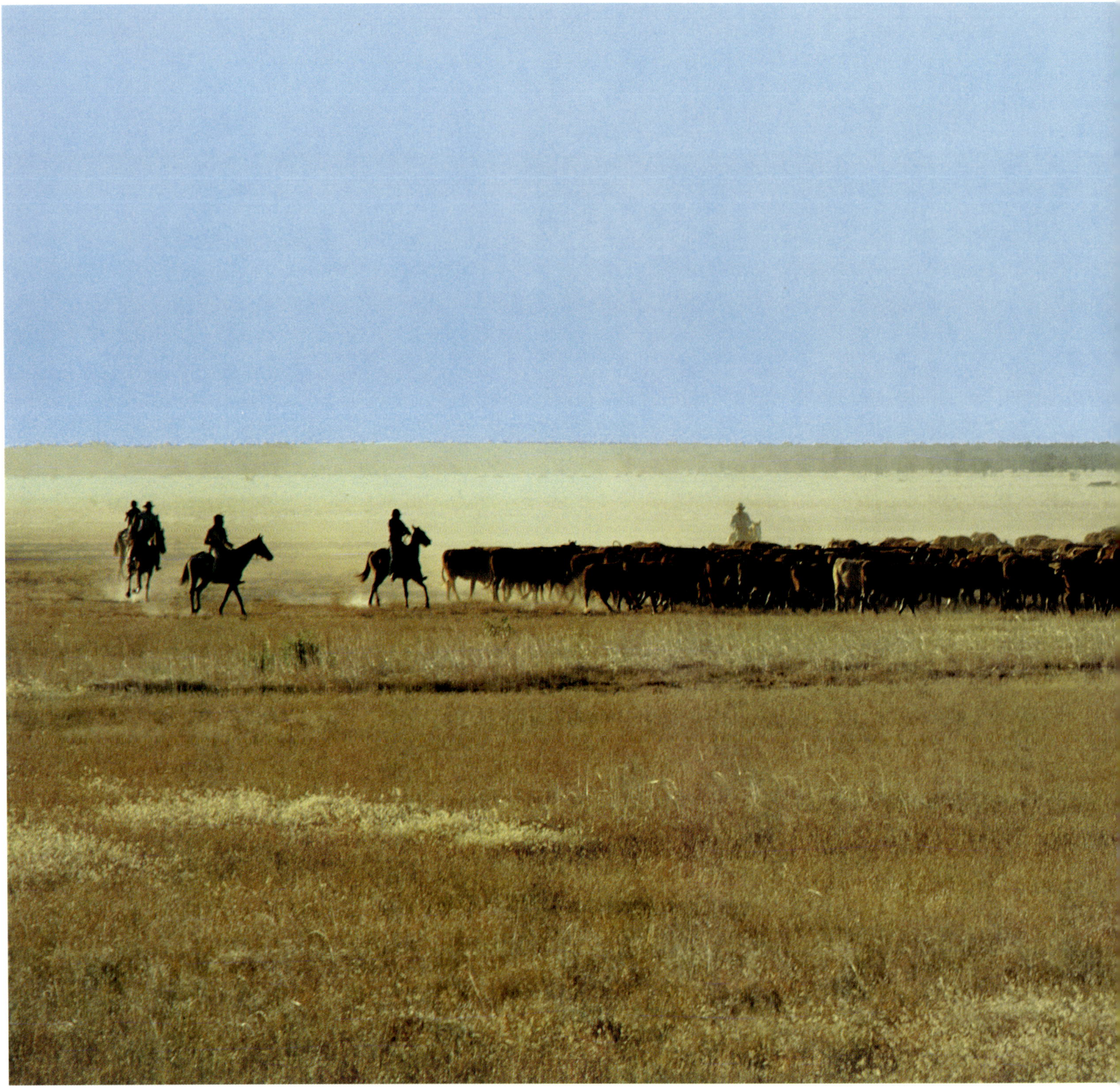

Moving the mob across a Kimberley plain, past a pair of Boab trees which, in winter, are devoid of leaves.

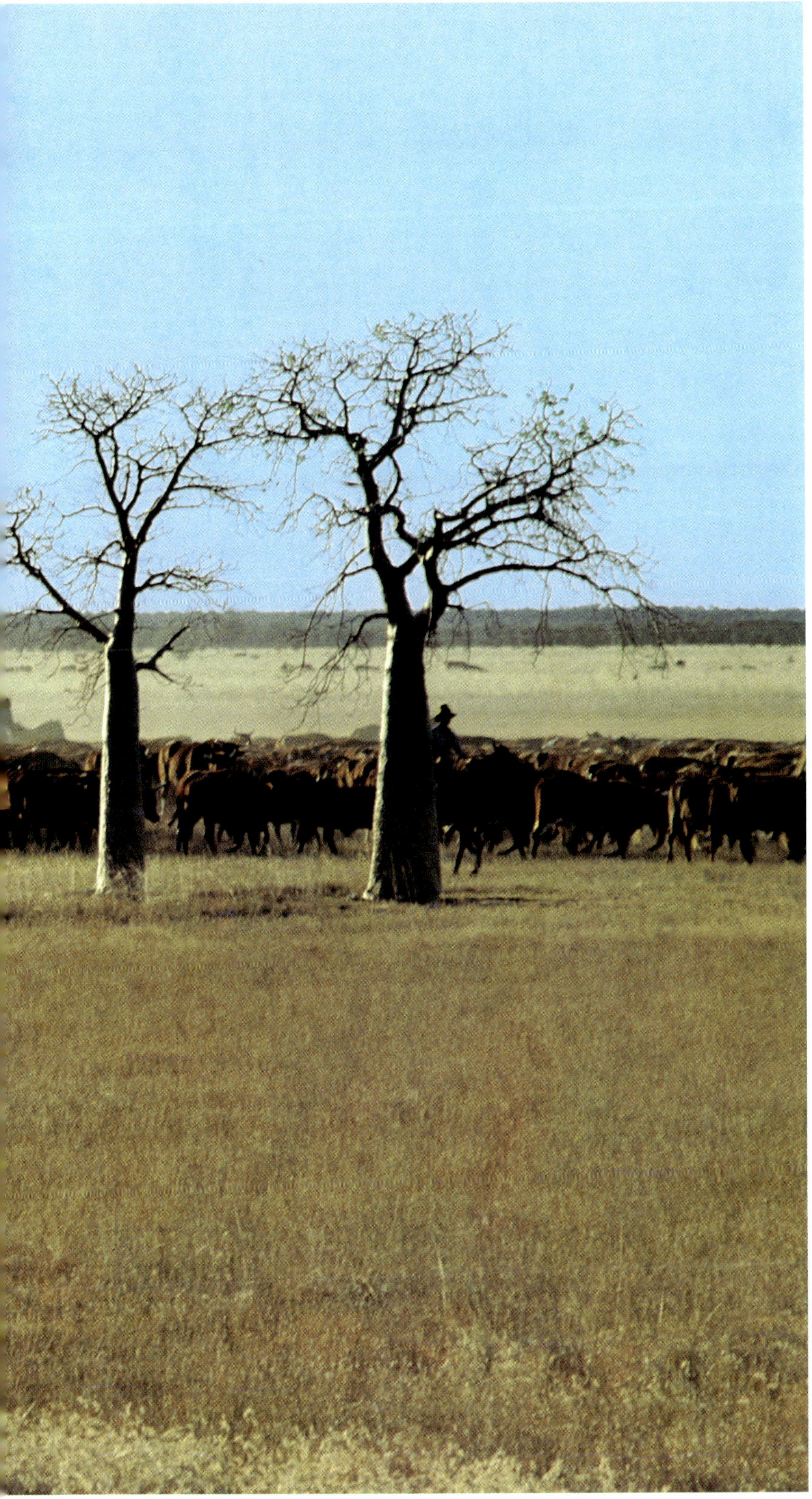

The Kimberley

The Kimberley is tropical monsoon country, where a warm dry winter sees trees drop their leaves and grasses brown off. With summer's bountiful tropical downpours, the land renews itself and cattle grow fat. Wildlife multiplies and rivers and billabongs are alive with birds – and crocodiles.

This is one of the world's final frontiers, a land of vast spaces, rugged ranges and wilderness, often inaccessible by road, and best visited in the cooler months of the year. In the Kimberley, there are still discoveries to be made and adventures to be lived.

Wilderness unparalleled

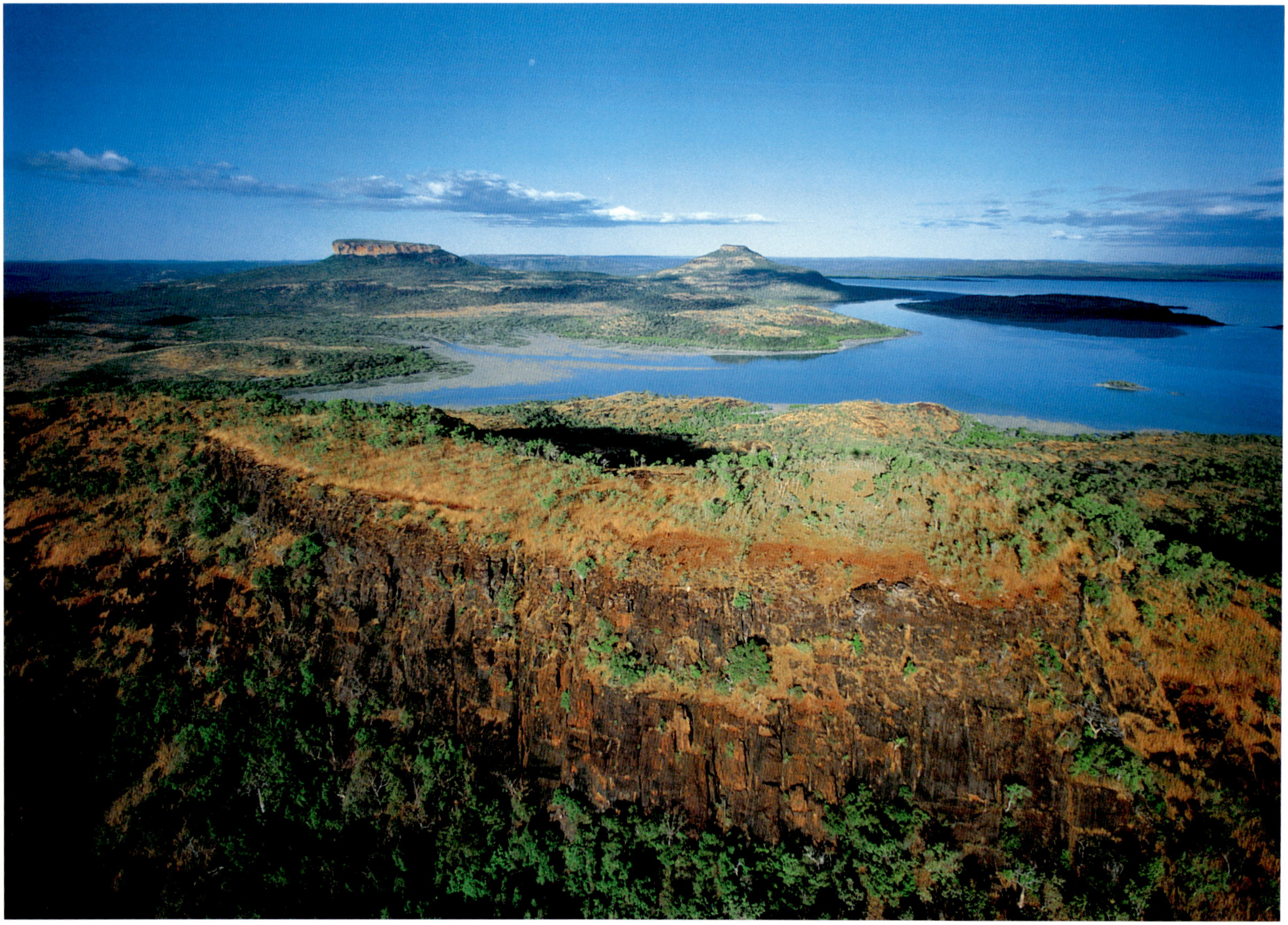

A stunning landscape in the Prince Regent Nature Reserve.

The Prince Regent River and its surrounding territory, in the north of the Kimberley, is an area of magnificent wilderness, classified as a World Biosphere Reserve.

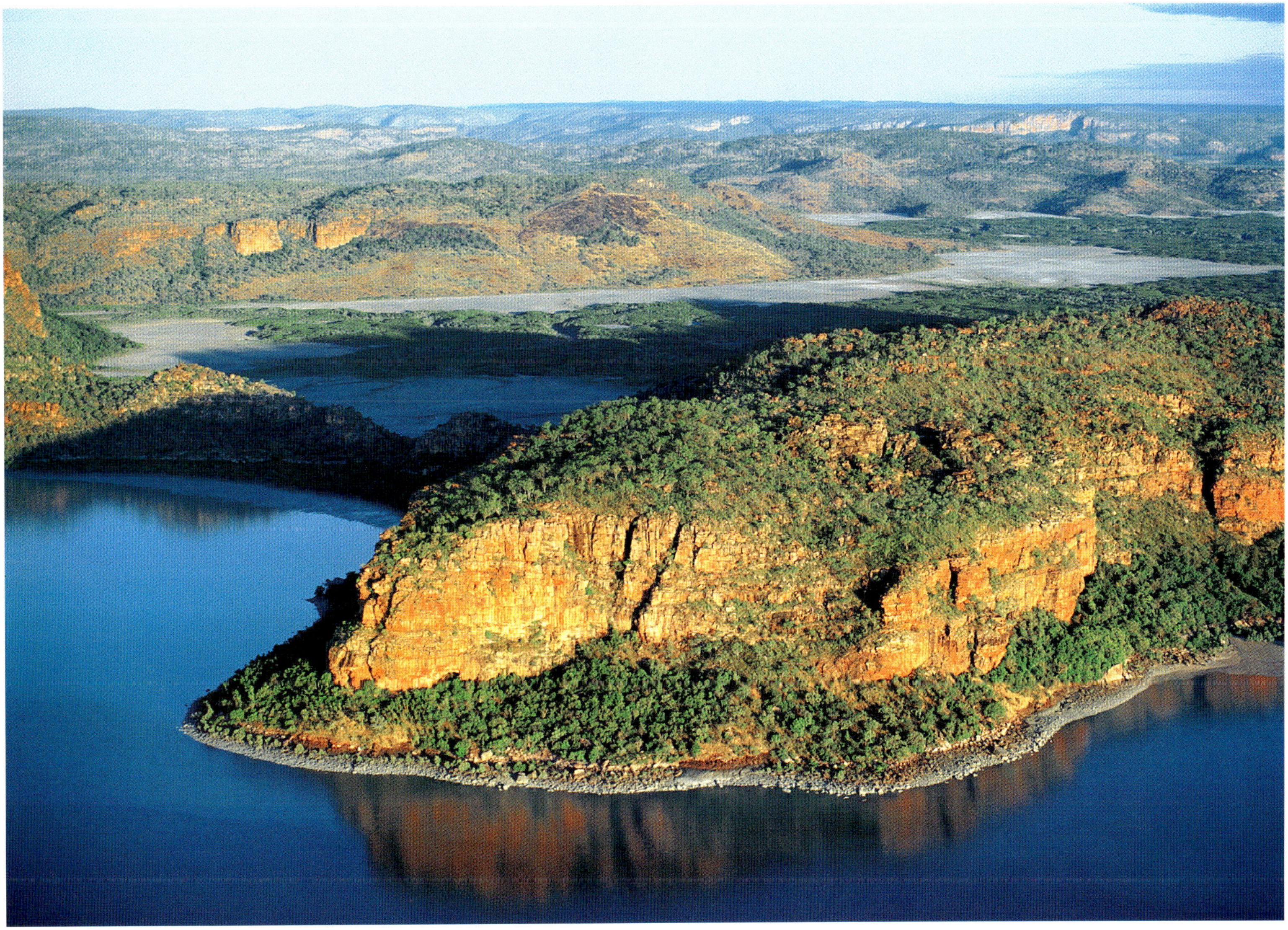

The tide rises and falls around 11 metres in Walcott Inlet.

Walcott Inlet, a drowned river valley, extends about 30 kilometres inland from Collier Bay. No roads penetrate this wild area, one of the world's most awe-inspiring landscapes.

Bell Creek Reserve

The Kimberley is a vast area, which includes landscapes as diverse as rugged ranges, flat-topped hills termed "jump-ups", wide grassy plains, and isolated rainforest remnants, in which live unique species of plants and animals. In the cooler dry season, it is comparatively easy to explore much of the Kimberley, except for the north-east, by vehicle. In the Wet, when monsoons bring frequent, torrential rain, unsealed roads become impassable. This is a country which keeps its secrets close, but which repays alert travellers with vistas of scenic grandeur, and cameos of beauty which linger in the memory long after the difficulties of the journey undertaken to discover them are forgotten.

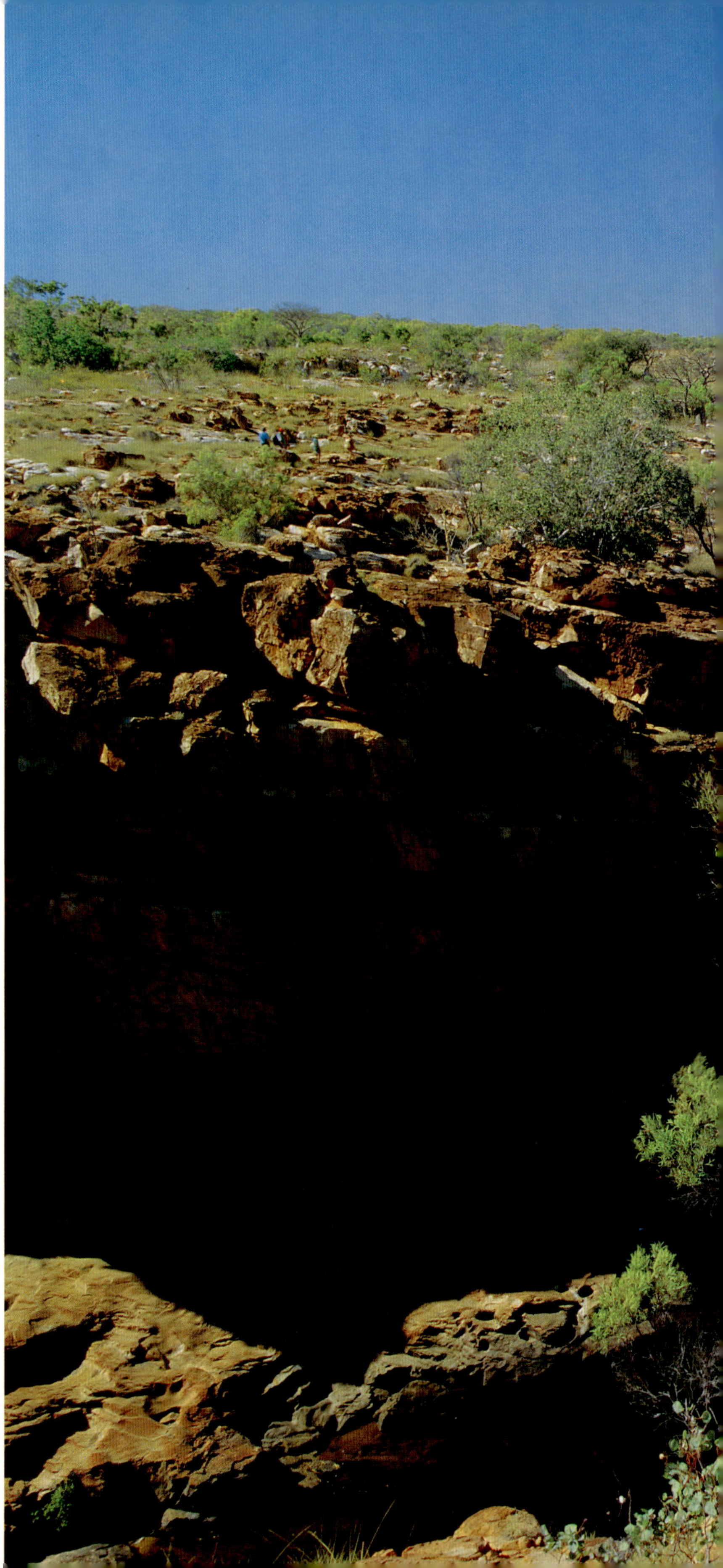

A place to cherish in Bell Creek Reserve.

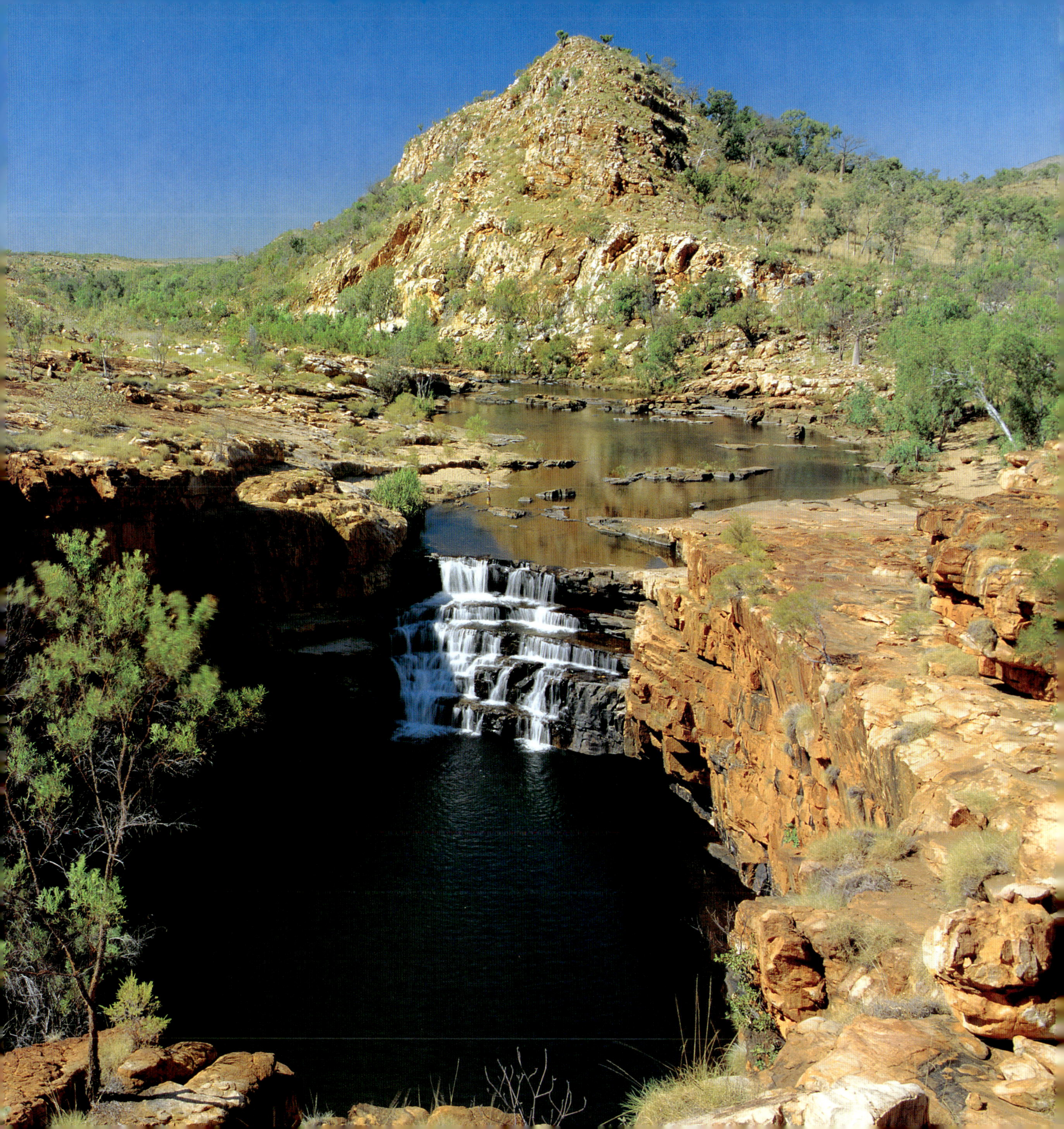

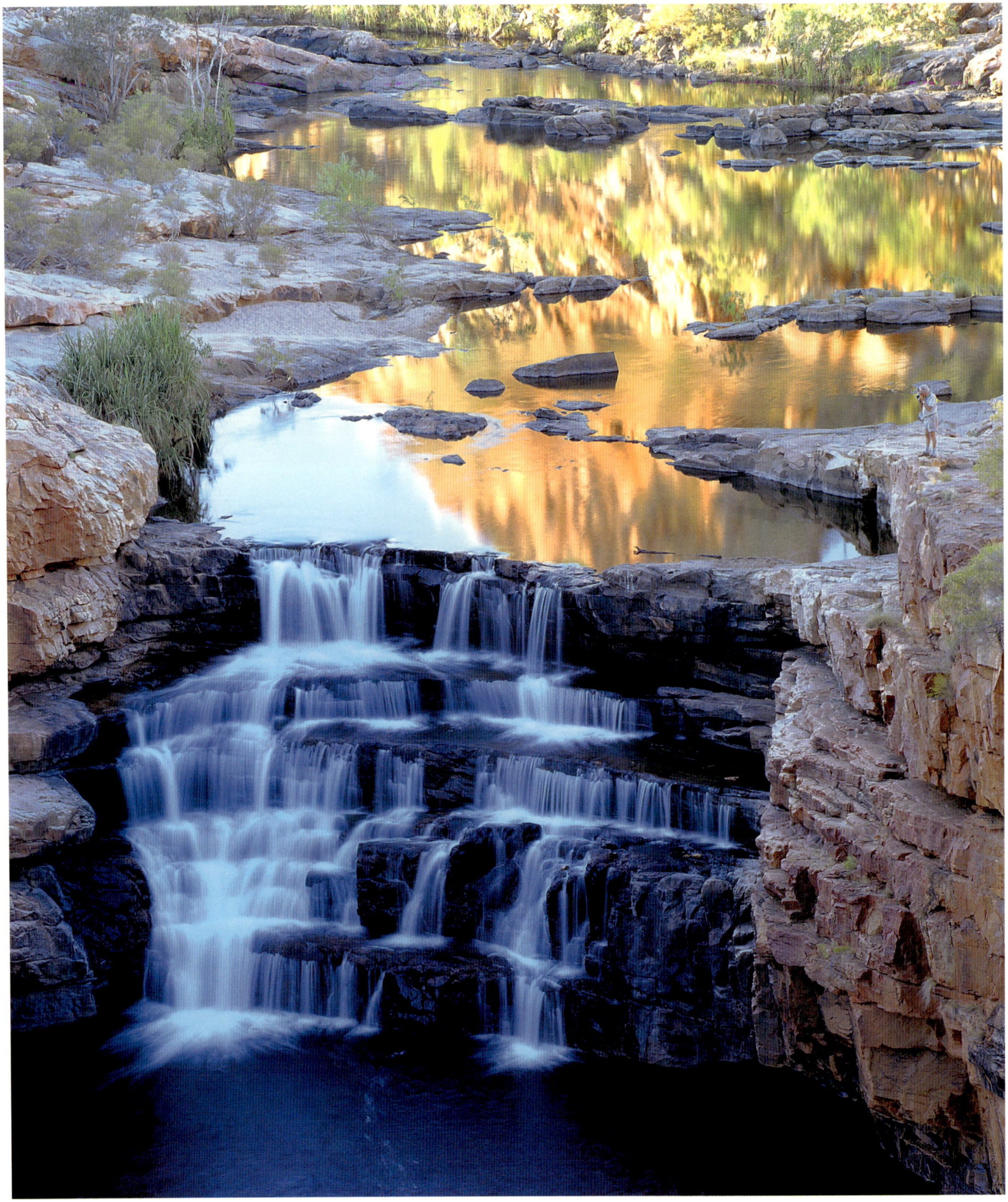

Waterfall, Bell Creek Reserve.

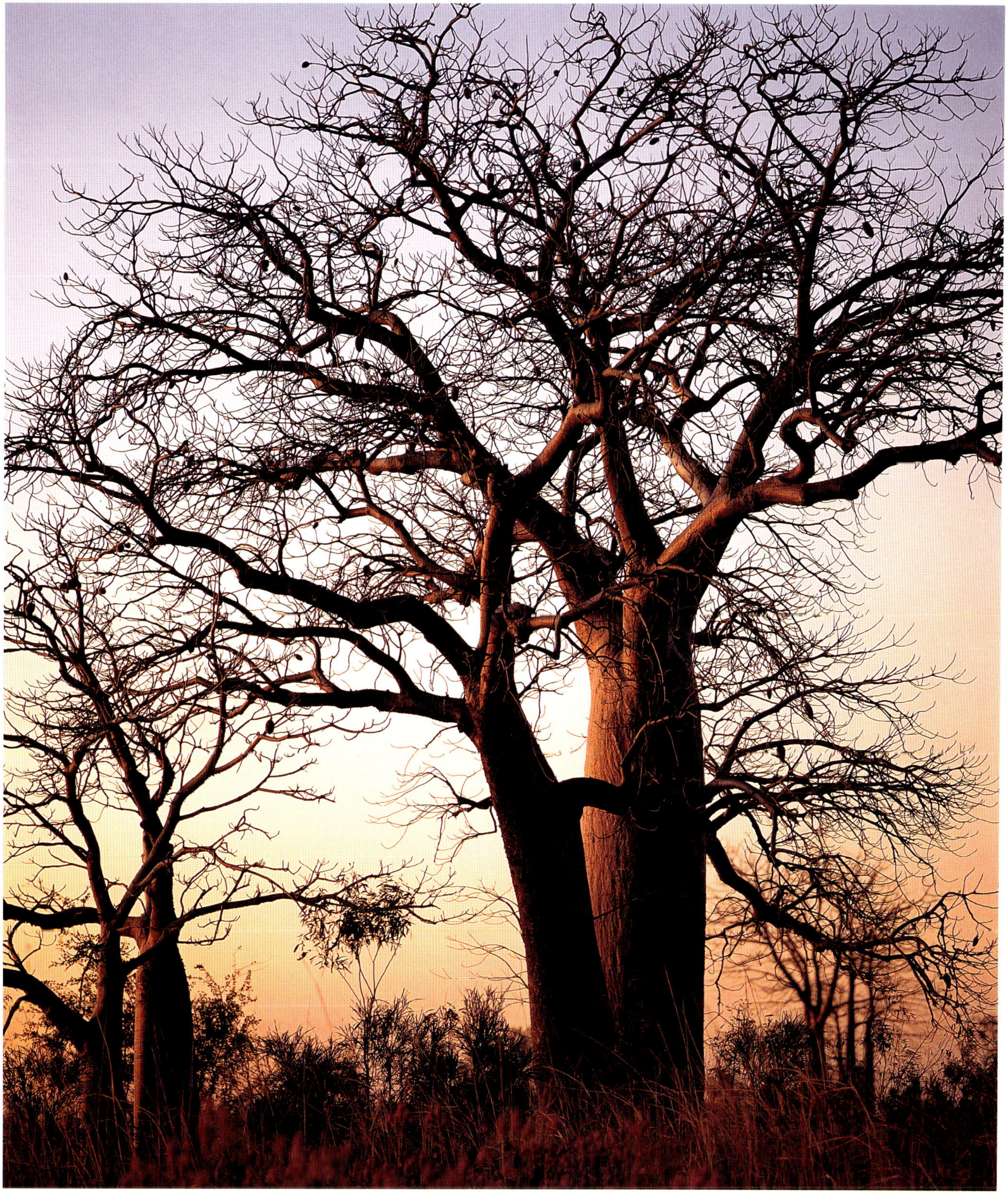

Above: Boab trees on the floodplain of the Fitzroy River, near Derby, a major port for the West Kimberley.

Following pages: Windjana Gorge National Park.

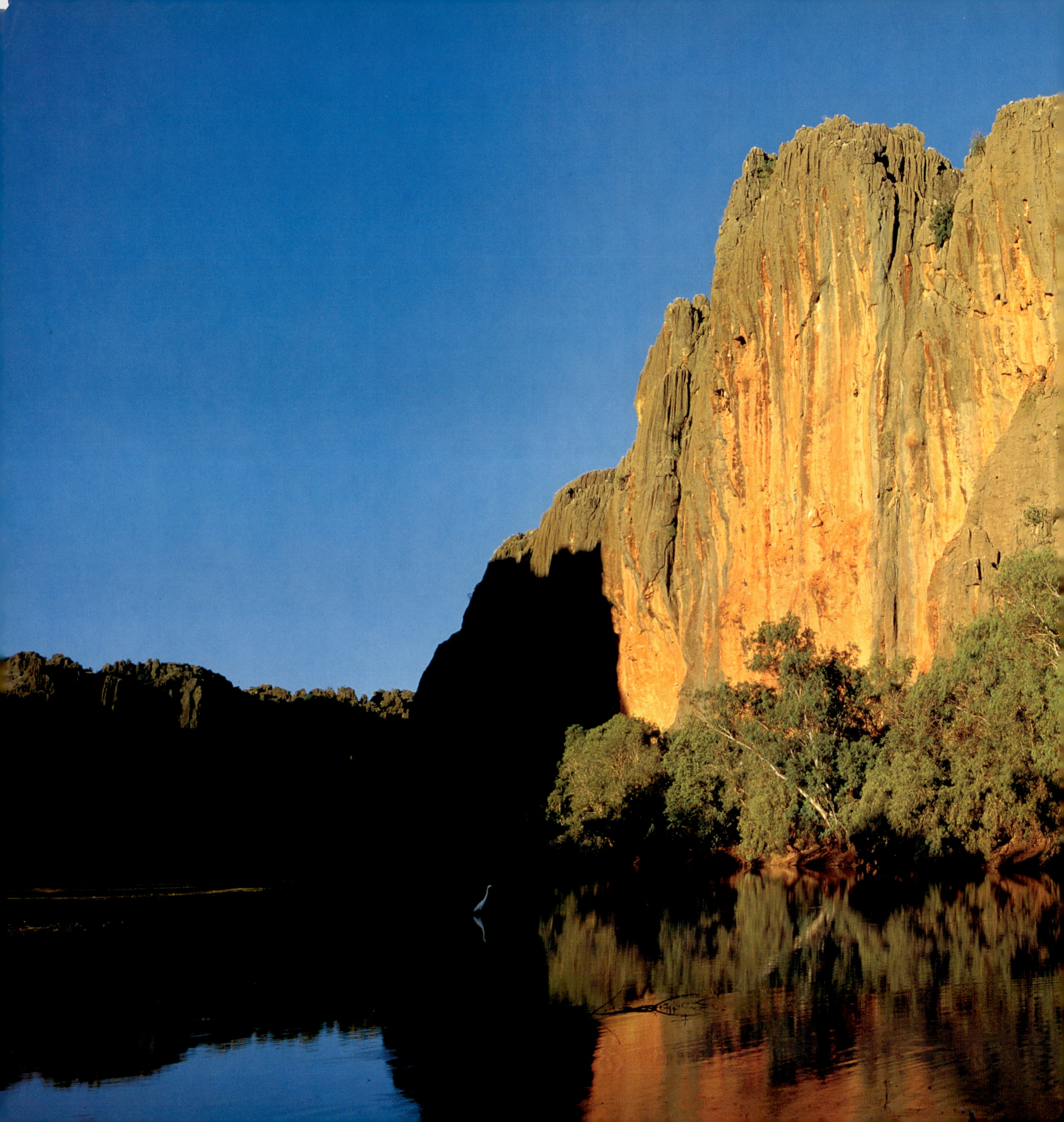

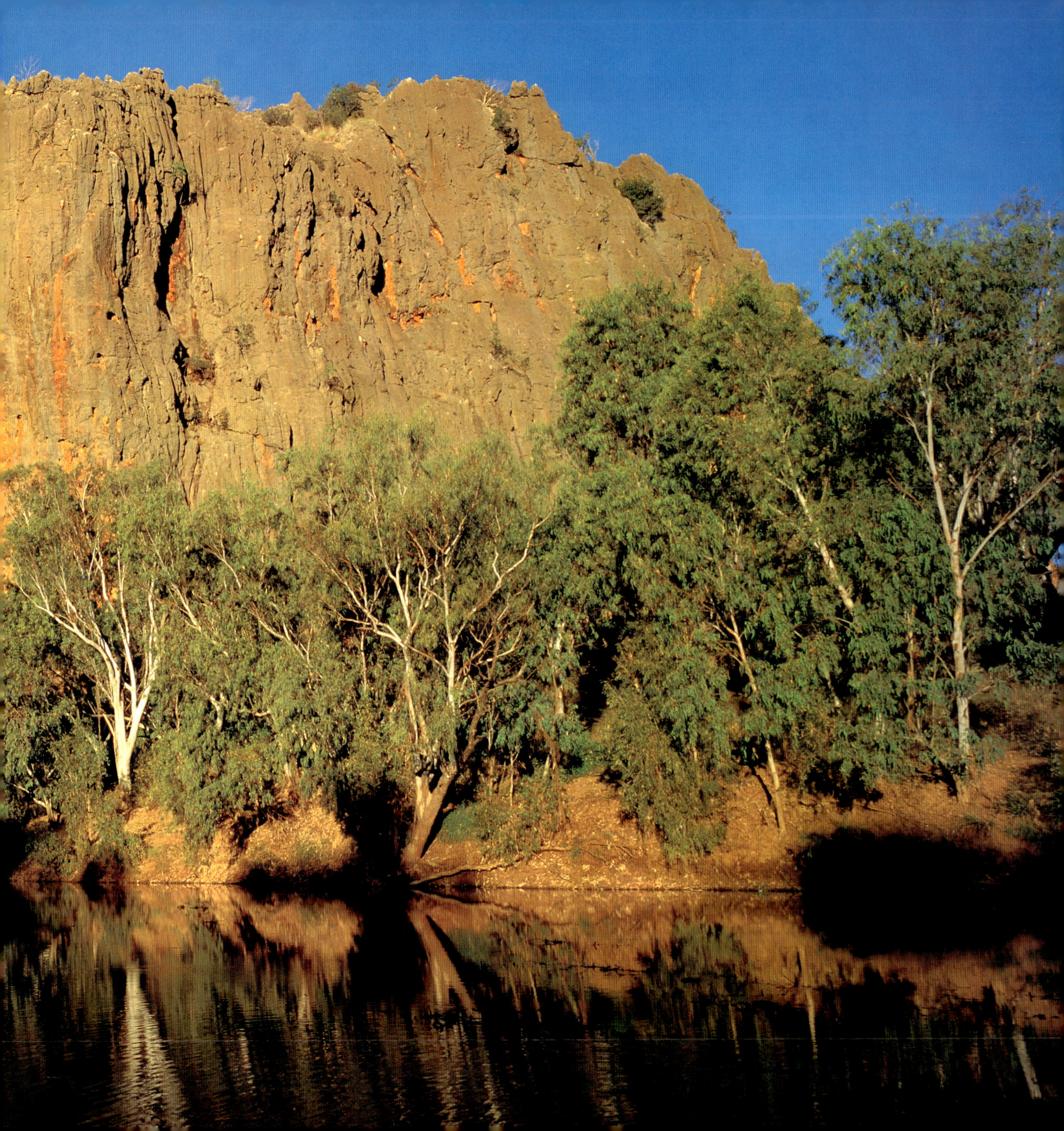

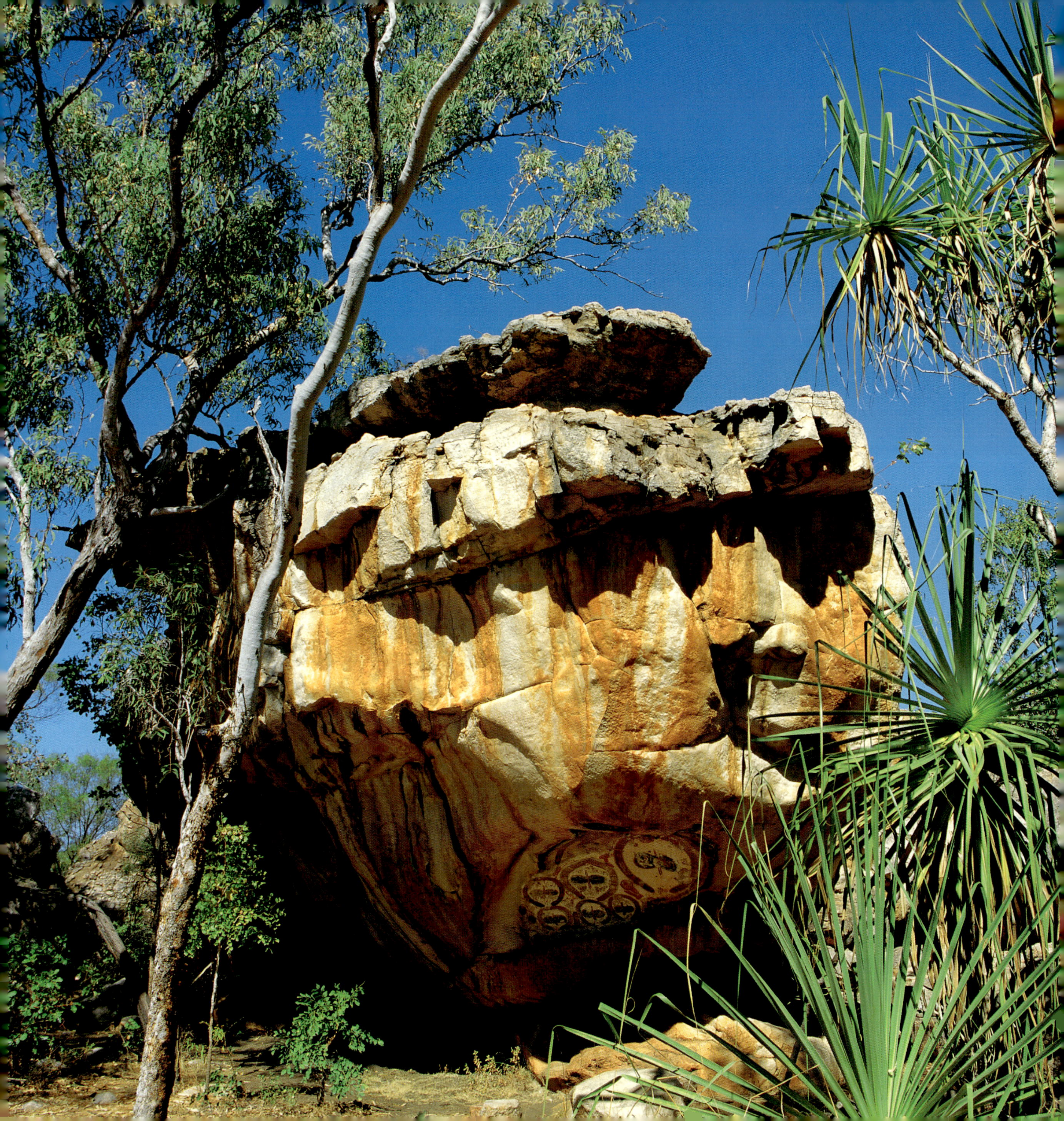

A spiritual heritage

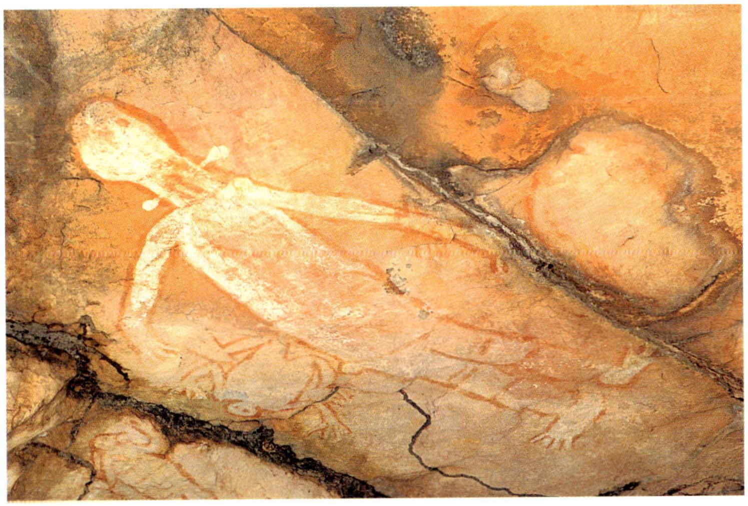

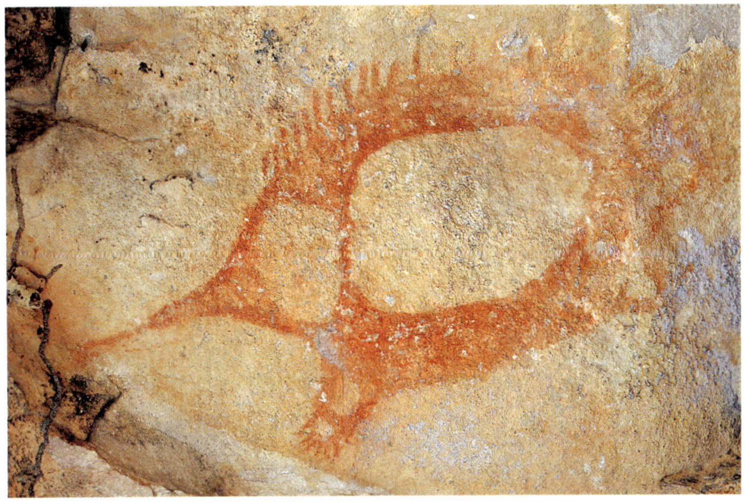

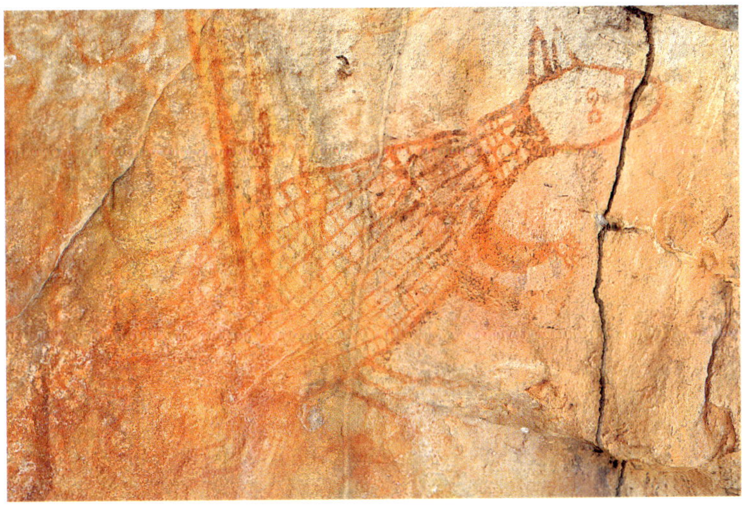

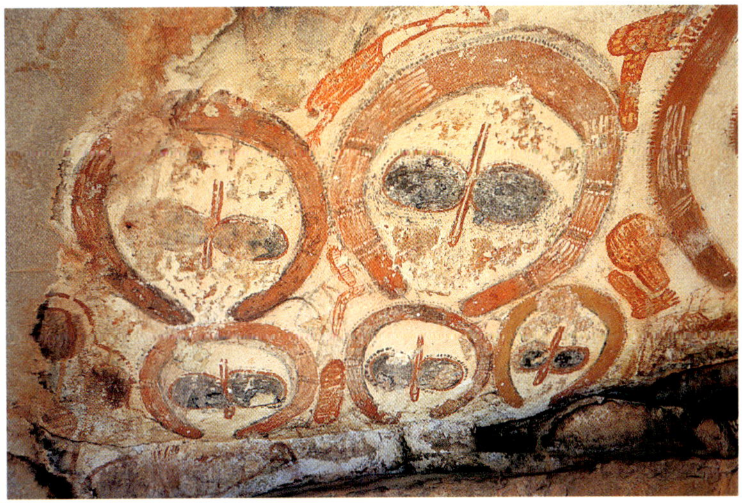

Aboriginal people have lived in the Kimberley for many tens of thousands of years. Their relationship with the land, and the spiritual and cultural heritage arising from this interaction, are reflected in their traditional rock art. This art was not created for entertainment and, if discovered, should be left exactly as it was when first sighted.

Opposite: Aboriginal artwork is sheltered by this rock's overhang.

Kimberley landscapes

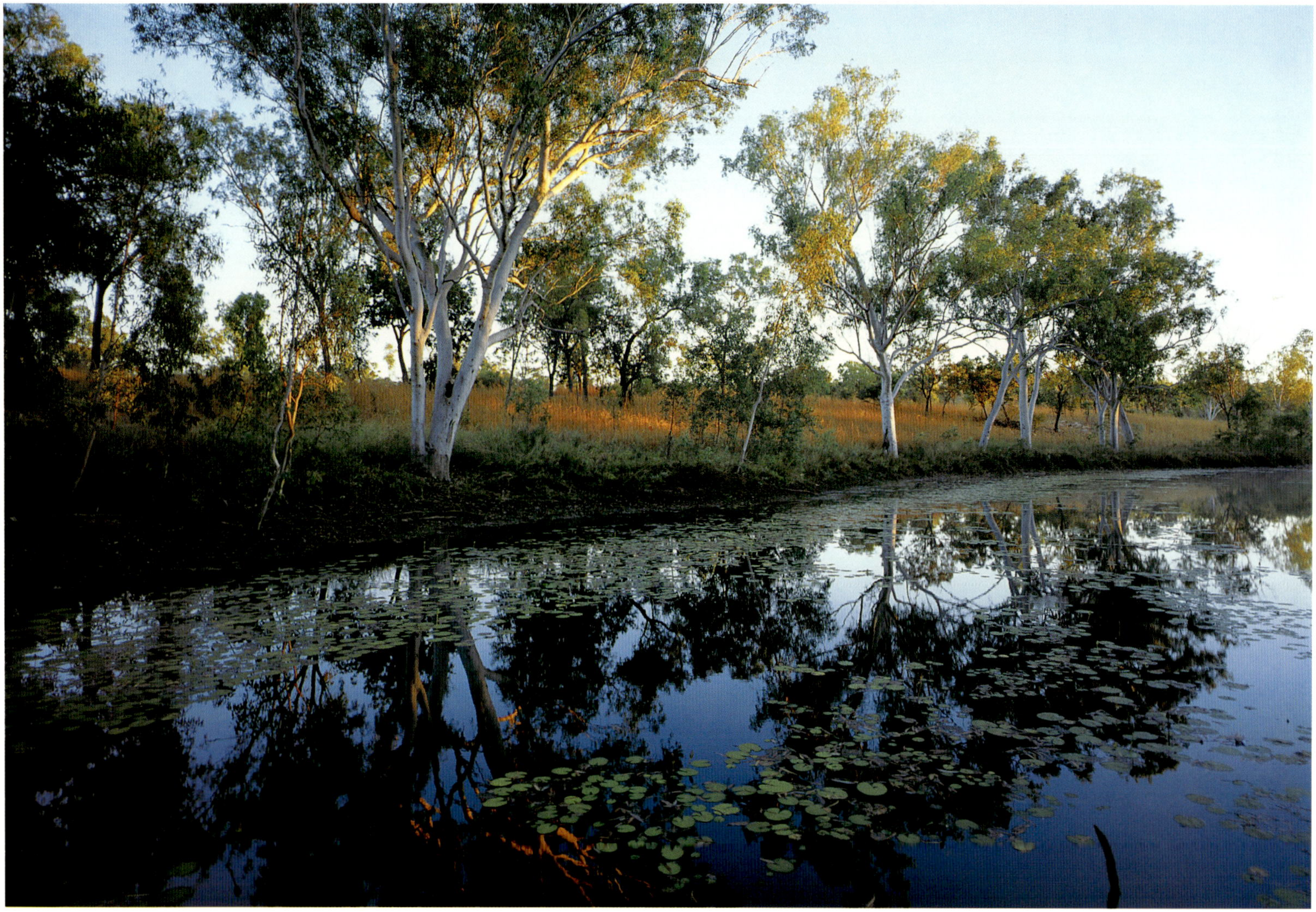

A billabong on the Bernet River.

A river winds across a plain in a series of S bends. Eventually it cuts through the middle section of the S, isolating a small, curved lake called a billabong. Kimberley billabongs are places to see waterbirds, waterlilies, kangaroos, fish — and crocodiles. The fish-eating Freshwater Crocodile is harmless to large animals unless provoked, but watch out for the larger broad-snouted, possibly man-eating Saltwater Crocodile.

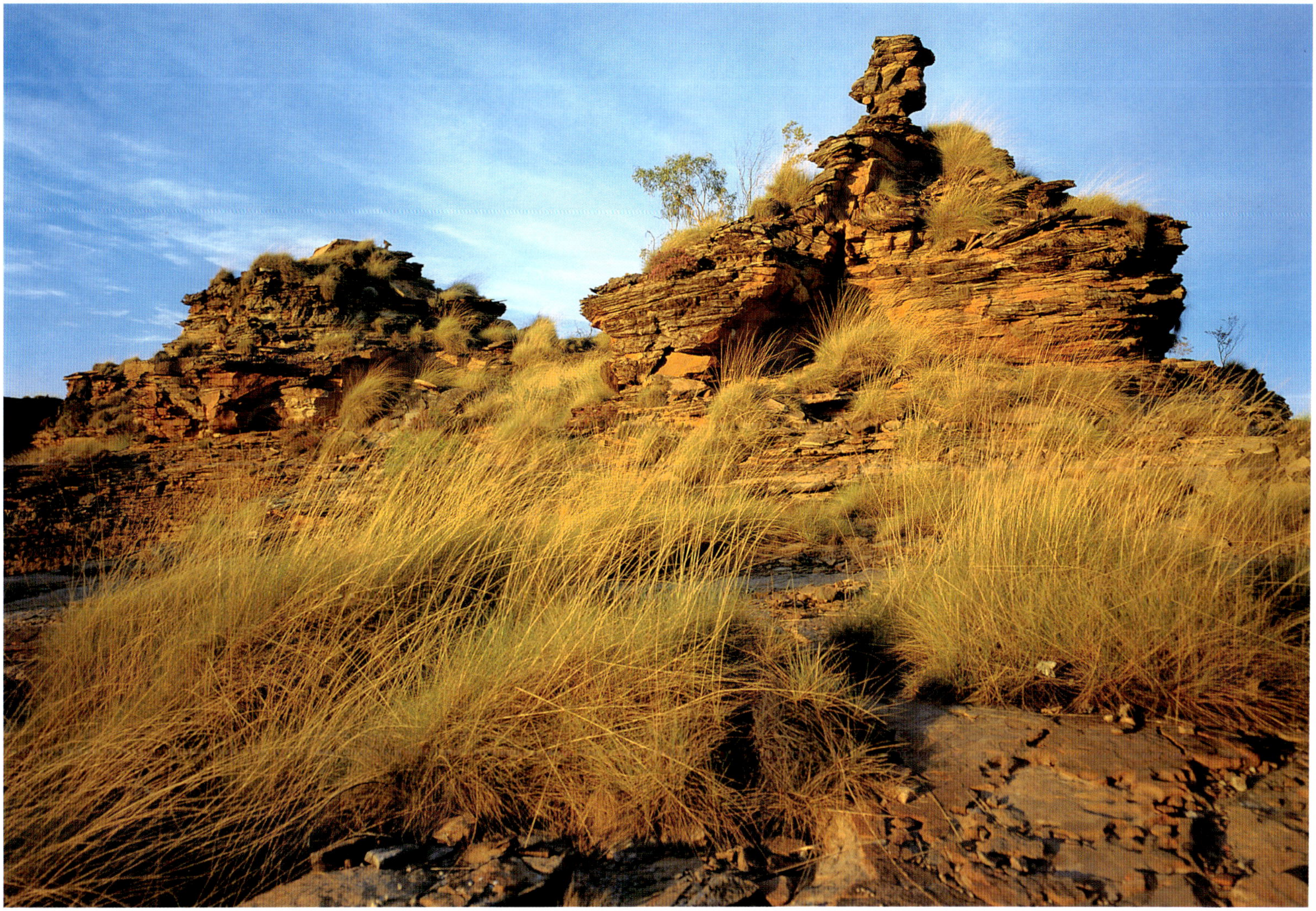

Above: Rock formations in Mirima National Park, near Kununurra.

Following pages: The Bungle Bungles, Purnululu National Park.

Around 350 million years ago, much of the Kimberley lay beneath a tropical sea. Sandstone was formed from sediment deposited on the floor of this sea: limestone is the remains of a primeval coral reef. Both are common in today's Kimberley. Formations like those shown above occur where a capping of harder rock protects the layered stone from weathering away at the same rate as the surrounding area.

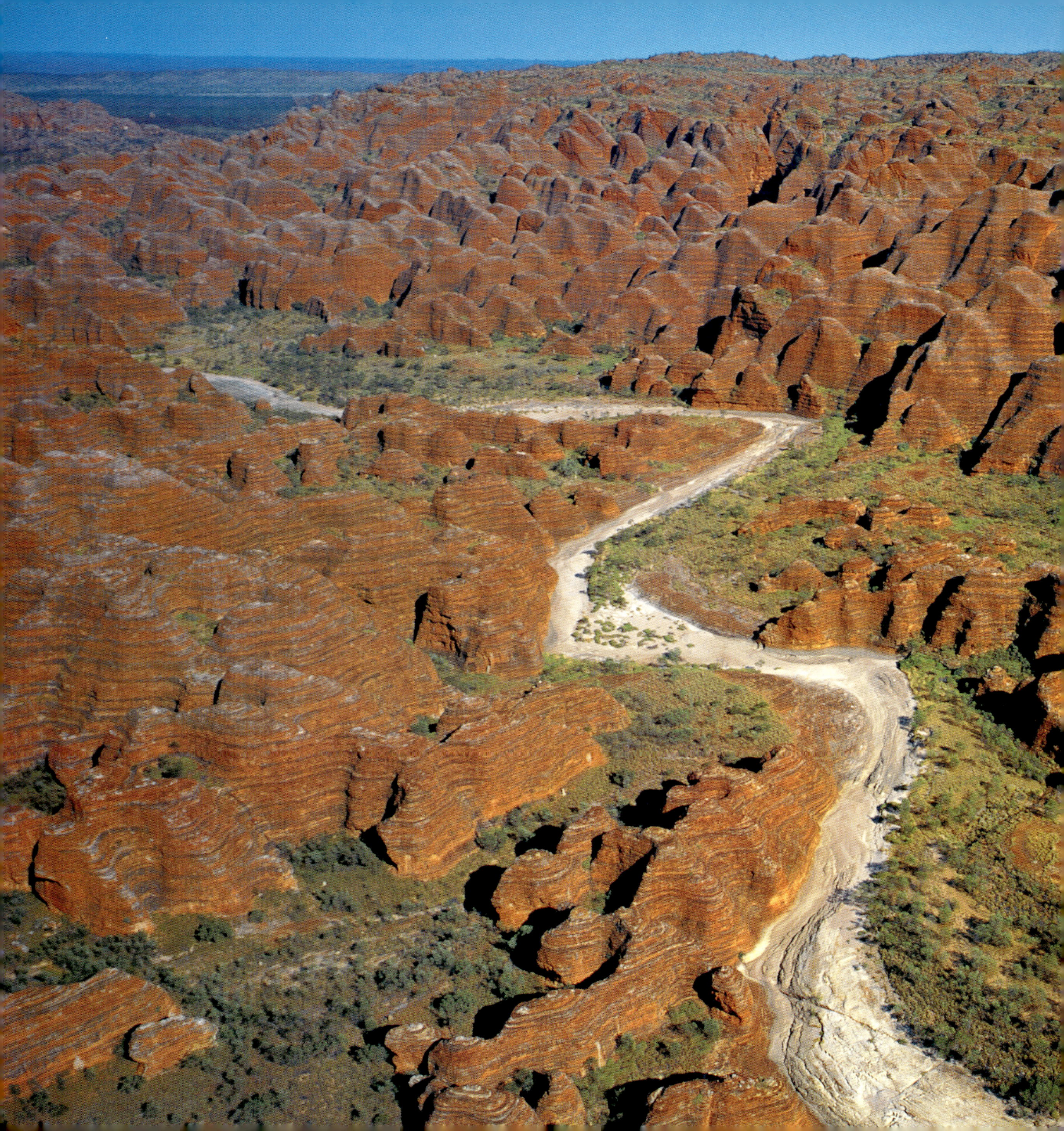

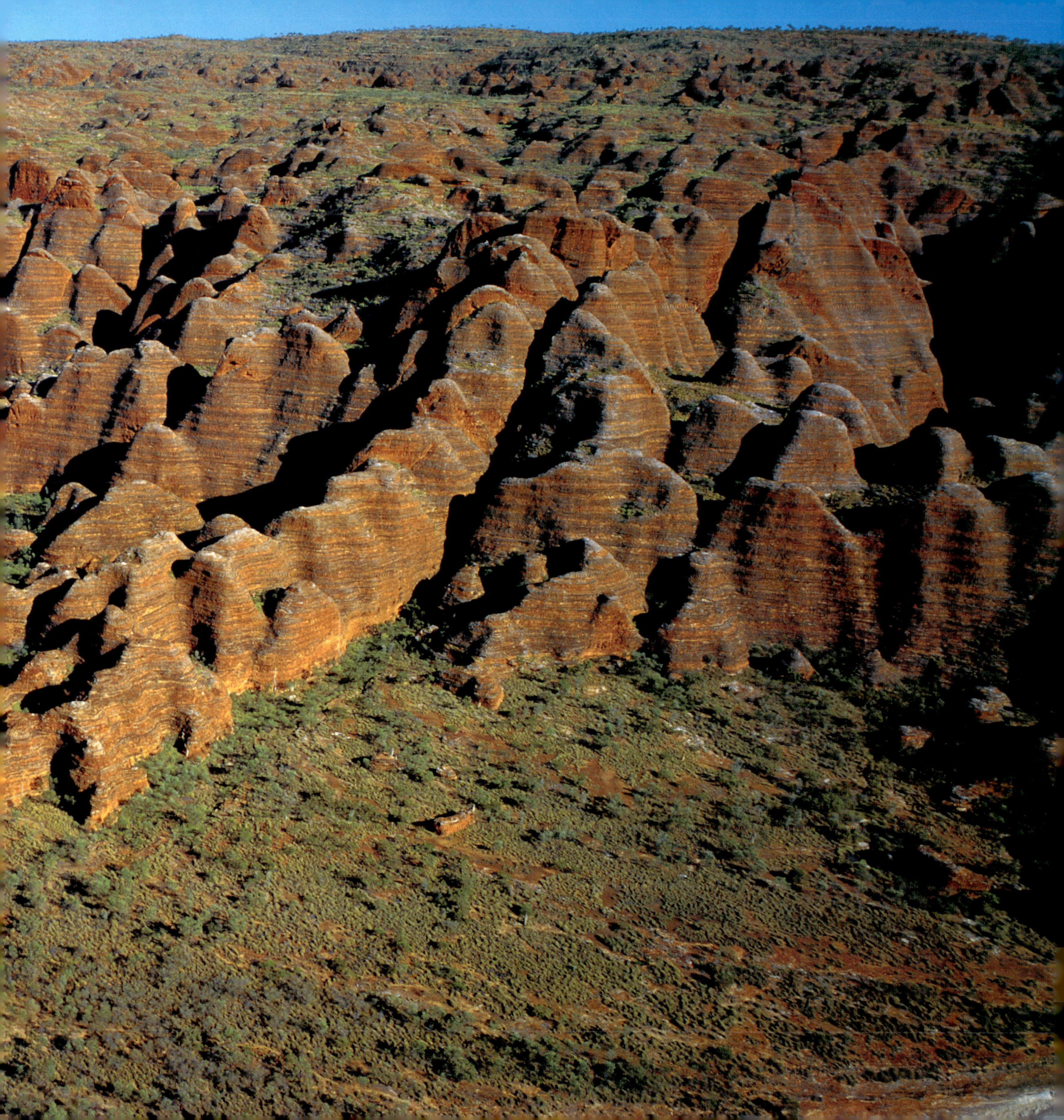

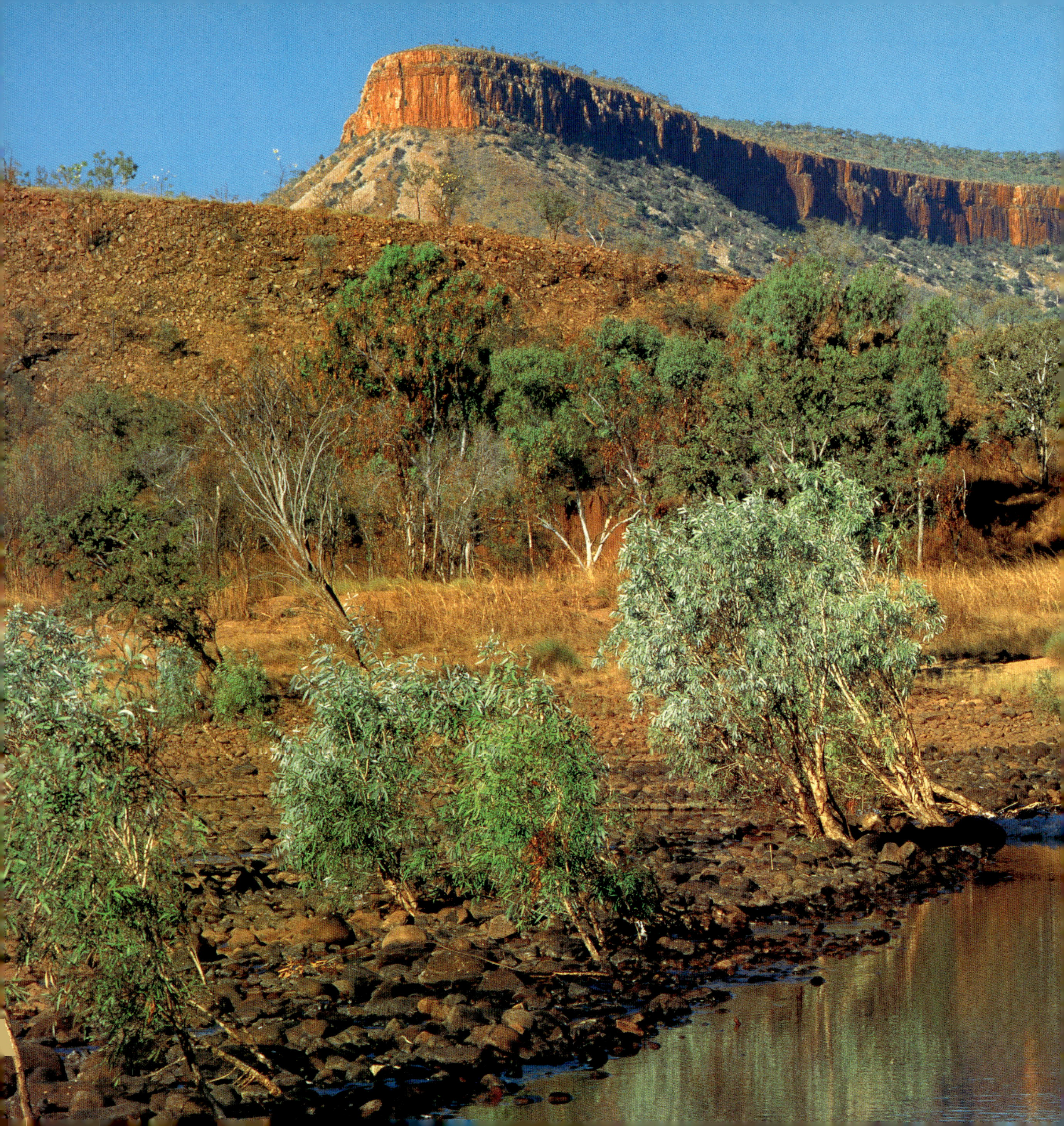

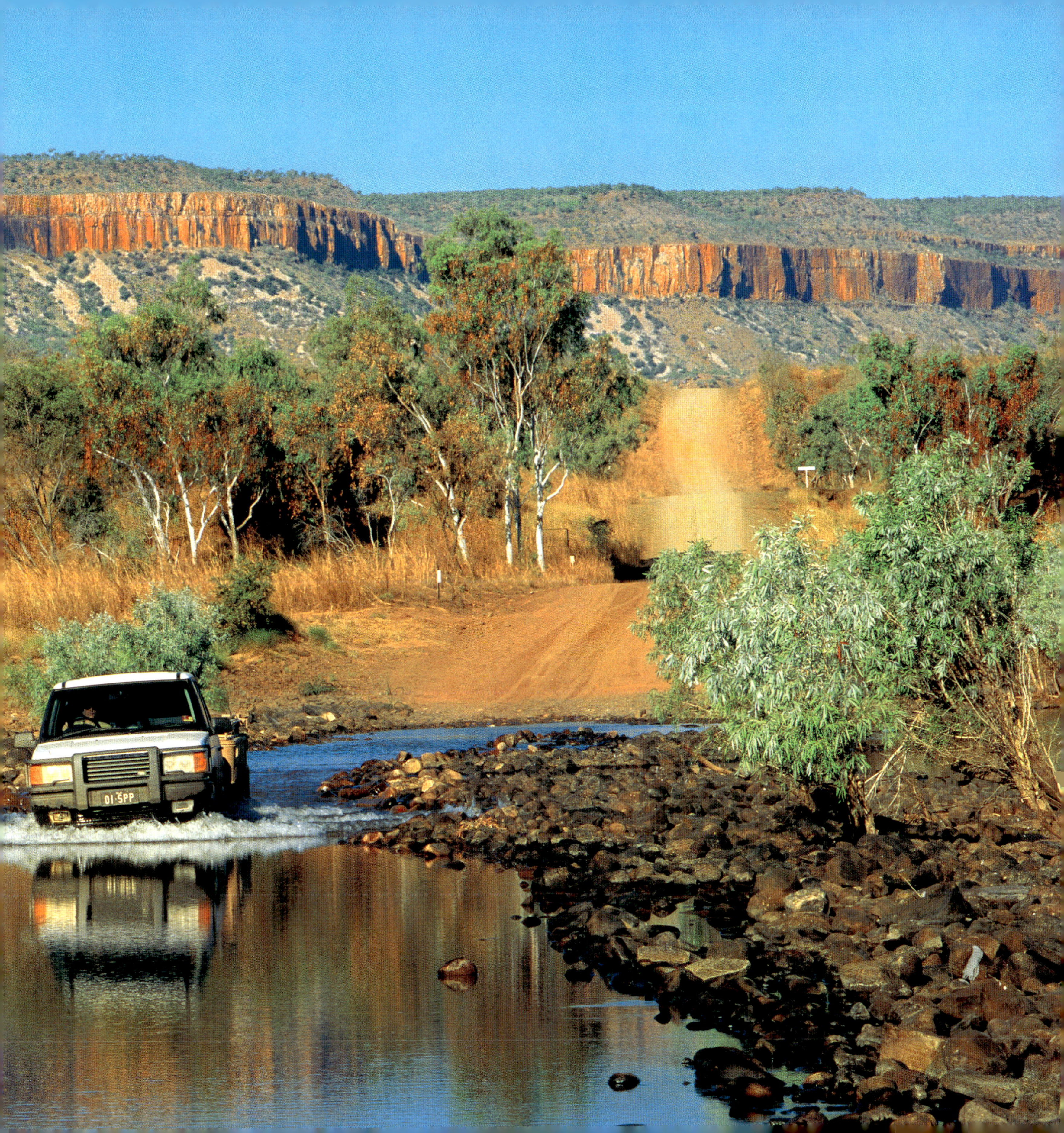

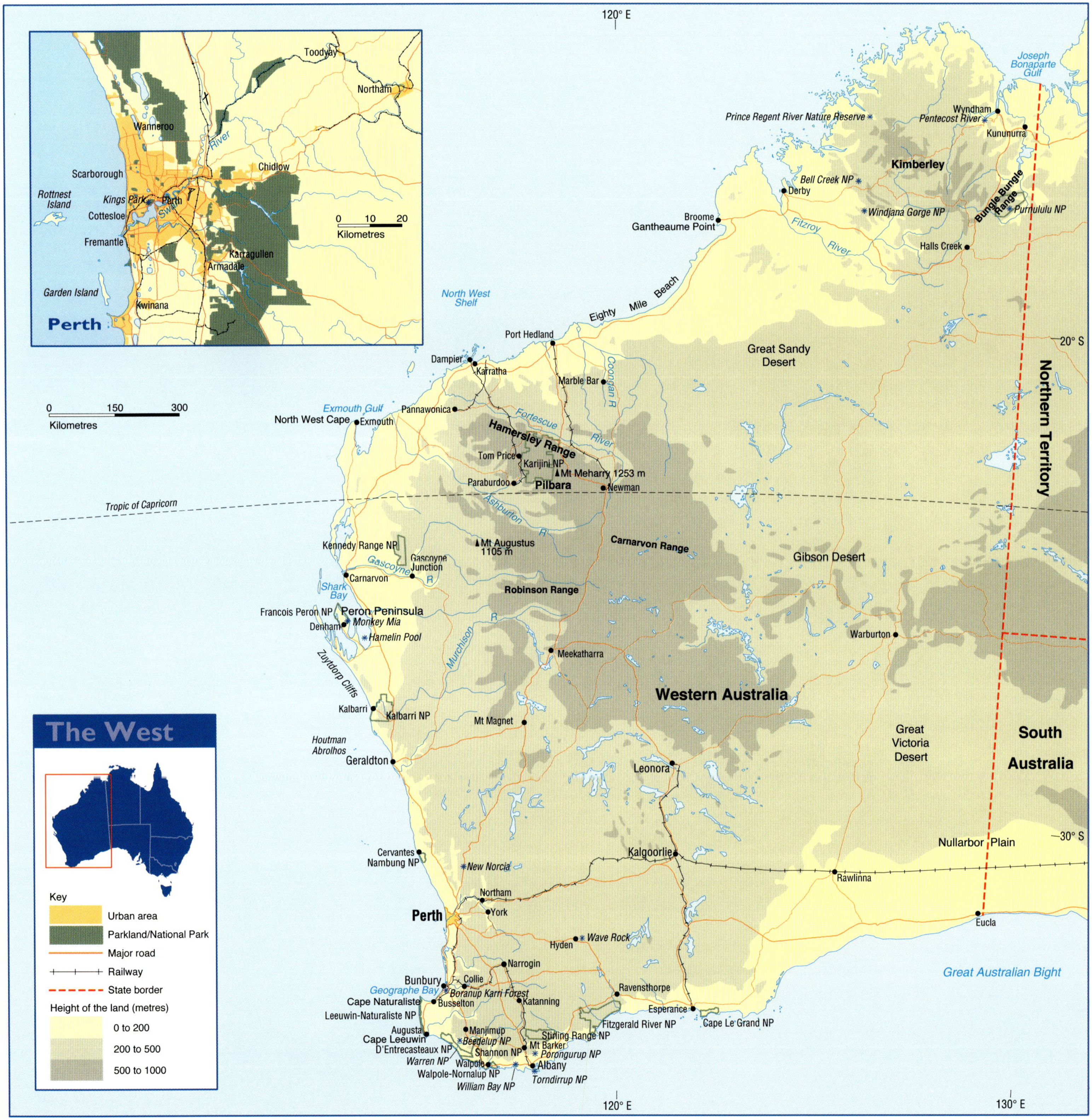
The West
Perth
Toodyay
Northam
Wanneroo
Chidlow
Scarborough
Rottnest Island
Kings Park
Perth
Cottesloe
Fremantle
Karragullen
Armadale
Garden Island
Kwinana
Swan River
0 10 20 Kilometres
0 150 300 Kilometres
Joseph Bonaparte Gulf
Prince Regent River Nature Reserve
Wyndham
Pentecost River
Kununurra
Kimberley
Bell Creek NP
Derby
Windjana Gorge NP
Bungle Bungle Range
Purnululu NP
Broome
Gantheaume Point
Fitzroy River
Halls Creek
North West Shelf
Eighty Mile Beach
Port Hedland
Great Sandy Desert
Dampier
Karratha
Marble Bar
Coongan R
Exmouth Gulf
Pannawonica
North West Cape
Exmouth
Fortescue River
Hamersley Range
Tom Price
Karijini NP
Mt Meharry 1253 m
Paraburdoo
Pilbara
Newman
Northern Territory
Tropic of Capricorn
Ashburton R
Kennedy Range NP
Mt Augustus 1105 m
Carnarvon Range
Gibson Desert
Gascoyne Junction
Gascoyne R
Carnarvon
Shark Bay
Robinson Range
Francois Peron NP
Peron Peninsula
Monkey Mia
Denham
Hamelin Pool
Murchison R
Warburton
Meekatharra
Zuytdorp Cliffs
Western Australia
Kalbarri
Kalbarri NP
Mt Magnet
Great Victoria Desert
South Australia
Houtman Abrolhos
Geraldton
Leonora
Nullarbor Plain
Cervantes
Nambung NP
Kalgoorlie
New Norcia
Rawlinna
Northam
Perth
York
Eucla
Wave Rock
Hyden
Narrogin
Great Australian Bight
Bunbury
Collie
Geographe Bay
Boranup Karri Forest
Ravensthorpe
Cape Naturaliste
Busselton
Katanning
Esperance
Leeuwin-Naturaliste NP
Fitzgerald River NP
Cape Le Grand NP
Augusta
Manjimup
Cape Leeuwin
Beedelup NP
Stirling Range NP
D'Entrecasteaux NP
Shannon NP
Mt Barker
Porongurup NP
Warren NP
Walpole
Albany
Walpole-Nornalup NP
Torndirrup NP
William Bay NP
120° E
130° E
20° S
30° S
Key
Urban area
Parkland/National Park
Major road
Railway
State border
Height of the land (metres)
0 to 200
200 to 500
500 to 1000

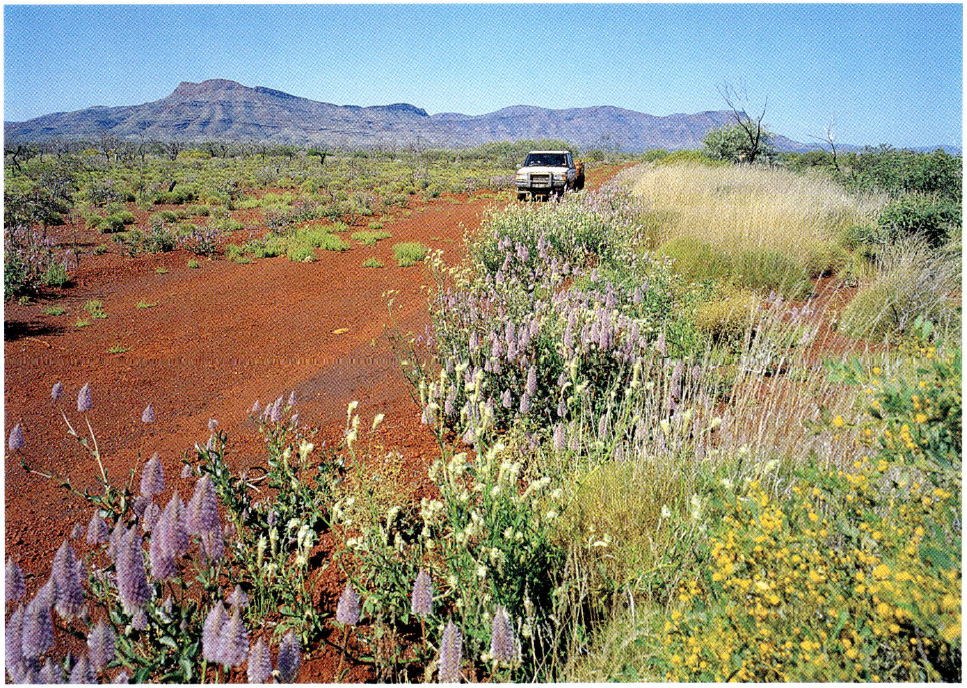

Wandering the West

At every turn of a Western Australian road, the traveller realises the magnificence of Australia's landscapes. Closer investigation highlights the unique relationships which have been established between plants and animals in this western part of the continent. It would take more than one lifetime to get to know Western Australia as it deserves. This third of the Australian continent keeps its secrets well, its fertile south-western corner separated from its tropical north by many kilometres of aridland. The coastal margin of Western Australia is now world-famous for its wildflowers, marine life and holiday atmosphere (witness the pilgrimages made to the springtime sandplains, to Monkey Mia and Rottnest Island). Now travellers are discovering the Pilbara, the Kimberley and the Goldfields. For the nature lover, the bushwalker, the photographer, or the adventurer, the West is a dream come true. Those who enjoy natural beauty, but who also savour the delights which civilisation has to offer, will find that warmth, friendliness and hospitality are all part of the Western Australian way of life.

Previous pages: Crossing the Pentecost River.

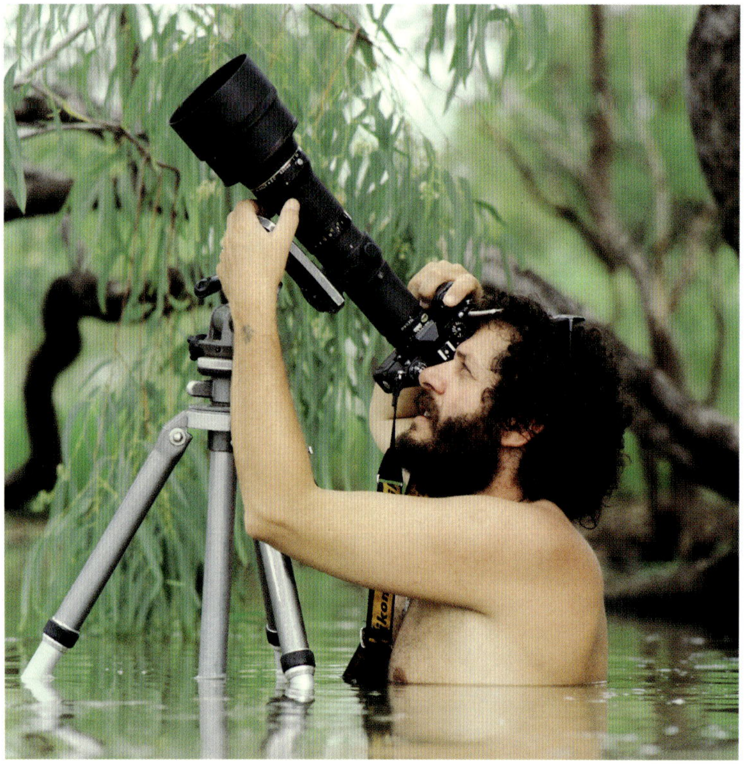

Steve Parish

World-famous photographer Steve Parish began his remarkable career by recording marine life off Australia's coasts. After discovering the fascinations of the rainforest and its wild creatures, he has spent much of his life journeying around Australia photographing the landscapes, plants, animals and the people of the land. Of recent years, he has extended the range of his subjects to include Australia's cities and towns.

The magnificent library of images which has resulted has become the heart of Steve Parish Publishing Pty Ltd. Through the firm's publications, Steve and his wife and partner Jan are realising their dream of sharing Australia with the world.

Celebrating Australia is a collection of titles which present the incomparable beauty of the southern continent in superb photographs and text. As Steve comments: "After a lifetime of travel and asking questions, I have only just begun to discover how much there is to learn about Australia. I hope these books arouse in others a desire like mine to explore and to appreciate this wonderful country."

Index

First published by Steve Parish Publishing Pty Ltd, 1997
PO Box 2160, Fortitude Valley BC, Queensland 4006, Australia

ISBN 1 875932 98 4

Photography: Steve Parish
Text: Pat Slater, Steve Parish Publishing, Australia

Map supplied by MAPgraphics
Editing, design: Steve Parish Publishing, Australia
Printed in Hong Kong
Colour separations by Steve Parish Publishing, Australia

Les expériences des DÉBROUILLARDS

TOME 2

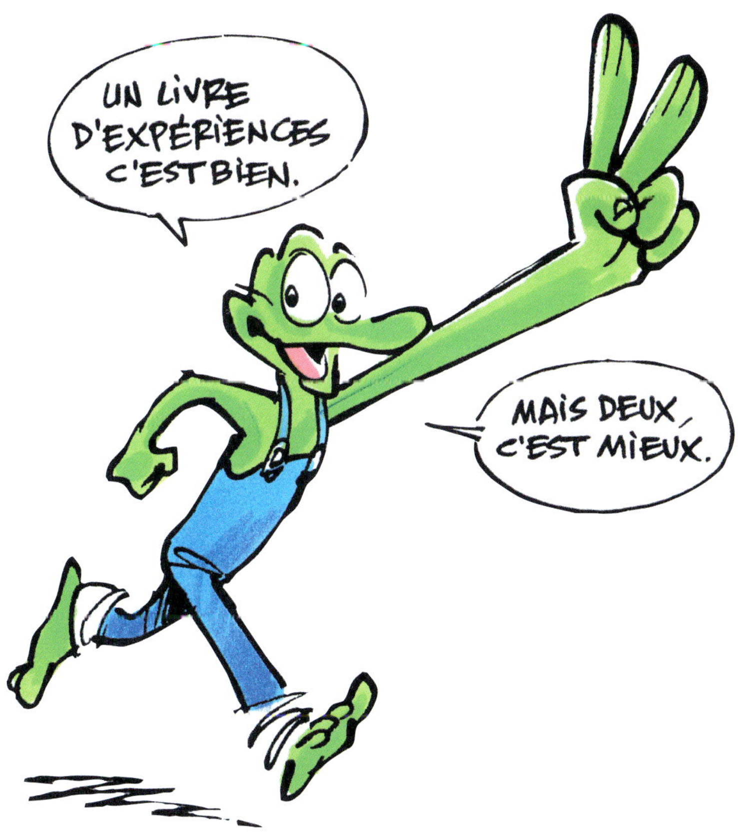

Par le professeur Scientifix
et son adjoint Yannick Bergeron

Catalogage avant publication de Bibliothèque et Archives Canada

Professeur Scientifix

Les expériences des Débrouillards

Pour les jeunes de 7 à 14 ans.

ISBN 2-89507-468-2 (v. 1)
ISBN 2-89579-089-2 (v. 2)

1. Sciences - Expériences - Ouvrages pour la jeunesse. 2. Jeux scientifiques - Ouvrages pour la jeunesse. 3. Sciences - Ouvrages pour la jeunesse. I. Goldstyn, Jacques. II. Titre.

Q164.P766 2004 j507.8 C2004-940458-X

Nous reconnaissons l'aide financière du gouvernement du Canada par l'entremise du Programme d'aide au développement de l'industrie de l'édition (PADIÉ) pour nos activités d'édition.

Conseil des Arts du Canada Canada Council for the Arts

Bayard Canada Livres Inc. remercie le Conseil des Arts du Canada du soutien accordé à son programme d'édition dans le cadre du Programme des subventions globales aux éditeurs.

Cet ouvrage a été publié avec le soutien de la SODEC.
Gouvernement du Québec – Programme de crédit d'impôt pour l'édition de livres – Gestion SODEC.

ISBN 2-89579-089-2
Dépôt légal – Bibliothèque et Archives nationales du Québec, 2006

Conception et réalisation des expériences : Yannick Bergeron et le professeur Scientifix, avec la participation de Johanne Champagne, Johanne David, Sarah Perreault et Isabelle Vaillancourt
Illustrations : Jacques Goldstyn
Photos : Laurence Labat et Marcel La Haye
Conception graphique : Espaceblanc.com
Recherche iconographique : Céline Lapointe
Recherche, édition des textes, coordination : Johanne Champagne
Révision des textes : Johanne Champagne et Hélène Veilleux
Direction, collection Les Débrouillards : Félix Maltais
Direction, Bayard Canada : Jean-François Bouchard
Photo de la page couverture : Laurence Labat
Débrouillards de la page couverture : Jacky Pyram et Shanie Beauchamp

Note
La majorité des expériences de ce livre ont paru dans le magazine **Les Débrouillards** entre 1998 et 2005. Pour découvrir d'autres expériences des Débrouillards, consultez le magazine **Les Débrouillards** ou le cédérom **Scientifix**.
Renseignements : www.lesdebrouillards.qc.ca. Téléphone : (514) 875-4444 ou 1 (800) 667-4444

4475, rue Frontenac
Montréal (Québec)
Canada H2H 2S2
Téléphone : (514) 844-2111 ou 1 866 844-2111
Télécopieur : (514) 278-3030
Courriel : edition@bayard-inc.com

Imprimé au Canada

Laboratoire du professeur Scientifix

25 ans d'expériences !

Cher Débrouillard,
Chère Débrouillarde,

Demande à tes parents : « À mon âge, avez-vous fait les expériences du livre **Le Petit Débrouillard** ? ». Il y a bien des chances qu'ils te répondent : « Oui, j'adorais ça, mais mes parents n'aimaient pas le désordre dans la cuisine après ! ».

C'est en effet il y a 25 ans, soit en 1981, qu'a été publié mon premier livre d'expériences, le petit livre bleu. Ce fut un tel succès qu'après, nous avons créé le magazine et le Club des Débrouillards.

Si tes parents ont gardé leur Petit Débrouillard bleu, tu verras beaucoup de différences avec ton livre à toi : le grand format, les photos, la couleur partout, des capsules d'informations supplémentaires, etc. Depuis un quart de siècle, nous nous sommes améliorés, mes adjoints et moi !

Mais ce qui n'a pas changé chez nous, c'est notre bonheur de faire découvrir aux Débrouillards comme toi les phénomènes scientifiques qui permettent de propulser une fusée ou de faire une butte d'eau. Et ce qui n'a pas changé chez les Débrouillards, c'est la curiosité... et le désordre dans la cuisine !

En terminant, je veux remercier les principaux adjoints qui depuis 25 ans m'ont aidé à faire des expériences toujours plus intéressantes : Robert Richards, Bernard Larocque, Marc Gingras, Sarah Perreault et le dernier mais non le moindre, Yannick Bergeron, qui a réalisé la majorité des expériences de ce livre.

Je te souhaite d'excellentes expériences scientifiques pour les prochaines semaines et pourquoi pas... pour les 25 prochaines années aussi !

Scientifiquement,

Prof Scientifix

Table des matières

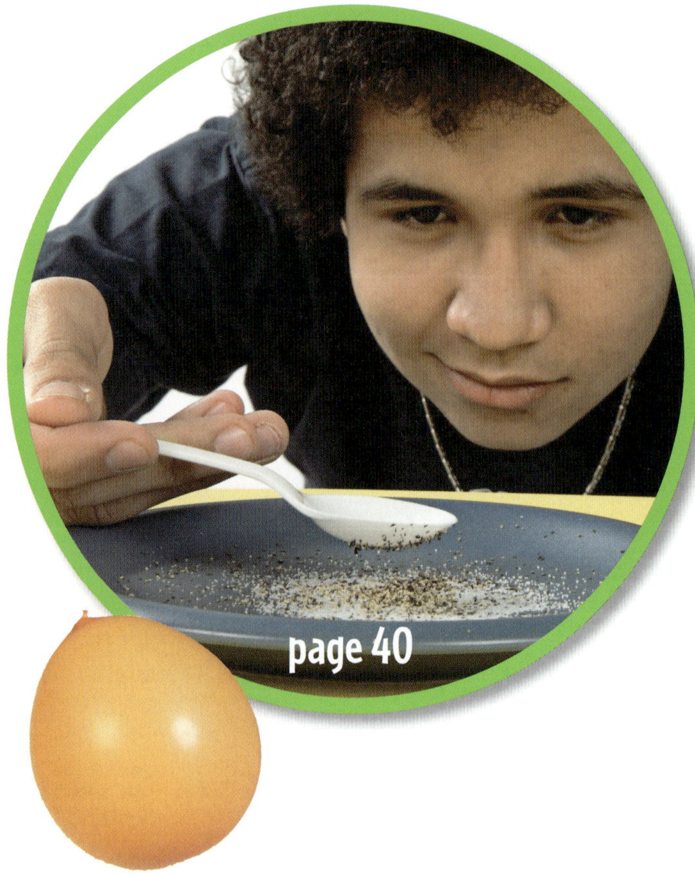

page 40

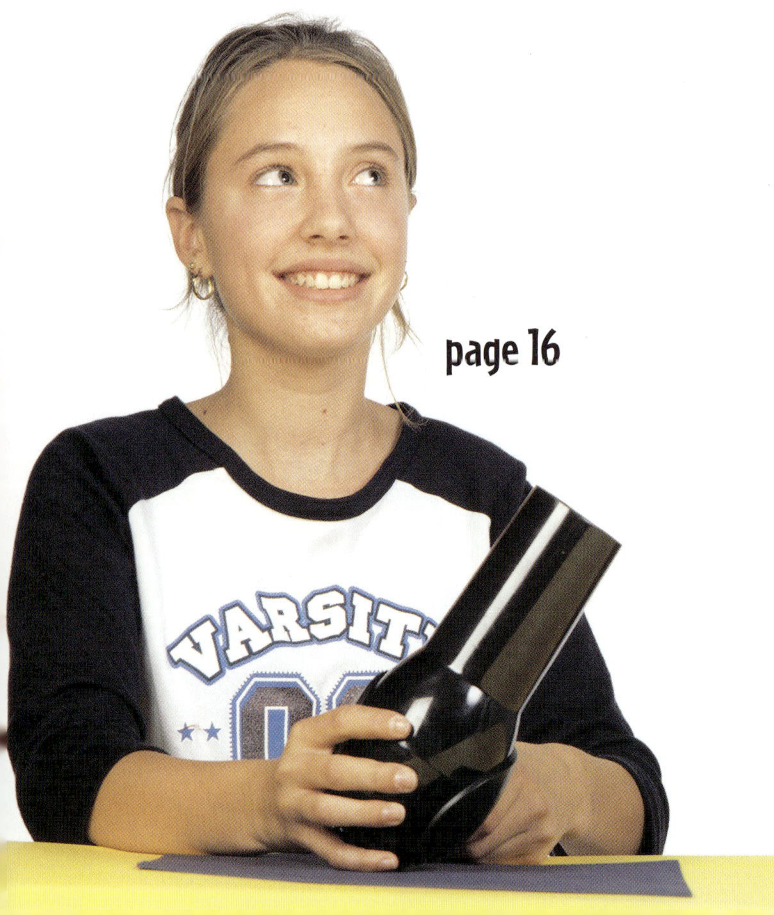

page 16

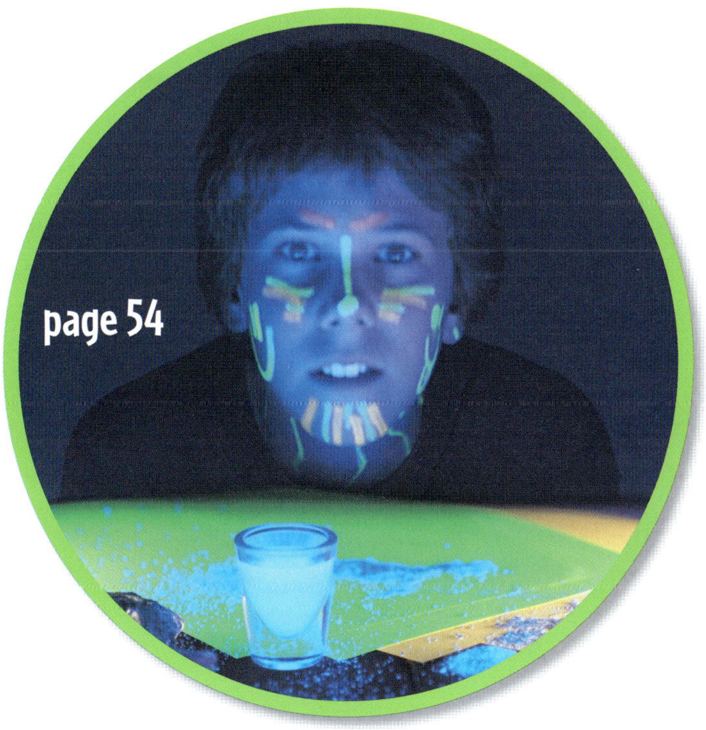

page 54

Expériences éclair !

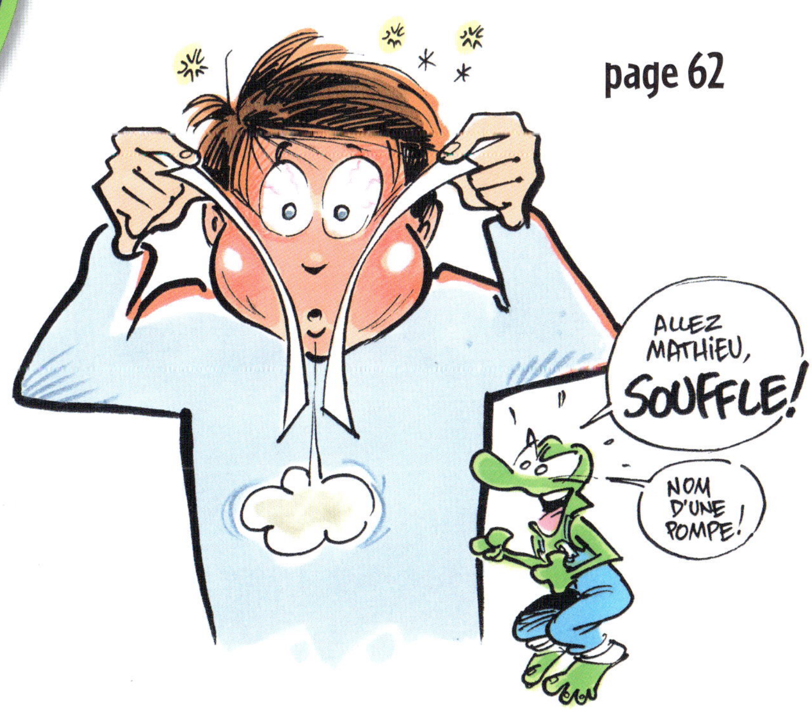

page 62

Le pendule hyperactif

Observe la course folle d'un pendule aux prises avec le magnétisme.

ATTENTION ! UTILISATION D'UN CLOU ET D'UN MARTEAU.

1

Découpe deux morceaux de carton de 20 cm sur 20 cm à l'aide du couteau ou des ciseaux. Trace quelques cercles concentriques à partir du centre du carton avec le compas. Repasse avec le crayon-feutre afin de rendre les cercles bien visibles.

Il te faut :

- du carton mousse (« foam core ») ou du carton rigide
- un couteau « exacto » (ou des ciseaux)
- un compas
- un crayon-feutre
- entre huit et 10 aimants ronds en céramique de 12 mm de diamètre (1 $ chacun au magasin à un dollar)
- de la colle blanche liquide
- quatre baguettes de bois de 2 cm de diamètre, longues de 20 cm
- une baguette de bois de 5 mm de diamètre, longue de 18 cm
- une aiguille de couture avec chas
- du fil à pêche
- un marteau et un clou de finition (très petit)
- de la pâte à modeler

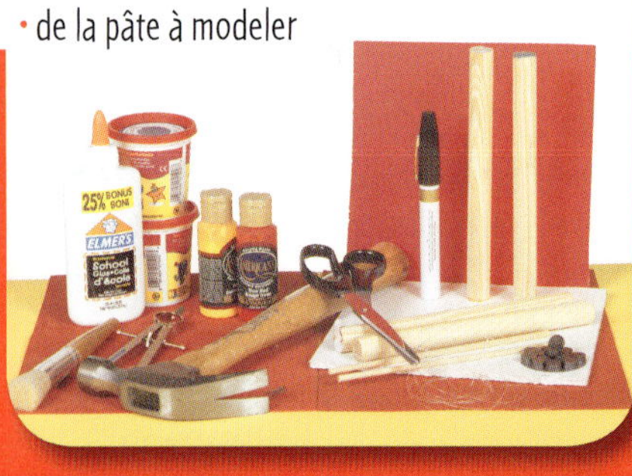

Débrouillard : Samuel Langlais Photos : Laurence Labat

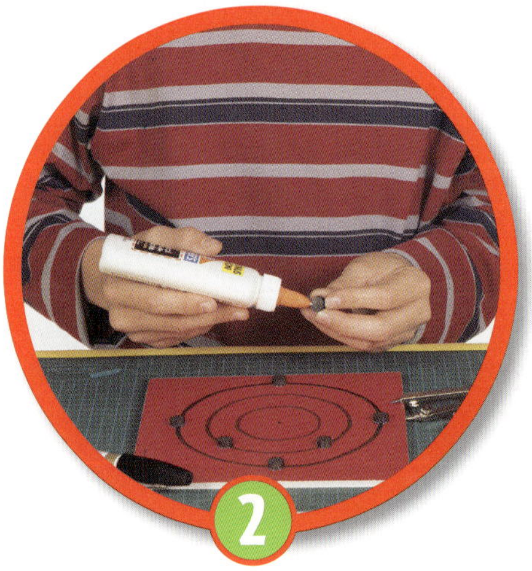

2

Colle les aimants sur les cercles à l'aide de la colle liquide (attention, tu dois en garder un pour le pendule). L'effet sera différent selon le côté de l'aimant que tu colles.

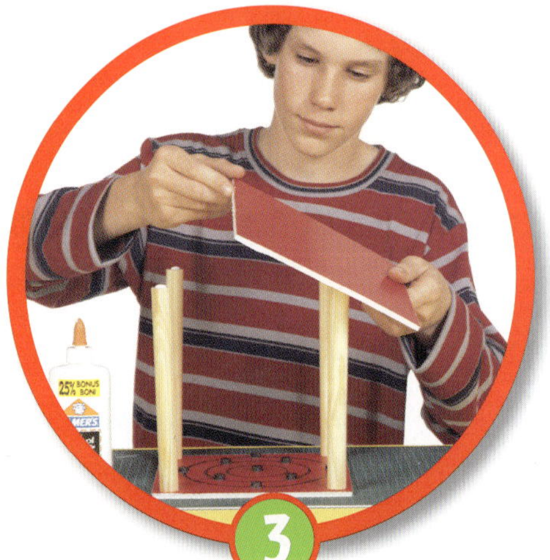

3

Colle les baguettes de 20 cm aux quatre coins du premier carton. Colle sur le dessus le second carton.

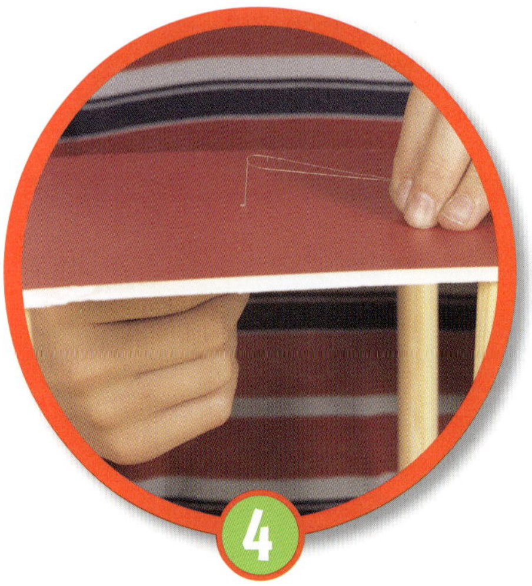

4

Enfile du fil à pêche dans l'aiguille. À l'aide de cette aiguillée, perce un trou en plein centre du carton du dessus. Fais passer 5 cm de fil à pêche à travers le trou central.

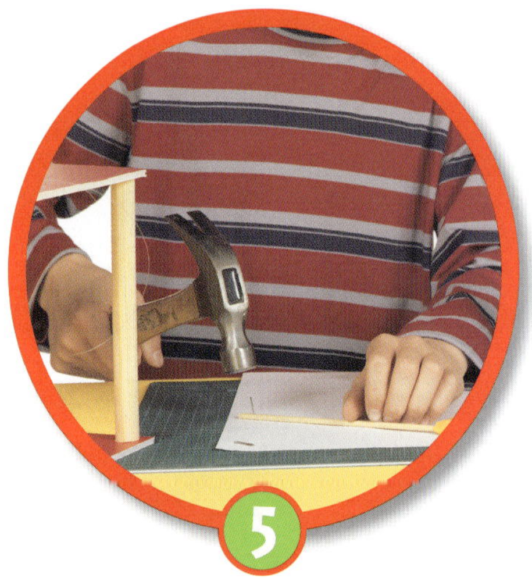

5

Perce un trou dans la petite baguette en te servant du marteau et du clou. Attention à tes doigts ! Le trou doit être à 1 cm d'une extrémité de la baguette. Mets une boule de pâte à modeler à l'autre extrémité et fixes-y un aimant circulaire.

Que se passe-t-il ?

Quand tu pousses le pendule, une série d'oscillations se produit. Étant donné la très courte distance qui sépare les aimants, les mouvements d'attraction et de répulsion se produisent sans arrêt. Pourquoi ? C'est parce que les aimants possèdent deux pôles magnétiques, le nord et le sud (voir page 30). Lorsque deux pôles identiques s'approchent, ils se repoussent. À l'inverse, deux pôles différents s'attirent. Ces forces d'attraction et de répulsion provoquent ces effets incroyables sur ton pendule !

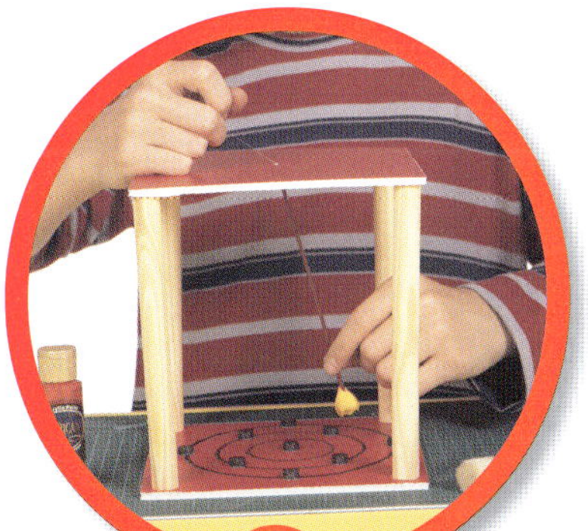

6

Passe le fil à pêche dans le trou de la baguette. Fais un nœud en t'assurant que l'aimant de la baguette est à 1 cm des aimants collés sur le plus petit cercle.

Donne une petite impulsion au pendule.

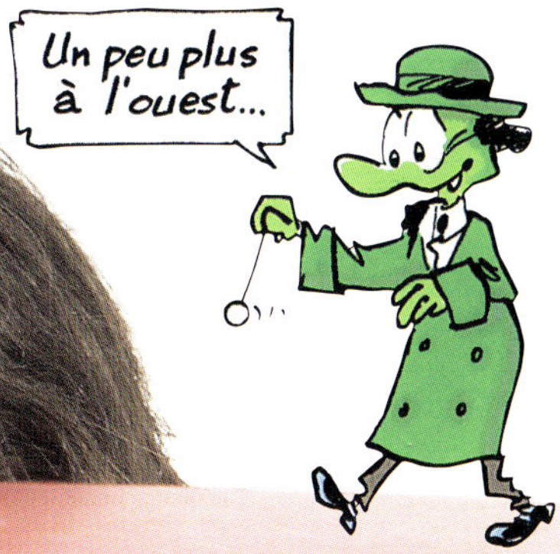

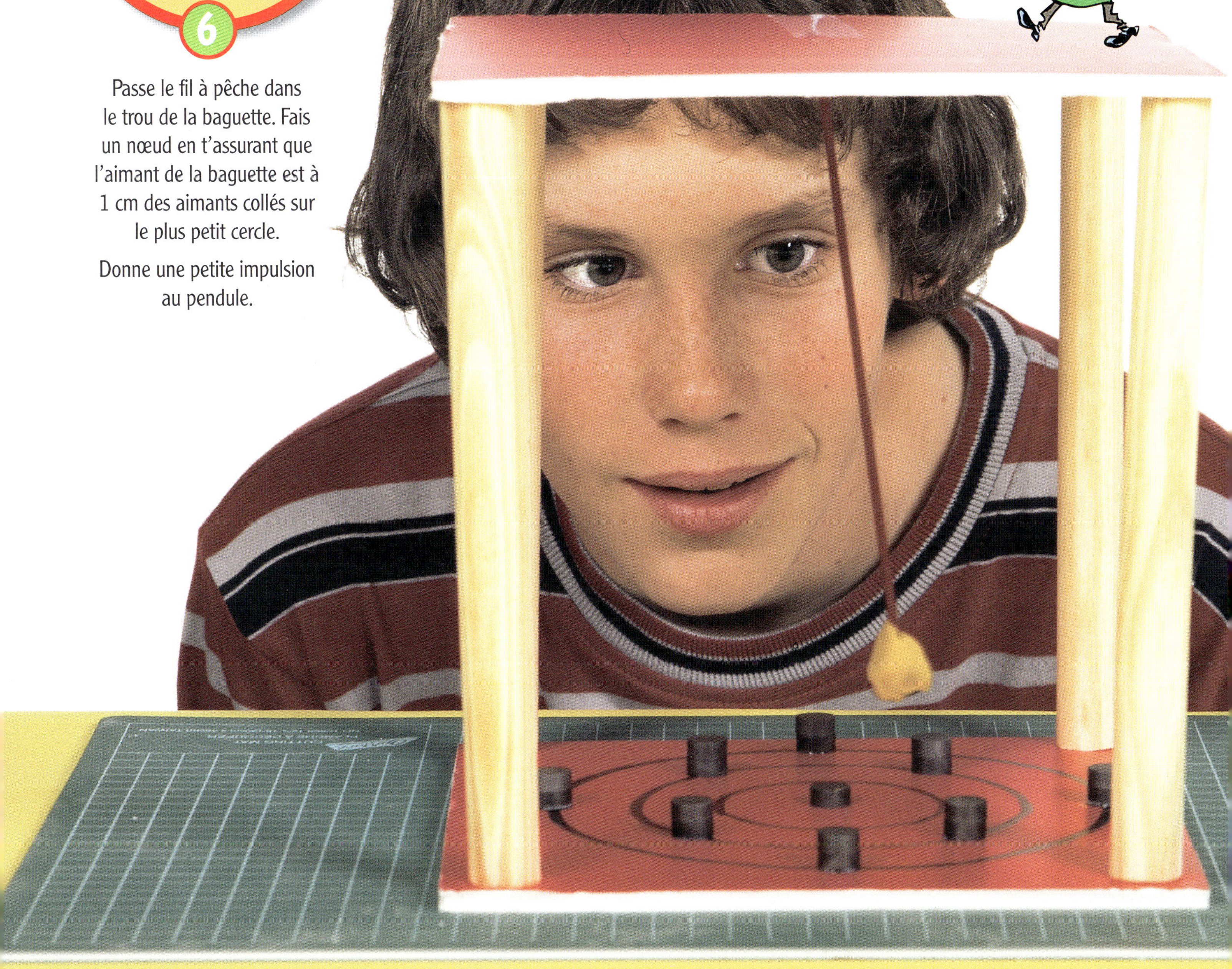

Ça ne marche pas ?

C'est sans doute parce que les aimants collés sur les cercles sont tous orientés dans le même sens (et opposés à l'aimant du pendule). Solution : retourne quelques aimants.

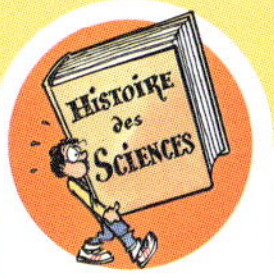

Le pendule

Le principe du pendule a été découvert en 1673 par le physicien et mathématicien néerlandais Christiaan Huygens (1629–1695). Un pendule simple est constitué d'un poids suspendu à un fil très léger. Quand on le déplace légèrement ou qu'on lui donne une impulsion, il produit un mouvement de va-et-vient, ou oscille. La durée d'une oscillation complète n'est pas influencée par le poids du pendule ni par la grosseur de son fil. Elle ne dépend que de la longueur du fil et de la gravité terrestre, cette force qui attire tous les objets vers le bas.

ATTENTION ! MANIPULATION DE VERRE BRISÉ.

Coule ton Nautilus

À l'époque où le romancier Jules Verne créa le Nautilus, on savait comment faire monter et descendre un submersible. C'est l'expérience qu'on te propose !

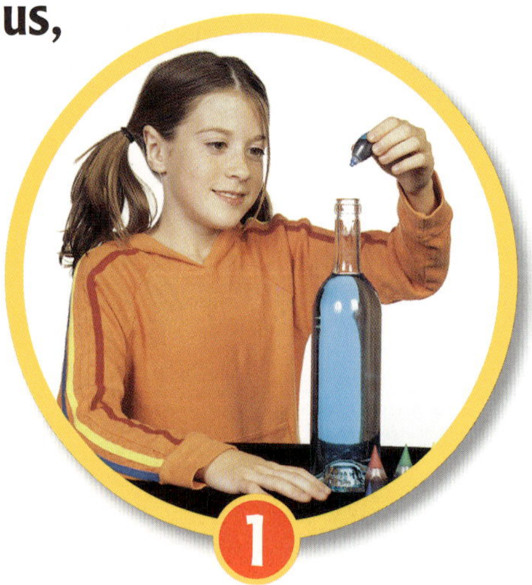

Remplis la bouteille d'eau jusqu'en haut en ne laissant que quelques centimètres d'air. Ajoute quelques gouttes de colorant alimentaire.

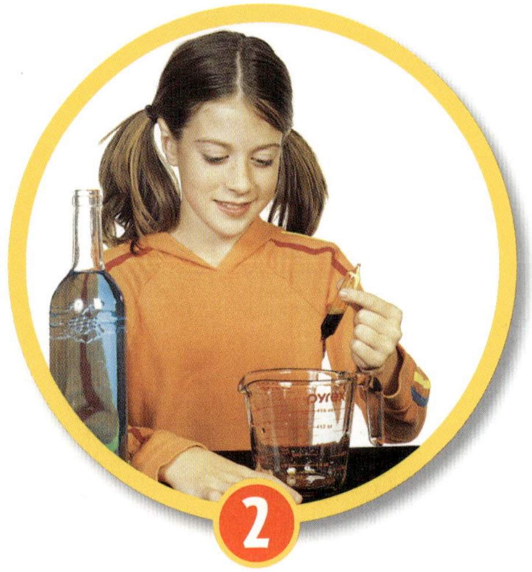

Brise les deux extrémités de la capsule et laisse s'écouler le contenu dans un verre.

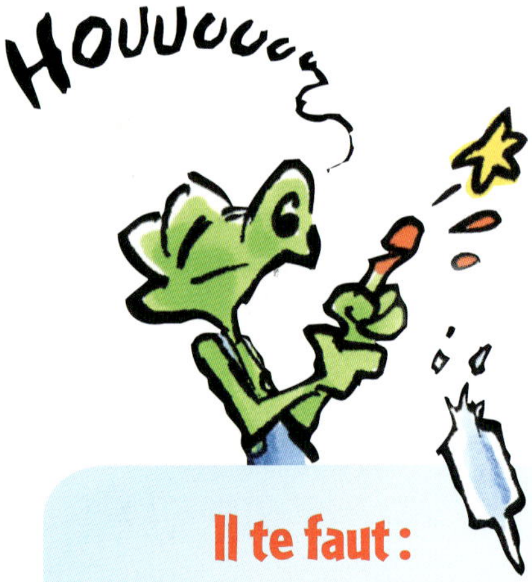

Il te faut :

- une bouteille en verre de 1,5 litre
- une ampoule (ou capsule) de verre, contenant des produits énergétiques ou des vitamines à boire
- une tasse à mesurer
- du colorant alimentaire
- un ballon gonflable
- de la pâte à modeler

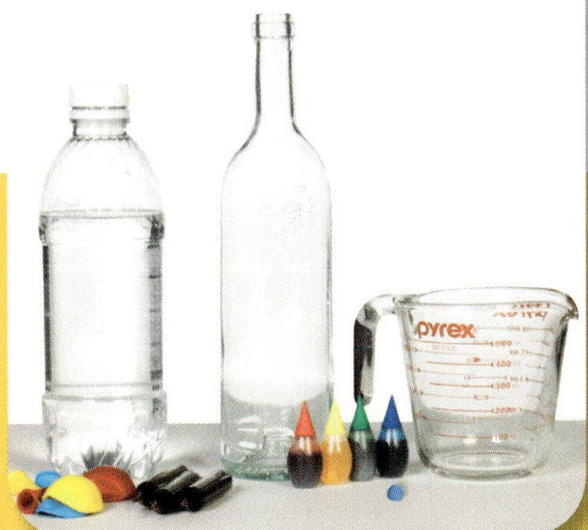

Débrouillarde : Shanie Beauchamp Photos : Laurence Labat

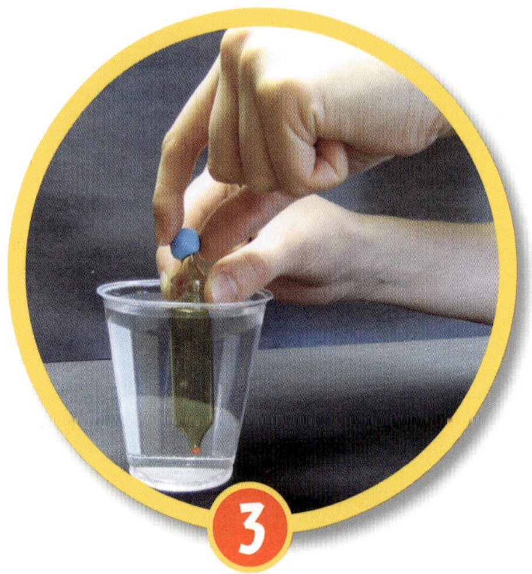

Plonge la capsule vide dans la tasse à mesurer afin de la remplir d'eau jusqu'aux trois quarts. Bouche l'une des extrémités de la capsule en te servant de pâte à modeler.

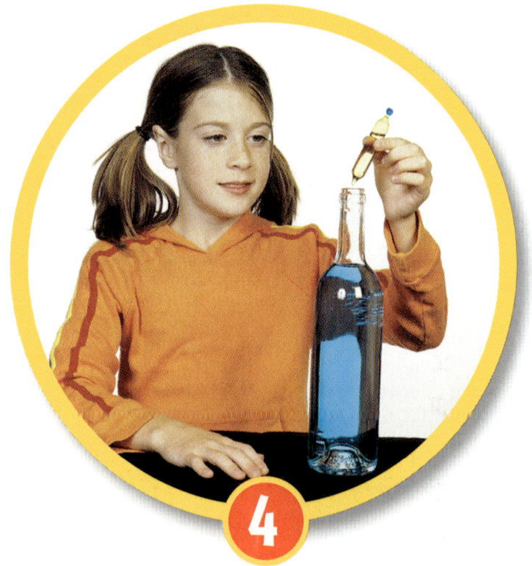

Insère ta capsule dans la bouteille d'eau en t'assurant que la partie sans pâte à modeler est vers le bas.

Que se passe-t-il ?

Quand tu appuies sur le ballon et que tu relâches, tu fais varier la pression à l'intérieur de la bouteille. Cette variation de pression fait entrer ou sortir l'eau de la capsule, ce qui modifie son poids. Lorsque le poids est plus faible, elle remonte. Lorsqu'il devient plus lourd, elle coule.

Les vrais sous-marins fonctionnent sur le même principe. Ils pompent de l'eau de mer dans de grands réservoirs, les ballasts, pour descendre. Pour remonter, ils vident leurs ballasts. Ainsi allégés, les sous-marins ne pèsent pas plus que l'eau qu'ils déplacent, donc ils flottent.

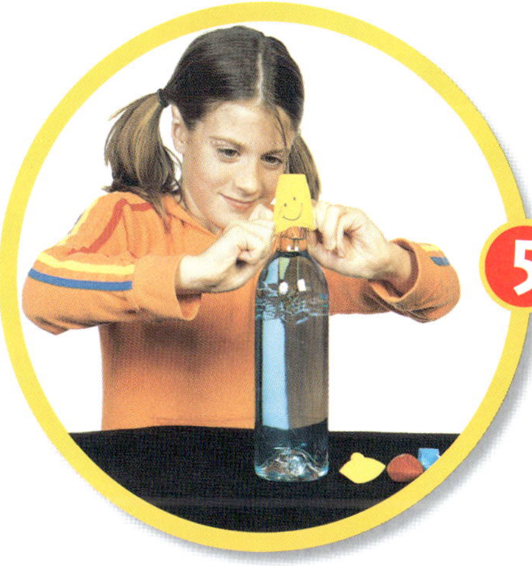

5

Installe le ballon gonflable sur le goulot de la bouteille.

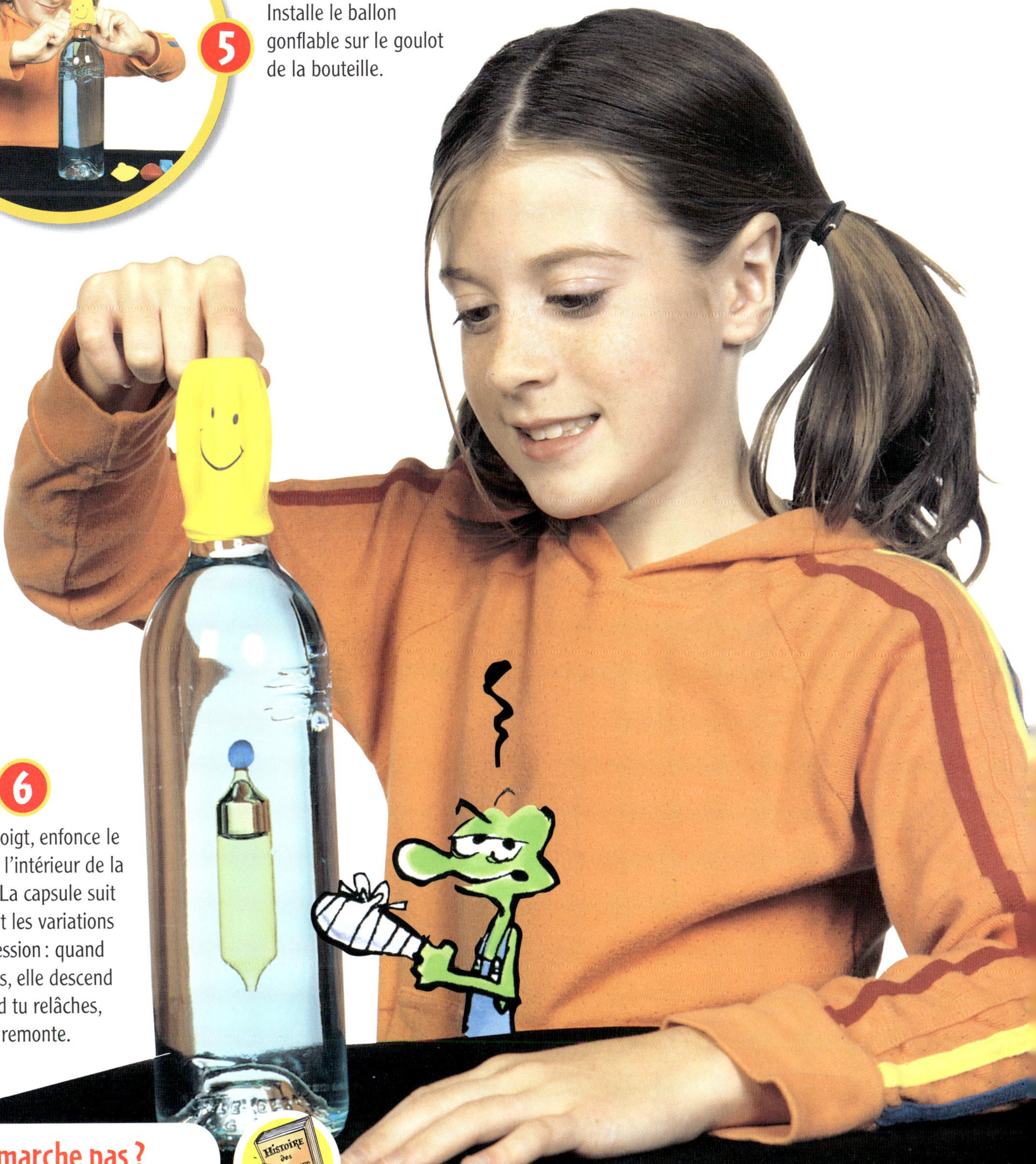

6

Avec ton doigt, enfonce le ballon vers l'intérieur de la bouteille. La capsule suit fidèlement les variations de la pression : quand tu appuies, elle descend et quand tu relâches, elle remonte.

Ça ne marche pas ?

Si la capsule ne coule pas, ajoute de l'eau à l'intérieur.

Si la capsule coule au fond, retire de l'eau de la capsule.

Si le fait de varier la pression ne change rien à la situation, retire un peu d'eau de la bouteille.

Histoire des Sciences

Le premier sous-marin

En 1775, l'Américain David Bushnell (1742–1824) met au point le Turtle (la tortue), un petit sous-marin en bois. Mais c'est à un autre Américain, l'ingénieur Robert Fulton (1765–1815), qu'on doit la conception du premier sous-marin réellement utilisable. En 1797, Fulton construit le Nautilus, un sous-marin en métal propulsé par une hélice actionnée à la main par trois hommes. Comme tous les sous-marins de l'époque, le Nautilus était un navire de guerre.

Sonate pour verre et fer

Transforme-toi en musicien et joue du... verre !

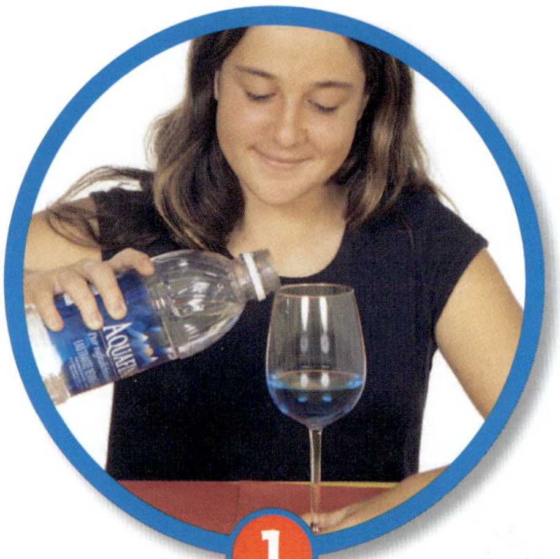

1

Verse de l'eau dans un verre et ajoute quelques gouttes de colorant alimentaire.

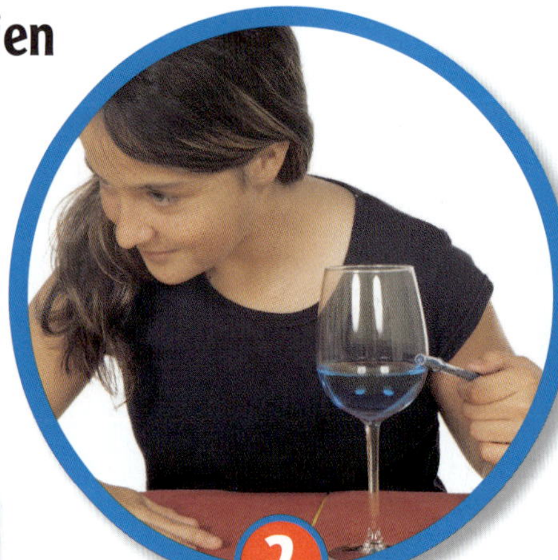

2

Frappe légèrement avec le crayon contre le verre. Tu entendras une note de musique.

3

Verse la même quantité d'eau dans un second verre et frappe-le légèrement pour t'assurer que les deux verres produisent exactement la même note. S'il y a une différence, ajoute de l'eau à l'un des verres et vérifie encore une fois.

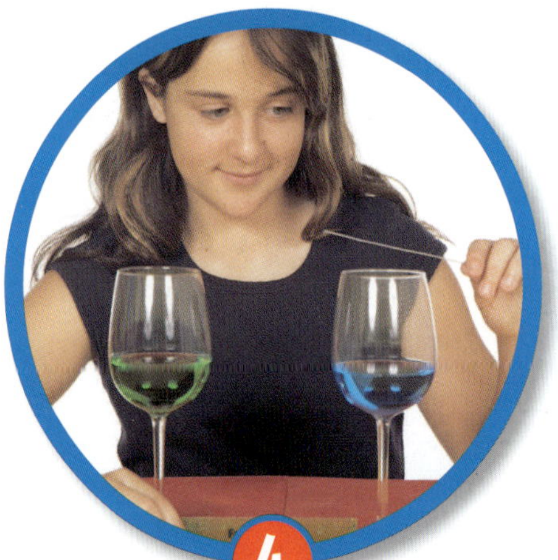

4

Place les verres à 10 cm l'un de l'autre. Dépose le fil métallique sur l'un d'eux.

Il te faut :

- entre deux et huit verres à vin
- de l'eau
- du colorant alimentaire
- un crayon
- un fil métallique très fin (grosseur d'un fil à coudre)
- une tasse à mesurer
- une règle

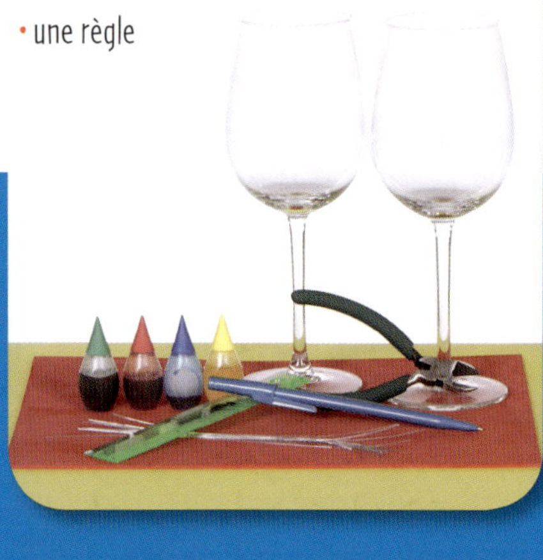

Débrouillarde : Ariane Fortin Photos : Laurence Labat

Poursuis l'expérience

Maintenant, remplis d'autres verres, mais à des niveaux différents. La tonalité du son varie selon le niveau d'eau : plus un verre contient d'eau, plus le son qu'il émet est grave. Humecte ton index et fais-le glisser sur le rebord du premier verre. Un son jaillira. Ton doigt agit sur le verre comme l'archet sur une corde de violon. Tu peux aussi simplement frapper les verres.

Passe d'un verre à l'autre pour jouer une mélodie.

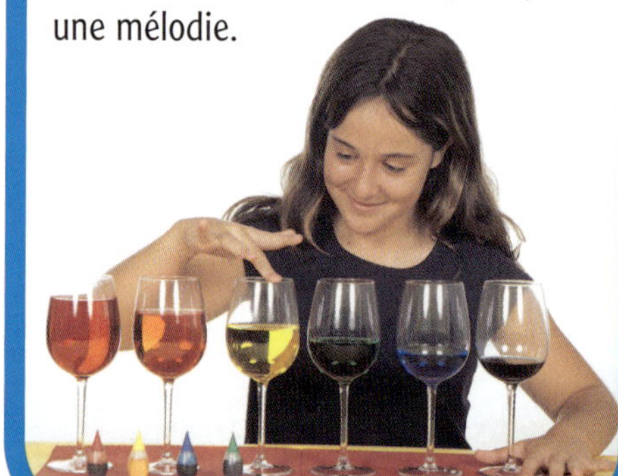

Que se passe-t-il ?

Un son est produit par un objet qui vibre, c'est-à-dire qui produit une suite de mouvements de va-et-vient rapides. Ces vibrations poussent l'air sous forme d'ondes. C'est ainsi qu'un son voyage dans l'air jusqu'à l'oreille. Quand tu frappes le verre, tu crées des vibrations. Les ondes sonores émises voyagent jusqu'à l'autre verre et le font vibrer à son tour. Les vibrations du deuxième verre sont transmises au fil métallique. Cela prouve que le son a un impact physique sur les choses qui l'entourent.

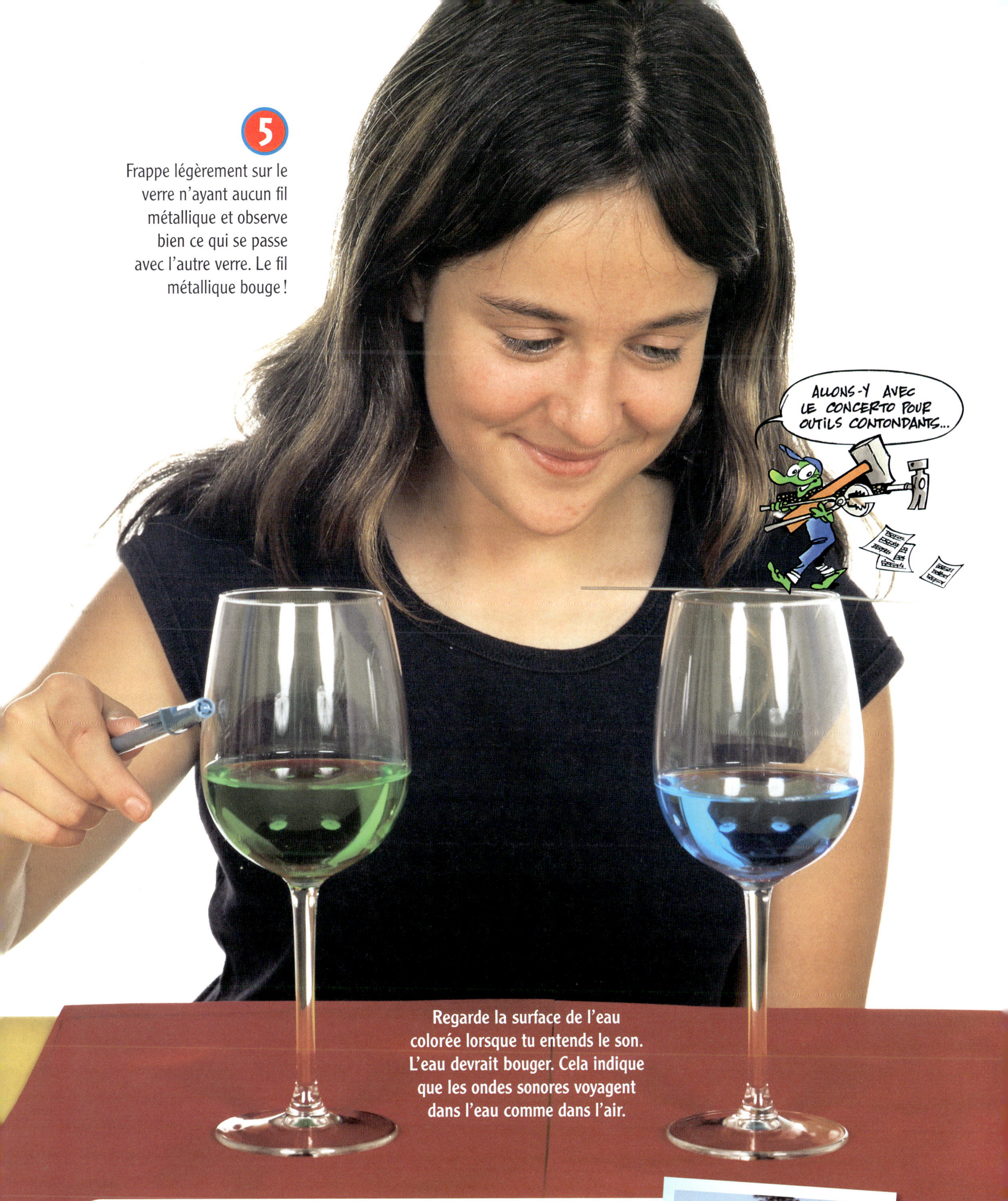

5

Frappe légèrement sur le verre n'ayant aucun fil métallique et observe bien ce qui se passe avec l'autre verre. Le fil métallique bouge !

Regarde la surface de l'eau colorée lorsque tu entends le son. L'eau devrait bouger. Cela indique que les ondes sonores voyagent dans l'eau comme dans l'air.

Comme tu as de grandes oreilles !

Une grande surface est nécessaire pour bien recueillir et concentrer les ondes sonores. C'est le rôle du pavillon de l'oreille. C'est pourquoi la plupart des animaux à l'ouïe fine, comme les chiens et les loups, sont dotés de grandes oreilles qu'ils orientent à leur gré, indépendamment l'une de l'autre.

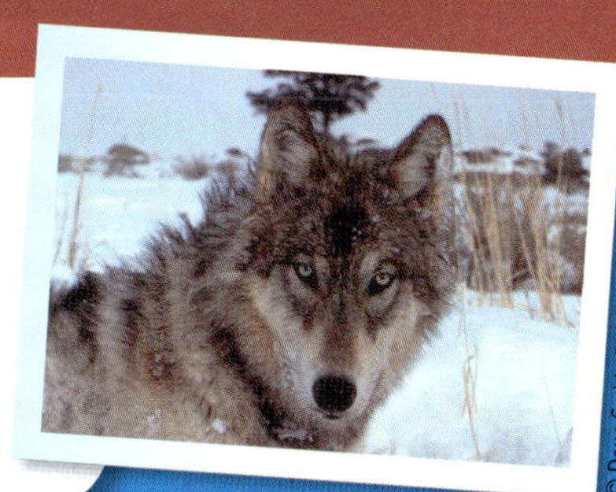

© Doug Smith/Yellowstone National Park

RÉSULTATS AU BOUT DE DEUX JOURS ENVIRON.
ATTENTION ! MANIPULATION DE MOISISSURES.

Par ici le moisi !

Les champignons microscopiques sont partout autour de nous. Ils sont si petits qu'on ne les voit pas… sauf quand ils nous envahissent !

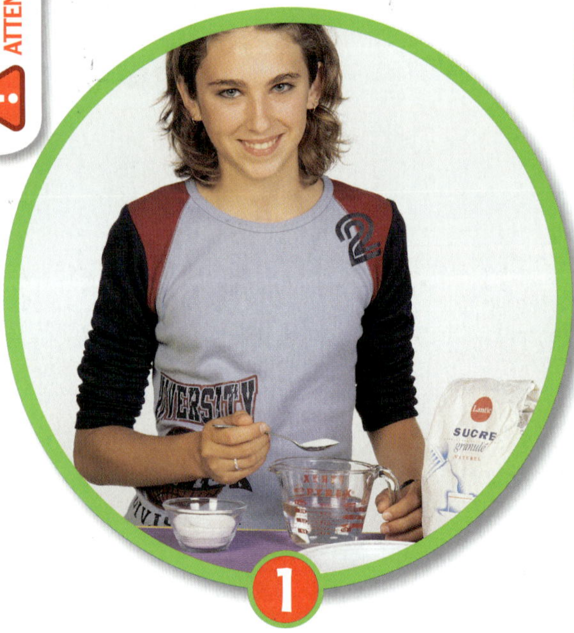

1 Ajoute deux cuillerées à table (30 ml) de sucre blanc à une tasse (250 ml) d'eau tiède.

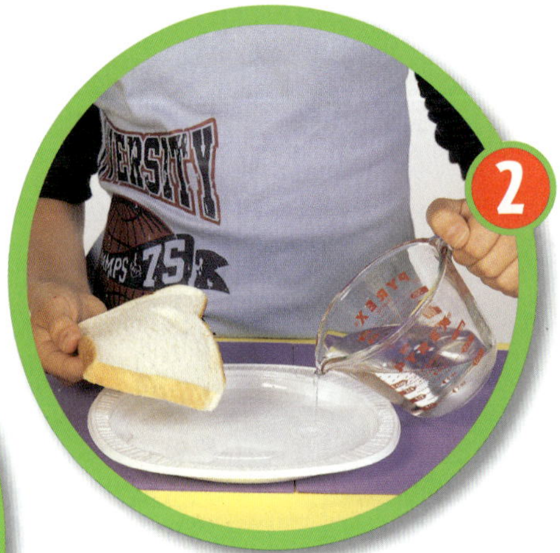

2 Verse 30 ml de cette solution sucrée dans une assiette de plastique. Déposes-y une tranche de pain sec et laisse le pain s'imbiber d'eau.

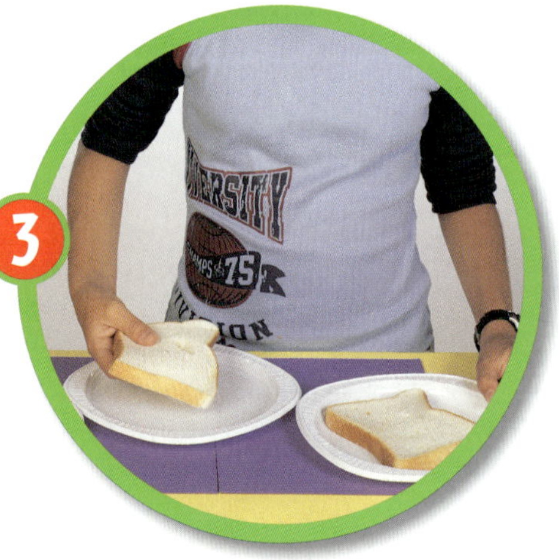

3 Dépose une deuxième tranche de pain sec dans une assiette de plastique contenant 30 ml d'eau du robinet. Dépose la troisième tranche dans une assiette de plastique, tout simplement.

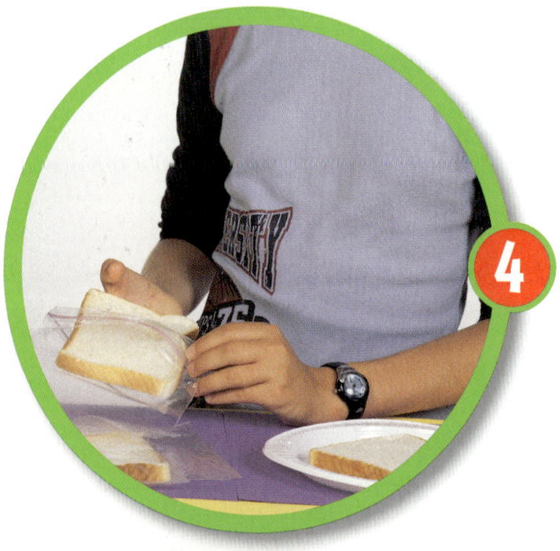

4 Au bout d'une journée à l'air libre, enferme chaque tranche de pain dans un sac de plastique. Ferme les trois sacs hermétiquement.

Il te faut :

- trois sacs à congélation (type « Ziploc[md] »)
- trois assiettes de plastique
- trois tranches de pain sec
- une tasse à mesurer
- du sucre blanc
- une cuillère à table
- de l'eau
- un microscope (facultatif)

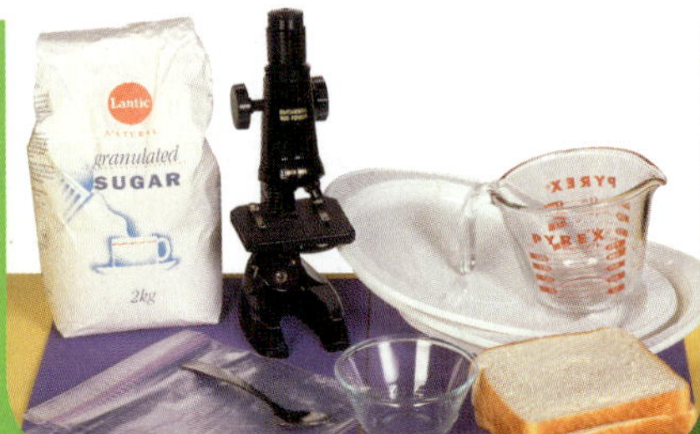

Débrouillarde : Mélodie Desjardins Photos : Laurence Labat

Que se passe-t-il ?

Les moisissures sont des champignons microscopiques qui se multiplient rapidement en présence de sucre, d'eau et d'oxygène.

Ici, les trois tranches de pain ont été privées d'oxygène. Par contre, la première des trois a eu assez de sucre et d'eau pour que des champignons se développent et prolifèrent.

La deuxième tranche n'ayant eu que de l'eau (pas de sucre), les moisissures se sont multipliées moins vite que sur la première.

Quant à la troisième tranche : pas de sucre, pas d'oxygène, pas d'eau… donc pas de bouffe, pas de moisissures !

5

Deux jours plus tard, compare les trois tranches de pain. Que remarques-tu ? Les deux tranches humides se sont couvertes de moisissures alors que le pain sec est resté… sec !

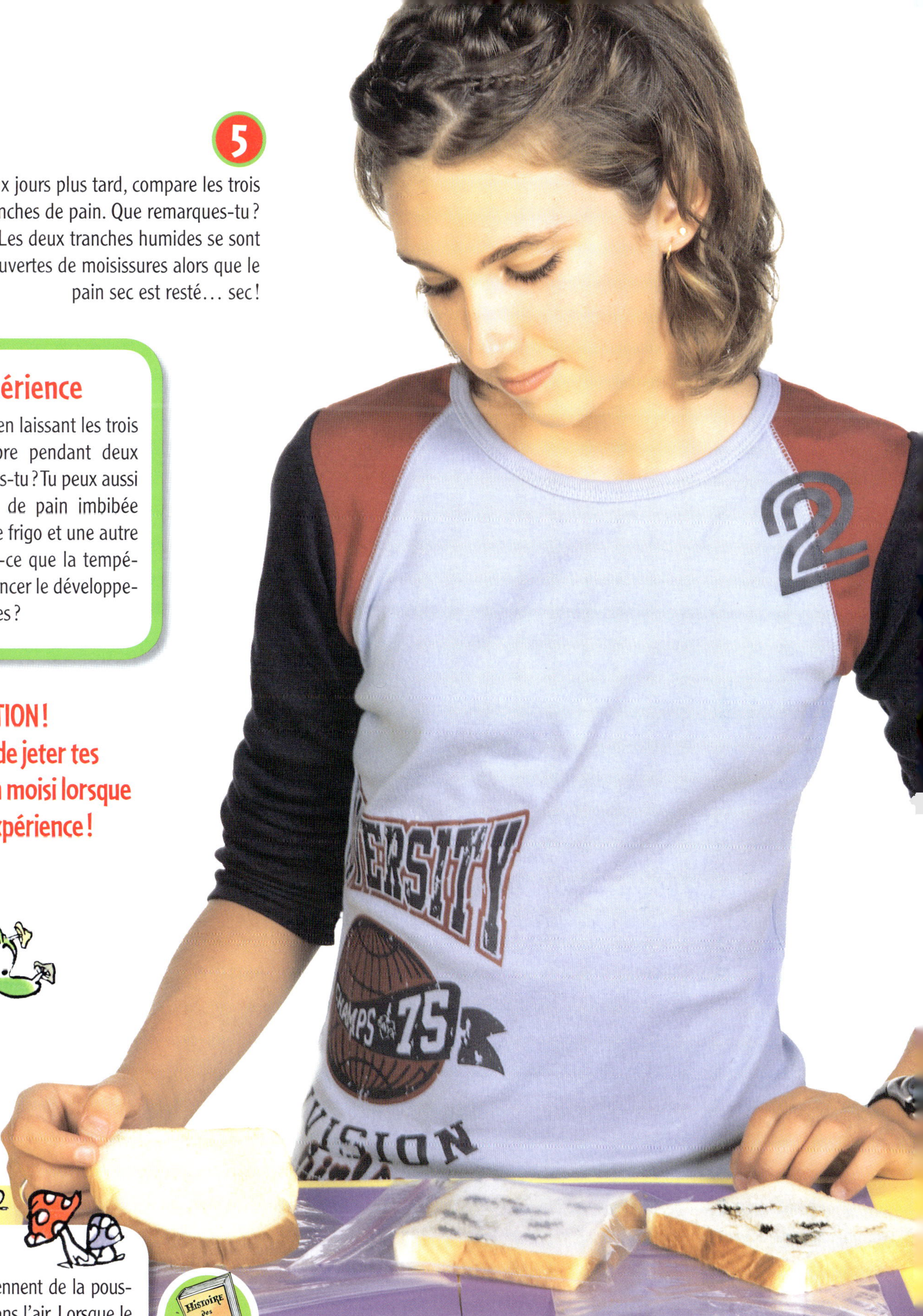

Poursuis l'expérience

Refais l'expérience en laissant les trois tranches à l'air libre pendant deux jours. Que remarques-tu ? Tu peux aussi placer une tranche de pain imbibée d'eau sucrée dans le frigo et une autre à l'air ambiant. Est-ce que la température semble influencer le développement des moisissures ?

ATTENTION !
Prends soin de jeter tes tranches de pain moisi lorsque tu as fini l'expérience !

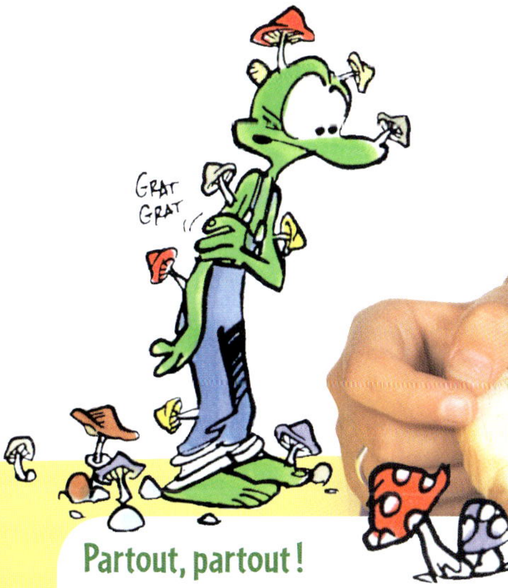

Partout, partout !

Les moisissures proviennent de la poussière en suspension dans l'air. Lorsque le milieu est favorable et qu'elles trouvent de quoi se nourrir, elles se développent. Ces champignons microscopiques poussent en un enchevêtrement de filaments, le mycélium, qui porte des petits sacs pleins de spores. Lorsque ces cellules reproductrices sont expulsées, elles se laissent porter par le vent à la recherche d'un endroit humide où se développer.

Histoire des Sciences

La découverte de la pénicilline

En 1928, le médecin et biologiste britannique Alexander Fleming (1881–1955) remarqua qu'une de ses cultures de bactéries avait été contaminée par une moisissure, le *Penicillium notatum*. Quelle ne fut sa surprise de constater que la moisissure avait empêché les bactéries de se développer ! Il venait de découvrir le premier antibiotique. Fleming essaya en vain d'extraire la substance produite par le *Penicillium*, qu'il baptisa pénicilline. Ce n'est qu'en 1942 que la pénicilline fut enfin utilisée par les médecins.

Un mini feu d'artifice

PEUT NÉCESSITER LA PRÉSENCE D'UN ADULTE (MANIPULATION DE FEU).

Crée un feu d'artifice... dans ta maison !

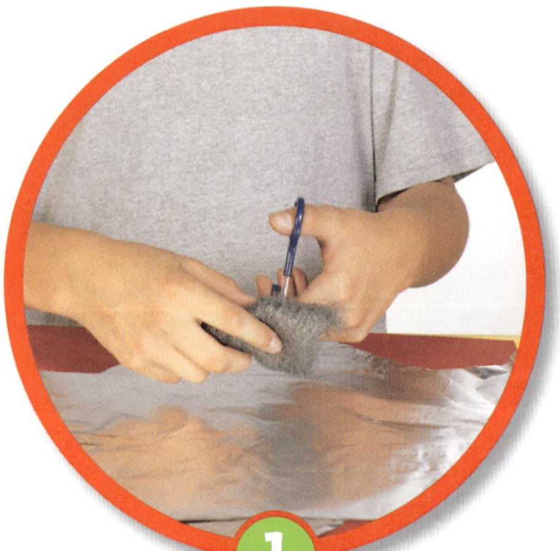

1

Étale quelques feuilles de papier d'aluminium sur une table. Au-dessus de cette surface, découpe un rouleau de laine d'acier à l'aide des ciseaux afin d'obtenir un morceau de 2 cm de largeur.

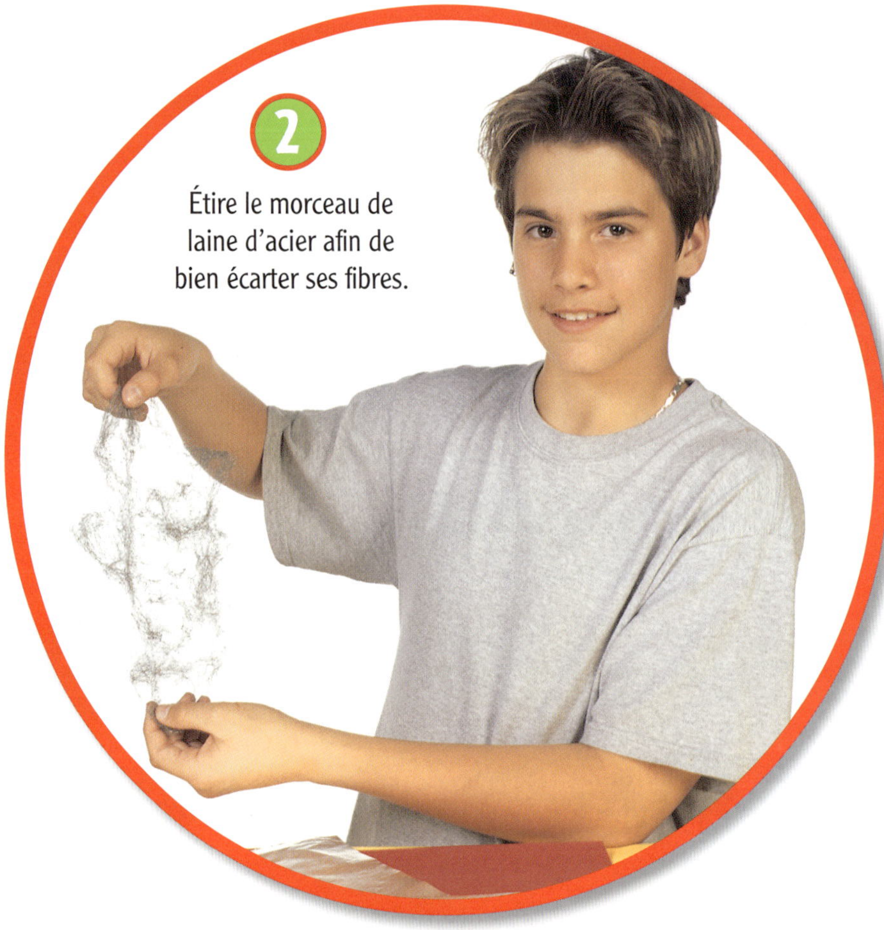

2

Étire le morceau de laine d'acier afin de bien écarter ses fibres.

Il te faut :

- du papier d'aluminium
- de la laine d'acier de type « moyen » sans nettoyant
- un bol en verre
- une bougie
- des ciseaux
- des pinces ou une fourchette
- des allumettes

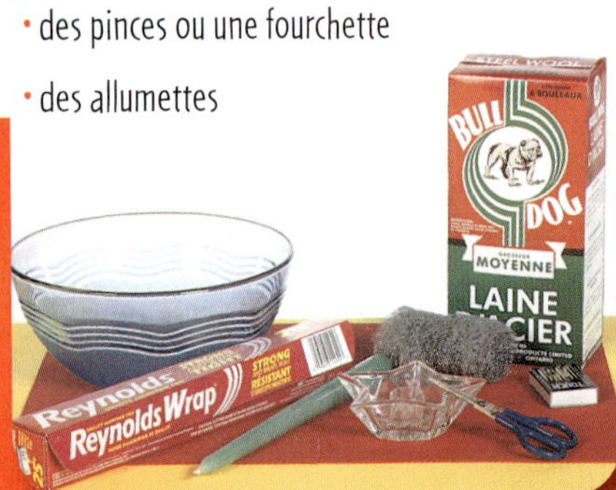

Débrouillard : Cédrik Lebrasseur Photos : Laurence Labat

La combustion de l'acier est possible seulement si une grande concentration d'oxygène est présente à travers les fibres. On appelle cela « augmenter la surface de contact ».

3

Allume la bougie et remplis le bol d'eau du robinet. En tenant le morceau de laine d'acier à l'aide de pinces ou d'une fourchette, fais-le brûler au-dessus du bol d'eau pour plus de sécurité.

Que se passe-t-il ?

Lorsqu'il est soumis à une chaleur intense, l'acier émet une lumière jaune visible. La chaleur dégagée par la combustion de ce métal a généré assez d'énergie pour déclencher une nouvelle réaction chimique. Il s'agit de la production de lumière. On appelle ce phénomène « incandescence ». Il est à l'origine, par exemple, de l'éclairage produit par les ampoules électriques classiques à filament.

D'où vient la couleur des feux ?

De nos jours, la coloration jaune des feux d'artifice provient de l'incandescence des sels de sodium. Les sels de magnésium produisent une intense couleur blanche. Quant à la lumière rouge, elle provient des sels de strontium. Ces mêmes sels se retrouvent dans les fusées éclairantes utilisées par les automobilistes en cas d'urgence.

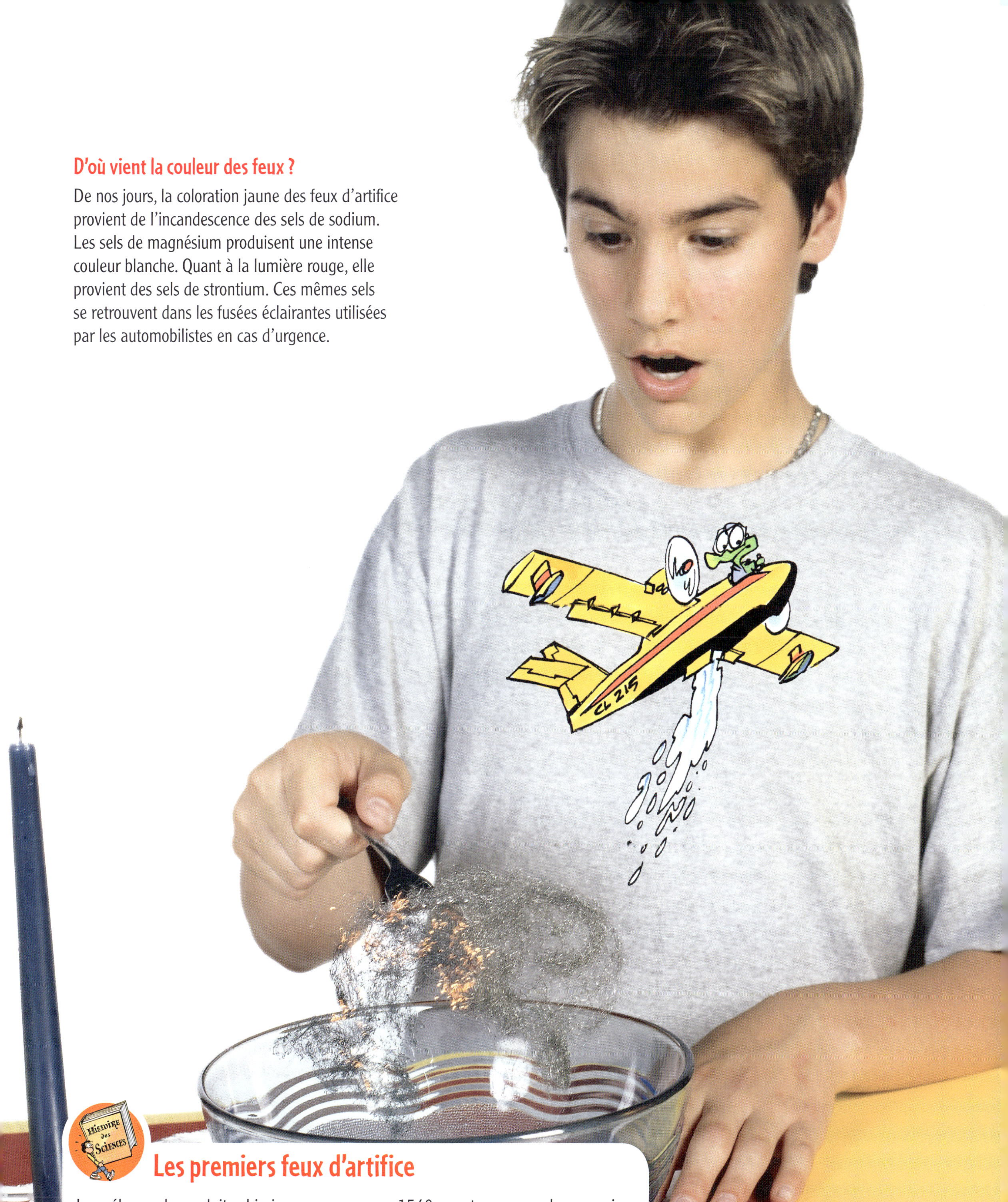

Les premiers feux d'artifice

Le mélange de produits chimiques pour fabriquer des feux d'artifice est un art ancien nommé pyrotechnie. Vers l'an 670, les Chinois ont mis au point les premiers feux d'artifice en s'inspirant d'armes rudimentaires qui projetaient du feu liquide sur les adversaires. Puis en Italie, en 1540, sont apparus les premiers feux colorés, après qu'on eût découvert que certains sels minéraux produisaient des effets de couleur en s'enflammant. La chimie du 20e siècle a permis de développer de nouveaux produits pyrotechniques plus performants.

Entre ciel et terre

Des balles restent en suspension dans le vide. Est-ce de la magie ? Non, c'est l'effet Bernoulli !

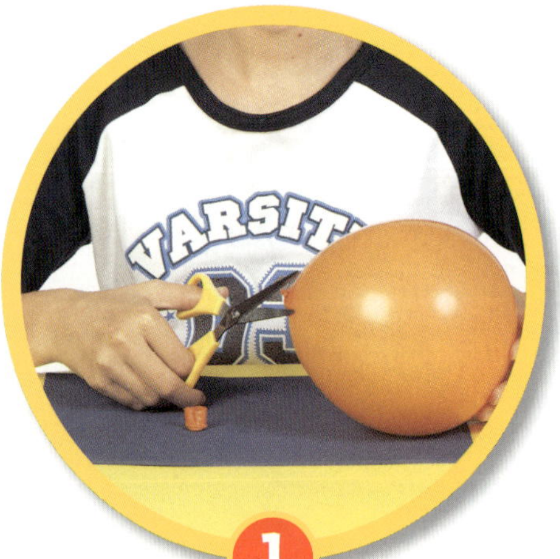

1

Gonfle le ballon de manière à obtenir un volume assez petit et fais un nœud. Coupe l'extrémité du nœud du ballon (pas trop !).

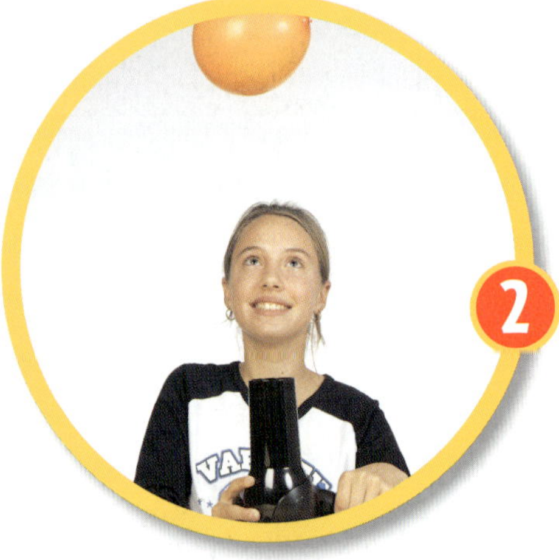

2

Tiens le sèche-cheveux à la verticale, le jet d'air chaud dirigé vers le haut. Place le ballon dans le courant d'air et lâche-le. Que se passe-t-il ? Le ballon reste en suspension dans l'air.

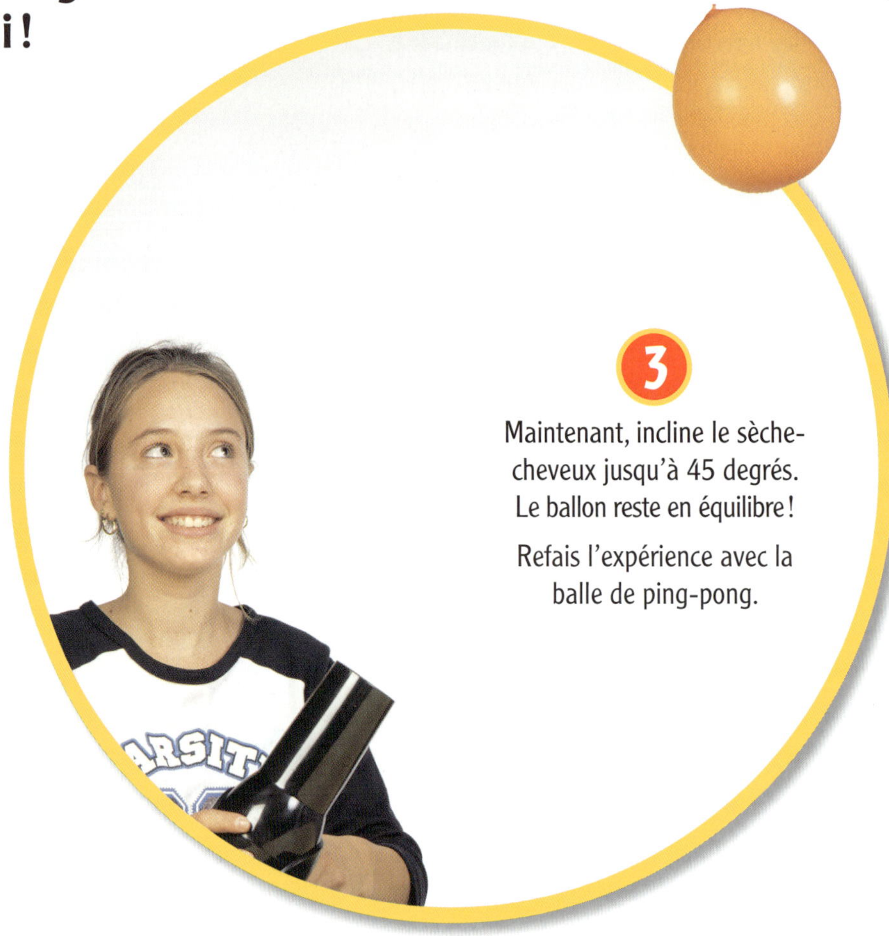

3

Maintenant, incline le sèche-cheveux jusqu'à 45 degrés. Le ballon reste en équilibre !

Refais l'expérience avec la balle de ping-pong.

MISE EN GARDE

Si tu inclines trop le sèche-cheveux, la balle va « décrocher » et tomber car l'équilibre entre la force gravitationnelle et la poussée d'air provenant du sèche-cheveux est rompu.

Il te faut :

- un sèche-cheveux
- une balle de ping-pong
- un ballon gonflable
- des ciseaux

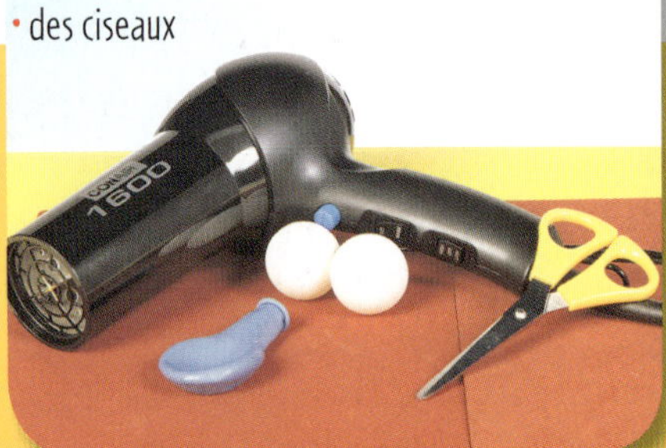

Que se passe-t-il ?

Il y a deux phénomènes dans cette expérience : 1) la balle (ou le ballon) s'élève et s'immobilise à une certaine hauteur, et 2) la balle reste à l'intérieur du jet d'air produit par le sèche-cheveux. Voici pourquoi :

1) La poussée de l'air du sèche-cheveux pointé sur la balle la fait monter. Cela, jusqu'au point où cette poussée est égale à la force gravitationnelle qui attire la balle vers le sol. À ce point, les deux forces s'équilibrent et la balle maintient sa position. Elle restera ainsi en suspension tant que le sèche-cheveux produira son jet d'air.

2) L'air qui passe à haute vitesse sur les côtés de la balle crée une zone de basse pression entre la balle et l'air ambiant. Or, la pression de l'air ambiant est plus élevée que la pression exercée par le filet d'air autour de la balle ; elle maintient la balle dans le jet d'air. Ce phénomène est appelé effet Bernoulli.

Débrouillarde : Josiane Douillard   Photos : Laurence Labat

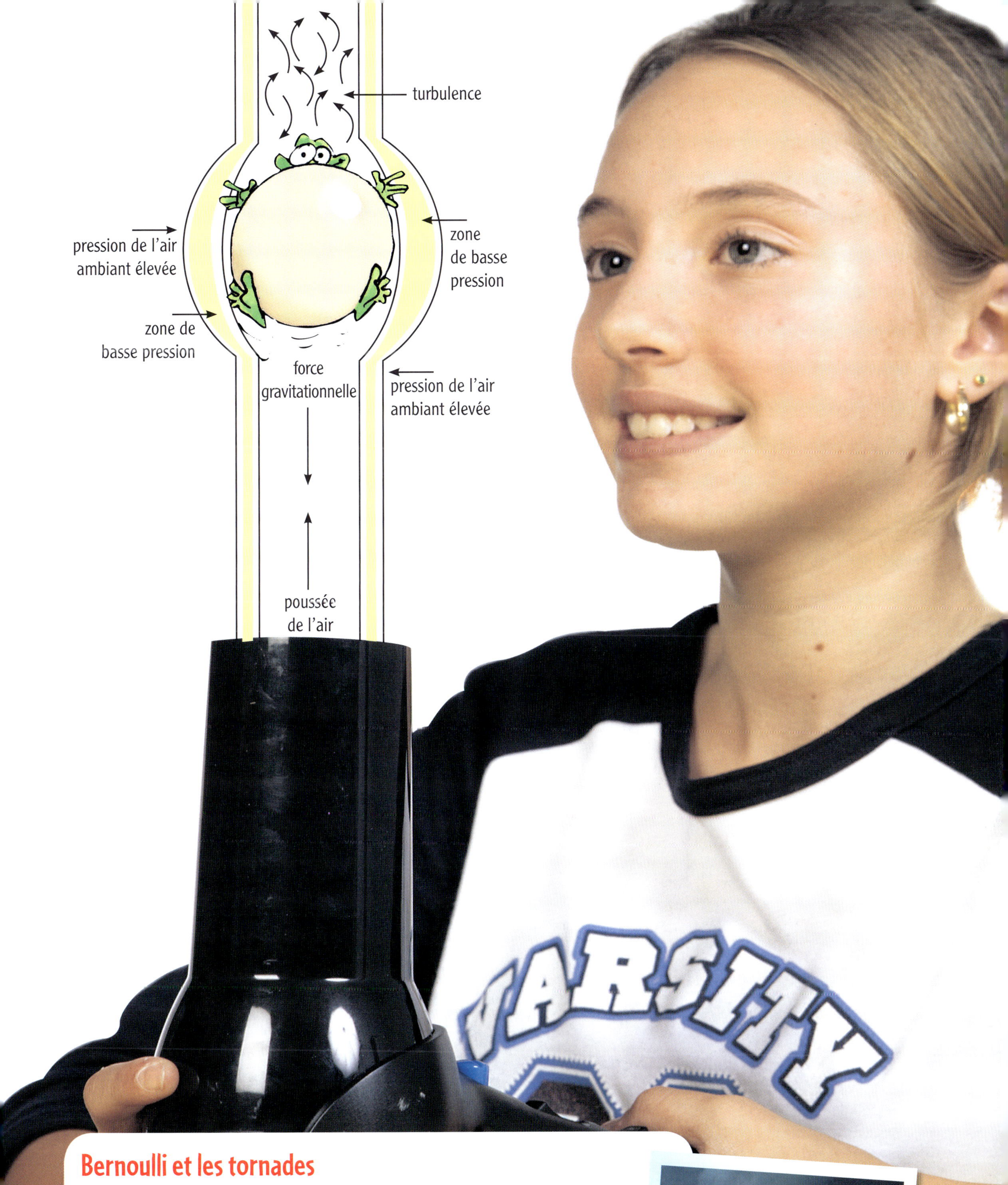

Bernoulli et les tornades

Le mathématicien suisse Daniel Bernoulli (1700–1782) s'intéressa tout particulièrement à l'étude du mouvement des fluides, ces corps sans consistance comme les gaz et les liquides. Il découvrit que la pression de l'air diminue quand sa vitesse augmente. Cette baisse de pression provoquée par le déplacement rapide de l'air est une des causes des destructions engendrées par les tornades. La pression de l'air à l'intérieur d'une tornade est si basse que les objets se trouvant sur son chemin peuvent être écrasés.

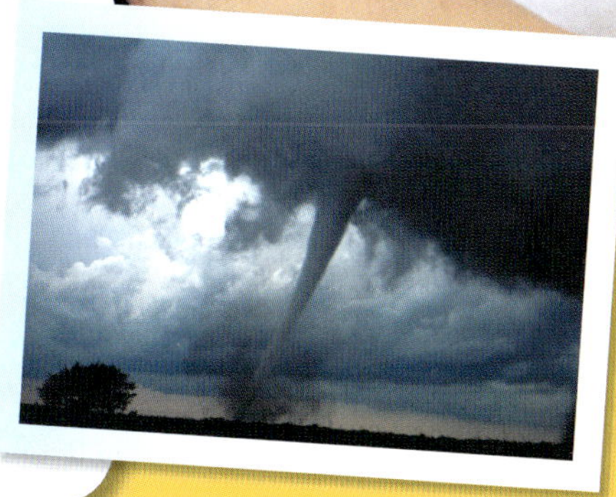

Fabrique du papier recyclé

ATTENTION ! MANIPULATION D'UN FER À REPASSER CHAUD.

Il y a 2 100 ans, les Chinois ont inventé le papier. Au 21e siècle, c'est le temps de le recycler !

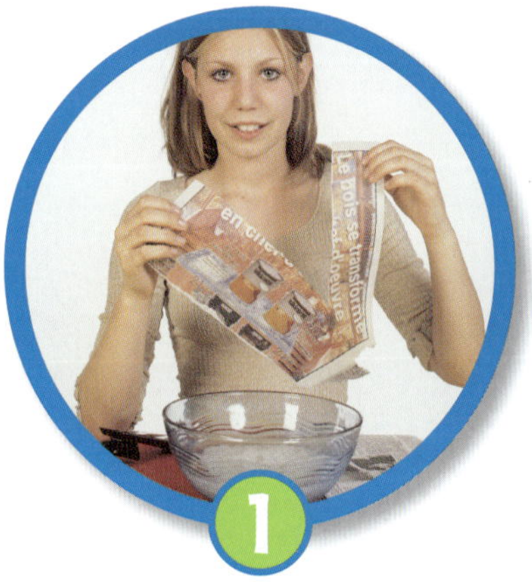

1

Déchire le papier en petits morceaux. Dépose les morceaux dans le bol et ajoute de l'eau chaude. Laisse tremper le papier pendant au moins 10 minutes.

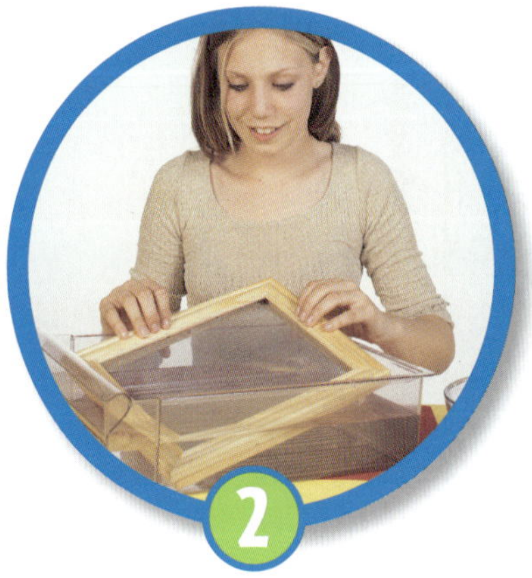

2

Agrafe la moustiquaire sur un des deux cadres en bois. Dépose ce cadre dans la bassine remplie d'eau en plaçant le côté moustiquaire vers le haut. Pose le deuxième cadre par-dessus. Tu as maintenant un moule à feuilles.

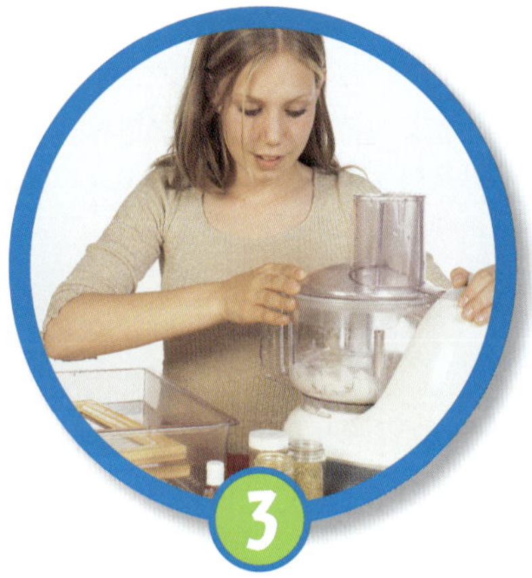

3

Au robot culinaire, réduis en purée le papier mouillé. Tu peux ajouter des fines herbes, des fleurs séchées ou du colorant alimentaire.

Il te faut :

- six à 12 feuilles lignées usagées ou du papier journal
- deux cadres pour photos en bois* (2 $ chacun au magasin à un dollar)
- de la toile moustiquaire en nylon (1 $ à la quincaillerie)
- des chiffons ou linges à vaisselle
- un récipient plus grand que les cadres (bassine)
- un robot culinaire
- une agrafeuse
- un fer à repasser
- un bol
- du colorant alimentaire (facultatif)
- des fines herbes ou fleurs séchées (facultatives)

* retire la vitre et le dos des cadres.

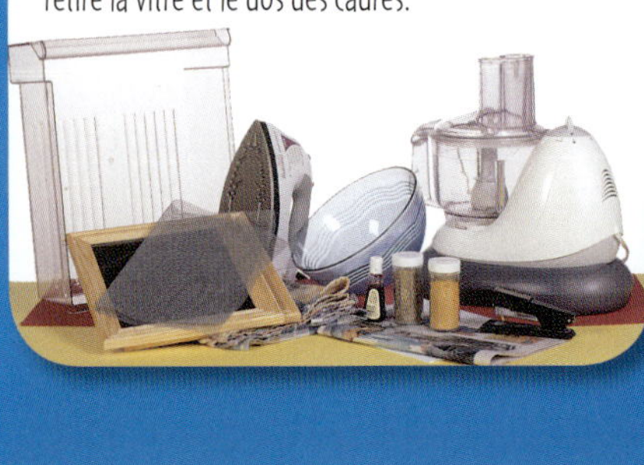

Débrouillarde : Cassandra Godin-Bergeron Photos : Laurence Labat

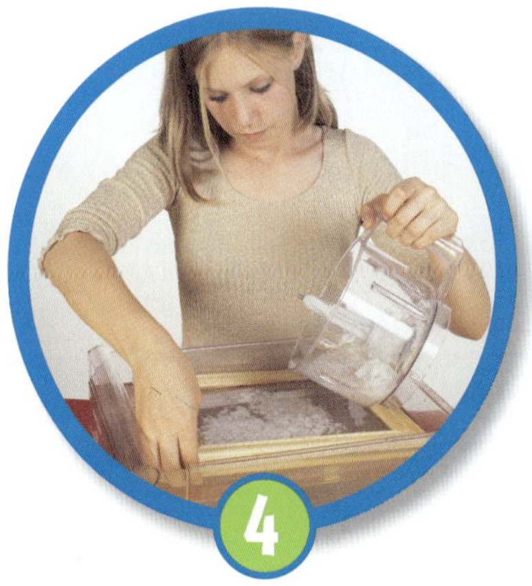

4

Dépose un peu de cette purée dans le moule. La pâte devrait se mélanger avec l'eau de la bassine. Secoue le moule pour étendre la pâte uniformément. Retire ensuite le moule de la bassine et laisse égoutter quelques minutes.

5

Retire le cadre du dessus (celui qui est sans moustiquaire). Remplace-le par un linge à vaisselle. En tenant bien le linge et le cadre-moustiquaire, retourne-les doucement pour déposer la feuille sur le linge. Retire ensuite le cadre.

Que se passe-t-il ?

En réduisant le papier mouillé en purée, on libère les fibres qui le composent. Tout en retenant ces fibres, le cadre-moustiquaire du moule permet à l'eau de s'égoutter. En séchant, les fibres emmêlées restent collées ensemble, durcissent et forment une feuille de papier.

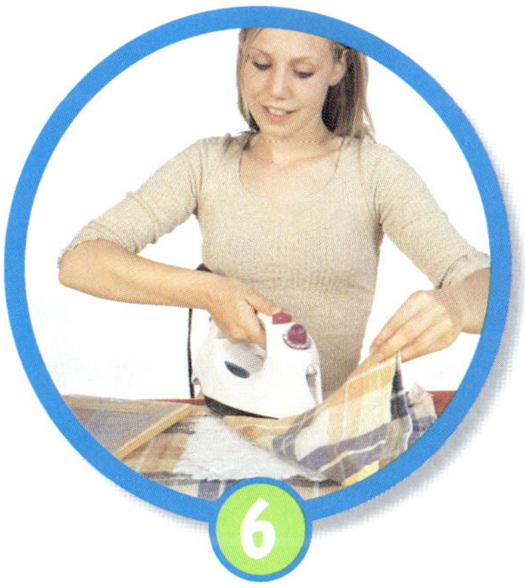

6

Pour le séchage, dépose le linge sur la planche à repasser. Recouvre ton papier d'un autre linge. Repasse à basse température, pendant au moins 15 minutes. Cela fait sécher le papier et l'aplatit.

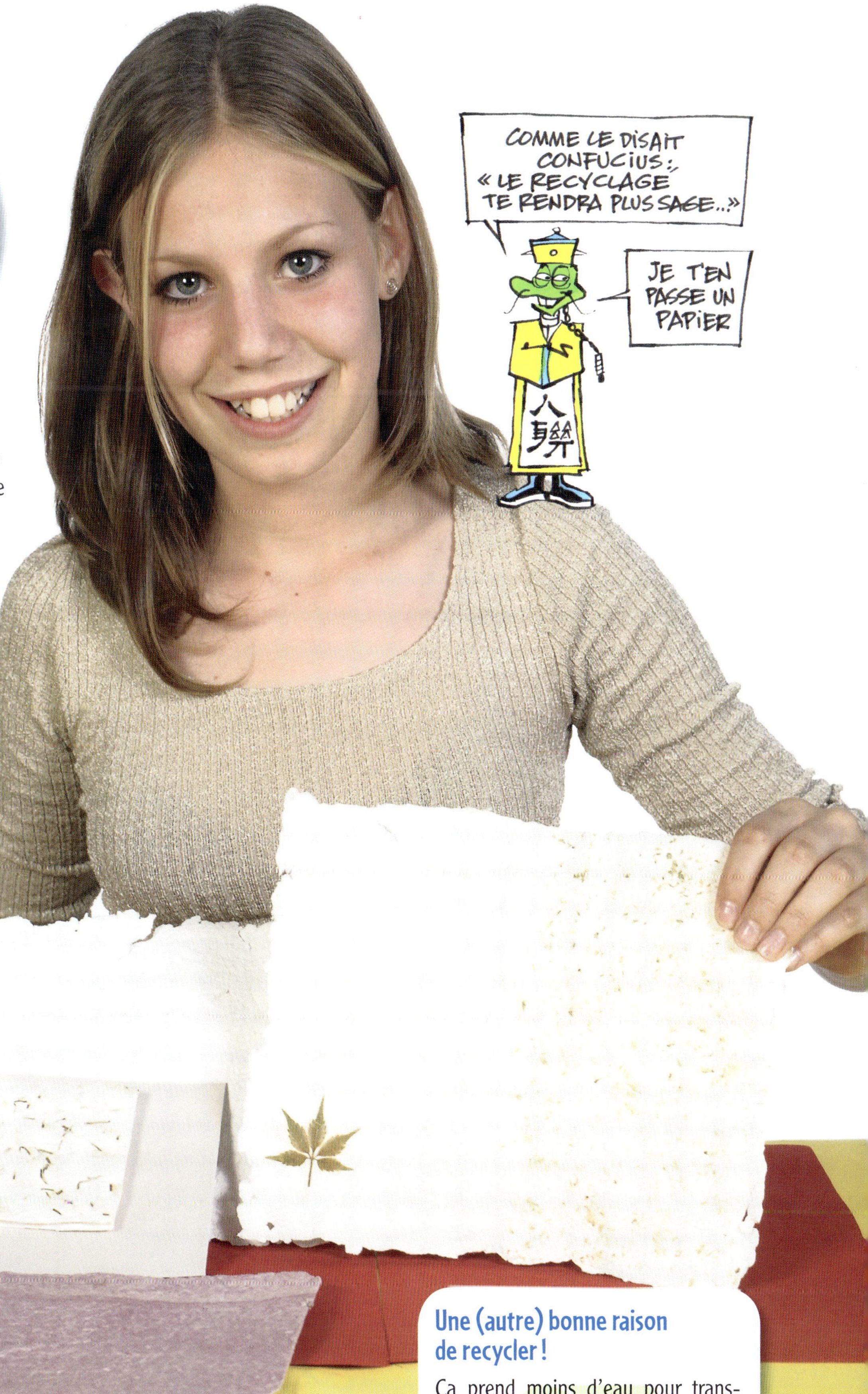

Pour faire un motif de dents, appuie sur le papier encore mouillé avec un peigne.

L'histoire du papier

La tradition chinoise rapporte qu'un certain T'sai Lun, alors fonctionnaire à la cour de l'empereur Ho Ti, aurait présenté la première feuille de papier en l'an 105. On ignore encore si cet homme est l'inventeur du papier ou s'il a tout simplement divulgué la nouvelle.

Une chose est certaine, ce sont les Chinois qui ont inventé une méthode pour fabriquer du papier à partir de fibres végétales. D'abord gardée secrète, cette technique pratique et peu dispendieuse fut peu à peu adoptée par tous les peuples de la Terre.

Une (autre) bonne raison de recycler !

Ça prend moins d'eau pour transformer les fibres du papier récupéré en pâte que pour en produire à partir du bois. En plus de sauver 17 arbres, la fabrication d'une tonne de pâte recyclée requiert environ 80 % moins d'énergie qu'une tonne de pâte neuve. Enfin, la récupération du papier contribue à diminuer l'enfouissement ou l'incinération des déchets.

Des objets électrisants

Tu marches sur un tapis, puis tu touches une personne. Ayoye ! Ce choc qui pique, c'est l'électricité statique. Voici une expérience qui utilise cette forme piquante d'électricité.

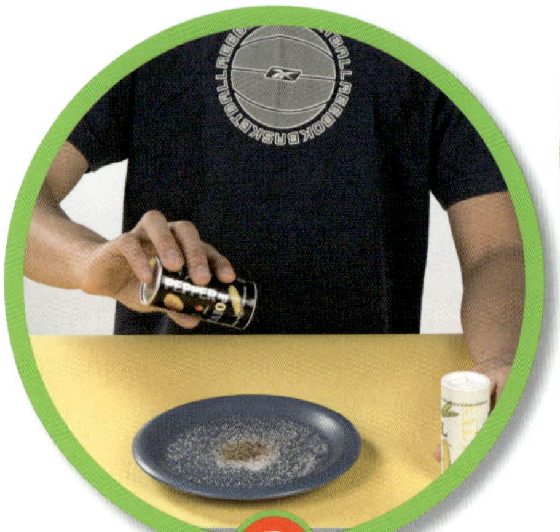

1 Verse une petite quantité de sel dans l'assiette. Ajoute du poivre et mélange-le au sel.

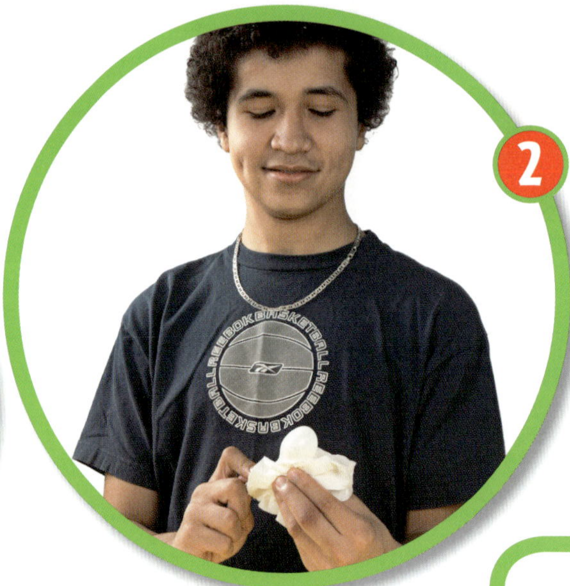

2 Frotte la partie bombée de la cuillère avec le mouchoir de papier. Tu peux aussi la frotter sur un chiffon de laine ou sur tes vêtements.

3 Approche la partie bombée de la cuillère de l'assiette. Ne touche pas à son contenu ! Les grains de poivre viennent se coller à la cuillère. Le sel, lui, ne bouge pas.

Ça ne marche pas ?

Change de cuillère de plastique. Certains plastiques sont plus difficiles à électriser que d'autres. Cette expérience fonctionne encore mieux par temps sec.

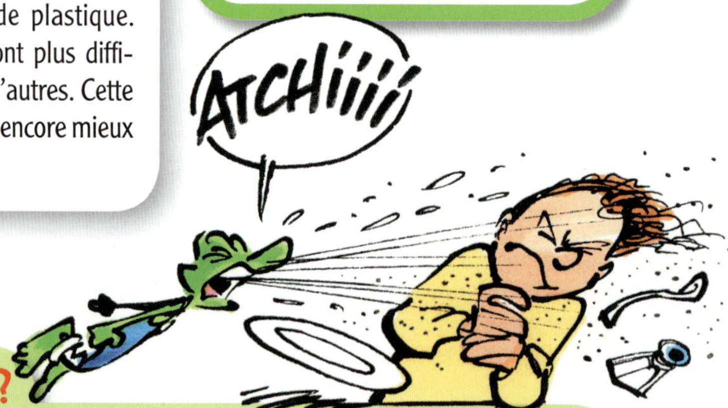

Il te faut :

- du sel
- du poivre
- une cuillère de plastique
- un papier mouchoir (ou un chiffon de laine)
- une petite assiette

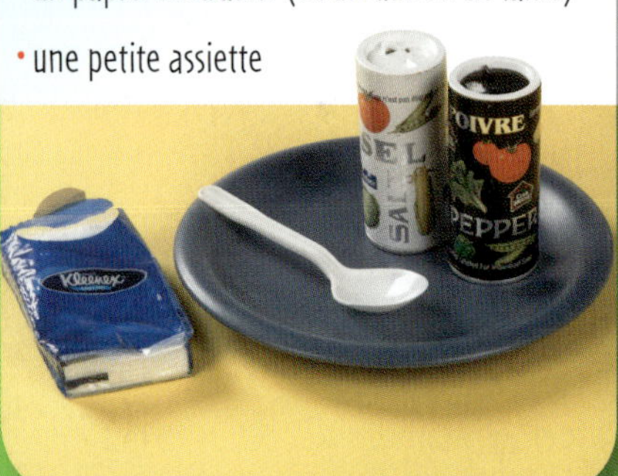

Que se passe-t-il ?

En général, les objets comme une cuillère ou une paille à boire contiennent autant de charges négatives que de charges positives. On dit qu'ils sont neutres. En frottant la cuillère ou la paille, tu as détruit cet équilibre.

Les deux objets se sont chargés négativement. Ils attirent ensuite les charges positives des objets neutres. Le sel aussi est attiré par la cuillère chargée. Mais comme il est plus lourd que le poivre, il ne quitte pas l'assiette.

Débrouillard : Mohammed El Malki Photos : Laurence Labat

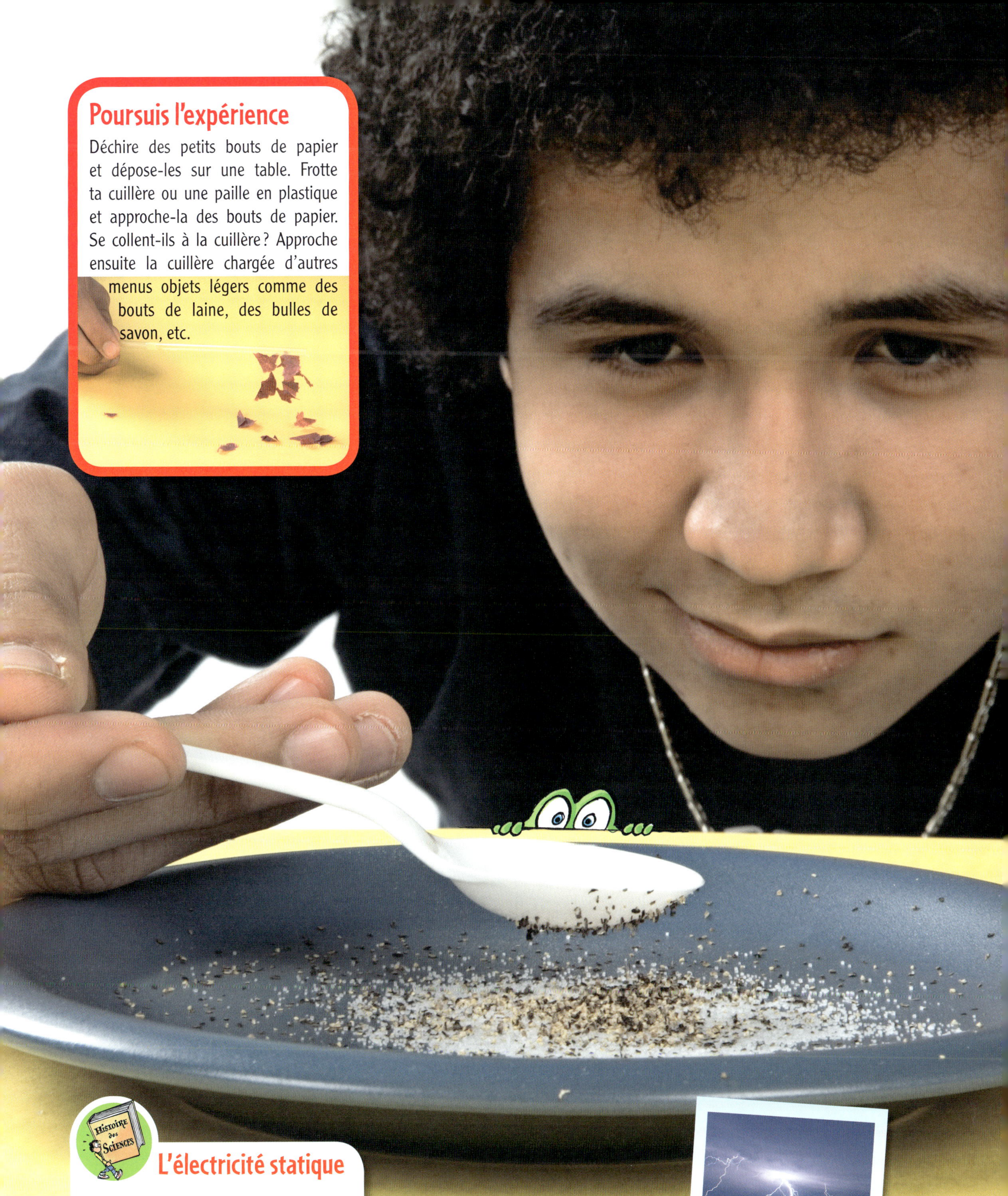

Poursuis l'expérience

Déchire des petits bouts de papier et dépose-les sur une table. Frotte ta cuillère ou une paille en plastique et approche-la des bouts de papier. Se collent-ils à la cuillère ? Approche ensuite la cuillère chargée d'autres menus objets légers comme des bouts de laine, des bulles de savon, etc.

L'électricité statique

Il y a près de 2600 ans, le savant et philosophe grec Thalès a constaté qu'en frottant de l'ambre (une résine fossilisée) sur du tissu, il attirait des petits brins de paille. Il venait de découvrir l'électricité statique. Le mot électricité vient du mot *elektron*, qui signifie « ambre » en grec.

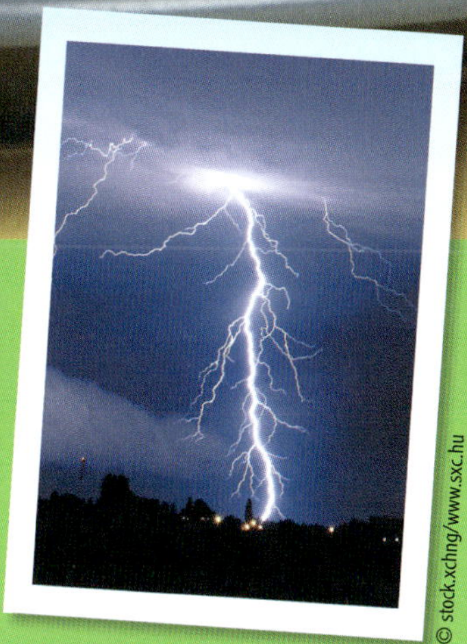

Les éclairs
Des charges électriques s'accumulent parfois dans les nuages. Elles sont causées par le frottement des gouttelettes d'eau et des cristaux de glace en formation. L'électricité reste emmagasinée jusqu'à ce que l'attraction entre les charges positives et négatives soit si forte qu'un éclair se produit entre les deux.

Une roche artisanale

La Terre a mis des millions d'années à créer les roches. Défie le temps et fabrique une roche en quelques minutes !

ATTENTION ! MANIPULATION D'EAU BOUILLANTE.

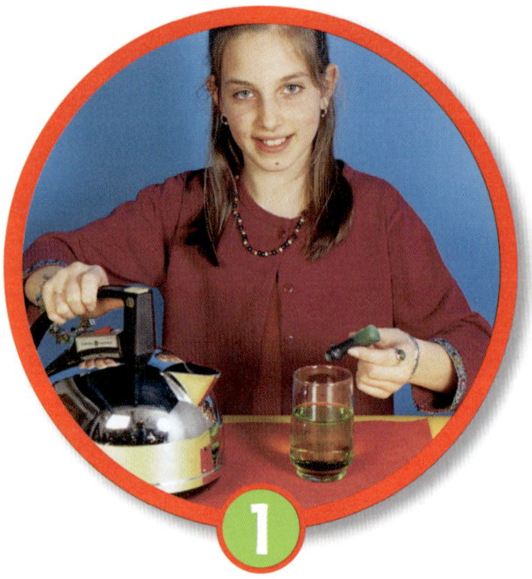

1 Verse une tasse (250 ml) d'eau bouillante dans un des récipients. Ajoute 15 cuillerées à table de sel d'Epsom et quelques gouttes de colorant alimentaire.

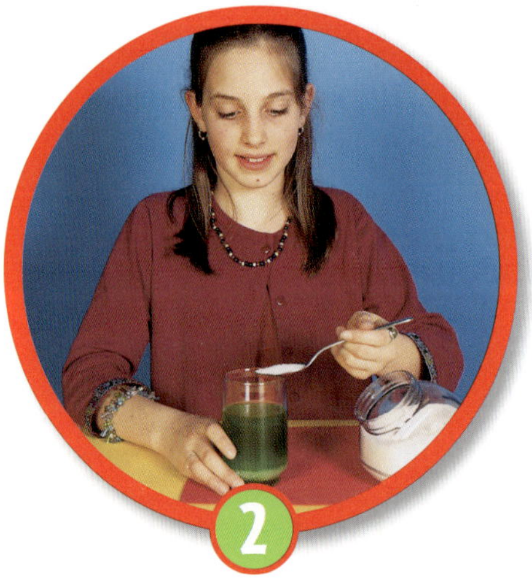

2 Dans le second récipient, dépose quatre cuillerées à thé de sable (sur la photo, nous avons ajouté des roches d'aquarium pour un effet plus spectaculaire). Verse trois cuillerées à thé de la solution salée sur le sable puis mélange afin d'obtenir la consistance d'une pâte à crêpe.

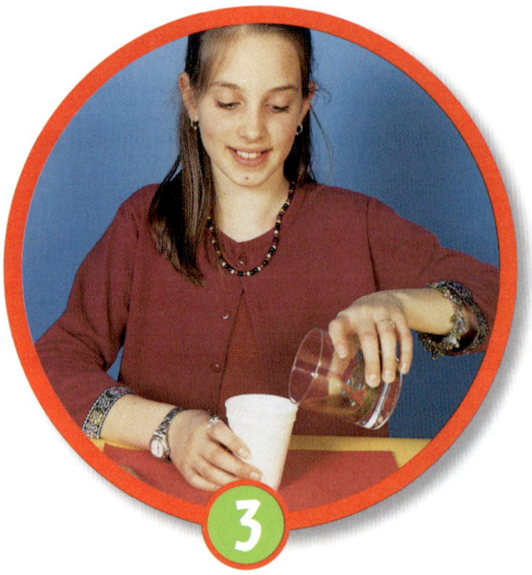

3 Verse ta pâte dans un verre en styromousse et fais-la chauffer au micro-ondes* pendant sept minutes à la puissance maximale ou jusqu'à ce que le surplus d'eau s'évapore.

*Tu n'as pas de four à micro-ondes ? Ce n'est pas grave ! Laisse sécher ta pâte quelques jours à l'air ambiant.

Il te faut :

- deux petits récipients allant au four à micro-ondes
- un verre de styromousse
- une cuillère à table
- une cuillère à thé
- 250 ml (1 tasse) de sel d'Epsom (disponible en pharmacie)
- 250 ml (1 tasse) de sable
- une tasse à mesurer
- un four à micro-ondes
- du colorant alimentaire

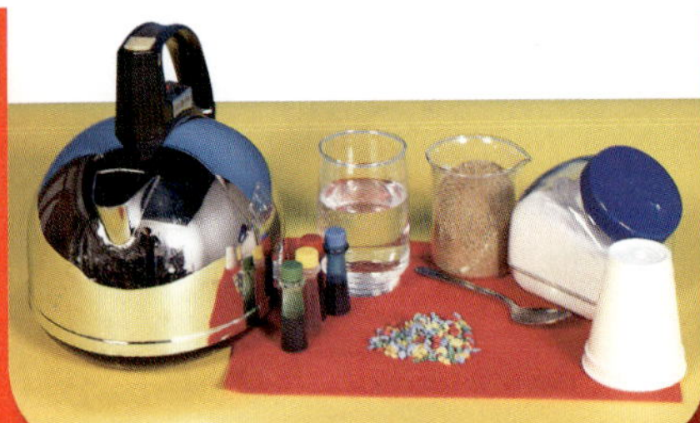

Débrouillarde : Audrey Bergeron   Photos : Laurence Labat

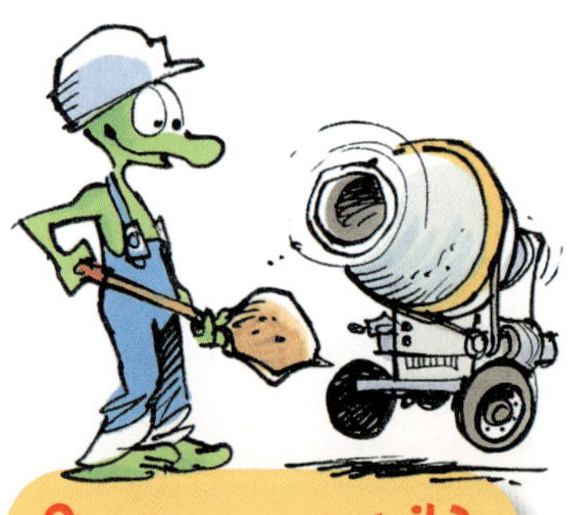

Que se passe-t-il ?

Tu as fait chauffer ta pâte jusqu'à ce que l'eau s'évapore complètement. En refroidissant, le sel a cristallisé autour des grains de sable. Il les a liés entre eux, comme un ciment. On dit que le sel est un ciment et le sable est un sédiment.

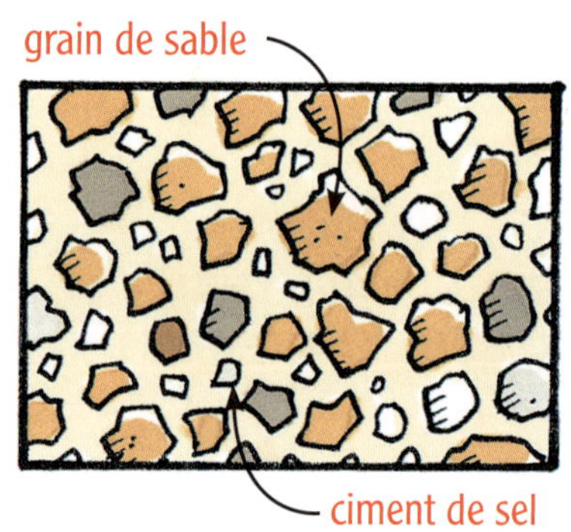

Dans la nature, il existe des roches faites de grains de sable compactés et liés ensemble par un ciment (surtout un ciment de silice). Ces roches sédimentaires portent le nom de grès.

4

Retire ta pâte du four. Laisse-la reposer quelques minutes, puis retire-la du verre en styromousse (déchire-le). Voilà ta roche !

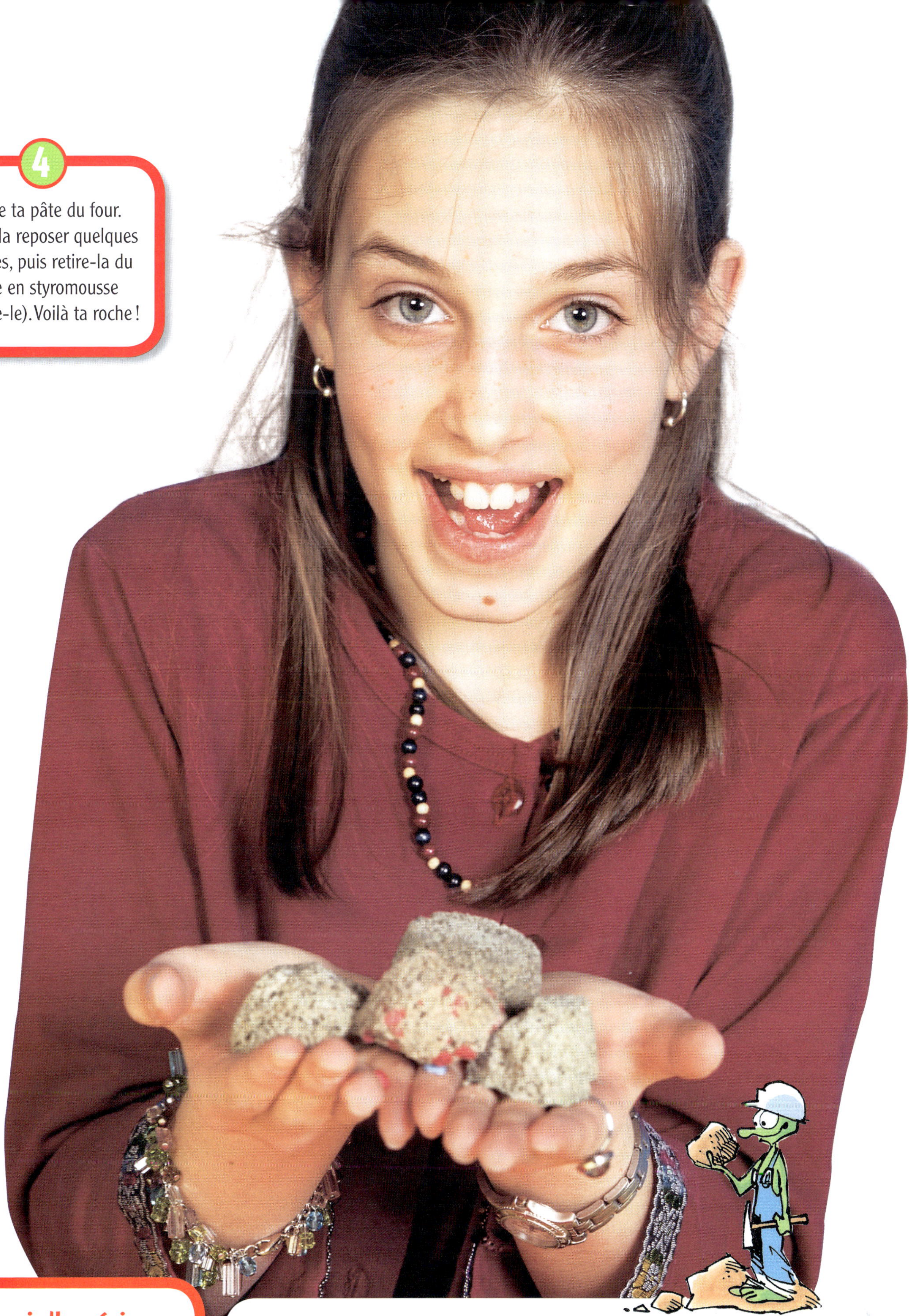

Poursuis l'expérience

Pour obtenir de jolis motifs, ajoute de la poudre de craie de couleur à ta pâte. Pour obtenir cette poudre, frotte la craie sur un tamis… au-dessus d'une assiette, bien sûr !

Les roches sédimentaires

Au fil du temps, l'érosion désagrège les roches en grains de plus en plus petits (sable). Ces petits grains peuvent s'accumuler en couches successives. Chaque couche qui s'ajoute comprime davantage les premières. La pression finit par souder les grains, formant ainsi un nouveau type de roches : les roches sédimentaires. Étant donné leur mode de formation, on retrouve souvent des fossiles dans ce type de roches. Le grès et le calcaire sont des exemples de roches sédimentaires.

Un potage multicolore

ATTENTION ! UTILISATION D'UNE CUISINIÈRE ET D'UN COUTEAU.

Cuisine un potage au chou et change sa couleur sans ajouter de colorant alimentaire !

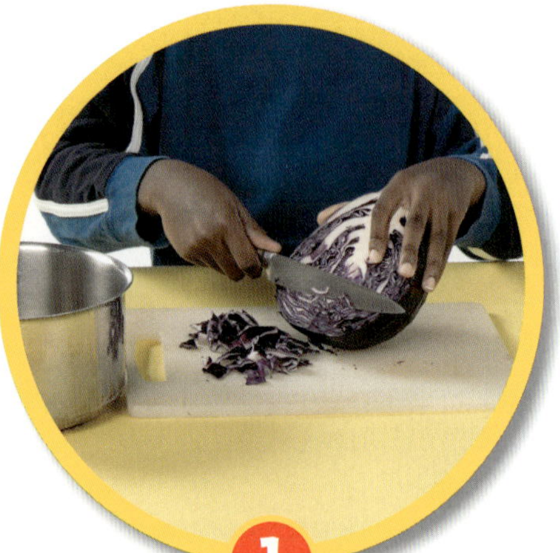

1

Hache un demi-chou rouge en menus morceaux. Transfère le chou dans une casserole et recouvre-le d'eau.

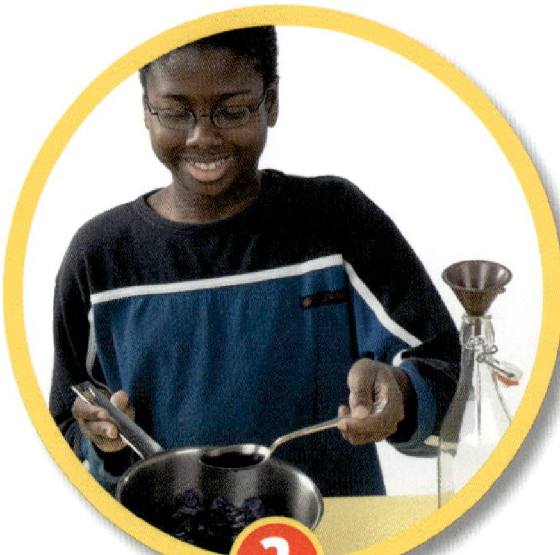

2

Porte le tout à ébullition et laisse bouillir une dizaine de minutes.

Si tu désires utiliser un four à micro-ondes, emploie un contenant de verre et règle le four à la puissance maximale pendant une dizaine de minutes.

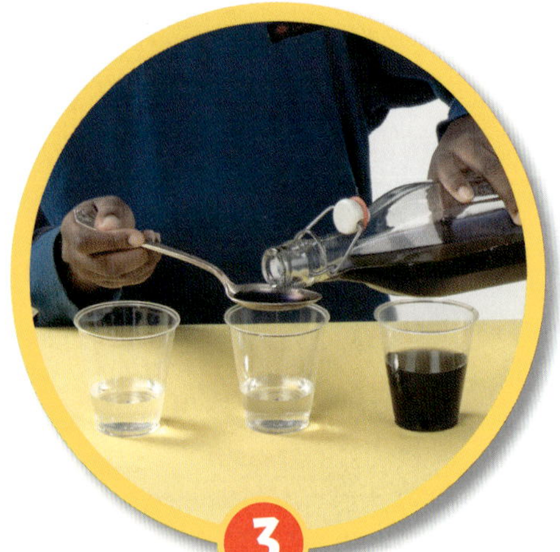

3

Lorsque ta soupe est refroidie, verse trois cuillerées à table de bouillon dans trois verres contenant trois cuillerées d'eau. À ce stade-ci, le bouillon est violet. Mets de côté un premier verre. Ce sera ton témoin.

Il te faut :

- du chou rouge
- de l'eau
- trois petits verres ou bocaux de verre
- une cuillère à table et une cuillère à thé
- une casserole
- du vinaigre
- du bicarbonate de soude (petite vache)

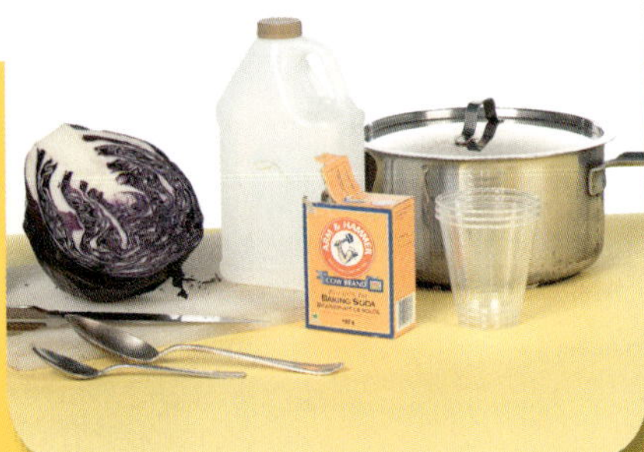

Débrouillard : Jacky Pyram Photos : Laurence Labat

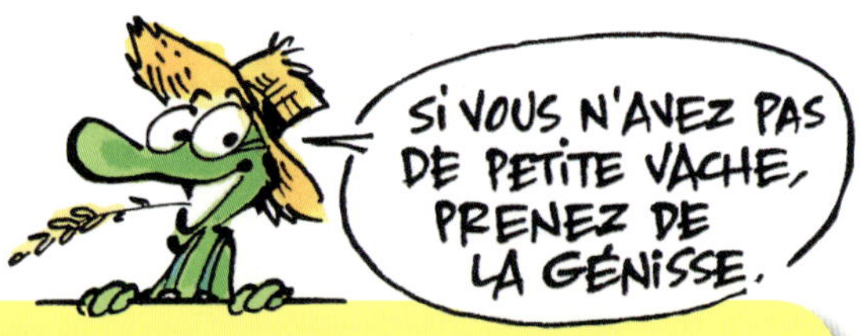

Que se passe-t-il ?

Le chou rouge contient des pigments qui changent de couleur sous l'effet des acides et des bases. Le vinaigre rend le bouillon plus acide, le faisant passer au rouge. De son côté, le bicarbonate est basique, et fait passer le bouillon du violet au vert. Ton témoin, intact, te permet de différencier l'acide (rouge) de la base (vert). Le bouillon de chou rouge est donc un bon indicateur chimique.

Joue au chimiste

Tu peux, comme un chimiste, suivre la progression de la réaction entre le vinaigre et le bicarbonate de soude en observant la couleur changer. Verse lentement le bouillon vert (basique) dans le bouillon rouge (acide). Le vinaigre et le bicarbonate réagissent ensemble. Observe bien le changement de couleur. Que peux-tu conclure ?

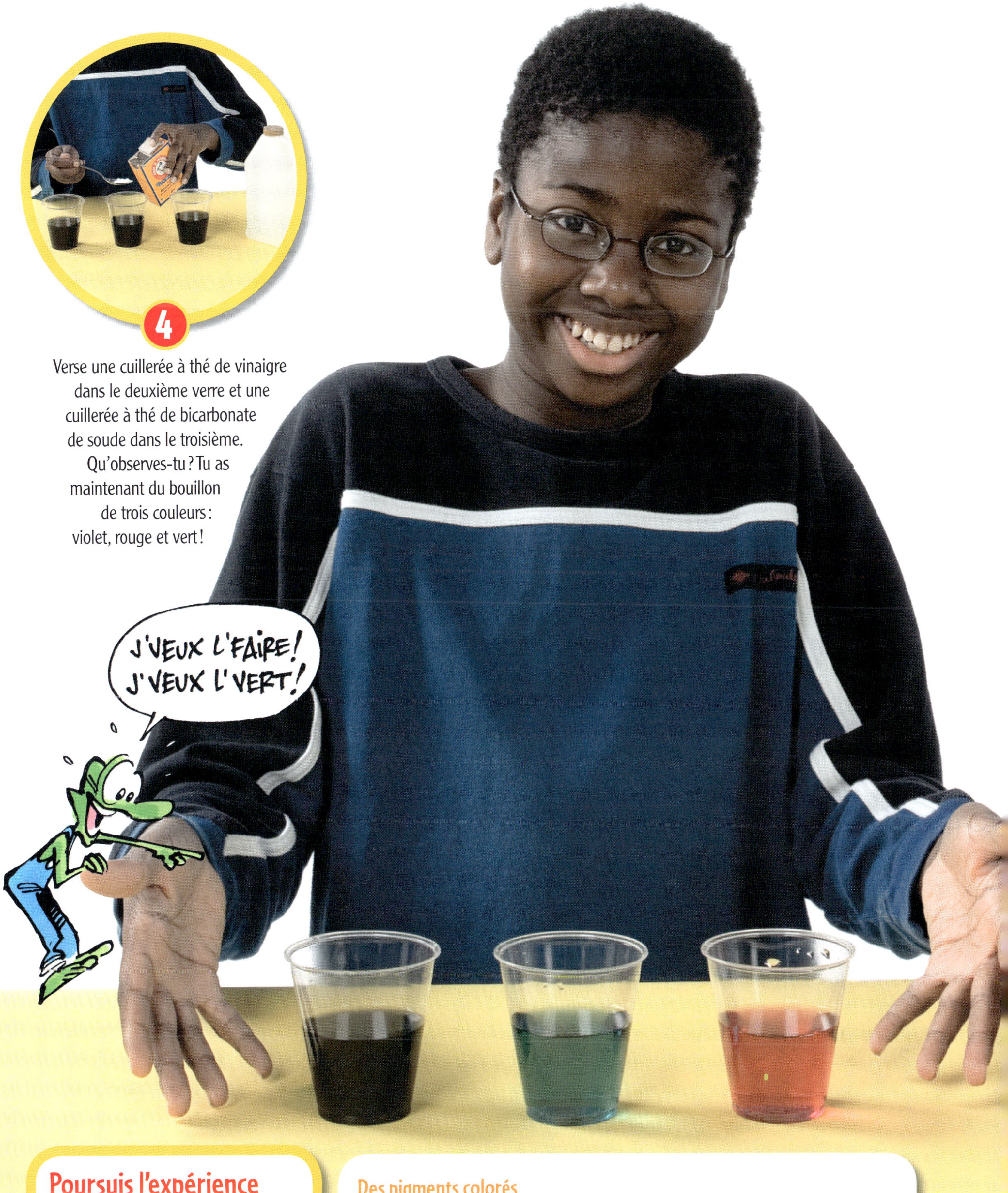

4

Verse une cuillerée à thé de vinaigre dans le deuxième verre et une cuillerée à thé de bicarbonate de soude dans le troisième. Qu'observes-tu ? Tu as maintenant du bouillon de trois couleurs : violet, rouge et vert !

Poursuis l'expérience

Tu peux aussi utiliser ton bouillon de chou pour tester d'autres produits comme du jus d'orange, du dentifrice, du yogourt, de la limonade ou du savon à lessive. Sont-ils neutres, acides ou basiques ?

Des pigments colorés

Ce sont des pigments qui donnent leur couleur aux plantes, aux légumes et aux fruits. Par exemple, le vert du feuillage est dû à la présence d'un pigment appelé chlorophylle, alors que l'orangé de la carotte provient du carotène. Plusieurs pigments changent de couleur selon l'acidité. Ainsi, les fleurs de l'hortensia sont bleues lorsque le sol est acide, mais blanches ou roses lorsque le sol est basique.

ATTENTION ! MANIPULATION D'UN COUTEAU ET D'UN SAVON TRÈS CHAUD.

Le secret de l'île flottante Ivory

Pourquoi le pain de savon Ivory flotte-t-il, alors que les autres coulent ? Cette expérience te révélera un secret bien gardé… et tu auras de quoi rigoler pour ton prochain bain !

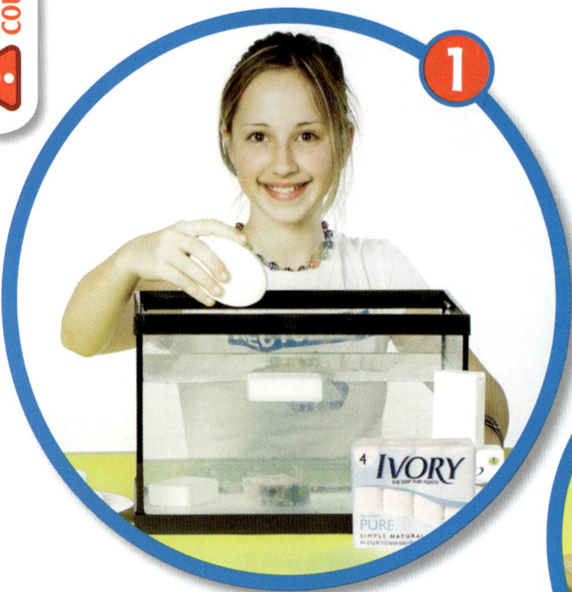

1

Remplis l'aquarium avec de l'eau. Déposes-y quelques pains de savon dont le savon Ivory. Observe ce qui se passe : le pain Ivory est le seul à flotter. Peut-être y a-t-il des bulles d'air à l'intérieur ?

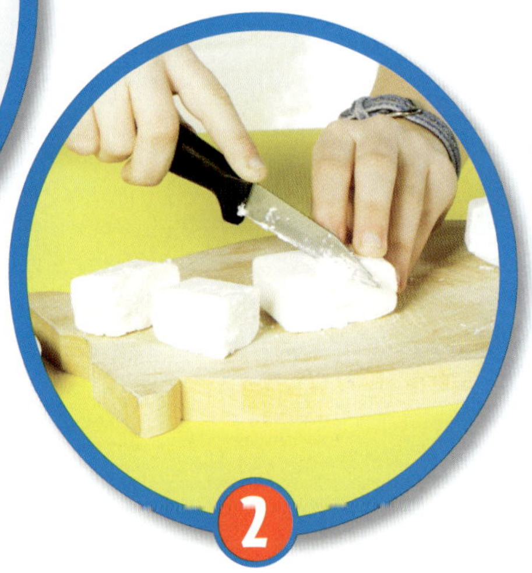

2

Pour vérifier, retire le savon Ivory de l'aquarium et dépose-le sur la planche à découper. Coupe le pain en deux. Vois-tu des bulles ? Non. S'il y en a, il faudra utiliser une nouvelle stratégie pour les découvrir.

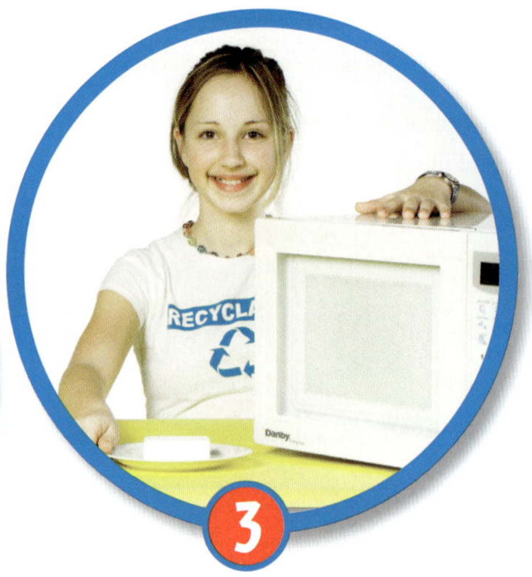

3

Dépose les morceaux ou une nouvelle barre de savon Ivory dans une grande assiette ou dans un plat allant au micro-ondes. Place le tout au centre du four.

Il te faut :

- un pain de savon Ivory
- un ou plusieurs pains de savon d'autres marques
- une planche à découper en bois
- un aquarium ou un bol transparent
- un couteau
- une assiette ou un plat de plastique allant au micro-ondes
- un four à micro-ondes

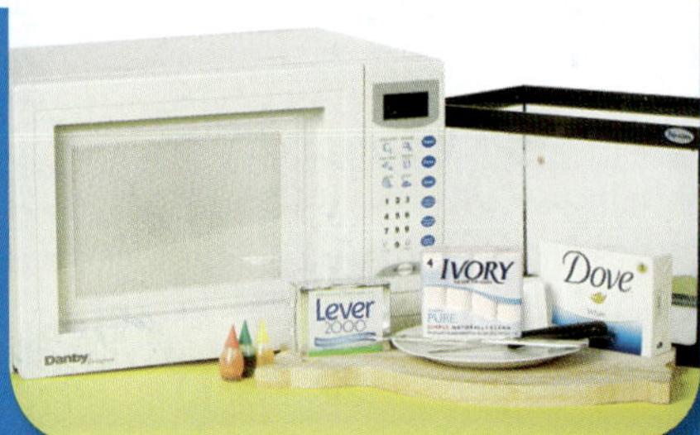

Débrouillarde : Justine B. Gravel Photos : Laurence Labat

Que se passe-t-il ?

Le savon de marque Ivory flotte car il est moins dense que l'eau. En d'autres mots, il pèse moins lourd que le même volume d'eau. Cela, parce qu'on a ajouté de l'air dans le mélange pendant la fabrication. Quand tu chauffes le savon au micro-ondes, les minuscules bulles d'air emprisonnées commencent à bouger plus rapidement. Ce mouvement s'intensifie, jusqu'à ce que les particules d'air réchauffé n'aient plus d'autre choix que de prendre de l'expansion. Le savon gonfle !

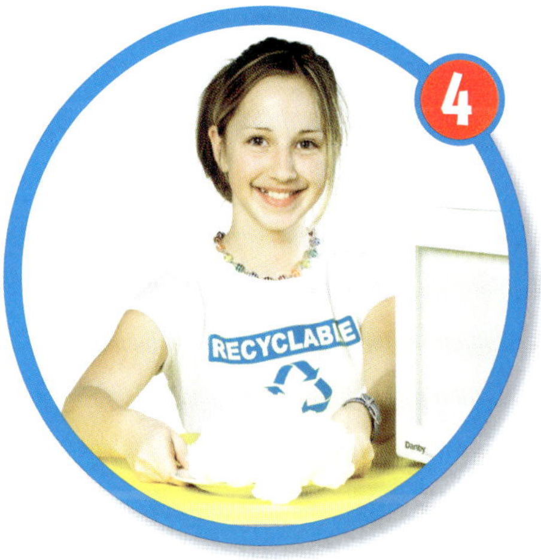

4

Programme ton four à micro-ondes à la puissance maximale pour une durée de deux minutes. Sois toujours prêt à intervenir car la puissance des fours à micro-ondes peut varier. De magnifiques structures ressemblant à des nuages jailliront du savon. Sois prudent et ne fais pas chauffer ton savon trop longtemps.

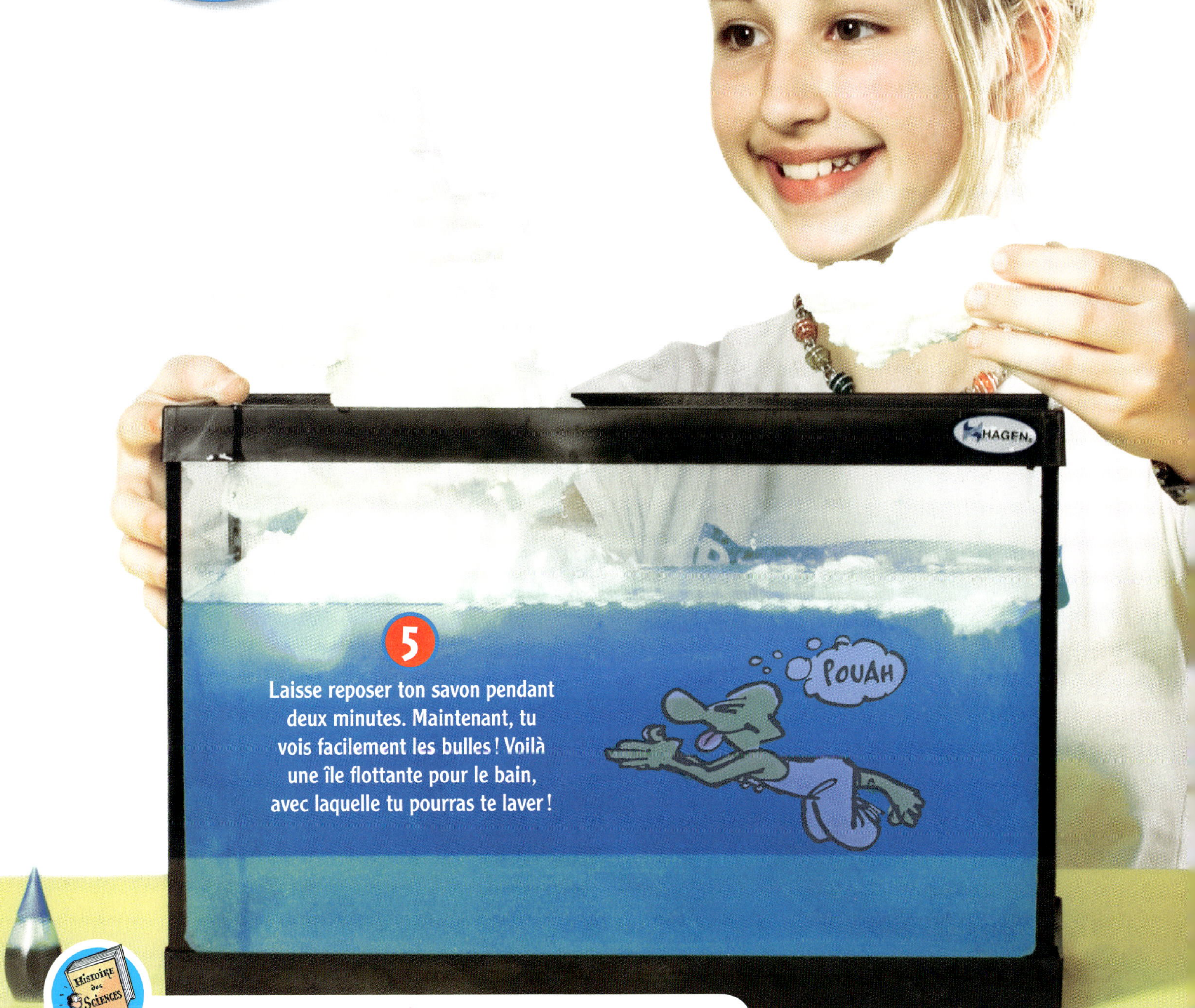

5

Laisse reposer ton savon pendant deux minutes. Maintenant, tu vois facilement les bulles ! Voilà une île flottante pour le bain, avec laquelle tu pourras te laver !

Les premiers savons flottants

Les savons flottants ont été découverts par accident en 1890. Un employé d'une usine de savons aurait oublié d'arrêter la machine qui brassait les ingrédients d'un pain de savon pendant l'heure du dîner. À son retour, le savon n'avait plus les mêmes propriétés qu'auparavant : il flottait. Les gens ont tellement aimé ce savon qu'on breveta peu après le procédé de fabrication.

Un ballon à réaction

Comment les fusées et les avions à réaction sont-ils propulsés ? Voici une expérience toute simple pour le découvrir.

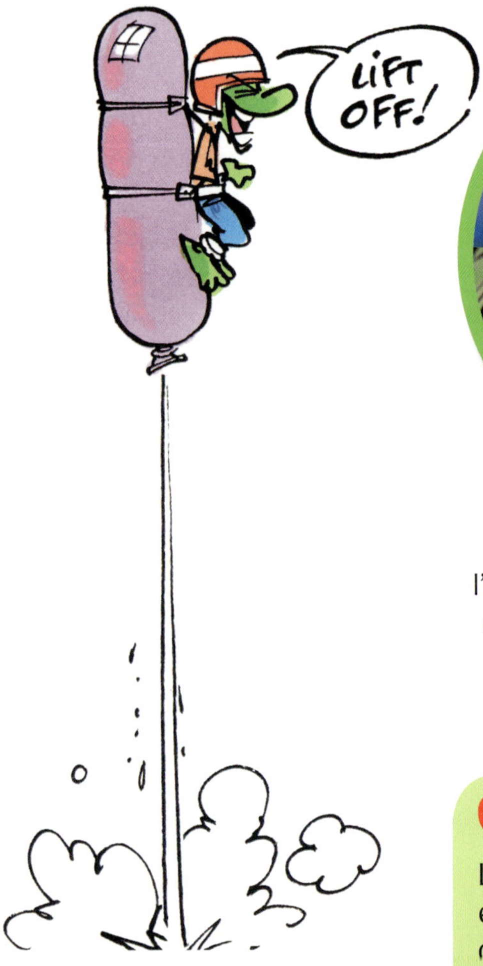

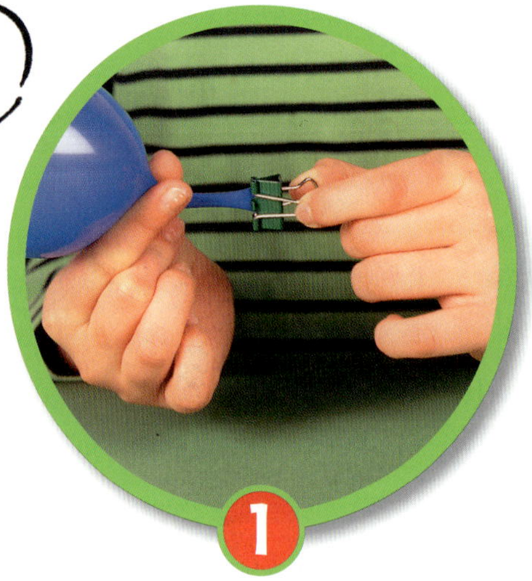

1

Gonfle le ballon et ferme son col à l'aide d'une pince. Surtout, ne fais pas de nœud. Si tu le désires, décore ton ballon avec des crayons-feutres.

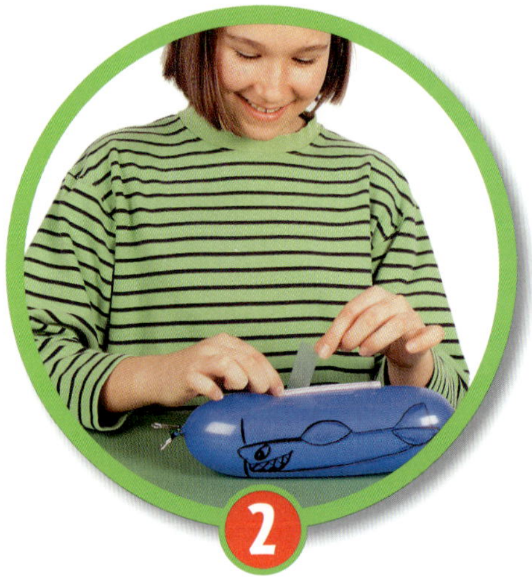

2

Coupe un bout de paille d'environ 10 cm de long. Fixe-le sur le ballon avec du ruban adhésif.

Débrouillarde : Stéphanie Faucher Photos : Laurence Labat

Il te faut :

- un ballon gonflable (allongé)
- une grosse paille à boire
- environ 3 m de ficelle très fine (ou de fil à pêche)
- des ciseaux
- du ruban adhésif
- une pince à papier
- des crayons-feutres non solubles dans l'eau (facultatif)

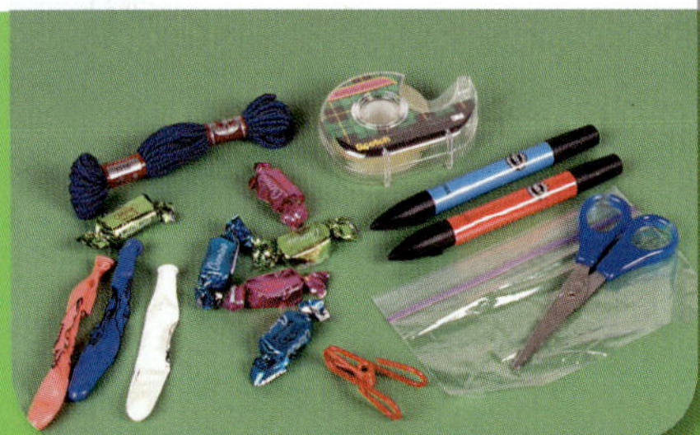

Que se passe-t-il ?

L'air dans le ballon exerce une pression en tous points de la paroi. Les poussées opposées s'annulent. Conséquence : le ballon est immobile. En retirant la pince, l'air s'échappe par l'ouverture arrière, et le ballon est propulsé vers l'avant.

Ton ballon répond ainsi à une loi physique fondamentale : **action = réaction**. La force de l'air qui s'échappe vers l'arrière (action) crée une force égale de sens contraire (réaction) qui agit vers l'avant et le propulse.

Ça ne marche pas ?

Ta ficelle est sans doute trop grosse pour le diamètre de la paille. Utilise une ficelle plus fine. Ou du fil à pêche. Évite la laine : si nous l'avons utilisée sur la photo, c'est seulement pour que tout soit bien visible.

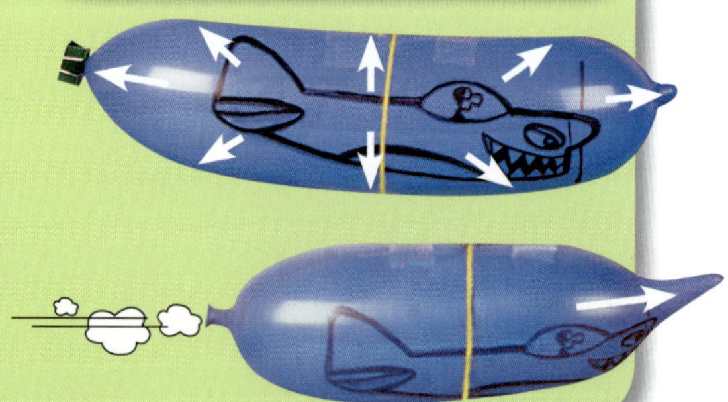

Et dans une fusée ?

Le même phénomène est à l'œuvre dans une fusée. Sauf que ce n'est pas de l'air comprimé qui fournit la poussée ; ce sont les gaz produits par la combustion rapide d'un mélange de carburant et d'oxygène. Les moteurs produisent ainsi une immense quantité de gaz chauds qui sont éjectés vers le bas. La fusée est alors propulsée vers le ciel, dans la direction opposée.

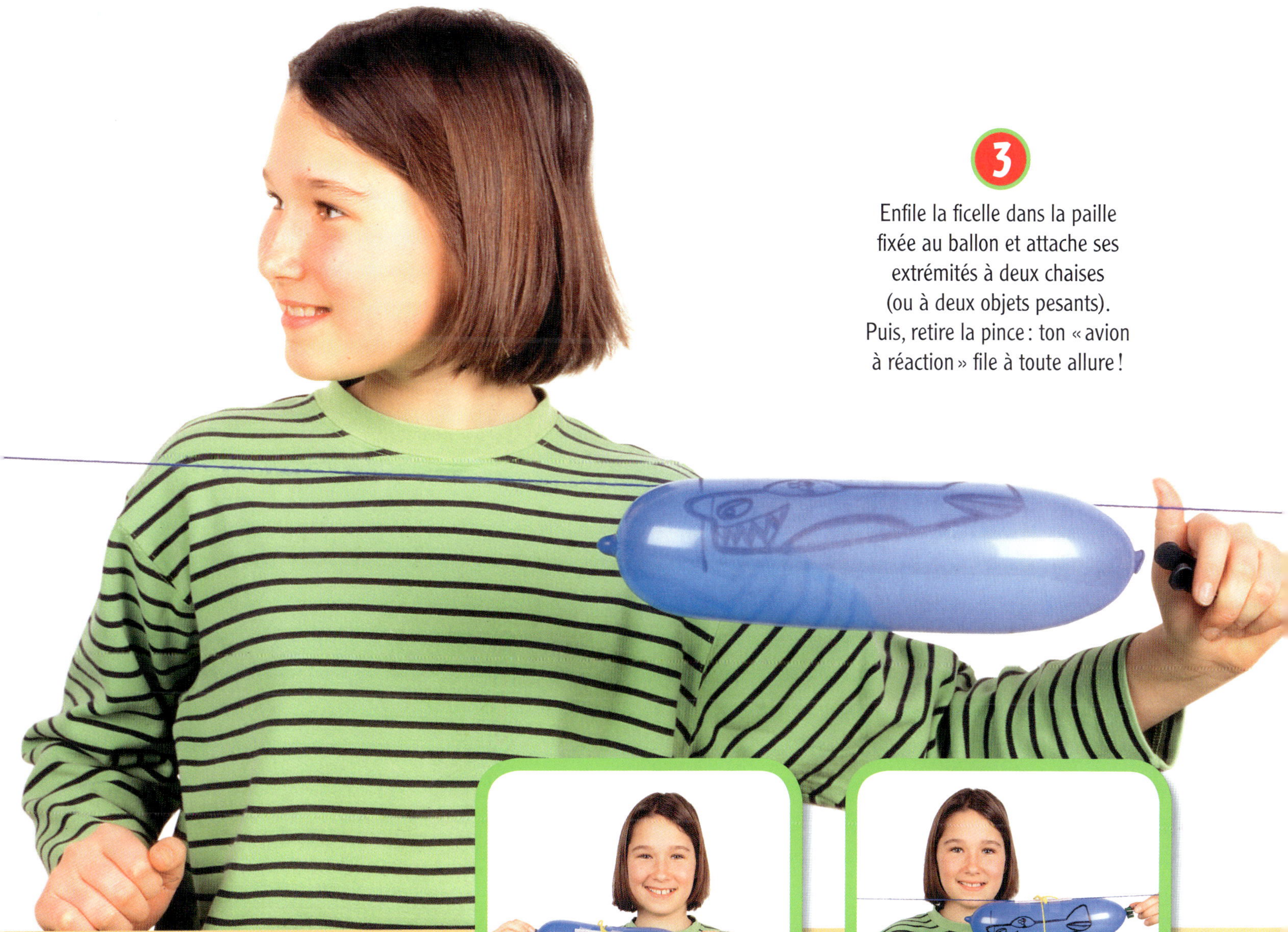

3

Enfile la ficelle dans la paille fixée au ballon et attache ses extrémités à deux chaises (ou à deux objets pesants). Puis, retire la pince : ton « avion à réaction » file à toute allure !

Poursuis l'expérience

Ton « avion » est-il assez puissant pour transporter du matériel ? Essaie ce qui suit !

Il te faut :

- un petit sac de plastique
- des bonbons (ou des gommes à effacer)

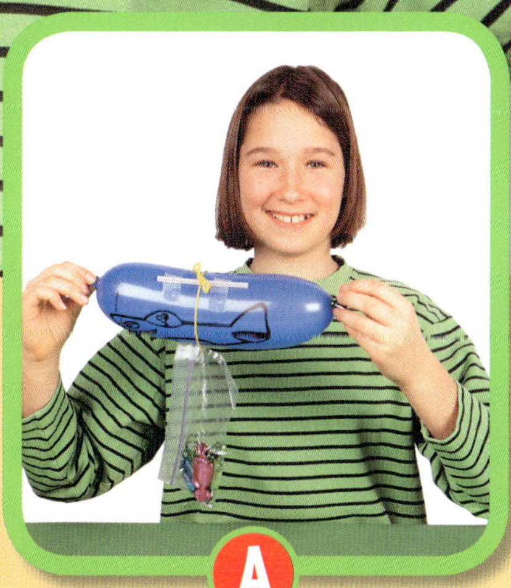

A

Mets quelques bonbons dans le sac de plastique. Perce le sac avec un poinçon ou la pointe d'un ciseau. Attache le sac au ballon à l'aide d'une ficelle.

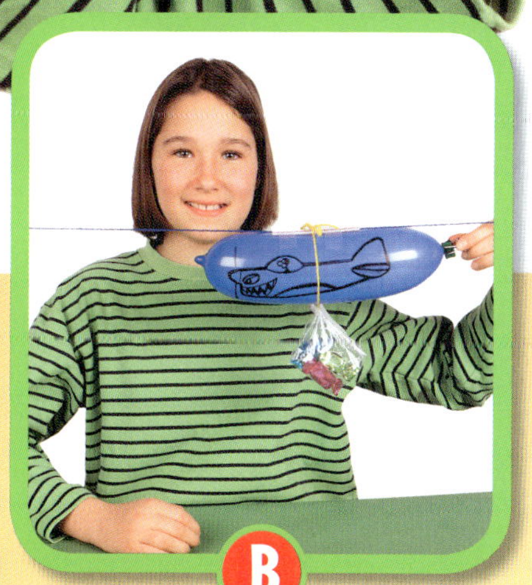

B

Répète l'expérience. Ton « avion » va-t-il aussi loin ? Comprends-tu pourquoi les modules de la Station spatiale internationale transportés par la navette spatiale sont faits d'aluminium, un métal léger ?

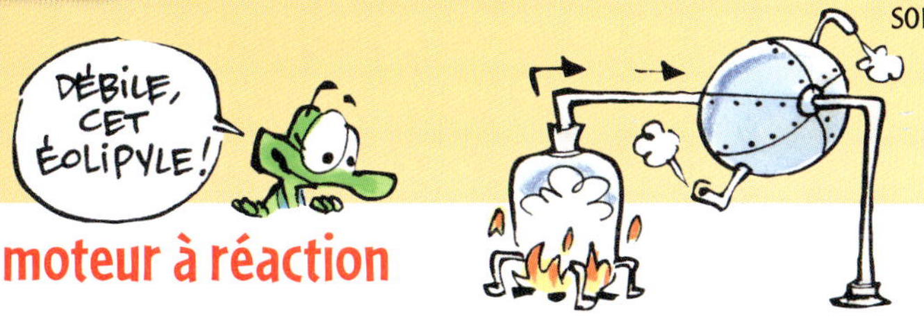

Histoire des Sciences

Le premier moteur à réaction

La création du premier moteur à réaction remonte à presque 2 000 ans. L'invention de Héron d'Alexandrie, l'éolipyle, comportait une chaudière remplie d'eau placée sur un feu. La vapeur produite était dirigée vers une sphère pivotante qui tournait lorsque la vapeur s'en échappait par deux conduits diamétralement opposés. De nos jours, les turboréacteurs des avions à réaction fonctionnent selon le même principe.

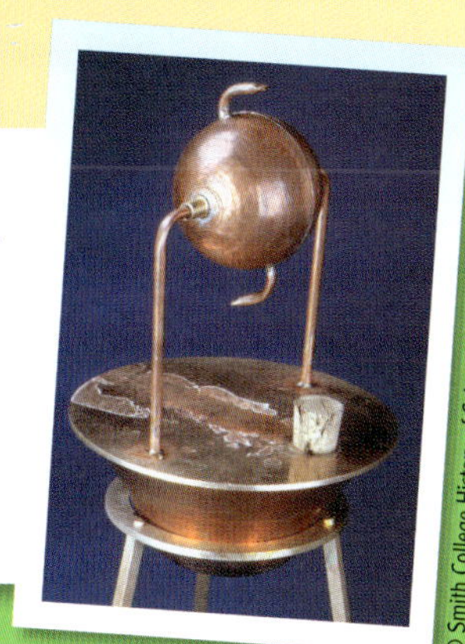

Une expérience attirante

Découvre les secrets d'une force invisible : le magnétisme.

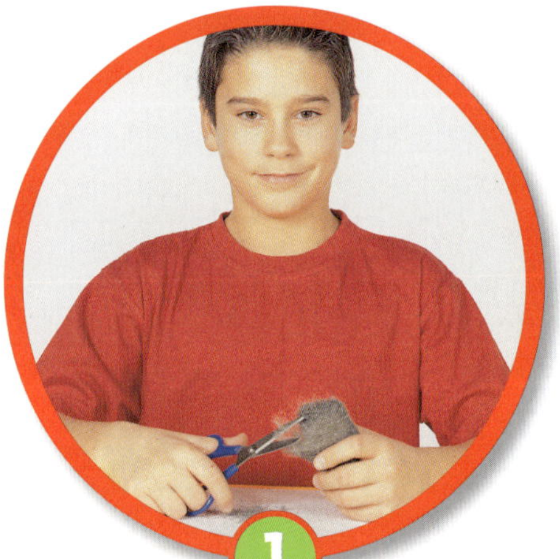

1 Si tu n'as pas de limaille de fer, coupe de la laine d'acier en morceaux minuscules.

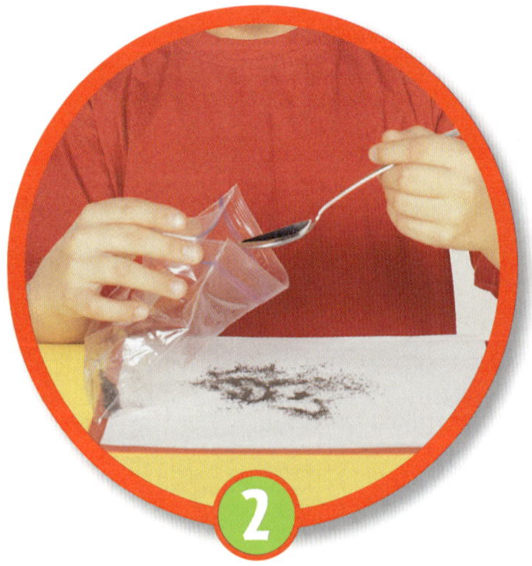

2 Dépose la limaille de fer ou les morceaux de laine d'acier dans le sac.

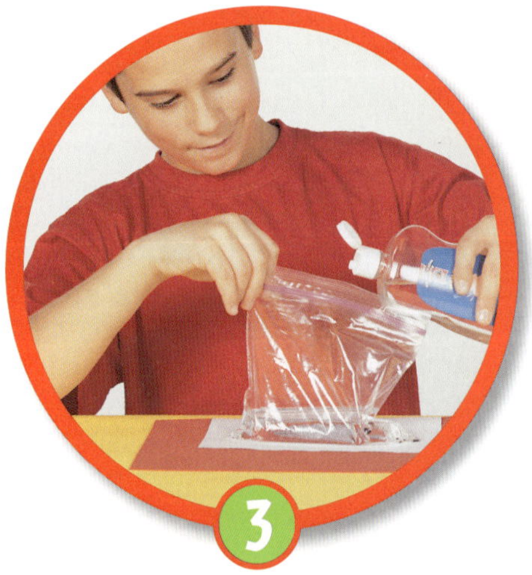

3 Verse cinq à six cuillerées à table d'huile (environ 80 ml) dans le sac et referme-le.

Il te faut :

- un sac de plastique avec fermeture (type « Ziploc[md] »)
- de l'huile pour bébé ou huile minérale
- de la laine d'acier sans nettoyant ou de la limaille de fer (disponible dans une quincaillerie)
- des ciseaux
- un aimant
- un carton blanc

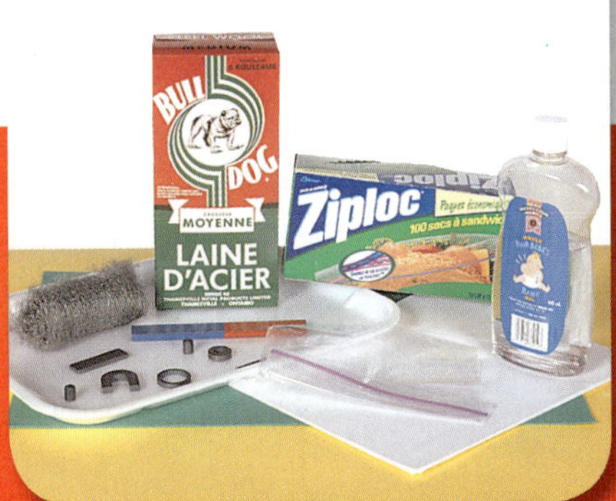

Débrouillard : PierLuc Dubé · Photos : Laurence Labat

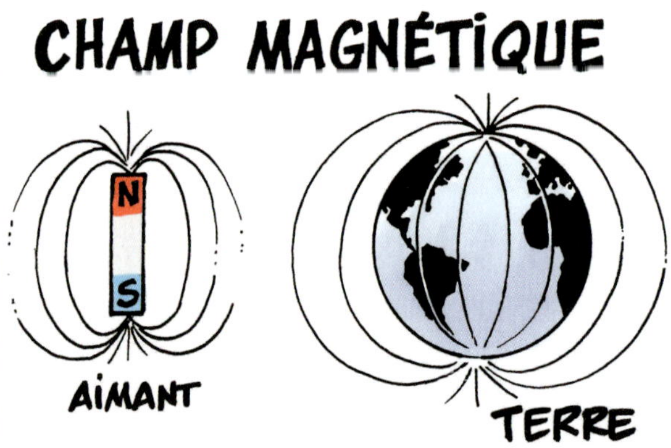

Un immense aimant

La Terre se comporte comme un gigantesque aimant droit, avec un pôle nord et un pôle sud magnétiques. Pourquoi ? Probablement à cause des métaux liquides constituant une partie de son noyau. C'est pour cela qu'une boussole indique toujours le nord. Son aiguille aimantée est attirée par le pôle nord magnétique de la Terre.

Que se passe-t-il ?

Le magnétisme se manifeste à l'intérieur d'une zone entourant l'aimant qu'on appelle champ magnétique. La limaille de fer s'oriente selon les lignes de force de ce champ. Or, les lignes de force d'un aimant vont de son pôle nord à son pôle sud. La limaille a permis de voir ces lignes.

Pourquoi ajouter de l'huile ?

Quand tu éloignes l'aimant du plat, l'huile garde la limaille dans la même position et l'empêche de retomber dans le désordre.

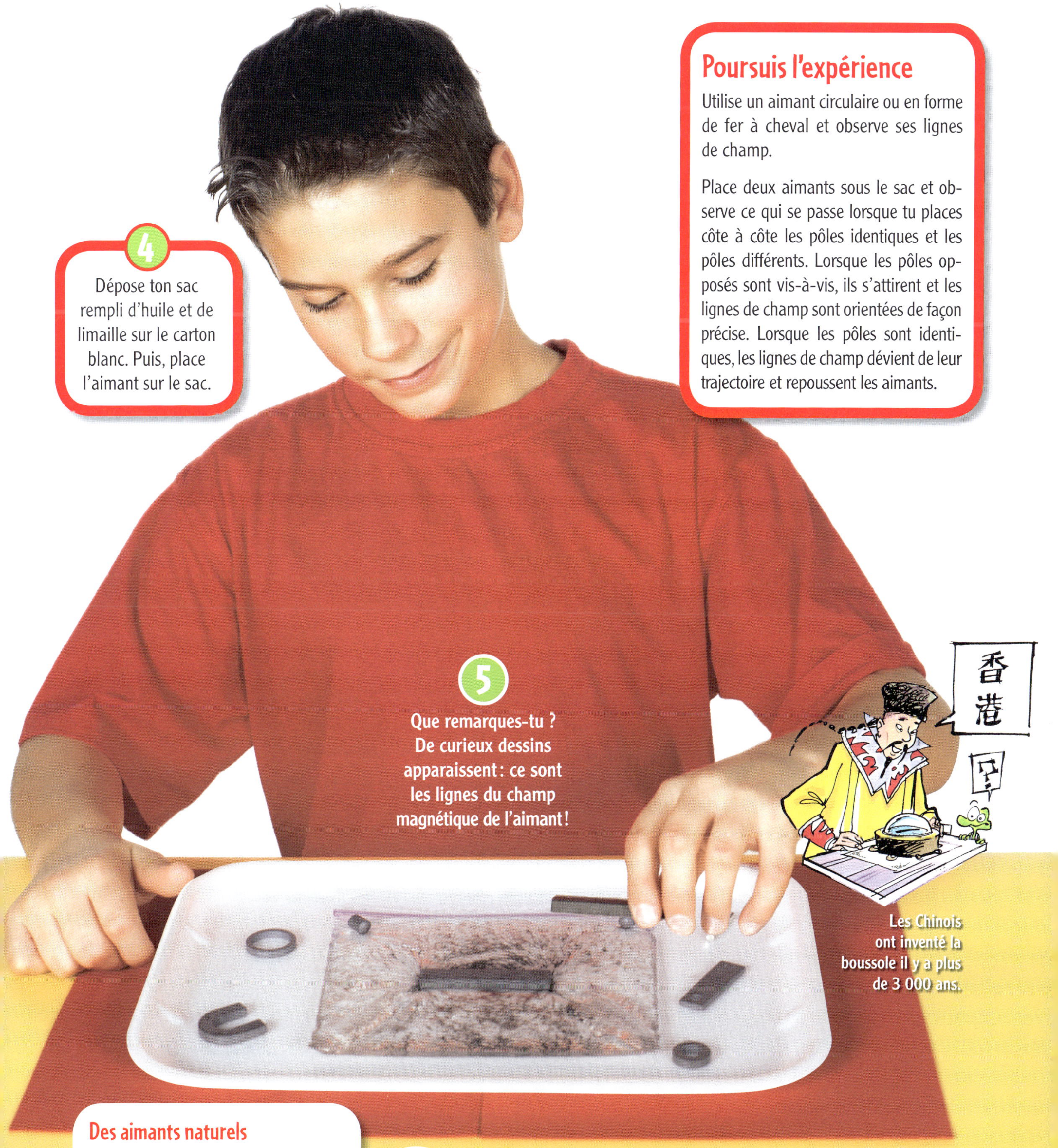

Poursuis l'expérience

Utilise un aimant circulaire ou en forme de fer à cheval et observe ses lignes de champ.

Place deux aimants sous le sac et observe ce qui se passe lorsque tu places côte à côte les pôles identiques et les pôles différents. Lorsque les pôles opposés sont vis-à-vis, ils s'attirent et les lignes de champ sont orientées de façon précise. Lorsque les pôles sont identiques, les lignes de champ dévient de leur trajectoire et repoussent les aimants.

4

Dépose ton sac rempli d'huile et de limaille sur le carton blanc. Puis, place l'aimant sur le sac.

5

Que remarques-tu ? De curieux dessins apparaissent : ce sont les lignes du champ magnétique de l'aimant !

Les Chinois ont inventé la boussole il y a plus de 3 000 ans.

Des aimants naturels

Il existe des aimants naturels. Ce sont des roches de magnétite. Leur structure est composée d'atomes dont les électrons tournent tous dans le même sens. C'est cet alignement particulier qui génère un champ magnétique. Certains matériaux, comme le fer et l'acier, deviennent aussi des aimants lorsqu'on les magnétise.

Histoire des Sciences

Le magnétisme

Il y a environ 2 500 ans, les Grecs ont fait la découverte d'une curieuse pierre qui avait la propriété d'attirer le fer. Ils croyaient que les morceaux de fer collaient à la pierre grâce à de minuscules crochets. Évidemment, ce n'était pas le cas ! Cette pierre noire était un oxyde de fer appelé magnétite. On qualifia alors tous les objets capables d'attirer le fer de « magnétiques ».

Frais, frais, le fromage

PEUT NÉCESSITER LA SUPERVISION D'UN ADULTE (UTILISATION DE LA CUISINIÈRE).

Faire du fromage, c'est une expérience culinaire vieille comme le monde.

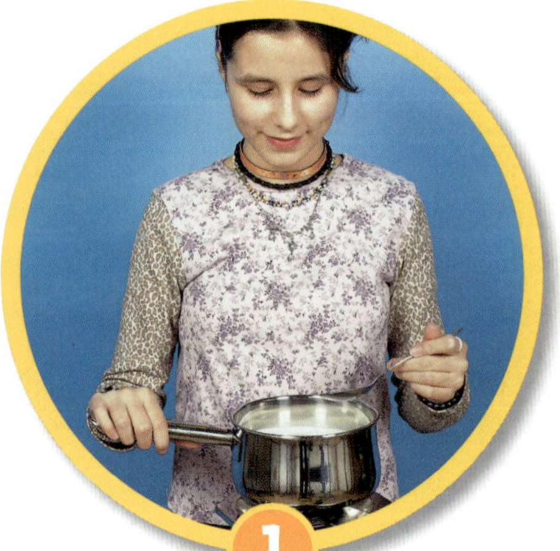

1

Fais chauffer un litre de lait. Amène-le à ébullition en brassant. Attention : réduis le feu dès que ça bout.

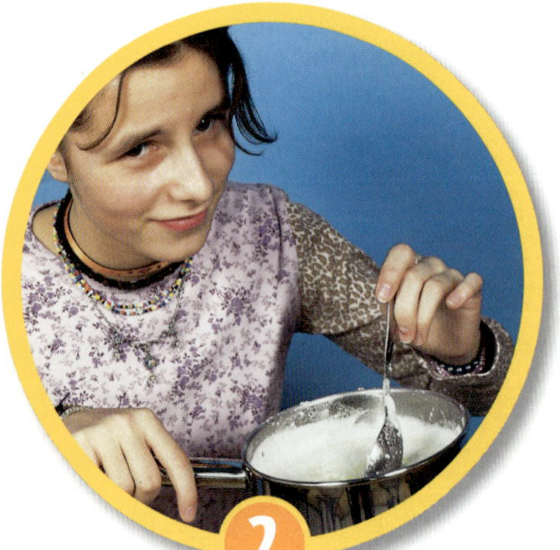

2

Ajoute le vinaigre et l'eau au lait. De petits caillots devraient se former. Laisse mijoter jusqu'à ce que le liquide se sépare du solide (environ cinq minutes).

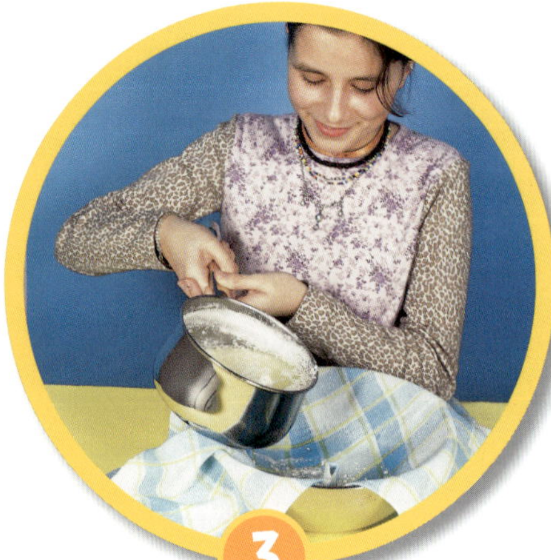

3

Retire du feu et verse ce mélange sur le linge à vaisselle déposé dans le bol.

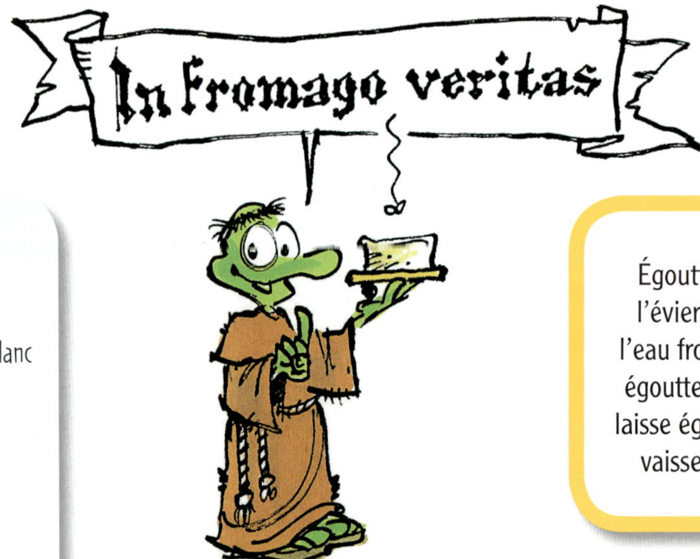

4

Égoutte et vide l'eau dans l'évier. Rince le mélange à l'eau froide à deux reprises et égoutte chaque fois. Ensuite, laisse égoutter dans un linge à vaisselle une demi-heure.

Il te faut :

- un litre de lait 3,25 %
- 45 ml (3 cuillerées à table) de vinaigre blanc
- 30 ml (2 cuillerées à table) d'eau froide
- deux linges à vaisselle (propres !)
- un bol à mélanger
- une casserole

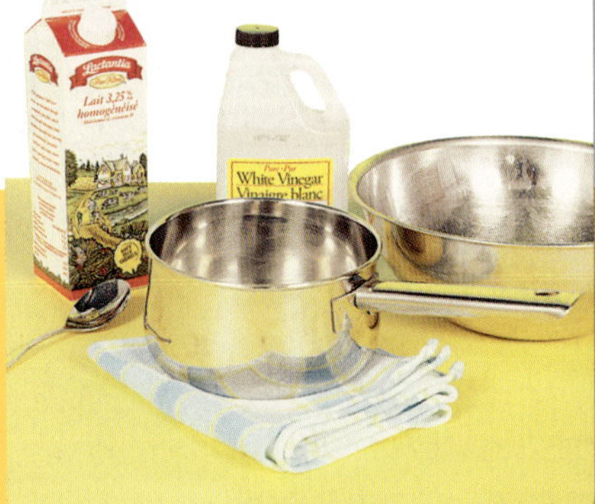

Débrouillarde : Karine Sicot Photos : Laurence Labat

Que se passe-t-il ?

Le lait est constitué d'eau, de lactose (un sucre), de caséine (une protéine), de graisse et de sels minéraux. À l'air ambiant, le lait s'acidifie. Cela est dû à la présence de champignons microscopiques. En se nourrissant du lactose du lait, ces champignons produisent un acide qui fait coaguler la caséine. La masse granuleuse contenant cette caséine s'appelle le caillé et le liquide qui se sépare est appelé le petit-lait. De la même façon, le vinaigre fait tourner le lait et favorise la formation rapide du caillé. Tous les fromages sont élaborés à partir de lait caillé.

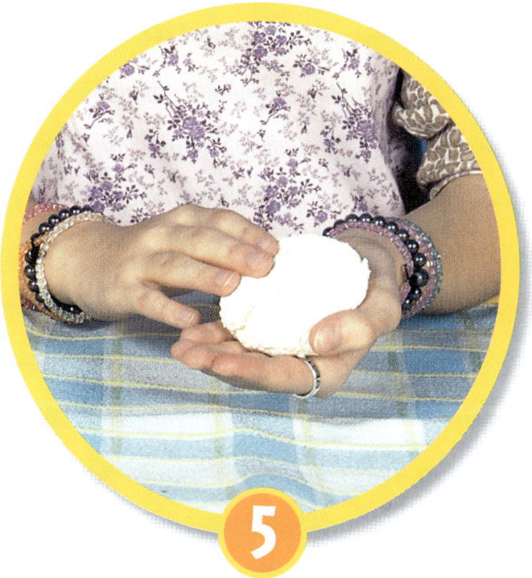

5

Pétris le fromage de façon à former une galette. Enveloppe cette galette dans le linge sec. Puis, déposes-y un objet lourd de façon à ce que la galette soit écrasée. Attends quelques heures.

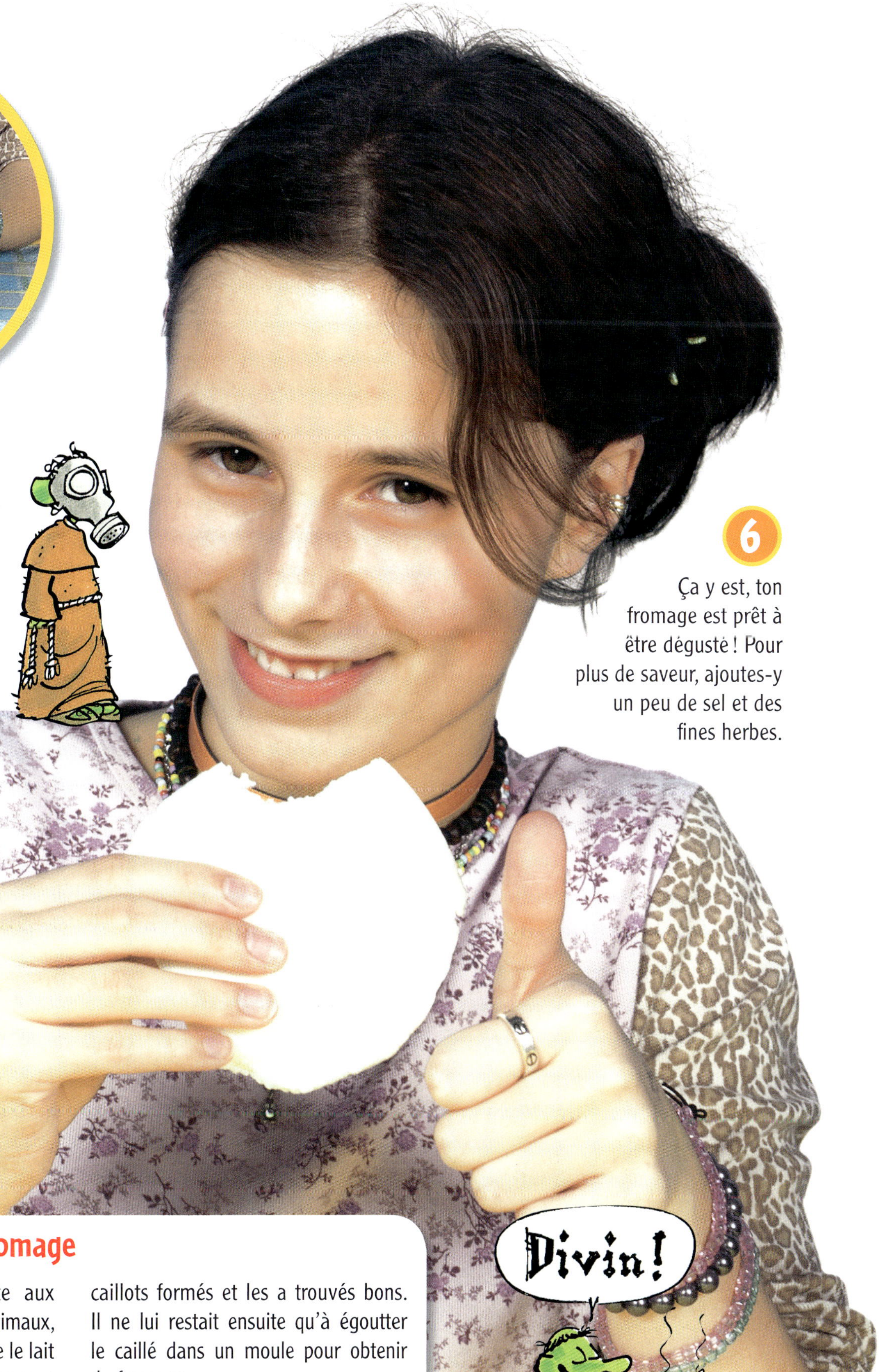

6

Ça y est, ton fromage est prêt à être dégusté ! Pour plus de saveur, ajoutes-y un peu de sel et des fines herbes.

L'origine du fromage

L'histoire du fromage remonte aux débuts de la domestication des animaux, il y a environ 10 000 ans. Comme le lait aigrit rapidement, surtout dans les pays chauds, on a vite trouvé des façons de le conserver. L'invention, ou plutôt la découverte du fromage fut probablement le fruit du hasard. Après avoir observé du lait coaguler, quelqu'un a sûrement décidé de goûter aux caillots formés et les a trouvés bons. Il ne lui restait ensuite qu'à égoutter le caillé dans un moule pour obtenir du fromage.

Beaucoup plus tard, au Moyen Âge, les moines ont mis au point plusieurs recettes de fromages et techniques d'affinage, ou maturation, encore utilisées de nos jours.

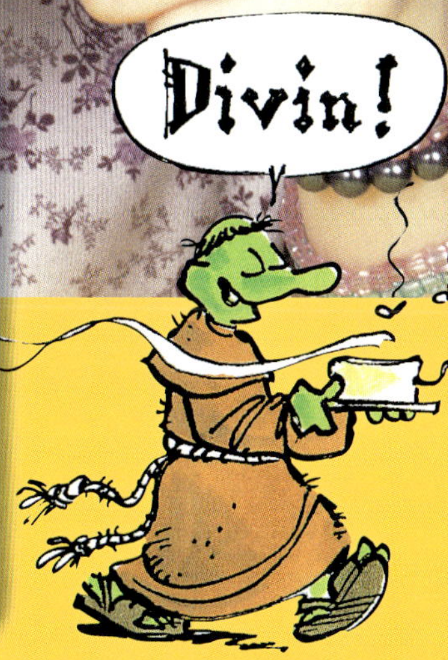

La poussée d'Archimède

Flotter sur l'eau c'est bien, mais flotter entre deux liquides, c'est encore mieux ! Voici comment relever ce défi.

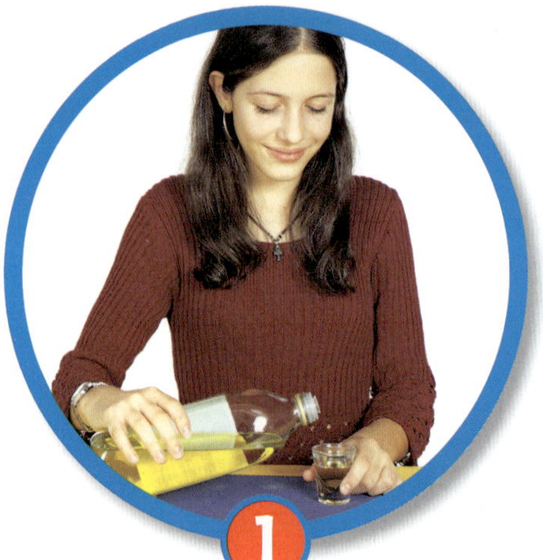

1

Verse de l'huile d'olive dans le petit verre jusqu'à ras bord. Dépose le petit verre dans le grand verre (ou le vase).

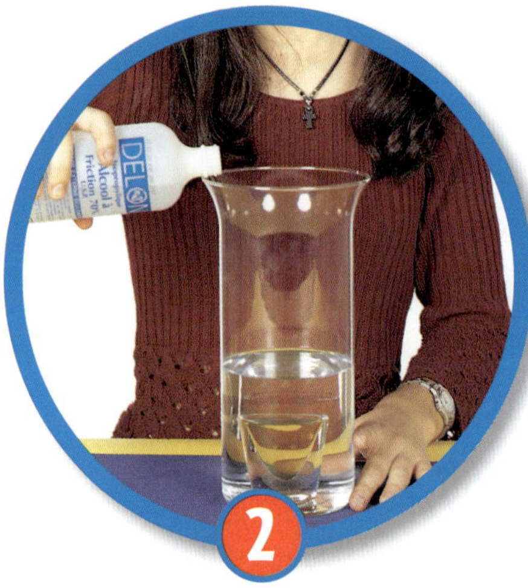

2

Remplis à moitié le grand verre d'alcool à friction. Fais couler l'alcool le long de la paroi pour éviter les turbulences. Le petit verre doit être entièrement recouvert d'alcool à friction.

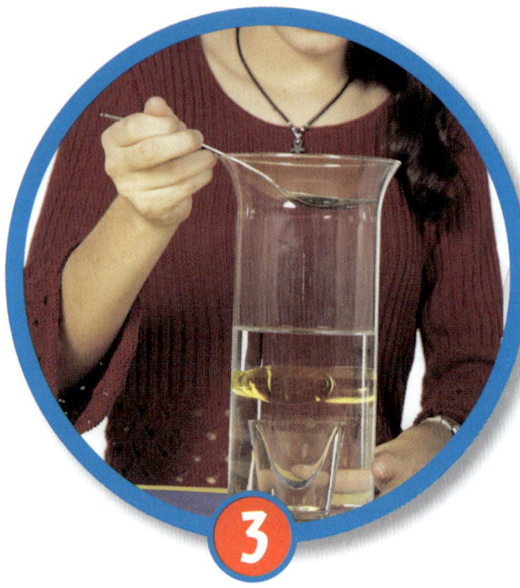

3

Ajoute de l'eau à l'aide d'une cuillère, en la faisant glisser sur la paroi. (Ici, nous avons ajouté du colorant.)

Débrouillarde : Cassandra Rivet-Therrien Photos : Laurence Labat

Il te faut :

- de l'huile d'olive
- un petit verre à liqueur
- un grand verre ou vase (à fleurs)
- de l'alcool à friction
- une cuillère
- du colorant alimentaire (facultatif)

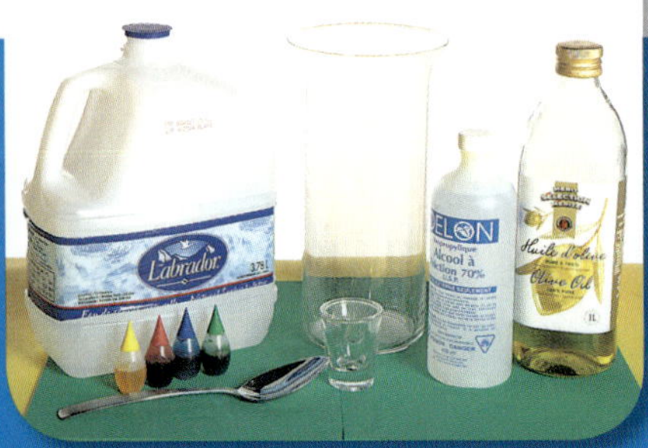

Que se passe-t-il ?

Quand un objet est plongé dans un liquide, il est soumis à deux forces : la gravité (ou son poids), qui le tire vers le bas, et la poussée d'Archimède, qui le tire vers le haut. C'est le fameux principe d'Archimède !

Le célèbre savant grec constata que la force de cette poussée de bas en haut était égale au poids de l'eau déplacée. Si l'objet est plus dense que le liquide, le poids l'emporte sur la poussée d'Archimède et l'objet coule. Si l'objet est moins dense, il flotte. Si l'objet est de même densité que le liquide et qu'il est complètement immergé, il demeure immobile.

L'huile est plus dense que l'alcool et moins dense que l'eau. Elle coule donc dans l'alcool et flotte dans l'eau. Or, lorsque tu ajoutes de l'eau à l'alcool, tu augmentes la densité du mélange (eau et alcool) jusqu'à atteindre la même densité que l'huile. À ce moment, l'huile est soumise à deux forces opposées de même intensité. L'huile reste donc immobile.

Pourquoi l'huile prend-elle la forme d'une boule ?

La goutte d'huile cherche à minimiser sa surface de contact avec le liquide. La sphère est la forme qui présente la plus petite surface.

Ils flottent !

D'autres liquides que l'huile, comme le pétrole et l'essence, sont moins denses que l'eau. C'est pourquoi le pétrole qui s'écoule accidentellement des pétroliers est si dommageable pour l'environnement. Comme il flotte, il reste à la surface de l'eau et s'étend sur de grandes distances. C'est aussi pourquoi il est difficile d'éteindre un feu d'essence avec de l'eau car l'essence flotte sur l'eau en restant enflammée.

Que remarques-tu ?

Dans le petit verre, la surface de l'huile se courbe de plus en plus. Lorsque la quantité d'eau est suffisante, une boule d'huile flotte dans le mélange.

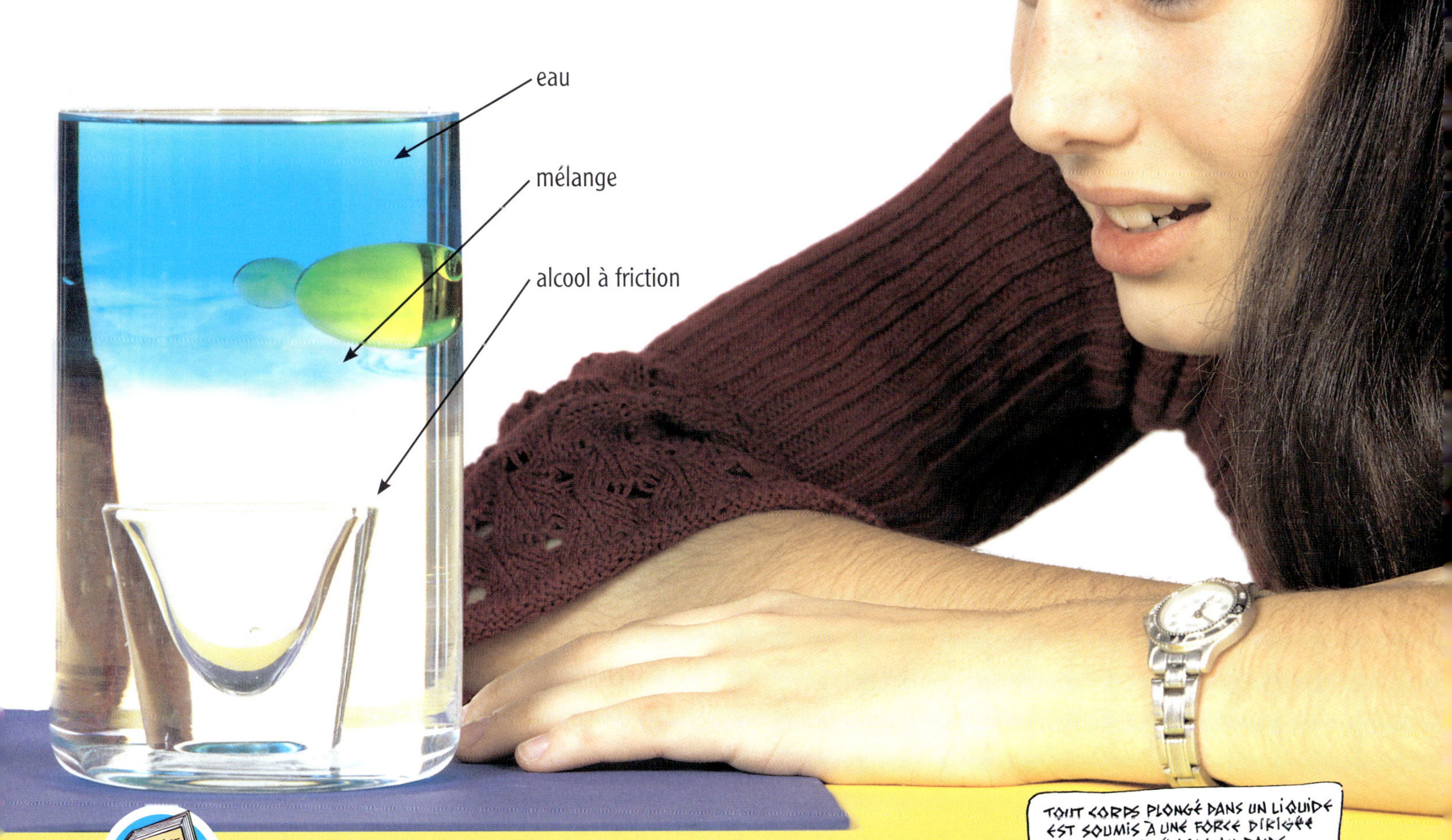

Le savant Archimède

Il y a environ 2 200 ans, Archimède étudia la géométrie et inventa toutes sortes de machines. On raconte que c'est en prenant son bain que le savant grec a élaboré son fameux principe. En entrant dans sa baignoire, il remarqua que plus il s'enfonçait dans l'eau, plus le niveau de l'eau montait. Il serait alors sorti dans la rue, tout nu, en s'écriant « *Eurêka !* », ce qui signifie « J'ai trouvé ! » en grec. Il venait de constater que la quantité d'eau déplacée avait un rapport avec les dimensions (le volume) et le poids de l'objet immergé. Ses observations allaient ensuite donner naissance au principe d'Archimède expliquant, entre autres, comment les objets flottent.

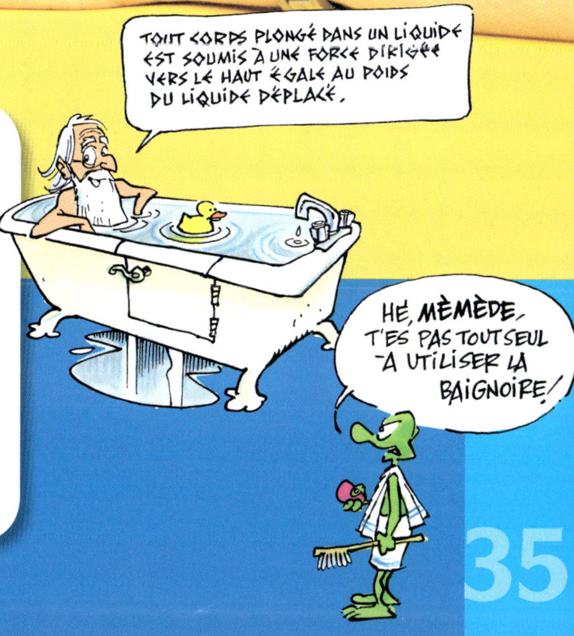

ATTENTION ! IL EST PRÉFÉRABLE DE RÉALISER CETTE EXPÉRIENCE DEHORS !

Le geyser jaillissant

Voici ce qui arrive quand on mélange bonbons et boisson gazeuse…

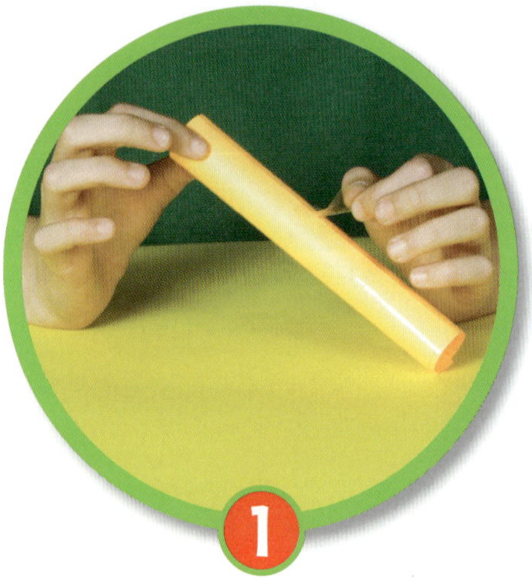

1

Enroule le papier pour faire un petit cylindre puis colle-le.

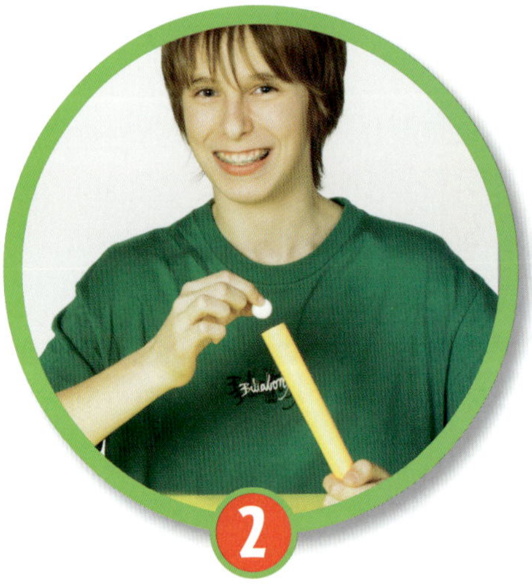

2

Plie une des extrémités du cylindre et mets toutes les menthes « Mentos » à l'intérieur.

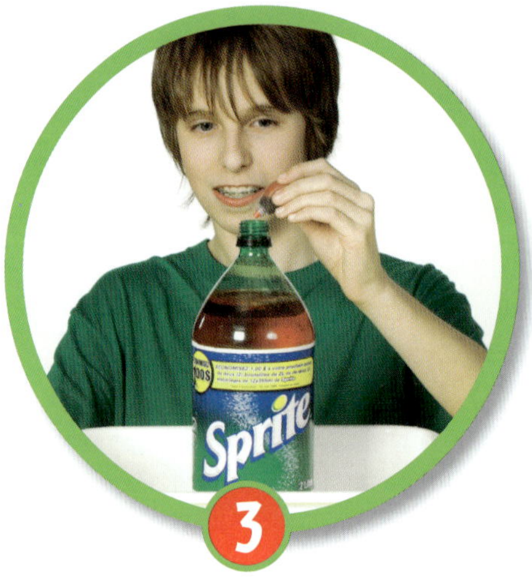

3

Place la bouteille de boisson gazeuse ouverte dans un grand bol. Si tu le désires, ajoute quelques gouttes de colorant alimentaire. Attention ! NE BRASSE PAS LA BOUTEILLE !

Il te faut :

- une bouteille de 2 litres de boisson gazeuse pas encore ouverte
- un paquet de menthes « Mentos »
- un grand bol
- du ruban adhésif
- une feuille de papier
- du colorant alimentaire (facultatif)

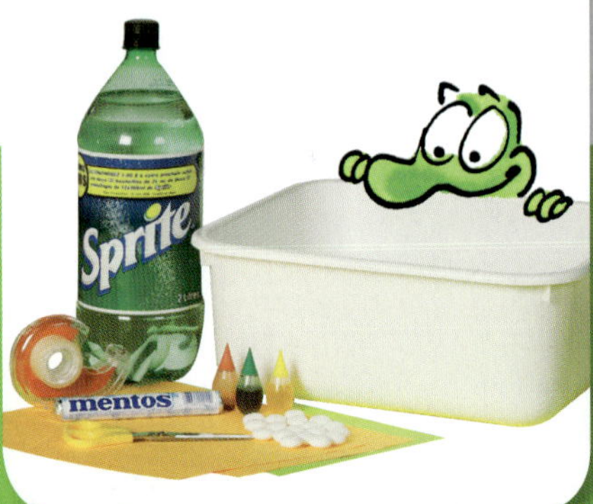

Débrouillard : Hugo Roy Photos : Laurence Labat

Que se passe-t-il ?

Les boissons gazeuses sont faites d'eau, de sucres, de saveurs artificielles, d'agents de conservation et d'autres ingrédients aux noms bizarres. Toutefois, un ingrédient les différencie des autres boissons : le gaz carbonique.

Dans une boisson gazeuse, l'eau entoure les bulles de gaz carbonique. Cette force se nomme la tension superficielle. Lorsque tu agites vigoureusement une boisson gazeuse, cette tension est rompue et le gaz s'échappe. Les bonbons « Mentos » contiennent du sucre, une saveur naturelle de menthe et de la gomme arabique. La gomme arabique est l'ingrédient mystérieux qui déclenche la fontaine : elle détruit la tension de surface qui unit l'eau au gaz carbonique. Le gaz carbonique s'échappe alors de la bouteille en entraînant le liquide.

Ça ne marche pas ?

C'est probablement parce que tu as brassé la bouteille ou que tu l'as laissée ouverte trop longtemps avant d'y plonger les menthes. Le gaz s'est déjà échappé. Recommence avec une nouvelle bouteille.

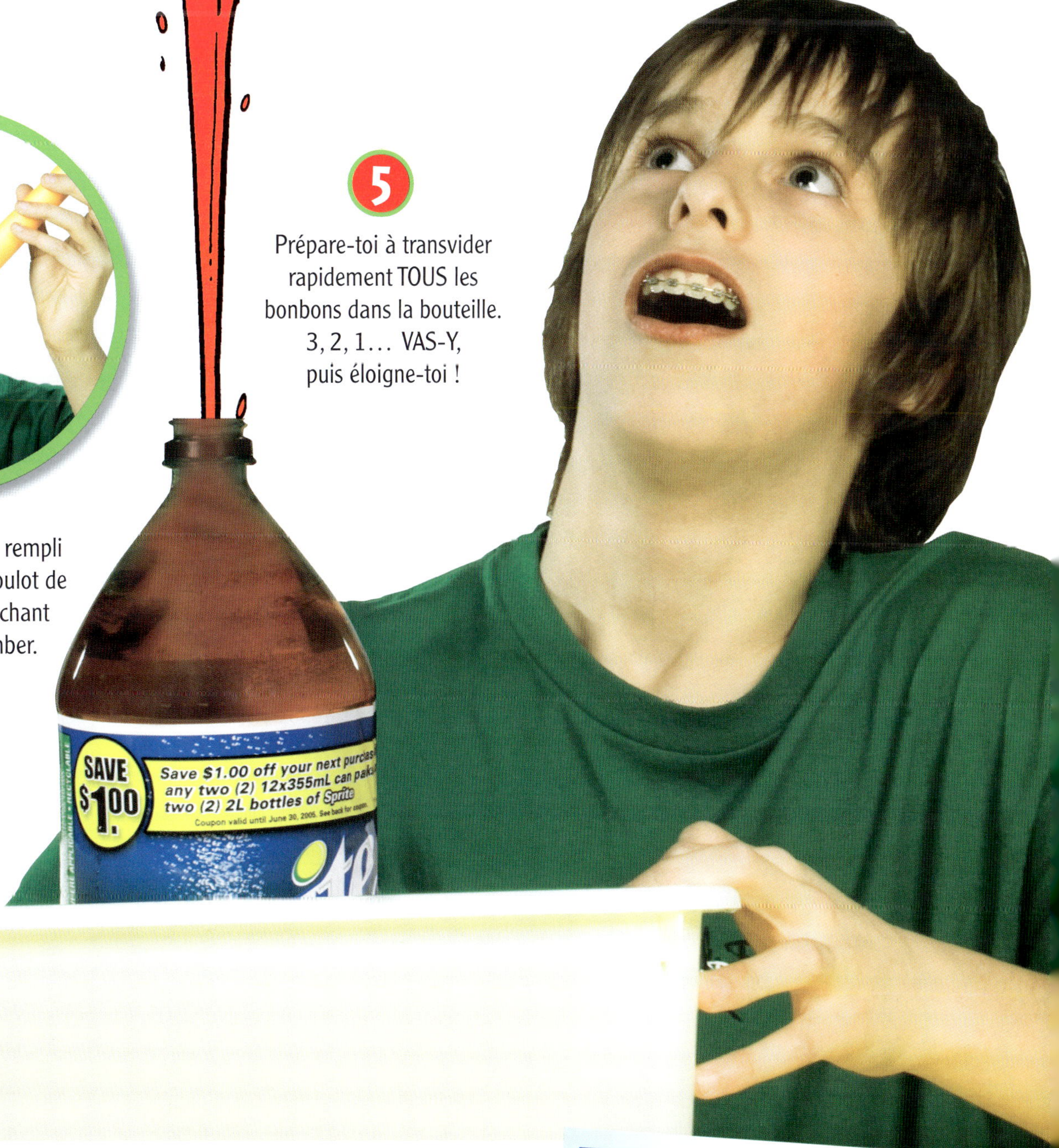

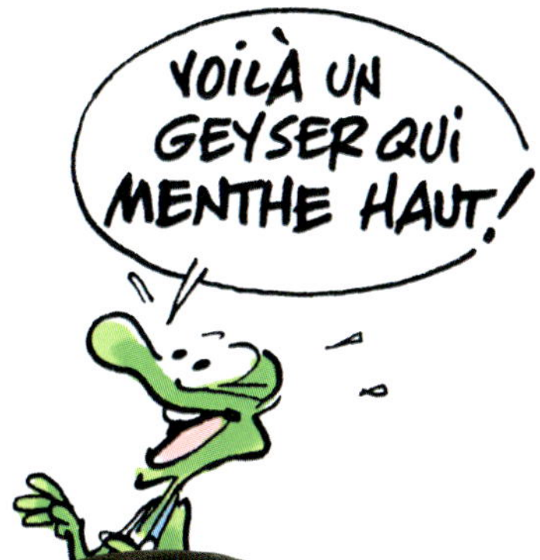

Quel dégât... mais c'est tellement drôle !

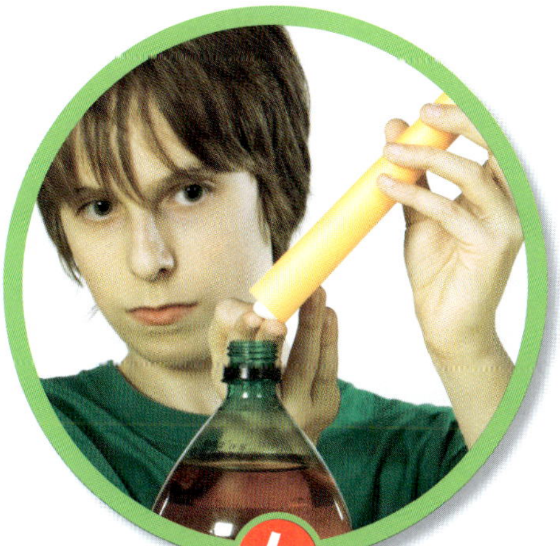

4

Approche ton cylindre rempli de bonbons près du goulot de la bouteille en empêchant les bonbons de tomber.

5

Prépare-toi à transvider rapidement TOUS les bonbons dans la bouteille. 3, 2, 1... VAS-Y, puis éloigne-toi !

Les geysers

Un geyser est une source qui jaillit de manière intermittente en un jet de vapeur et d'eau chaude. Ce jet peut dépasser 100 m de hauteur ! Les geysers se retrouvent en grande partie dans les régions où le magma souterrain est situé près de la surface. Quand l'eau de pluie s'infiltre profondément dans le sol, elle rencontre des roches chauffées par le magma brûlant. Ainsi chauffée, l'eau se transforme en vapeur et ressort alors par une faille sous forme de geyser.

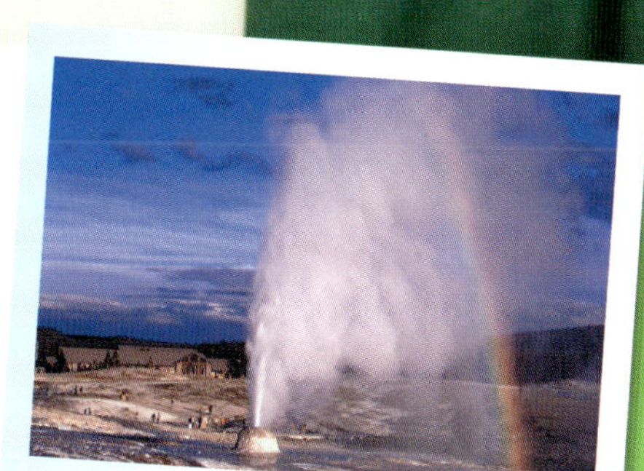

La crème glacée du prof

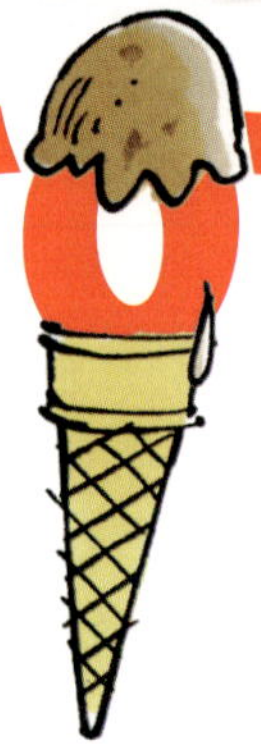

Il fait chaud ? Tu as une envie irrésistible d'une bonne crème glacée ? Comme le prof Scientifix, fabrique-la toi-même… grâce à la science !

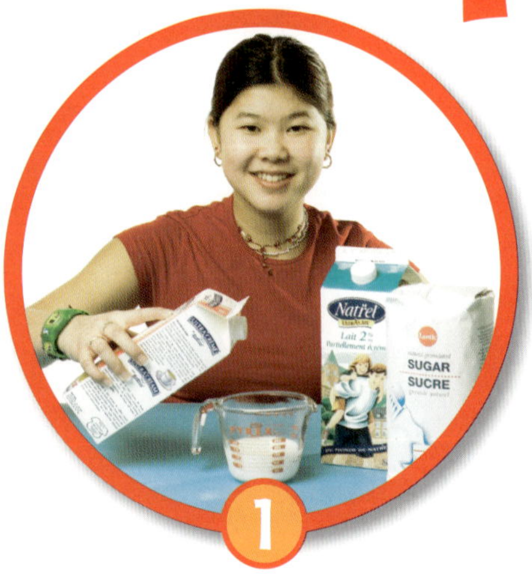

Verse le lait et la crème dans la tasse à mesurer. Ajoute le sucre, quelques gouttes d'arôme artificiel et, si tu le désires, quelques gouttes de colorant alimentaire. Brasse bien ton mélange.

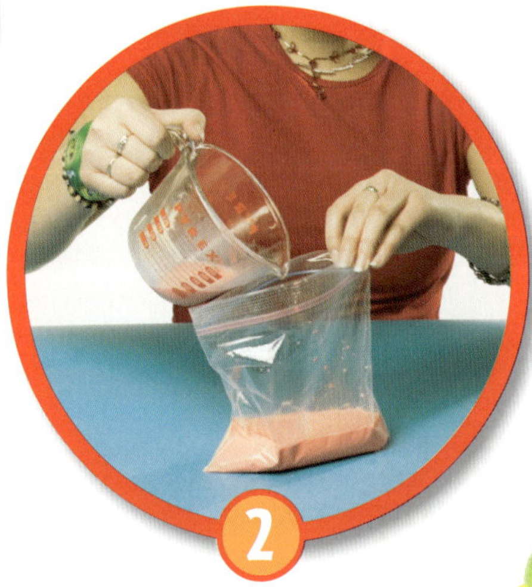

Transvide tout le contenu dans le petit sac de plastique. Referme-le bien en t'assurant qu'il y a le moins d'air possible à l'intérieur. S'il y a trop d'air, le sac pourrait s'ouvrir.

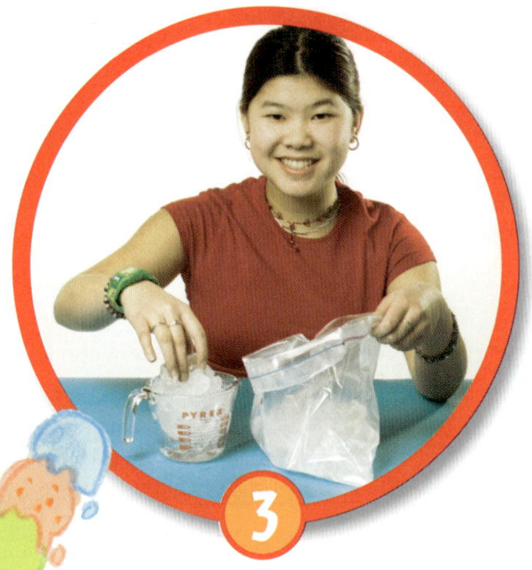

Dépose les glaçons dans le grand sac de plastique. Saupoudre le sel sur les glaçons.

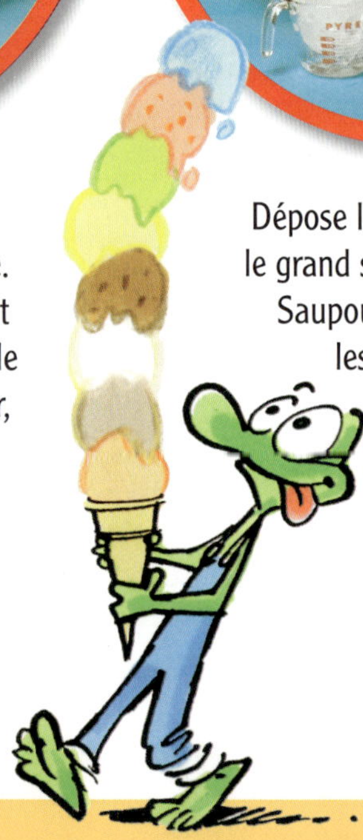

Il te faut :

- 125 ml (1/2 tasse) de lait 3,25 %
- 125 ml (1/2 tasse) de crème 10 %
- 45 ml (3 cuillerées à table) de sucre
- de l'arôme artificiel (extrait de vanille, d'érable, d'orange, d'amande, de citron, etc.)
- une tasse à mesurer
- 120 ml (8 cuillerées à table) de sel
- 1 litre (4 tasses) de glaçons
- un grand sac de plastique à congélation (type « Ziploc^md^ »)
- un petit sac de plastique (type « Ziploc^md^ »)
- des mitaines !
- du colorant alimentaire (facultatif)
- des pépites de chocolat, des noix hachées, de la confiture, des petits bonbons (facultatifs)

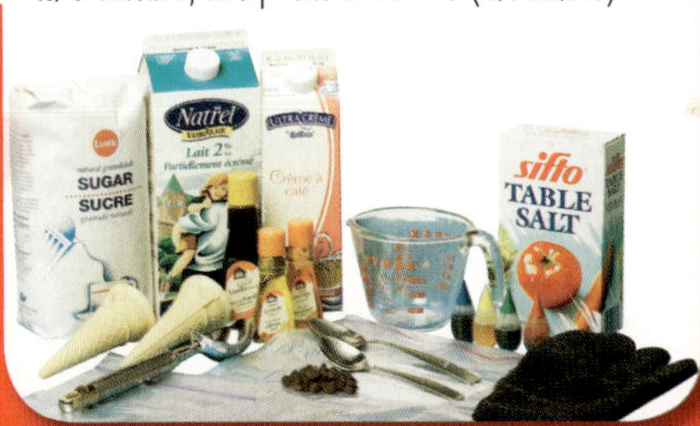

Débrouillarde : Ève DesRoches Photos : Laurence Labat

Que se passe-t-il ?

Le but de cette expérience est de congeler ton mélange sans congélateur. Pour geler, la future crème glacée doit perdre de la chaleur, c'est-à-dire de l'énergie. Qu'est-ce qui lui prendra son énergie ? C'est la glace saupoudrée de sel.

Le sel fait fondre la glace plus vite*. Ce passage de l'état solide (glace) à celui de liquide (eau) nécessite de l'énergie. Cette énergie provient de ta crème glacée qui, en perdant sa chaleur au profit de la glace, refroidit beaucoup et devient solide. Si tu n'avais pas mis de sel, cela aurait pris beaucoup plus de temps pour congeler ta crème glacée. Tu aurais probablement dû ajouter des glaçons pour y arriver.

* Le sel mélangé à la glace abaisse considérablement le point de congélation de la glace. Elle se forme alors entre - 15 et - 4 °C au lieu de 0 °C. C'est pourquoi on en épand sur les routes.

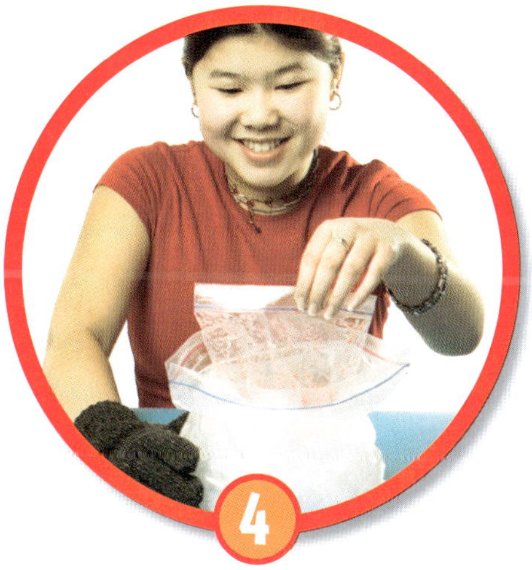

4

Insère le petit sac de plastique contenant ton mélange à crème glacée au centre de la glace du grand sac. Ferme le grand sac. Après avoir mis des mitaines, malaxe doucement le grand sac de plastique pendant cinq minutes.

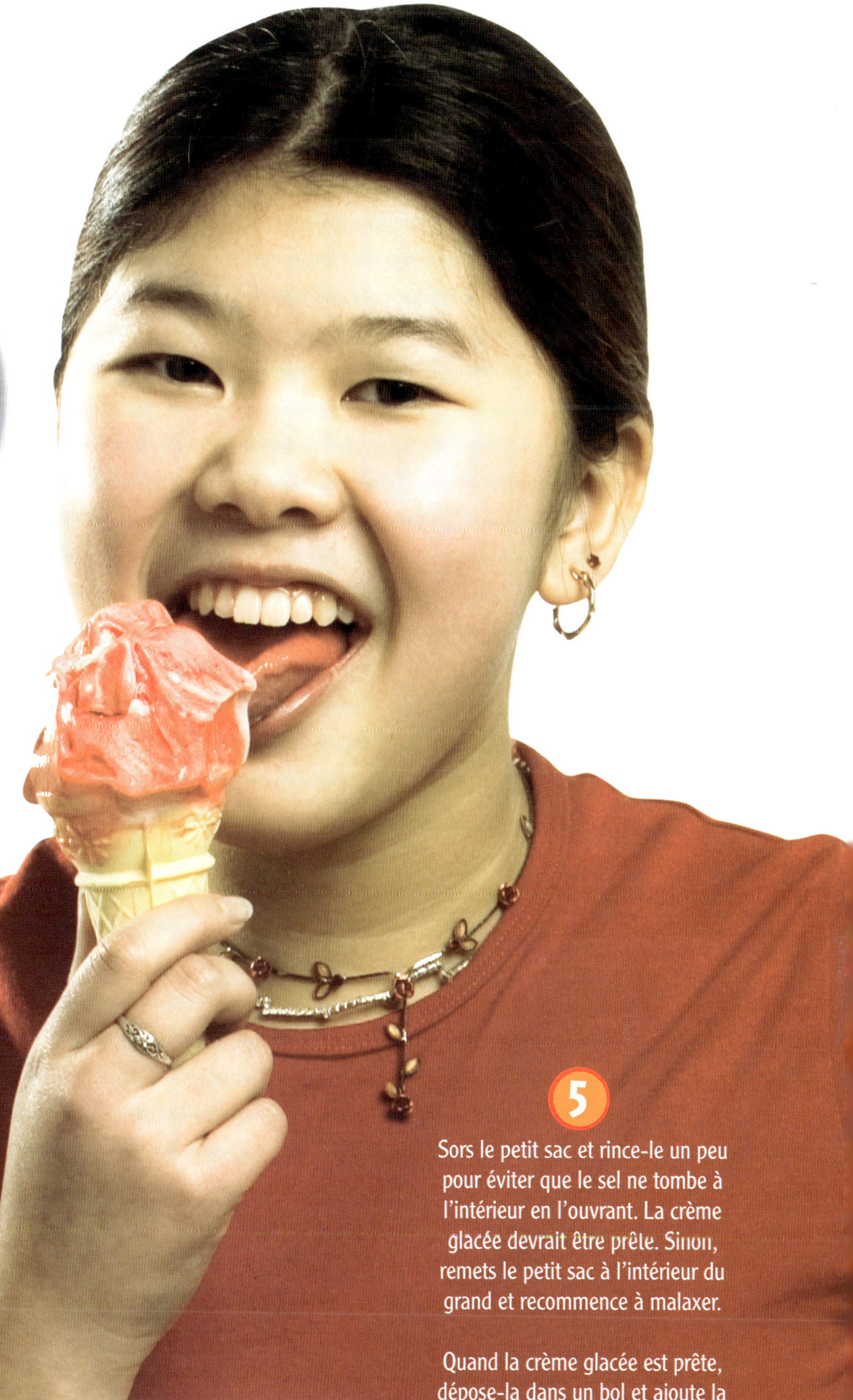

5

Sors le petit sac et rince-le un peu pour éviter que le sel ne tombe à l'intérieur en l'ouvrant. La crème glacée devrait être prête. Sinon, remets le petit sac à l'intérieur du grand et recommence à malaxer.

Quand la crème glacée est prête, dépose-la dans un bol et ajoute la garniture de ton choix. Bonne dégustation !

Histoire des Sciences

La crème glacée

Contrairement à ce qu'on pourrait croire, on fabriquait de la crème glacée bien avant l'invention du congélateur ! Ce sont les Chinois qui ont inventé la crème glacée il y a plus de 2 000 ans. La recette originale combinait un mélange de miel et de fruits à de la neige. Les Arabes ont été les premiers à prendre connaissance de ce procédé, suivis des Italiens. C'est Marco Polo qui introduisit ce délice en Italie au 13e siècle, alors qu'il revenait d'un voyage en Chine. D'abord réservée à la royauté, la crème glacée connût un succès immédiat et se répandit en Europe puis, plus tard, en Amérique.

De mystérieux anneaux

Peux-tu créer un anneau qui n'a qu'une seule face ?

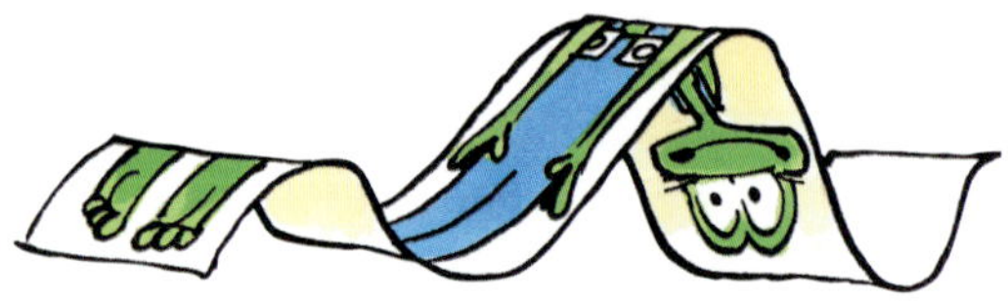

L'étrange anneau de Möbius

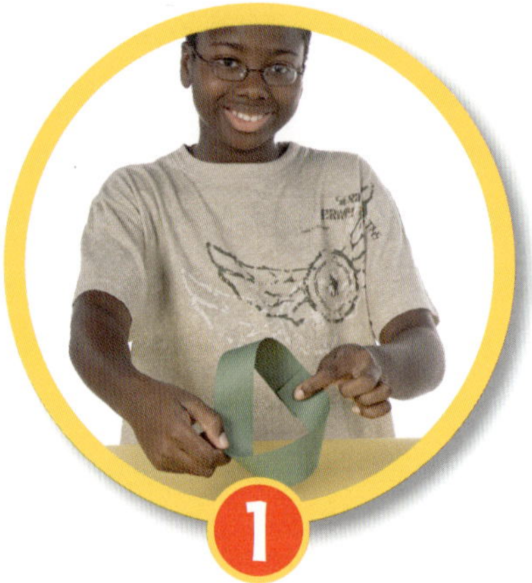

1

Retourne un des deux bouts de la bande de papier et joins ensuite les deux extrémités avec du ruban adhésif. Cette bande est l'anneau de Möbius.

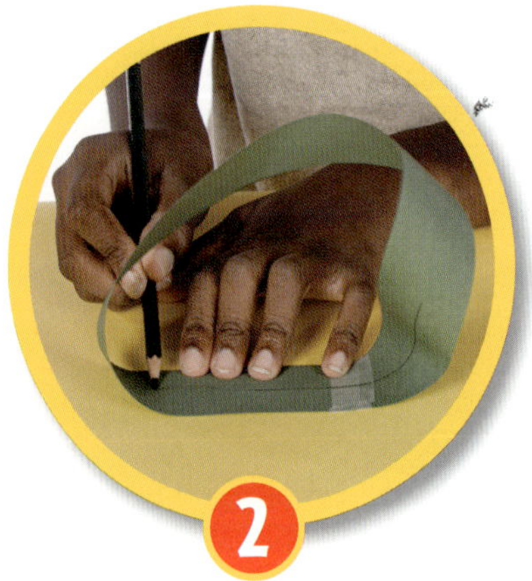

2

Trace une ligne au milieu de la bande de papier. Tu reviendras à ton point de départ sans avoir soulevé le crayon ! La raison en est simple : l'anneau de Möbius n'a qu'une seule face !

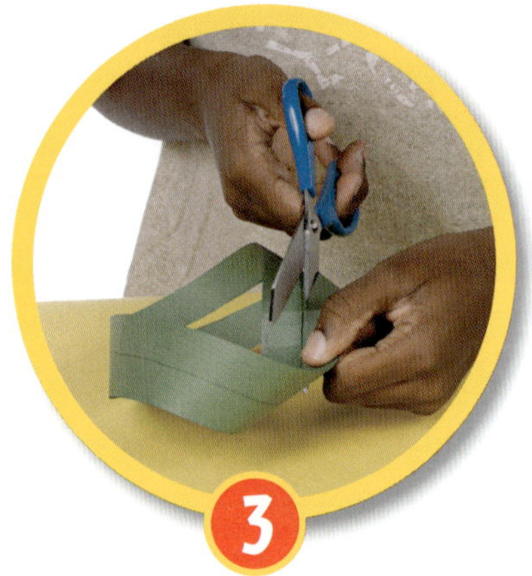

3

Découpe ensuite ton anneau le long de la ligne que tu as tracée au milieu. Qu'observes-tu ?

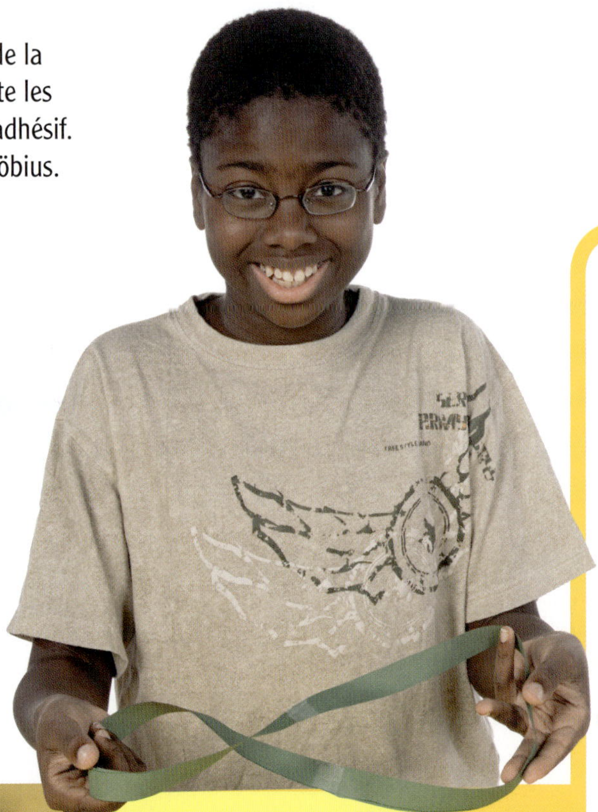

Il te faut :

- deux bandes de papier de 50 X 5 cm
- du ruban adhésif
- un crayon
- des ciseaux
- une feuille de papier de 21 X 28 cm

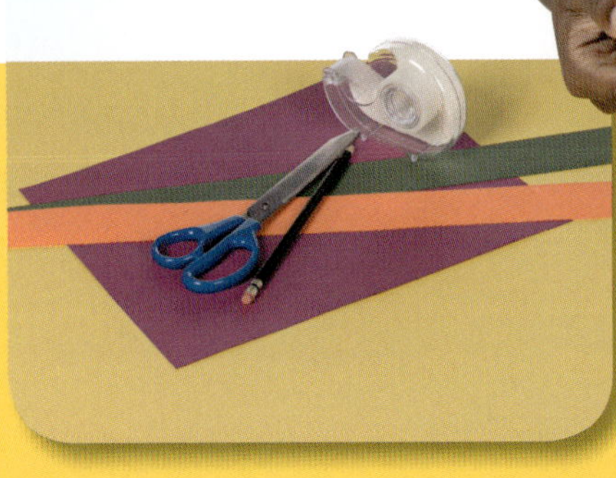

Poursuis l'expérience

Fais un autre anneau de Möbius mais cette fois, découpe-le à un tiers du bord de la bande et non pas au milieu. Les ciseaux feront deux fois le tour de la bande de papier avant de revenir au point de départ. Tu obtiens un autre résultat inattendu : deux bandes de papier l'une dans l'autre ! Et la plus petite est un nouvel anneau de Möbius.

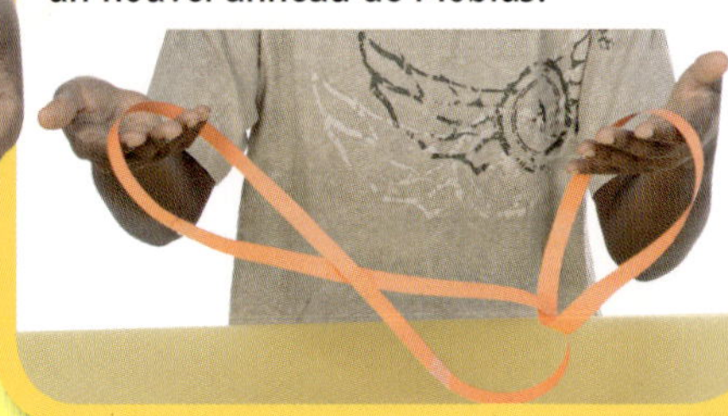

Que se passe-t-il ?

Au lieu de se diviser en deux bandes de papier séparées, comme tu pourrais t'y attendre, l'anneau reste en un morceau ! Il forme une nouvelle bande de papier deux fois plus grande que la première avec deux faces et deux côtés. Personne n'a jamais su expliquer ce tour étrange !

Débrouillards : Jacky Pyram et Elisa Liu Chien Kiow
Photos : Laurence Labat

Peux-tu passer au travers d'une feuille de papier sans la déchirer ?

Tout est dans la forme !

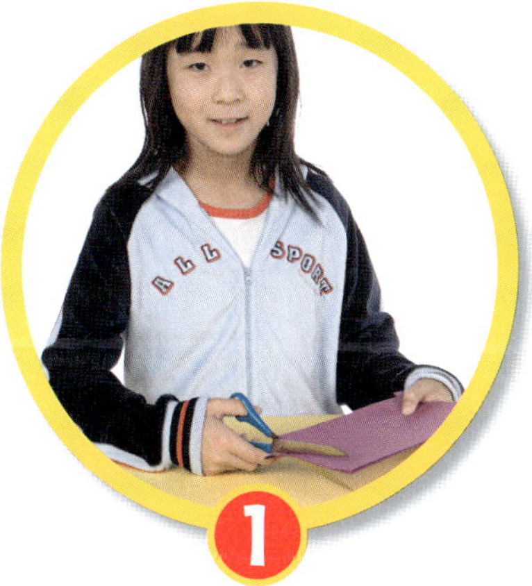

Joins le haut et le bas de la feuille et plie celle-ci au milieu.

Découpe une bande de papier le long du pli. Coupe ensuite 13 fentes dans la feuille, comme sur la photo, puis étire-la avec soin et… tu pourras passer au travers !

Poursuis l'expérience

Pour faire passer plusieurs personnes à la fois, prends une autre feuille de papier et fais un plus grand nombre (toujours impair) de fentes, tout en suivant le même modèle.

Savais-tu que...

l'anneau de Möbius a inspiré le logo des produits recyclés ?

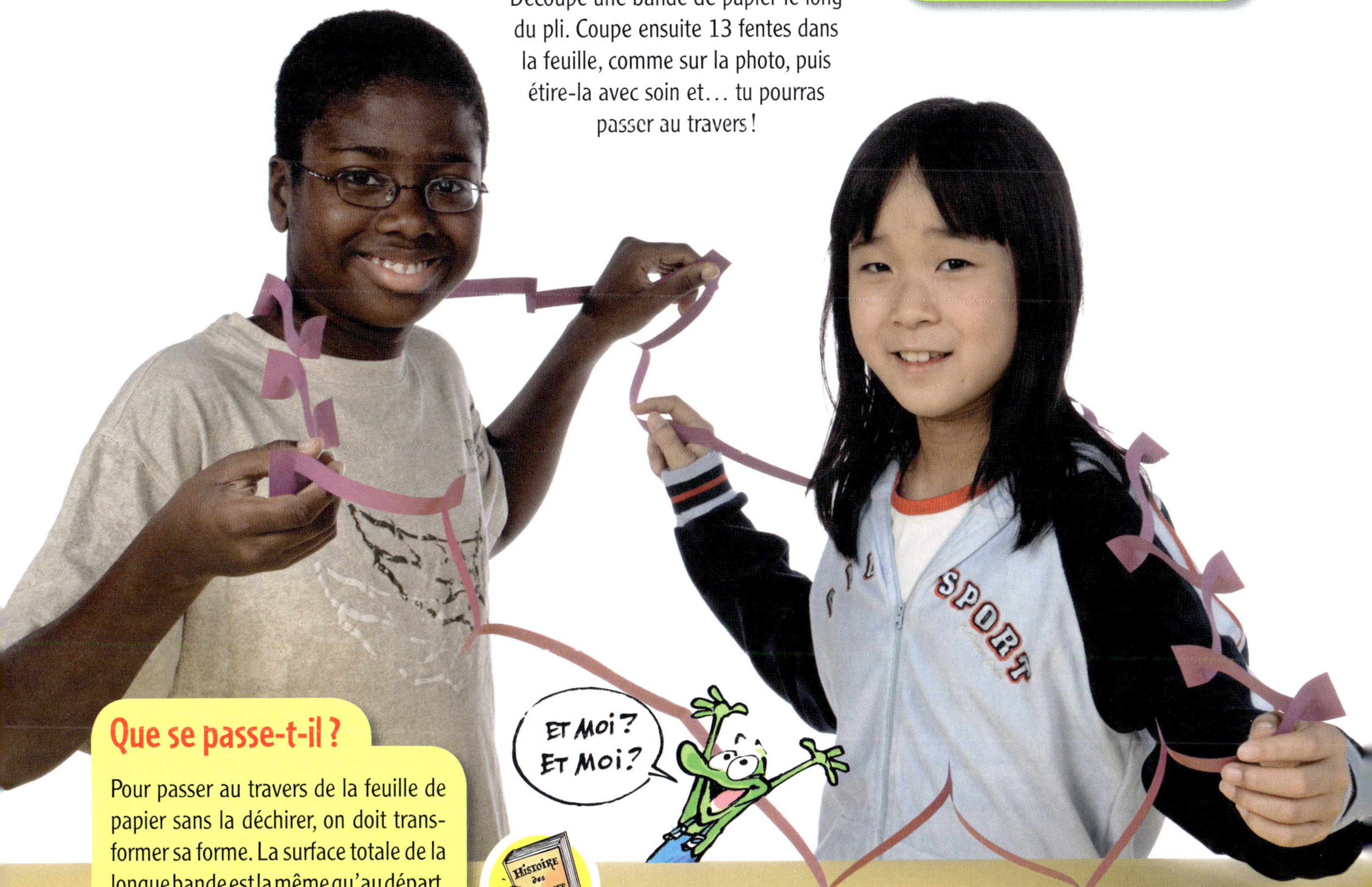

Que se passe-t-il ?

Pour passer au travers de la feuille de papier sans la déchirer, on doit transformer sa forme. La surface totale de la longue bande est la même qu'au départ. Elle n'est que répartie différemment. Grâce à la façon dont est découpé le papier, on peut l'étirer d'un côté et puis de l'autre sans qu'il se déchire.

Ces deux expériences illustrent en partie une branche des mathématiques, soit l'étude des formes, ou topologie.

L'anneau de Möbius

L'anneau, ou ruban, de Möbius a été nommé en l'honneur du mathématicien et astronome allemand qui l'a découvert au 19e siècle, Fernand Möbius (1790–1868). Ce pionnier de la topologie a découvert cette surface unique en 1858.

Depuis, l'industrie a trouvé des applications pratiques à cette forme munie d'un seul côté. Des anneaux de Möbius servent entre autres de courroies de ventilateur et de tapis roulants.

De l'eau sale...

RÉSULTATS PEUVENT VARIER SELON LA TEMPÉRATURE EXTÉRIEURE.

Transforme la boue en eau claire et potable, sans usine de filtration !

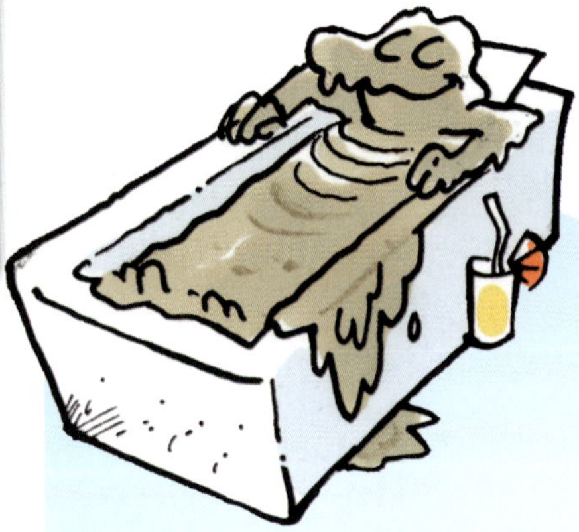

Il te faut :

Pour la première partie (distillateur)

- un bol
- un verre moins haut que le bol
- de l'eau boueuse
- un caillou assez lourd ou de la pâte à modeler
- un rouleau de pellicule plastique (papier cellophane)

Pour la deuxième partie (filtreur)

- un tube de caoutchouc d'environ 30 cm de long et 1,5 cm de diamètre (en vente dans les quincailleries)
- du charbon activé (en vente dans les animaleries)
- de la ouate
- un entonnoir
- des ciseaux
- un autre verre

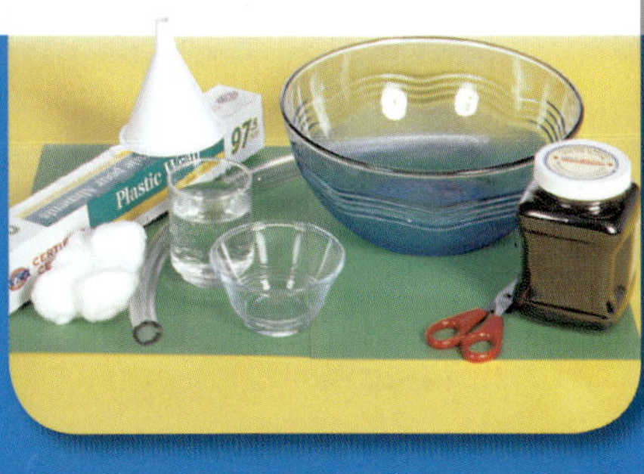

Débrouillarde : Kati Anna Larrieux Photos : Laurence Labat

Première partie : purifie l'eau avec un distillateur

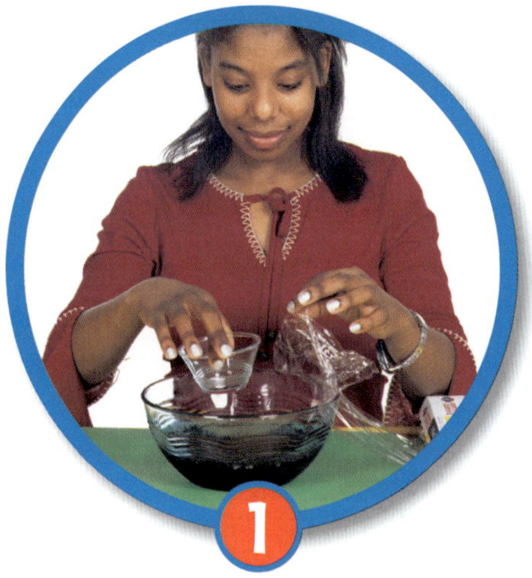

1 Verse l'eau boueuse dans le bol. Place le verre au milieu du bol. Recouvre le tout d'une pellicule plastique (il est très important que la pellicule ne soit pas complètement tendue).

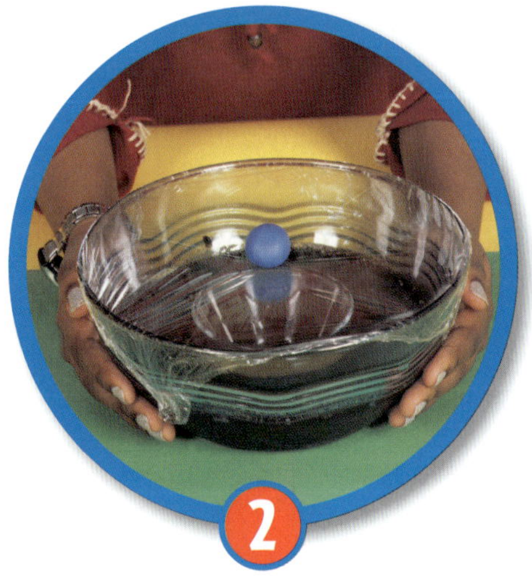

2 Dépose en plein centre du plastique un caillou (ou une boule de pâte à modeler) assez lourd pour incurver la pellicule de plastique vers l'intérieur du bol.

3 Place le distillateur dans un endroit ensoleillé pendant quelques heures. Et voilà ! L'eau que tu obtiens dans le verre ne contient que très peu d'impuretés.

Tu peux accélérer l'évaporation de l'eau en plaçant un carton noir sous le bol servant de distillateur.

Que se passe-t-il ?

Dans le distillateur, le soleil réchauffe l'eau qui s'évapore. Quand la vapeur atteint la face interne de la pellicule plastique, elle se condense et reprend la forme de gouttelettes d'eau, qui tombent finalement dans le verre. C'est la distillation. L'eau ainsi obtenue est très propre car seuls les éléments pouvant s'évaporer quittent la boue.

La distillation

On utilise souvent le processus de distillation lorsque les substances d'un mélange doivent être séparées, par exemple quand on veut obtenir de l'eau douce à partir d'eau salée, de l'essence à partir de pétrole ou du cognac à partir de vin.

à l'eau propre

Deuxième partie : désodorise l'eau avec un filtreur

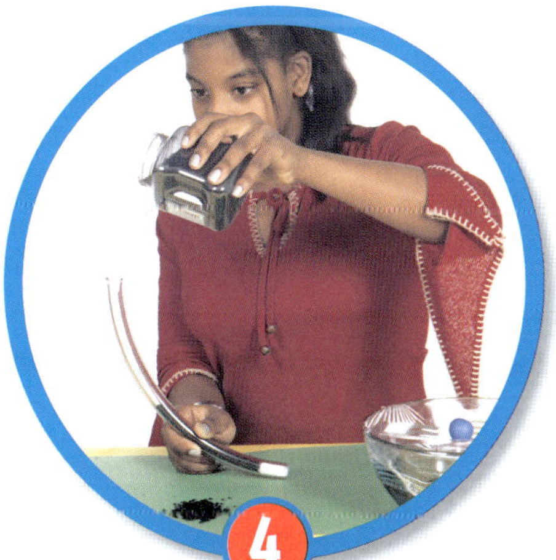

4

Insère une boule d'ouate dans une des extrémités du tuyau de caoutchouc. À l'aide de l'entonnoir, remplis le tuyau aux trois quarts de charbon activé. Bouche le tuyau avec une autre boule d'ouate.

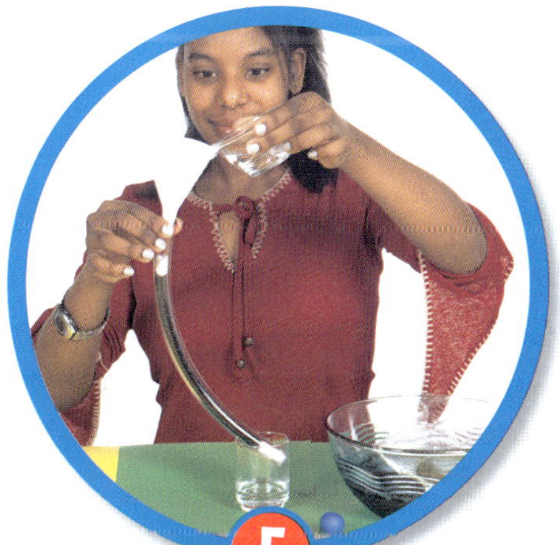

5

Place le tuyau dans un verre. Verse l'eau obtenue avec le distillateur dans le tube en t'aidant de l'entonnoir. L'eau qui ressort à l'autre bout est distillée et purifiée.

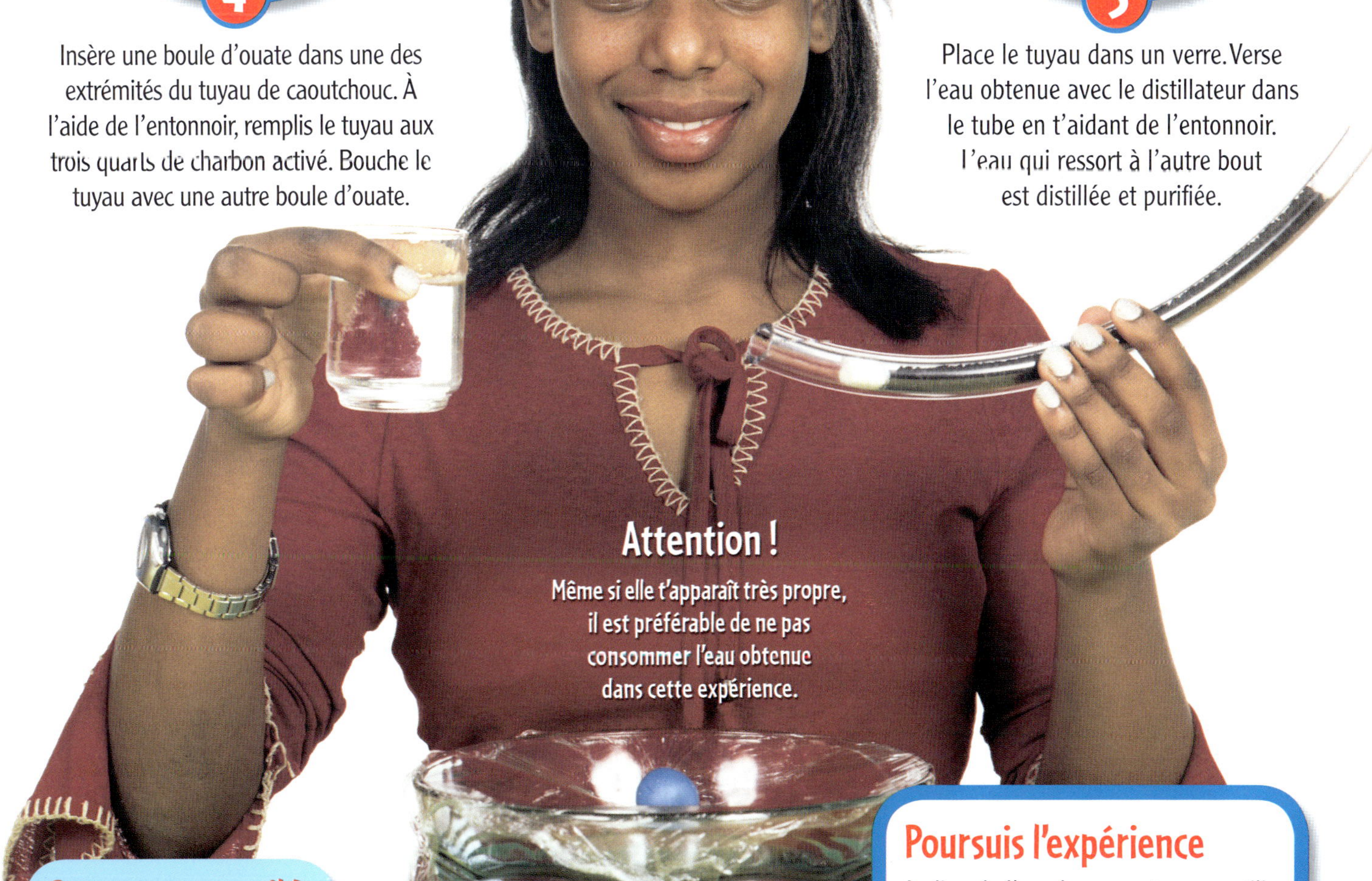

Attention !

Même si elle t'apparaît très propre, il est préférable de ne pas consommer l'eau obtenue dans cette expérience.

Poursuis l'expérience

Au lieu de l'eau boueuse, tu peux utiliser l'eau d'un lac ou de la mer.

Que se passe-t-il ?

Dans le filtreur, le charbon activé désodorise l'eau. Il agit à la manière d'une éponge en absorbant les particules qui donnent une odeur, une saveur ou une couleur à l'eau.

De l'eau usée à l'eau potable

Dans les grandes villes, l'eau potable est produite dans une usine de filtration qui utilise un procédé semblable. Des produits chimiques sont cependant ajoutés à différentes étapes pour tuer d'éventuelles bactéries.

Construis un pont

Découvre les différences entre un pont à poutres, un pont en arc et un pont à haubans.

NÉCESSITE LA PRÉSENCE D'UN ADULTE.

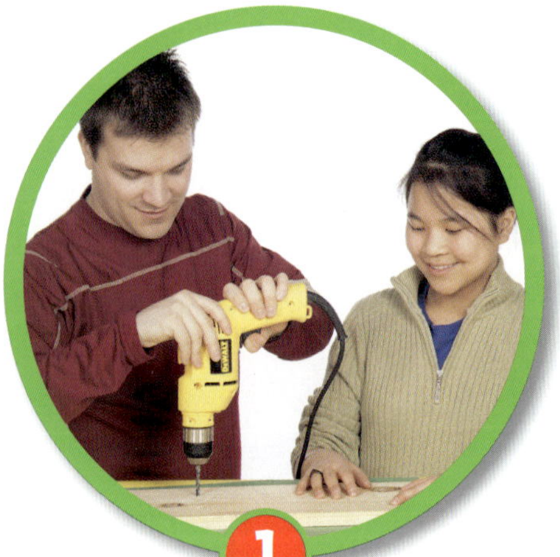

1

Avec la perceuse électrique, perce deux trous à chaque extrémité de la planche, à environ 10 cm du bord. La supervision d'un adulte est essentielle.

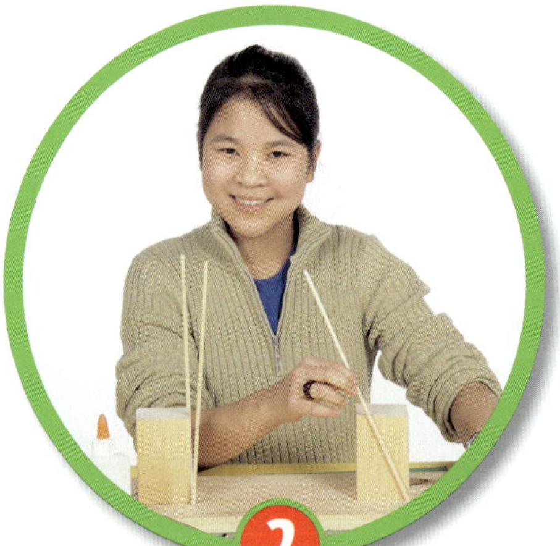

2

Colle les blocs de bois derrière les paires de trous. Colle les baguettes dans les trous. Si tu le désires, décore ton pont et aménage un paysage.

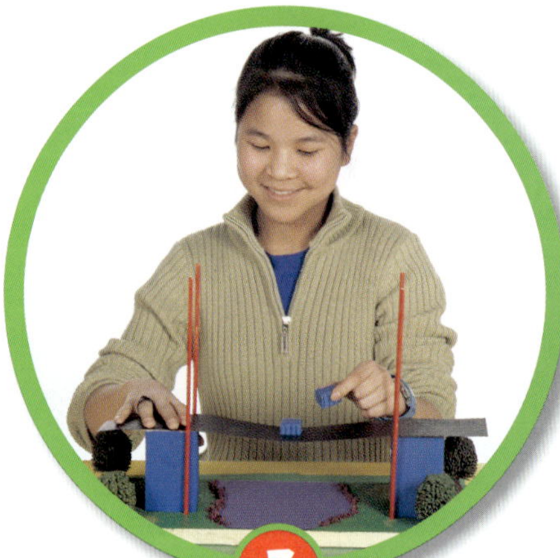

3

Le pont à poutres

Pour le plancher du pont, ou tablier, place un morceau de carton rigide entre les poutres sans le coller. Dépose quelques morceaux de pâte à modeler au centre du pont. Combien peut-il en supporter?

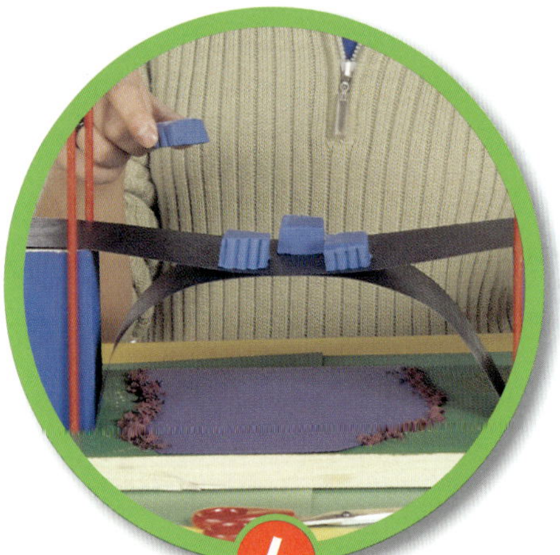

4

Le pont en arc

Insère un rectangle de carton rigide sous le tablier en lui donnant une forme d'arc. Combien peux-tu ajouter de morceaux de pâte à modeler sur ton pont sans qu'il s'écroule?

5

Le pont à haubans

Enlève l'arc du pont. Perce quatre trous dans le carton rigide du tablier qui sert de route. Attache un bout de ficelle à l'extrémité de chaque baguette et l'autre bout au trou le plus près. Combien de morceaux de pâte à modeler ton pont supporte-t-il cette fois ?

Il te faut :

- une perceuse électrique avec une mèche de 5 mm
- une planche de bois d'environ 50 cm de longueur sur 20 cm de largeur
- quatre baguettes de bois de 30 cm de longueur (5 mm de diamètre)
- quatre blocs de bois de 10 cm de hauteur
- une scie
- du carton rigide (type « boîte de céréales »)
- du papier de construction de couleur
- de la colle blanche liquide
- un poinçon
- de la ficelle
- des ciseaux
- un adulte !

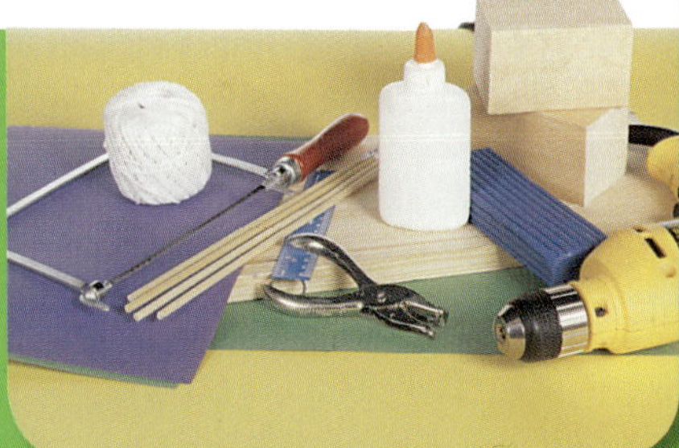

Débrouillarde : Oriane Gratton (aidée par Yannick Bergeron) Photos : Laurence Labat

Que se passe-t-il ?

Il y a plusieurs façons de construire un pont, dépendant du résultat visé. Ici, l'ajout de structures portantes comme l'arc ou les haubans augmente la résistance de ton pont aux lourdes charges.

En plus de la charge à supporter, les ingénieurs considèrent une multitude de facteurs dans la conception d'un pont. Parmi eux : la longueur de l'obstacle à franchir, le type de circulation prévu, la constitution du sol et les contraintes du vent.

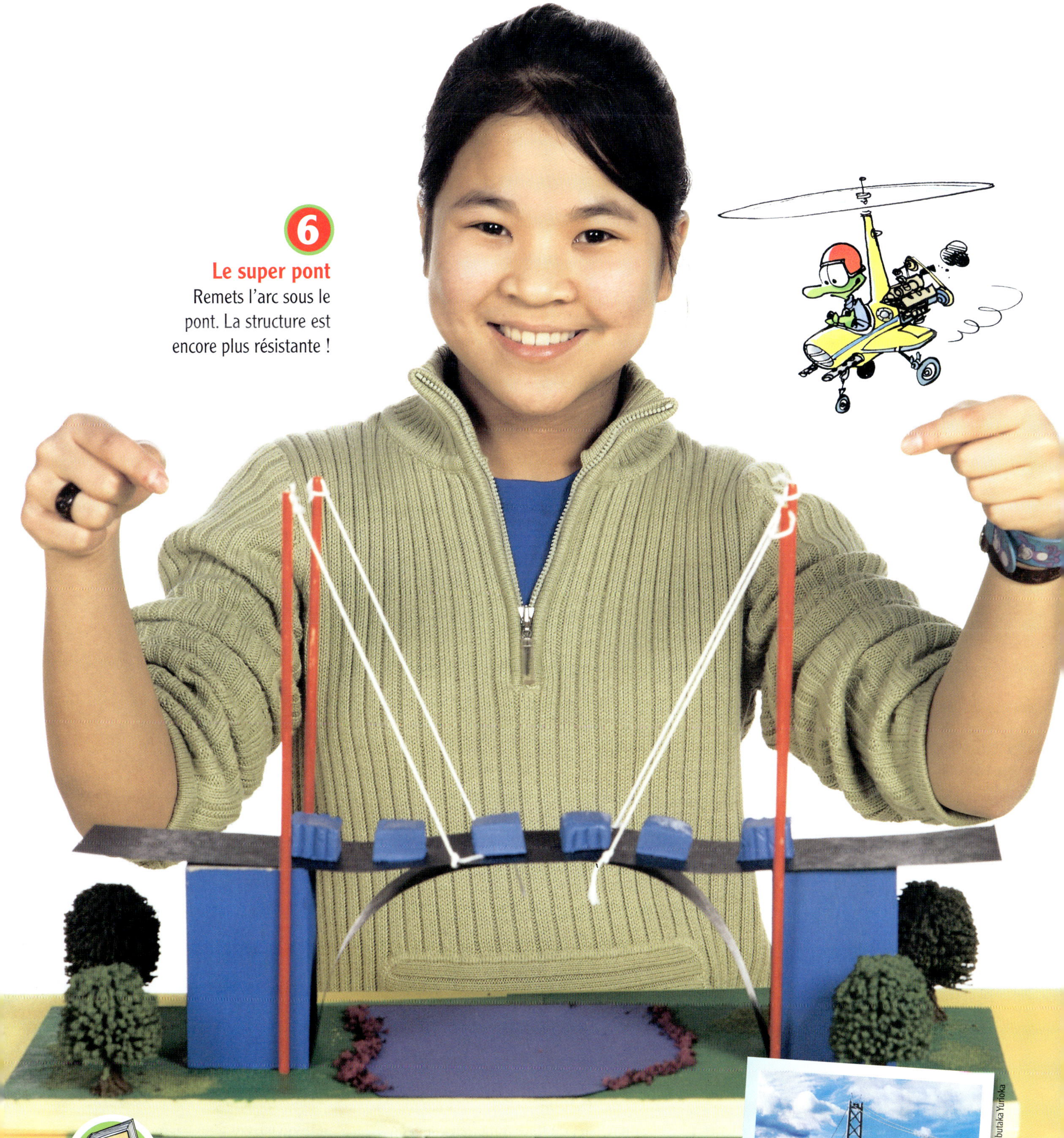

6

Le super pont

Remets l'arc sous le pont. La structure est encore plus résistante !

Les premiers ponts

Les tout premiers ponts étaient de simples troncs d'arbre abattus en travers d'une rivière ou d'un ravin étroit. Rapidement, les hommes ont probablement cherché à les rendre fixes en enfonçant des pieux dans les berges, par exemple. Pour traverser les obstacles naturels de grande largeur, on a dû trouver des façons de soutenir les ponts, comme l'ajout d'arches et de piliers. De nos jours, l'emploi judicieux de poutres, d'arches, de câbles et de matériaux solides offre d'immenses possibilités.

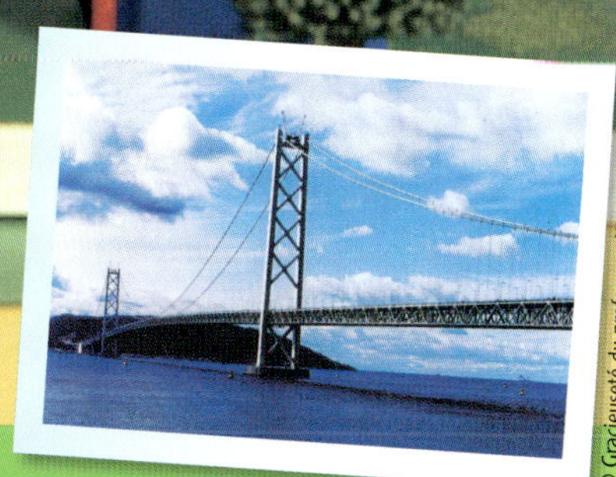

Le pont le plus long

Le pont Akashi Kaikyo, situé au Japon, est à ce jour le plus long pont. Inauguré en 1998, ce pont suspendu mesure 3,9 kilomètres de long, comprend six voies et est conçu pour résister aux séismes.

Un look unique

Conçois un vêtement artistique et un foulard pour un chien sympathique.

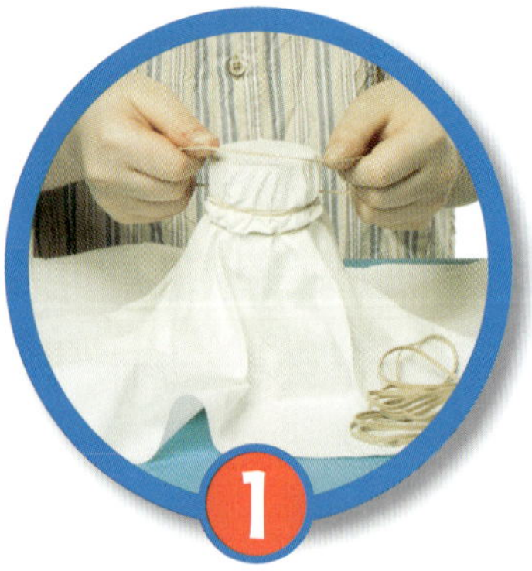

1

Place un verre au centre de la pièce de tissu. Attache le tissu sur l'ouverture du verre avec un élastique.

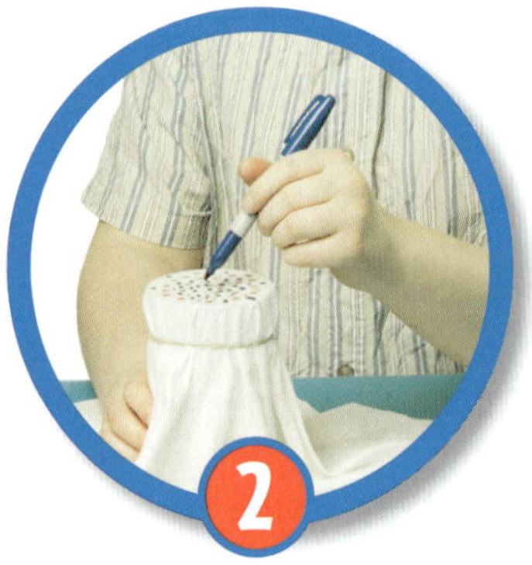

2

Avec les crayons-feutres, dessine des points, des traits ou des formes sur le cercle de tissu.

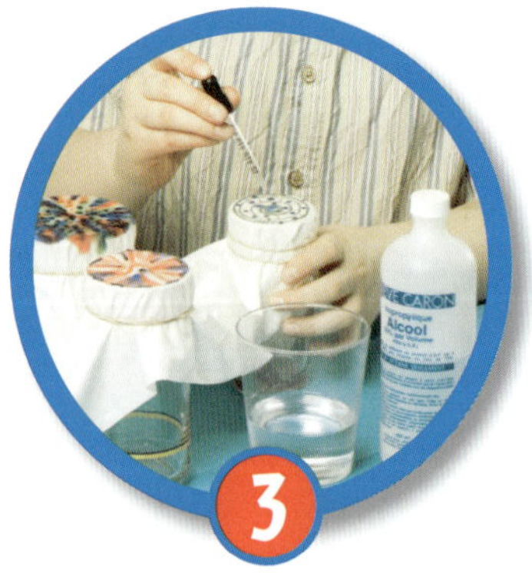

3

Avec le compte-gouttes, laisse tomber tout doucement une vingtaine de gouttes d'alcool à friction au centre du cercle. Laisse sécher avant de retirer l'élastique.

4

Répète les étapes précédentes sur d'autres endroits de ton morceau de tissu.

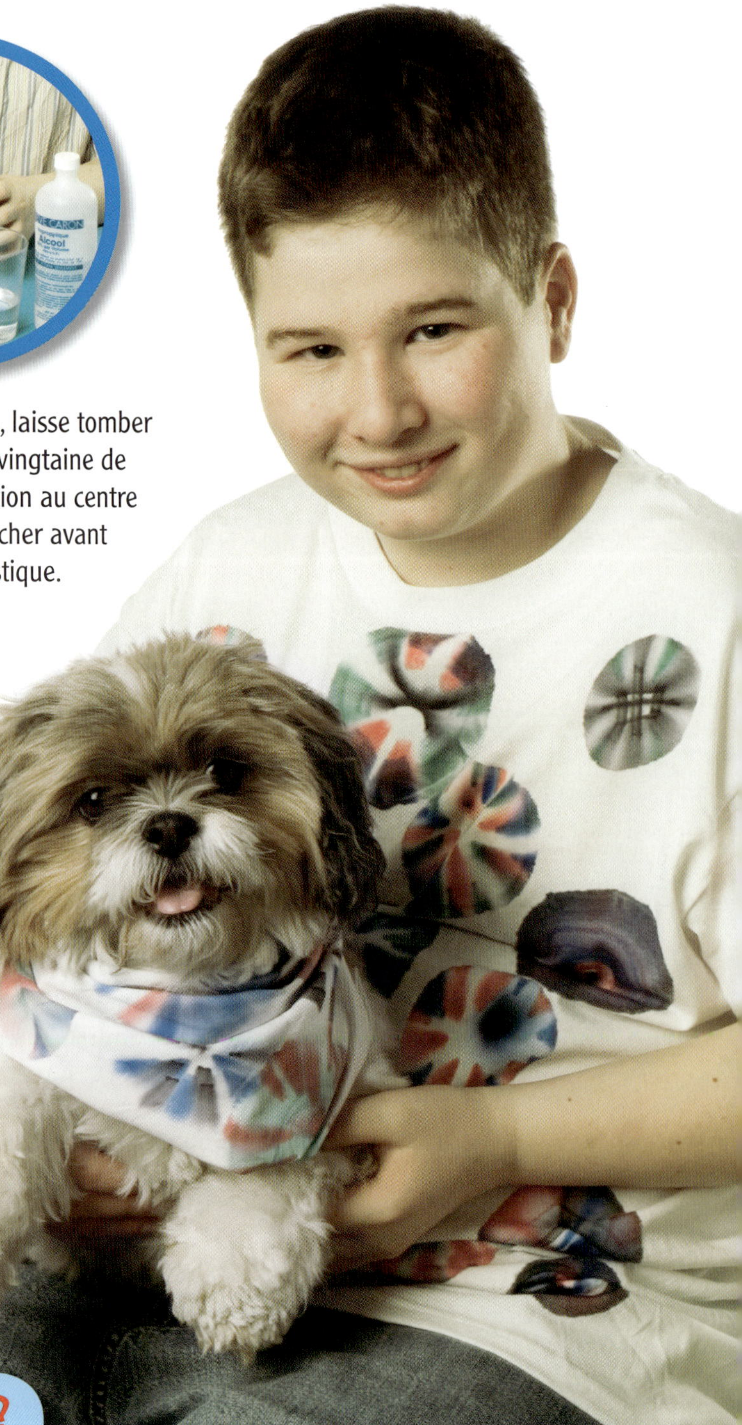

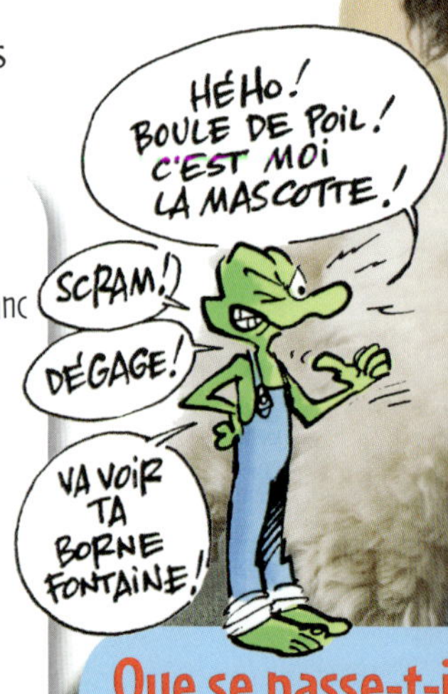

Débrouillard : Émille Kelly Chien : Pounkie Photos : Laurence Labat

Il te faut :

- un t-shirt, un fichu ou un morceau de tissu blanc
- des crayons-feutres à encre permanente de couleurs différentes
- des verres de différentes grosseurs
- des élastiques
- de l'alcool à friction (alcool isopropylique) concentré à 70 %
- un compte-gouttes
- un chien sympathique (facultatif)

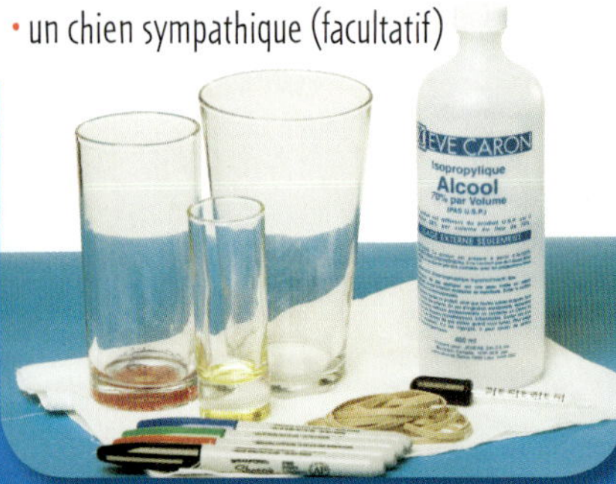

Que se passe-t-il ?

L'encre des crayons, pourtant insensible à l'eau, est soluble dans l'alcool. Ainsi, quand tu ajoutes les gouttes d'alcool, l'encre des crayons se dissout et se sépare en plusieurs couleurs. Même si l'encre semble de couleur uniforme, elle est généralement composée de pigments de couleurs différentes. Or, les différents pigments ne se comportent pas de la même façon dans l'alcool. Certains sont plus solubles et se dissolvent davantage. En se déplaçant sur la surface de tissu, l'alcool entraîne avec lui les différents pigments de couleur et crée des motifs. On appelle cette technique « chromatographie ».

Étrange à l'os !

Les os sont quatre fois plus résistants que le béton armé. Découvre comment les plier sans forcer !

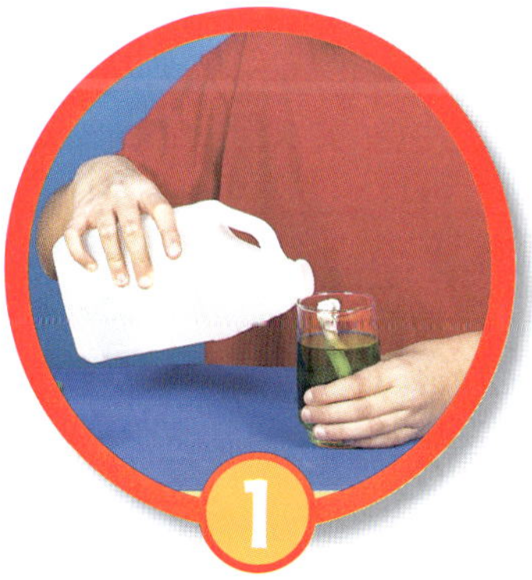

1. Verse une tasse (250 ml) de vinaigre dans le pot et déposes-y l'os.

2. Laisse tremper l'os pendant trois jours. Change la solution de vinaigre tous les jours.

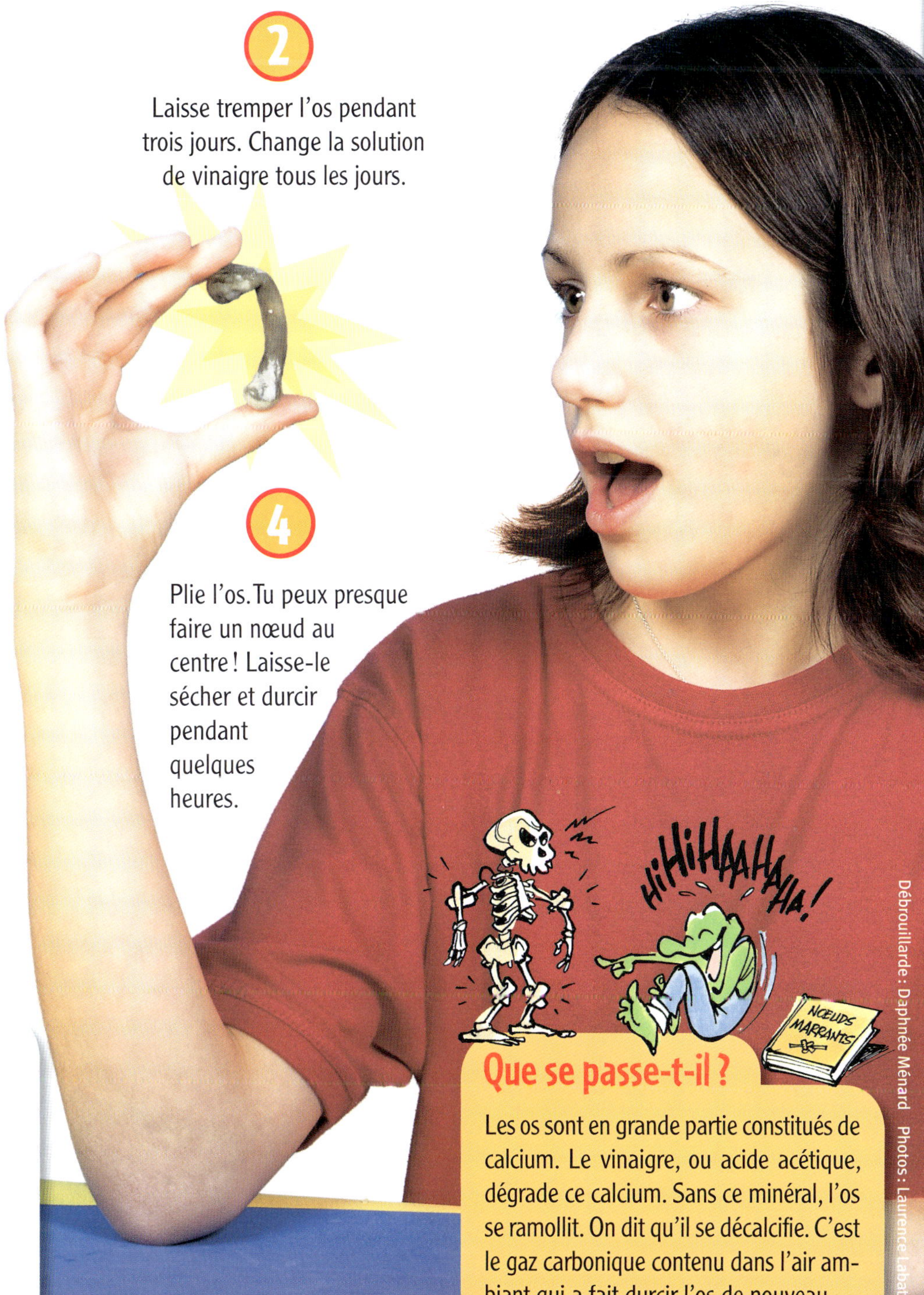

3. Retire l'os du vinaigre. Que remarques-tu ? Il est mou comme du caoutchouc !

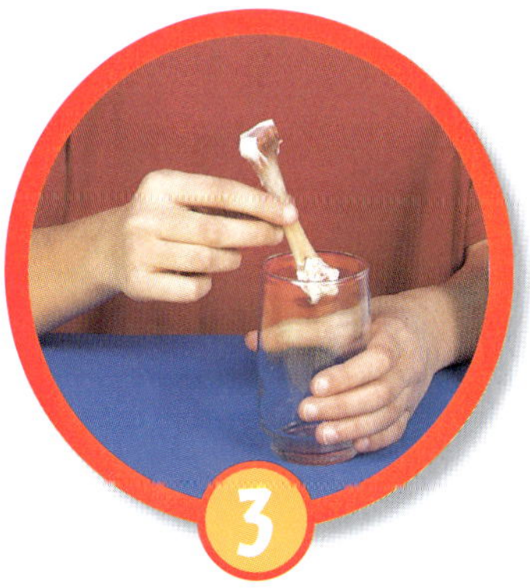

4. Plie l'os. Tu peux presque faire un nœud au centre ! Laisse-le sécher et durcir pendant quelques heures.

RÉSULTATS AU BOUT DE TROIS JOURS.

Il te faut :

- un grand pot transparent
- un os d'aile de poulet long, fin et propre (sur la photo, nous avons utilisé un plus gros os pour mieux le voir)
- 750 ml (3 tasses) de vinaigre blanc
- une tasse à mesurer

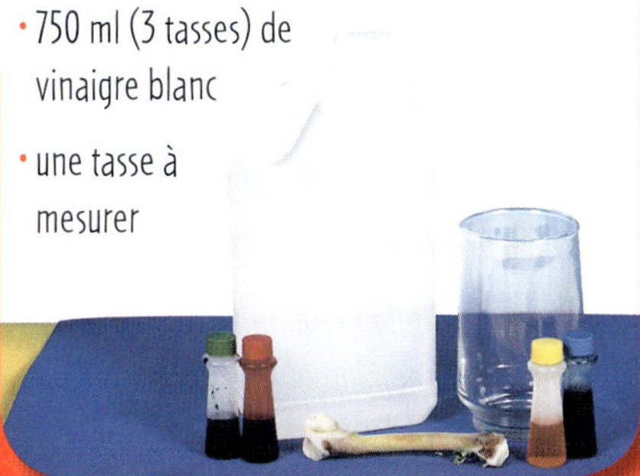

Que se passe-t-il ?

Les os sont en grande partie constitués de calcium. Le vinaigre, ou acide acétique, dégrade ce calcium. Sans ce minéral, l'os se ramollit. On dit qu'il se décalcifie. C'est le gaz carbonique contenu dans l'air ambiant qui a fait durcir l'os de nouveau.

Le calcium du corps

Un corps adulte contient environ 7,2 kg de calcium (99 % se trouve dans les os et les dents). Ton squelette est ainsi un véritable « réservoir » de calcium ! En plus de donner aux os leur solidité, le calcium sert aussi à la contraction des muscles et à la coagulation du sang. Quand l'organisme en a besoin et que l'alimentation ne lui en fournit pas suffisamment, il fouille dans ses réserves. Il est donc important de maintenir ton réservoir bien rempli ! La solution : consomme des produits laitiers et fais de l'exercice !

Débrouillarde : Daphnée Ménard Photos : Laurence Labat

La bouteille turbulente

Quand l'eau ne veut plus rien savoir du savon, ça fait des vagues !

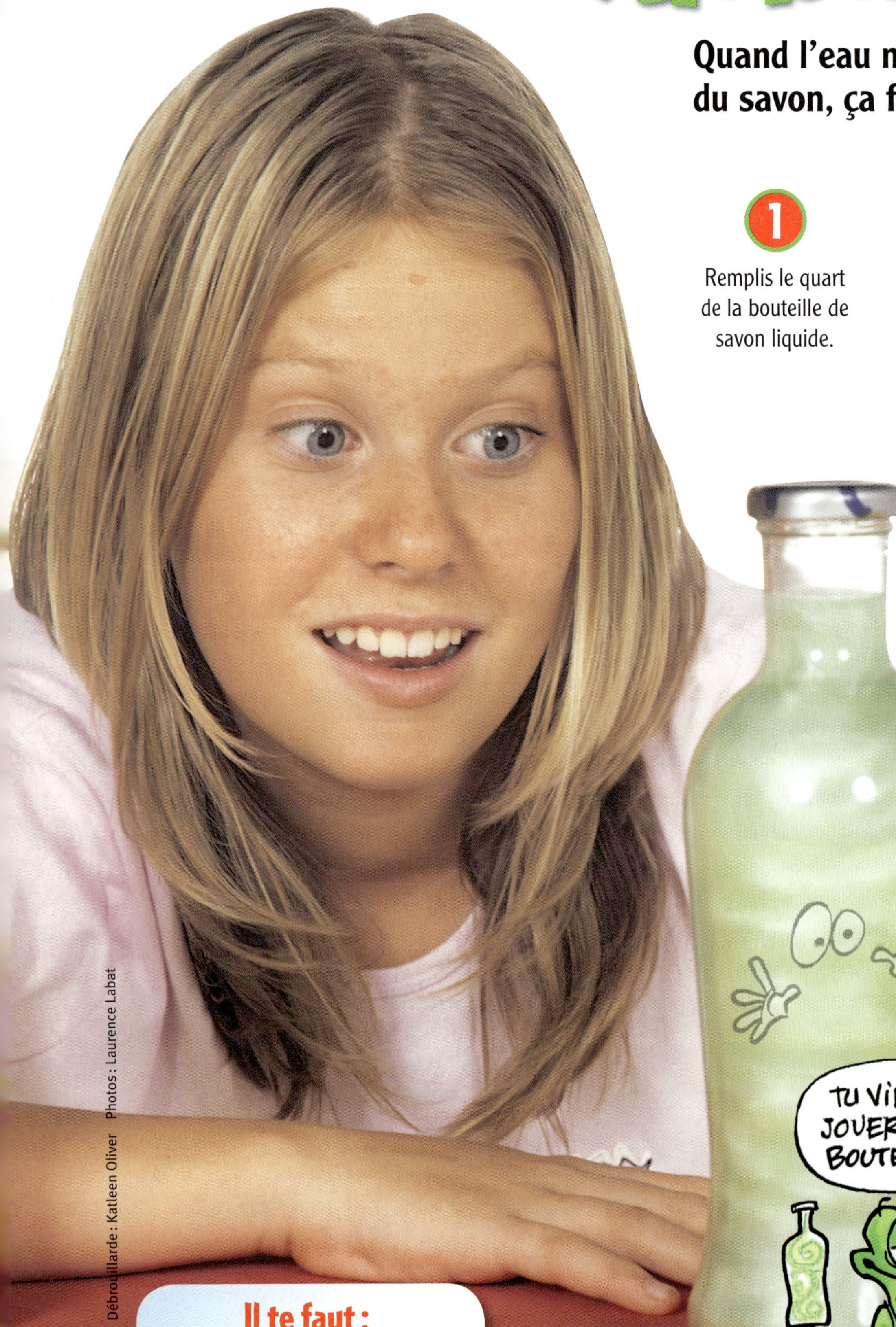

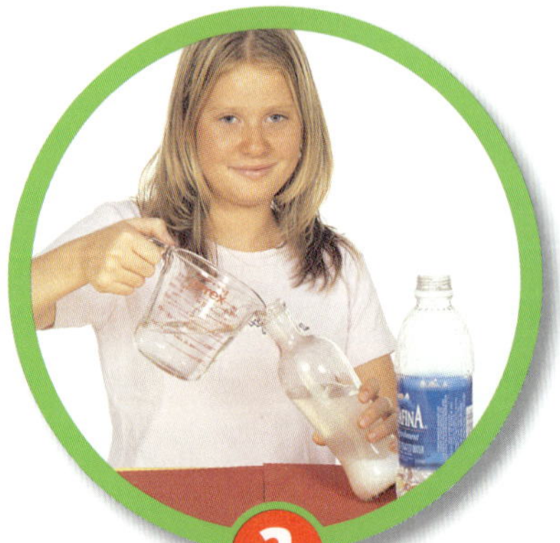

1 Remplis le quart de la bouteille de savon liquide.

2 Verse de l'eau tout doucement dans la bouteille, jusqu'au rebord du goulot.

3 Ajoute cinq gouttes de colorant alimentaire de la couleur de ton choix.

4 Replace le bouchon et agite la bouteille afin de bien mélanger les deux produits. Des vagues, des remous et des tourbillons se forment !

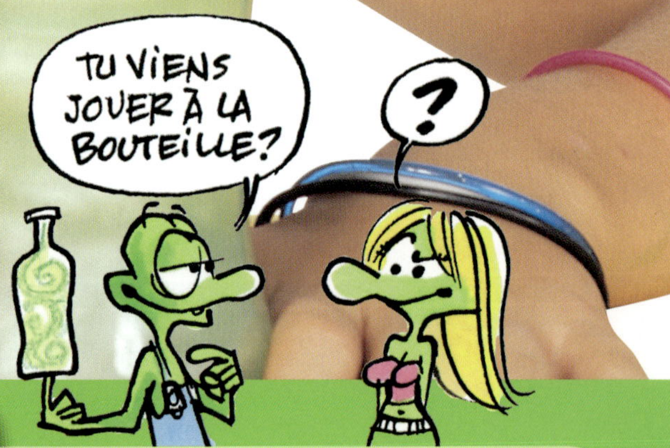

Débrouillarde : Katleen Oliver Photos : Laurence Labat

Il te faut :

- 250 ml de savon à mains liquide blanc perle, de marque « Softsoap »
- une bouteille transparente d'un litre
- du colorant alimentaire
- de l'eau

Que se passe-t-il ?

Pourquoi des vagues se forment-elles quand on agite la bouteille? C'est parce qu'il n'y a pas assez d'eau pour dissoudre complètement le savon. L'eau se faufile entre les particules de savon non dissoutes, créant des courbes intéressantes. Le colorant alimentaire rend le phénomène plus visible.

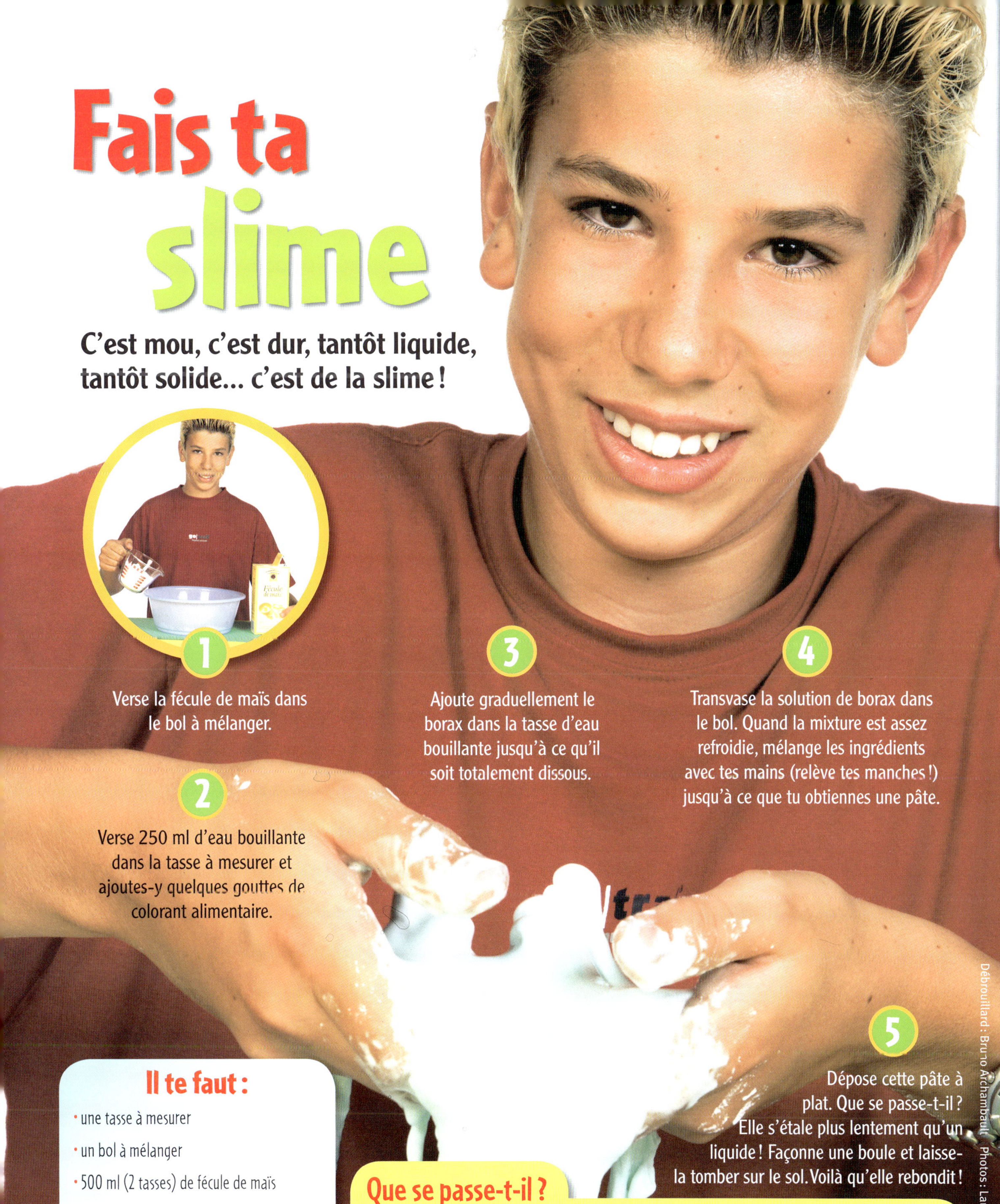

Fais ta slime

C'est mou, c'est dur, tantôt liquide, tantôt solide… c'est de la slime !

1 Verse la fécule de maïs dans le bol à mélanger.

2 Verse 250 ml d'eau bouillante dans la tasse à mesurer et ajoutes-y quelques gouttes de colorant alimentaire.

3 Ajoute graduellement le borax dans la tasse d'eau bouillante jusqu'à ce qu'il soit totalement dissous.

4 Transvase la solution de borax dans le bol. Quand la mixture est assez refroidie, mélange les ingrédients avec tes mains (relève tes manches !) jusqu'à ce que tu obtiennes une pâte.

5 Dépose cette pâte à plat. Que se passe-t-il ? Elle s'étale plus lentement qu'un liquide ! Façonne une boule et laisse-la tomber sur le sol. Voilà qu'elle rebondit !

ATTENTION ! LE BORAX IRRITE LA PEAU ET LES YEUX. SE LAVER LES MAINS APRÈS L'EXPÉRIENCE.

Il te faut :

- une tasse à mesurer
- un bol à mélanger
- 500 ml (2 tasses) de fécule de maïs
- 125 ml (1/2 tasse) de borate de sodium (ou borax*)
- de l'eau bouillante
- du colorant alimentaire

* disponible en pharmacie

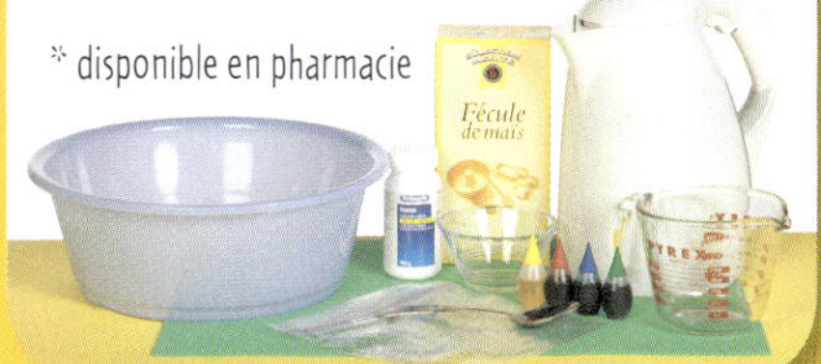

Que se passe-t-il ?

La slime commerciale contient de la « gomme de Guar », un ingrédient servant à épaissir les fromages. Ici, nous l'avons remplacée par la fécule de maïs, plus facile à trouver.

La fécule de maïs est composée de minuscules grains d'amidon. L'amidon est formé d'une très longue chaîne de molécules de glucose, un type de sucre. C'est un polymère.

En présence d'eau bouillante, l'amidon forme une colle. Lorsque cette « colle » est combinée au borax, des liens chimiques se forment entre le bore et les longues chaînes de glucose. En s'entremêlant, les chaînes forment une cotte de mailles… visqueuse !

Débrouillard : Bruno Archambault Photos : Laurence Labat

NÉCESSITE L'AIDE D'UN ADULTE.

Le conducteur a bonne mine

Transforme-toi en électricien chevronné et construis un rhéostat avec une mine de crayon !

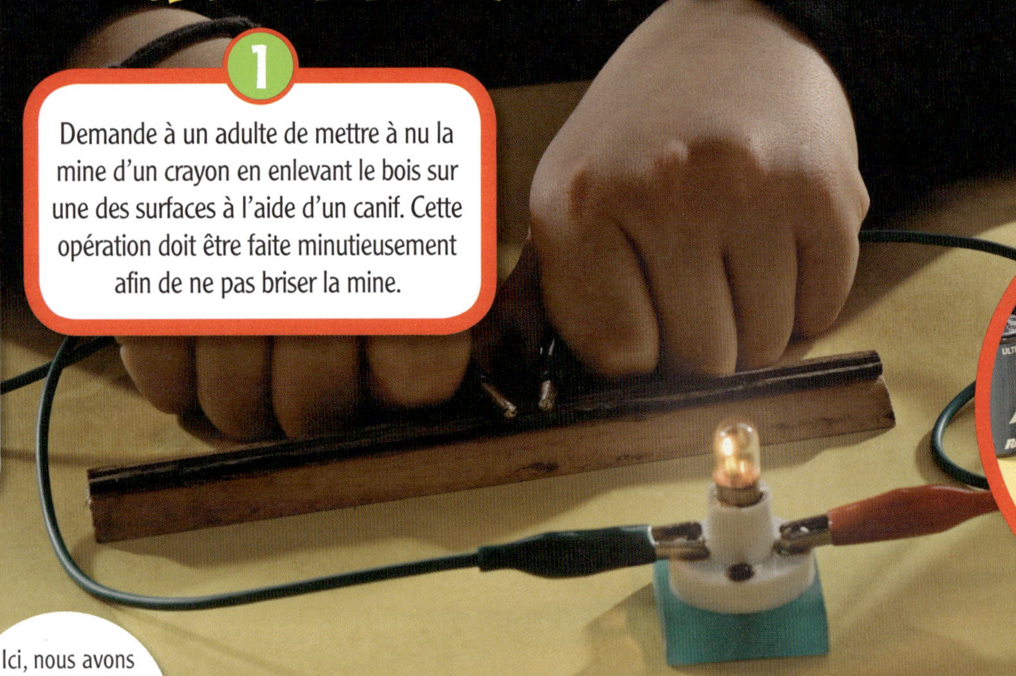

1

Demande à un adulte de mettre à nu la mine d'un crayon en enlevant le bois sur une des surfaces à l'aide d'un canif. Cette opération doit être faite minutieusement afin de ne pas briser la mine.

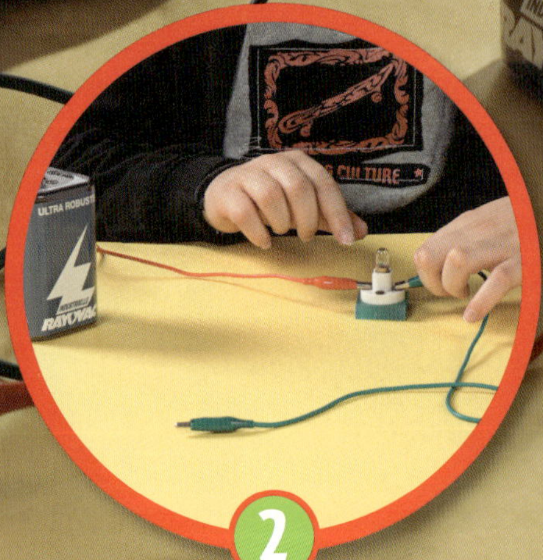

2

Visse l'ampoule sur son socle. Attache le fil A à la pile. Attache ensuite le fil C et l'extrémité libre du fil A aux vis du socle en suivant le schéma ci-dessous.

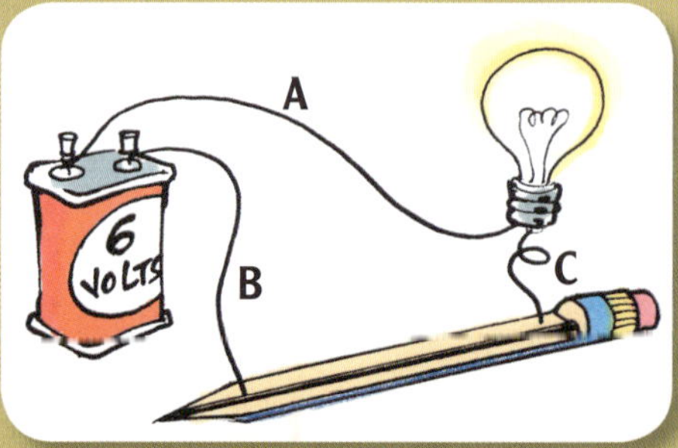

Ici, nous avons collé le crayon sur un bout de bois pour augmenter sa stabilité.

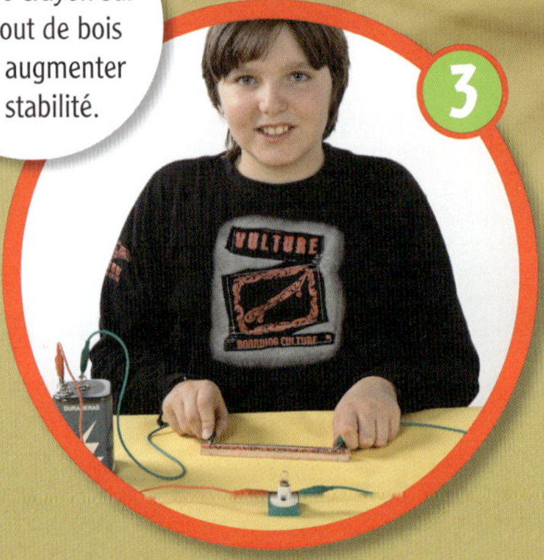

3

Attache une extrémité du fil B à la pile et joins l'autre extrémité de ce fil à la mine. Raccorde ensuite l'ampoule à l'extrémité libre de la mine par le fil C. L'ampoule brille-t-elle ?

4

En retenant avec tes doigts le fil C à une des extrémités de la mine, promène le bout libre du fil B le long de la mine. Que remarques-tu ? La lumière devrait s'allumer avec d'autant plus d'intensité que la distance entre les fils B et C sera plus courte.

Il te faut :

- une pile de 6 volts
- une ampoule électrique de 6 volts*
- un socle pour ampoule*
- trois fils électriques avec une « pince alligator » aux extrémités
- un crayon à mine le plus long possible (au moins 15 cm de longueur)
- un canif ou un couteau « exacto »

* vendus dans les magasins de fournitures électriques

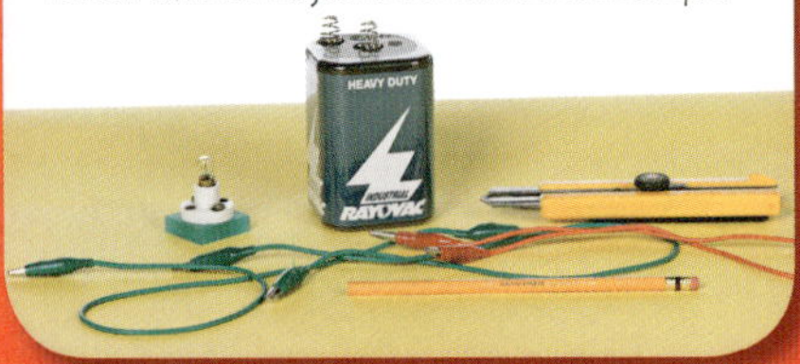

Que se passe-t-il ?

Le graphite de la mine de crayon conduit le courant électrique, mais avec une certaine résistance. Ici, la mine de crayon joue le rôle d'une résistance variable, ou rhéostat. En augmentant la longueur de la mine dans le circuit, la résistance est augmentée. Plus la résistance est élevée, moins l'ampoule brille. Le rhéostat permet ainsi de créer toute une gamme de luminosités allant de l'éclairage tamisé à la lumière vive.

Bons et mauvais conducteurs

Les métaux, comme l'aluminium et le cuivre, sont de bons conducteurs d'électricité alors que d'autres substances, comme le plastique et le caoutchouc, ne permettent pas le passage de l'électricité. On dit de ces dernières qu'elles sont des isolants électriques.

Entre les bons conducteurs et les isolants, il existe des substances dont la conduction électrique est moyenne, comme le graphite.

Débrouillard : Nicolas Muraton Photos : Laurence Labat

Une régate maison

Un bateau qui carbure au savon ? Oui, grâce à la tension !

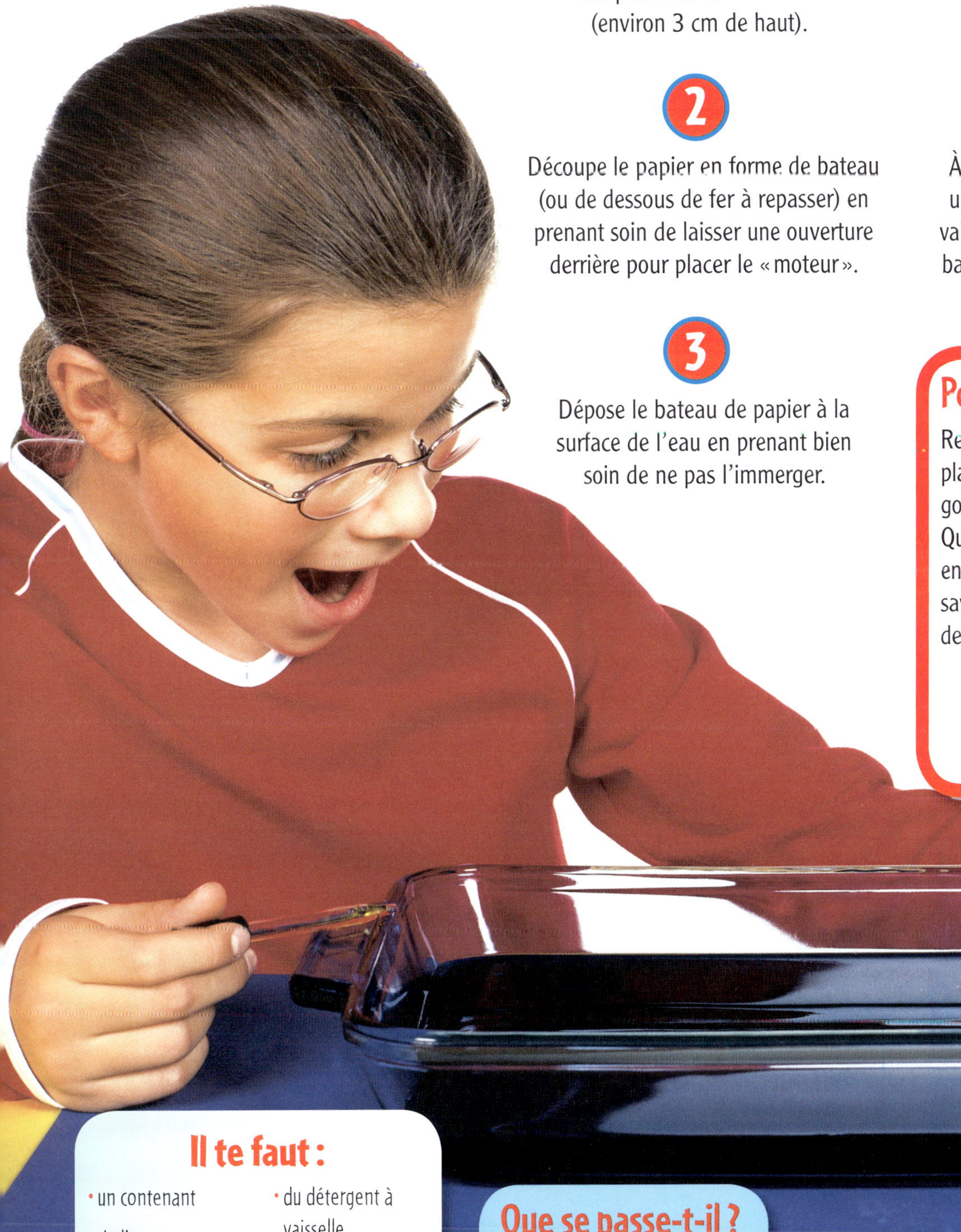

1

Remplis le contenant d'eau (environ 3 cm de haut).

2

Découpe le papier en forme de bateau (ou de dessous de fer à repasser) en prenant soin de laisser une ouverture derrière pour placer le « moteur ».

3

Dépose le bateau de papier à la surface de l'eau en prenant bien soin de ne pas l'immerger.

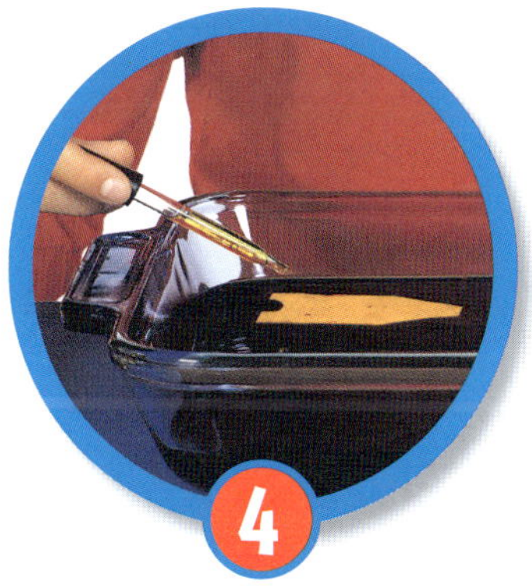

4

À l'aide d'un compte-gouttes, verse une ou deux gouttes de détergent à vaisselle dans le trou, à l'extrémité du bateau. Que se passe-t-il ? Le bateau file à toute vitesse !

Poursuis l'expérience

Refais l'expérience avec deux bateaux placés « dos à dos ». Verse quelques gouttes de savon entre les deux bateaux. Que se passe-t-il ? Chaque bateau file en sens opposé ! C'est parce que le savon se disperse dans l'eau en faisant des cercles (dispersion radiale).

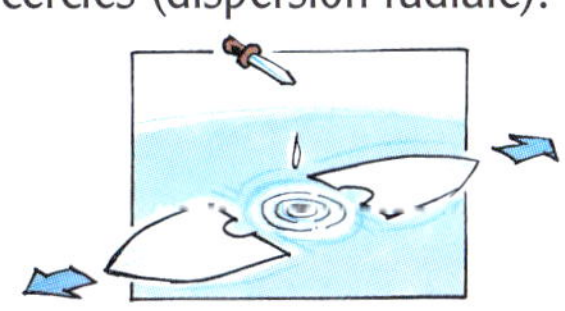

Il te faut :

- un contenant
- de l'eau
- du papier
- des ciseaux
- du détergent à vaisselle
- un compte-gouttes

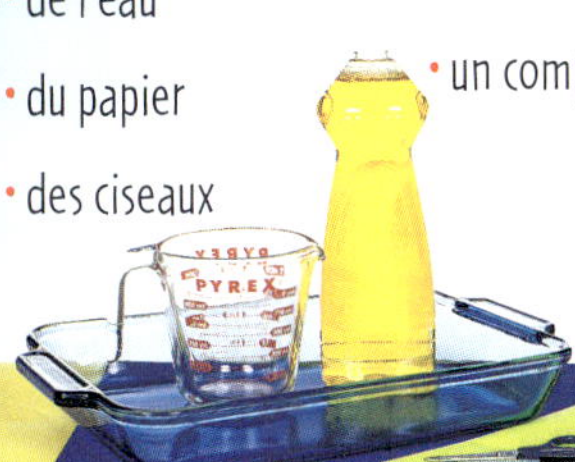

Que se passe-t-il ?

Le savon a réduit la tension superficielle de l'eau. La tension superficielle est due à l'attraction des molécules d'eau entre elles. Cette force « soude » les molécules d'eau de telle sorte qu'elles forment une fine pellicule. C'est cette pellicule qui supporte ton bateau de papier. En réduisant la tension à l'arrière du bateau, cela crée un déséquilibre. La tension à l'avant est devenue plus élevée qu'à l'arrière. Résultat : le bateau est tiré vers l'avant.

Débrouillarde : Catherine Bégin-Latour
Photos : Laurence Labat

Une banane sous pression

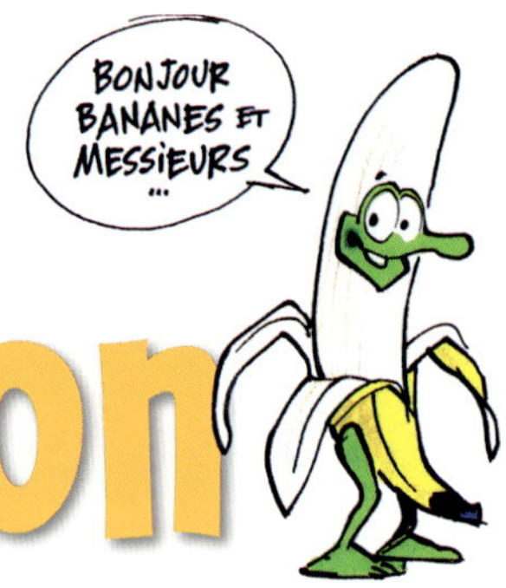

ATTENTION ! MANIPULATION D'EAU BOUILLANTE.

Peux-tu introduire une banane dans une bouteille sans la toucher ?

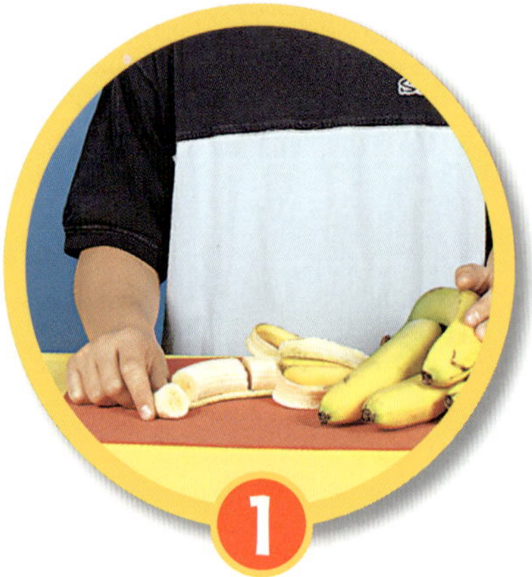

1 Coupe l'extrémité de la banane de façon à obtenir un morceau de 5 cm de long. Retire la pelure.

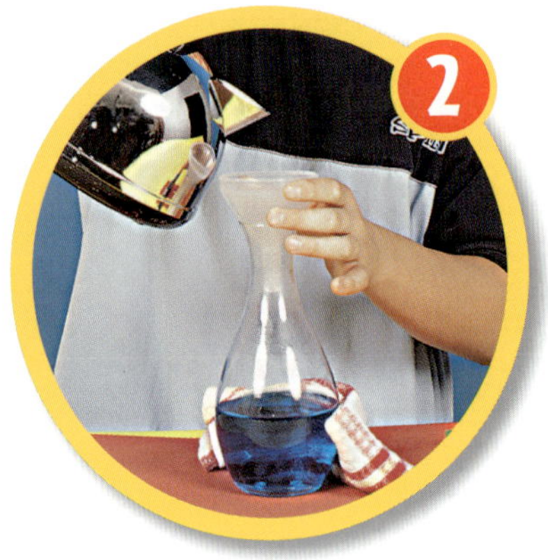

2 À l'aide de l'entonnoir, verse de l'eau bouillante jusqu'à la moitié de la bouteille. Tiens bien l'entonnoir pour ne pas te brûler.

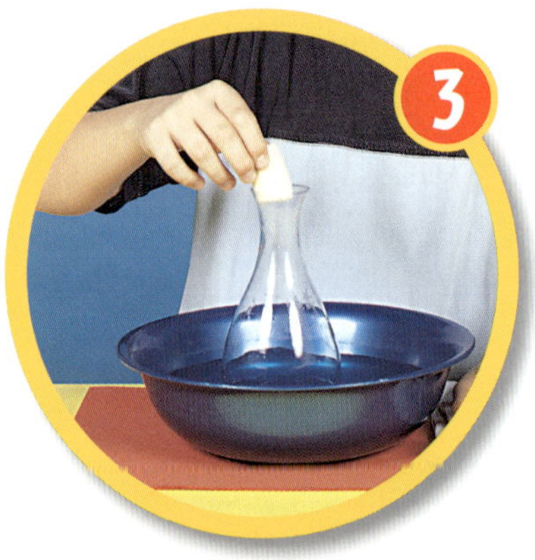

3 Dépose la bouteille dans un plat rempli d'eau chaude. Place la pointe de la banane dans le goulot de la bouteille.

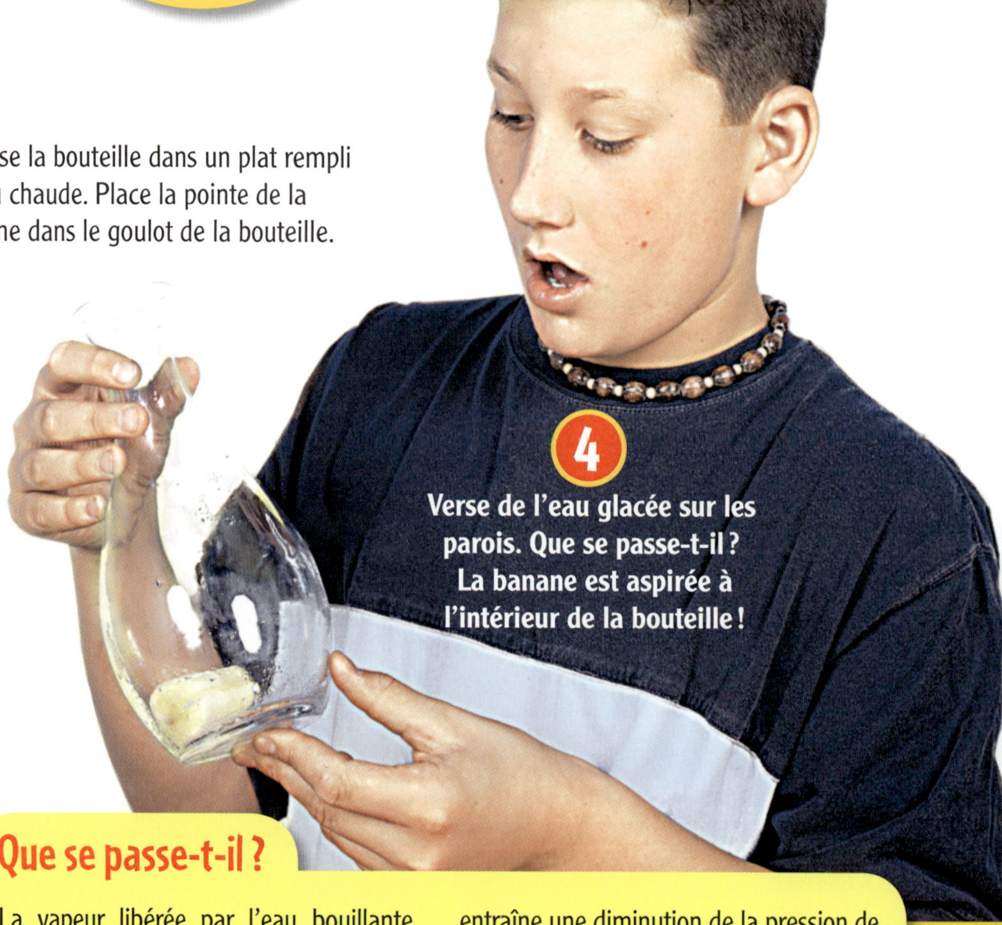

4 **Verse de l'eau glacée sur les parois. Que se passe-t-il ? La banane est aspirée à l'intérieur de la bouteille !**

Il te faut :

- une banane
- un couteau
- un entonnoir
- une bouteille en verre épais ayant un goulot d'un diamètre de 2 à 3 cm environ
- une tasse à mesurer
- un bol

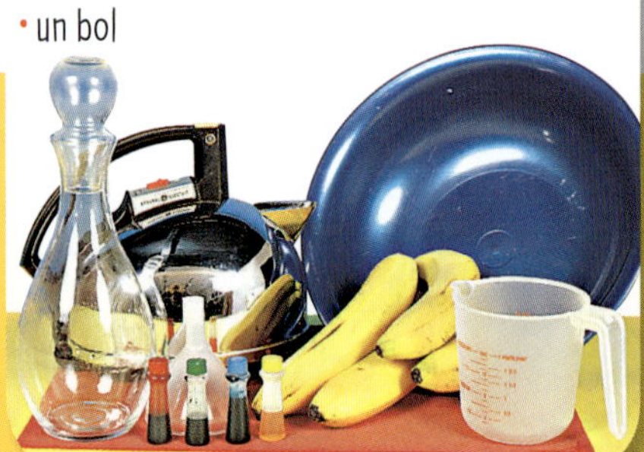

Que se passe-t-il ?

La vapeur libérée par l'eau bouillante est emprisonnée dans la bouteille par la banane. En ajoutant l'eau glacée sur les parois, la vapeur « prisonnière » se condense. Elle se transforme en gouttelettes d'eau. Or, ces gouttelettes occupent moins d'espace que la vapeur et cela entraîne une diminution de la pression de l'air dans la bouteille.

Résultat : la pression de l'air à l'extérieur de la bouteille est plus élevée que la pression à l'intérieur. C'est cette pression externe qui pousse la banane dans la bouteille.

Débrouillard : Vincent Bélanger-Dompierre Photos : Laurence Labat

Une expérience très absorbante

Voici comment de minuscules particules réussissent à absorber d'énormes quantités d'eau.

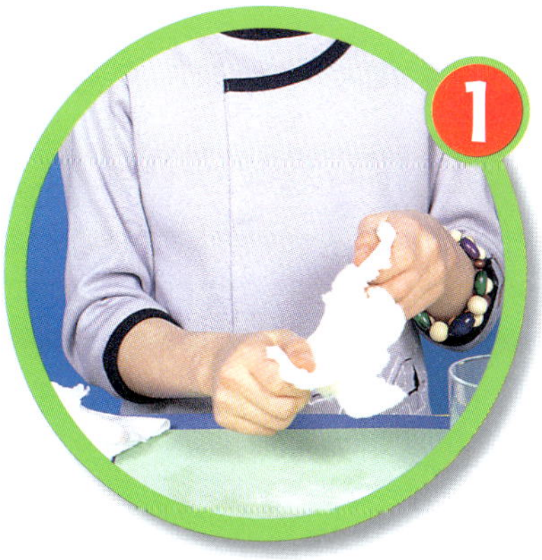

1 Découpe l'intérieur des couches à l'aide des ciseaux puis retire la bourre. Défais la bourre au-dessus d'une feuille de papier pour en recueillir la poudre. Récupère une cuillerée à thé de cette poudre et verse-la dans le verre.

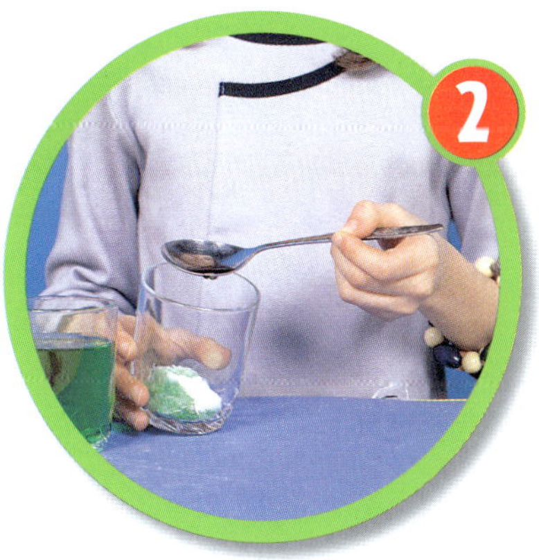

2 Verse trois cuillerées à table d'eau colorée dans le verre et brasse légèrement. Et hop ! l'eau disparaît en un clin d'œil !

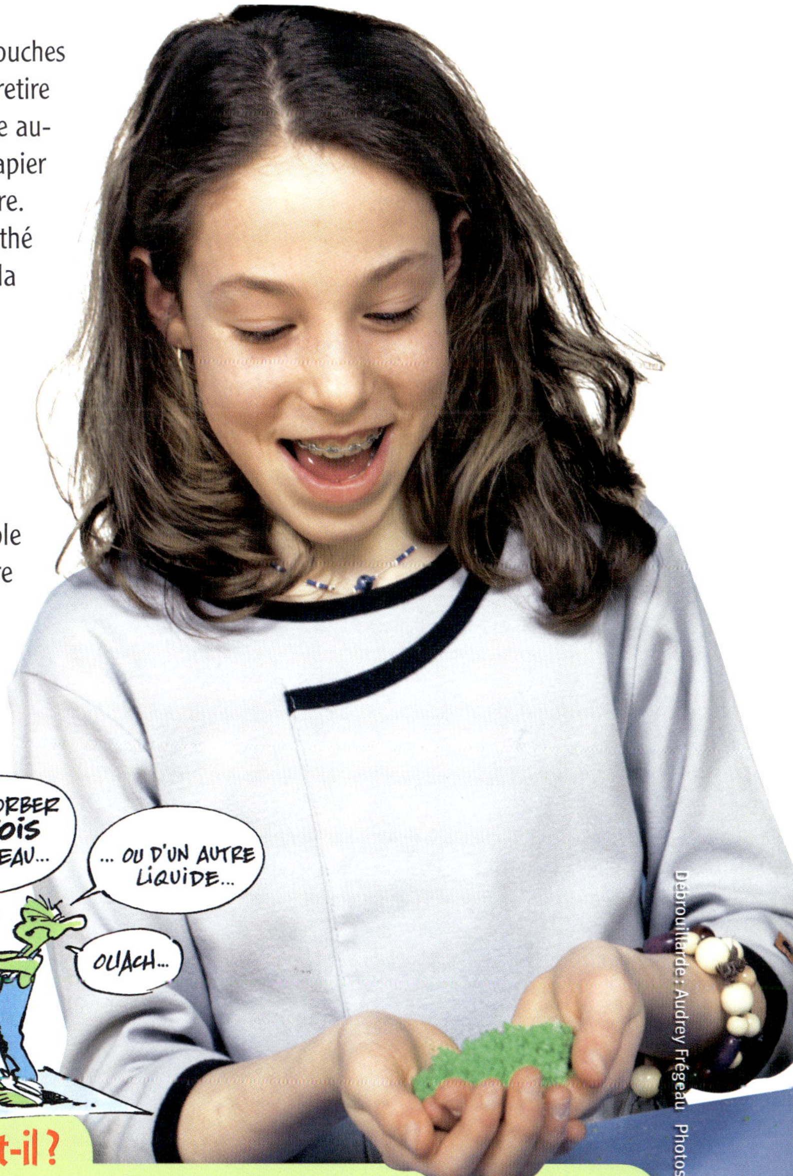

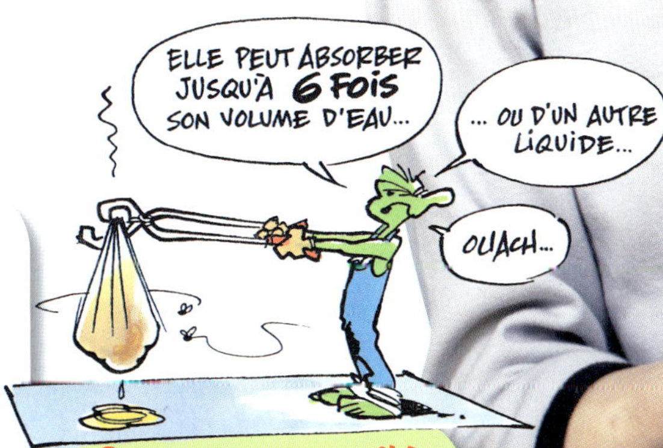

Débrouillarde : Audrey Frégeau Photos : Laurence Labat

Il te faut :

- quatre couches jetables pour bébé
- un morceau de papier
- de l'eau
- une cuillère à thé et une cuillère à table
- du colorant alimentaire
- des ciseaux
- un verre

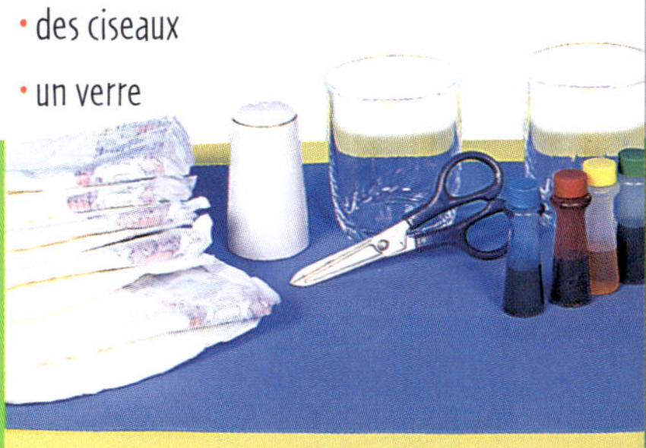

Que se passe-t-il ?

L'eau a été absorbée totalement par la poudre contenue dans les couches. Cette poudre particulière est constituée de minuscules granules d'un plastique appelé polyacrylate.

La particularité du polyacrylate est son grand pouvoir d'absorption. En effet, ce plastique peut absorber jusqu'à six fois son volume en eau !

Comme tous les plastiques, le polyacrylate est un polymère, une substance constituée de longues chaînes de molécules. Les grands espaces séparant les molécules du polyacrylate sont facilement comblés par des molécules d'eau. Voilà pourquoi les couches pour bébés sont si absorbantes !

La nuit, c'est fluo !

Pour ton party d'Halloween, une expérience qui se déroule dans le noir !

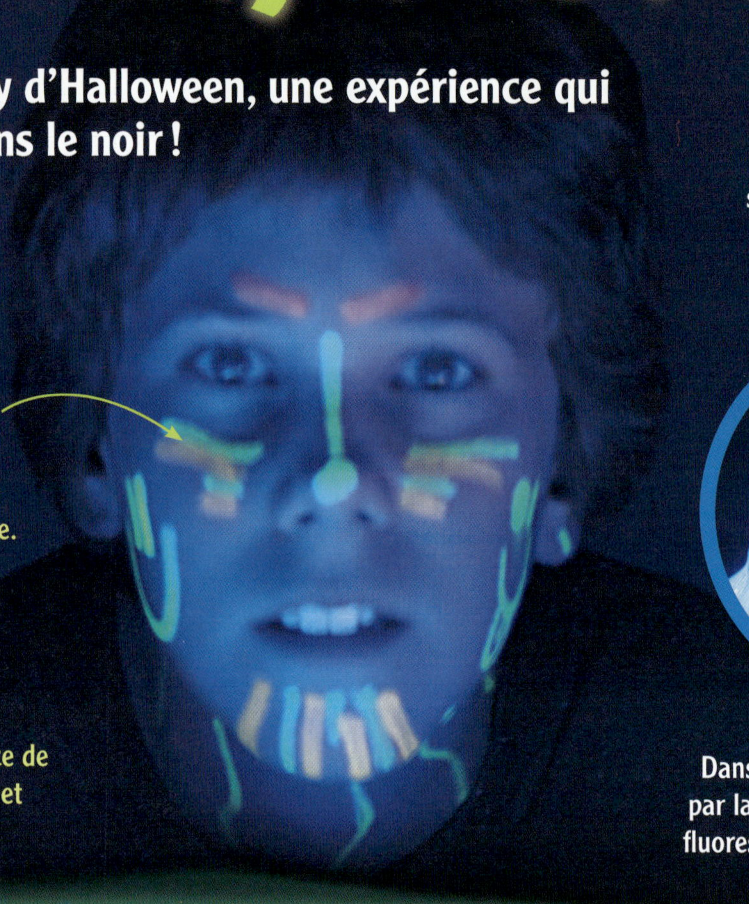

Les lignes faites avec des surligneurs fluorescents émettent une fluorescence incroyable.

Observe la fluorescence de divers papiers, roches et objets colorés.

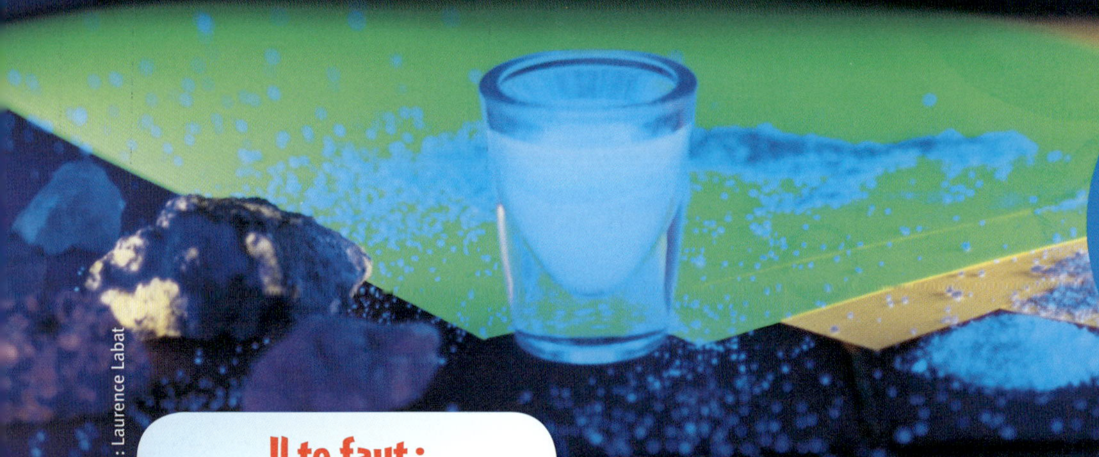

1

Verse environ 250 ml de soda tonique dans un verre de plastique transparent.

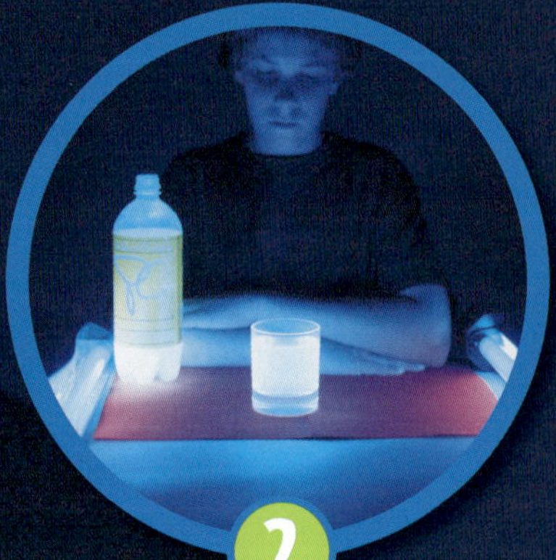

2

Dans une pièce éclairée seulement par la lumière noire, observe la forte fluorescence bleue qu'émet le liquide.

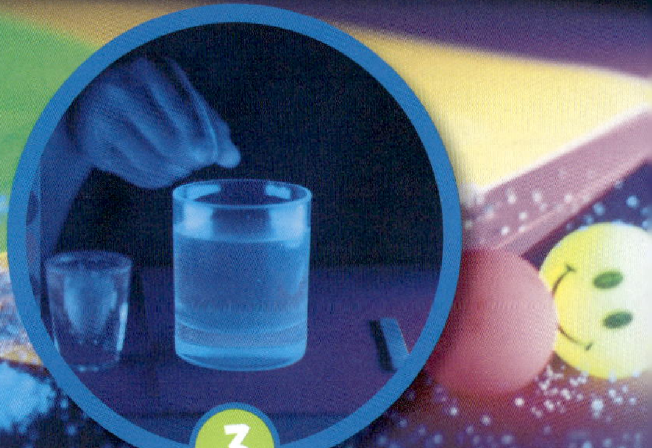

3

Ajoute du sel au soda. Que remarques-tu ? La solution est moins fluorescente.

Il te faut :

- une lumière noire (« Blacklight », de 5 $ à 15 $)
- un verre de plastique
- du soda tonique
- du sel de table

Facultatif : papier de couleur vive, crayons-feutres fluorescents, détergent à lessive, roches, t-shirt blanc...

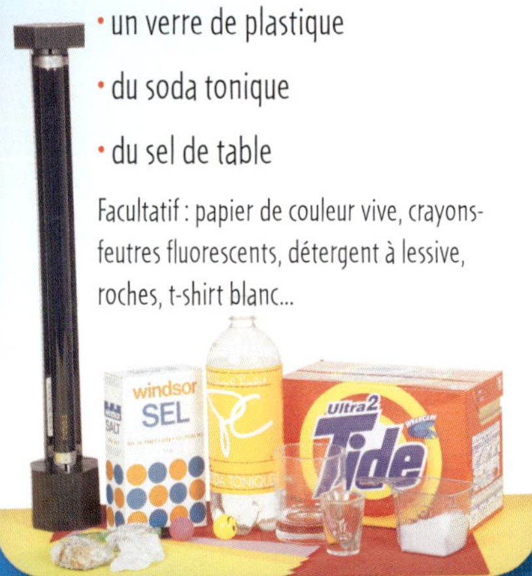

Que se passe-t-il ?

Le soda tonique est une boisson gazéifiée au goût amer. C'est à la quinine qu'il doit ce goût. Ce produit naturel provient de l'écorce d'un arbre poussant en Amérique du Sud, le quinquina.

La quinine est une molécule très fluorescente. Cela signifie qu'elle absorbe l'énergie de la lumière de ta lampe (elle devient « excitée »), puis qu'elle émet immédiatement une lumière visible plus énergétique. Voilà pourquoi une lumière bleutée apparaît.

L'ajout de sel de table (chlorure de sodium, ou NaCl) réduit la fluorescence. Cela, à cause d'une réaction chimique entre les particules de chlore et la quinine excitée. Ce phénomène est appelé « extinction de fluorescence ».

Débrouillard : Simon Lalande   Photos : Laurence Labat

Des objets biodégradables ?

RÉSULTATS AU BOUT D'UN MOIS.

Découvre les secrets de la terre en creusant… tes méninges !

1

À l'aide de la cuillère à table, creuse sept trous dans la terre du jardin* et enterres-y tous les objets.

* Ou encore, remplis de terre une boîte de carton recouverte de plastique. Attention, la terre doit provenir d'un jardin afin de renfermer des micro-organismes et d'autres animaux décomposeurs comme des vers.

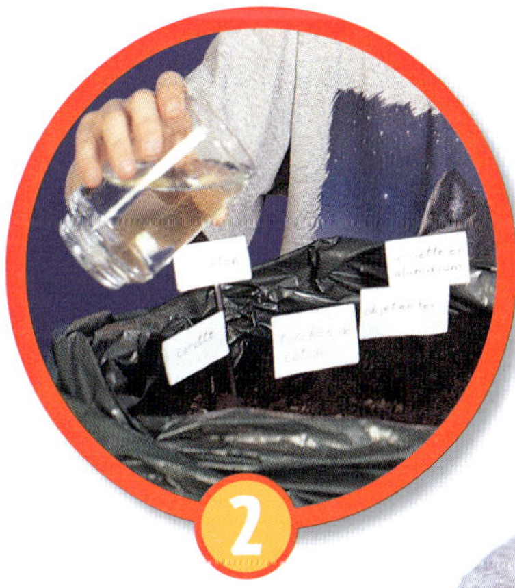

2

Plante les bâtons vis-à-vis les objets pour les identifier. Si la terre est sèche, humidifie-la.

3

Un mois plus tard, enfile des gants de caoutchouc et déterre les objets. Dans quel état sont-ils ? Certains ont-ils disparu ?

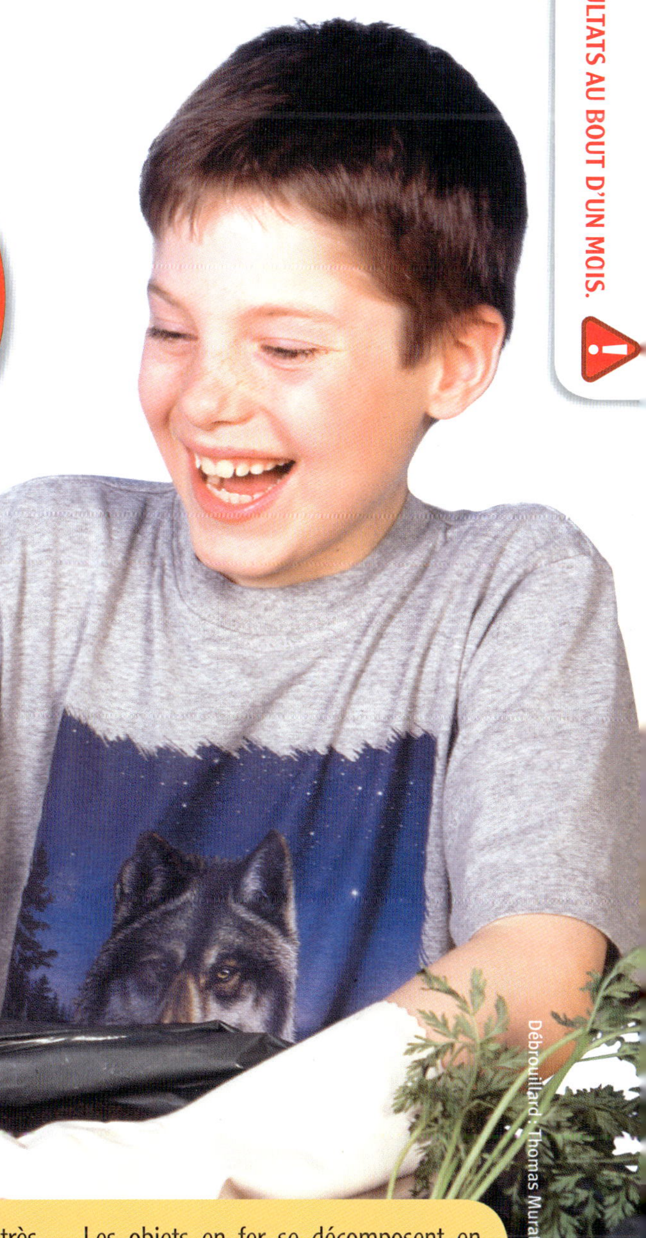

Il te faut :

- une cuillère de plastique, un morceau de pomme, un vieux torchon de coton, une carotte, un morceau de carton, un objet en fer et une assiette en aluminium
- une cuillère à table
- des gants de caoutchouc
- un vieux bac de plastique (45 X 60 cm)*
- de l'eau (facultatif)
- un arrosoir (facultatif)
- sept bâtons pour identifier tes objets (facultatif)

* Pour les photos, nous avons utilisé une boîte de carton recouverte d'un sac de plastique.

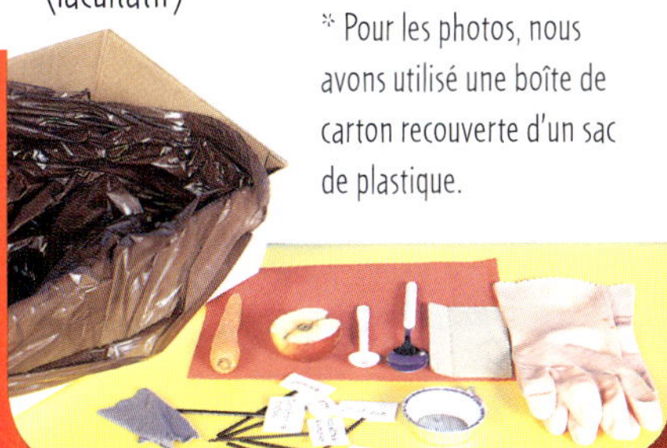

Que se passe-t-il ?

Certains objets se décomposent très vite car ils sont biodégradables. Ils sont faits de matière organique, c'est-à-dire provenant de plantes ou d'animaux. Les objets biodégradables servent de nourriture aux vers, insectes et autres micro-organismes vivant dans la terre.

Le coton, par exemple, est une fibre végétale et se décompose rapidement. On ne peut pas en dire autant du plastique ! La majorité des plastiques prennent plus de 50 ans à se décomposer dans l'environnement.

Les objets en fer se décomposent en rouillant. Le fer réagit avec l'oxygène et l'eau de l'air humide, et produit de la rouille (on dit qu'il s'oxyde).

Pourquoi la carotte ne s'est-elle pas décomposée complètement comme la pomme ? La carotte est une racine. Si on la met en terre, elle germe et une tige sort du sol. Dans le cas de la pomme, la chair se décompose et seuls les pépins germent.

Débrouillard : Thomas Muraton Photos : Laurence Labat

La miniserre à bouturage

RÉSULTATS AU BOUT DE QUELQUES JOURS.
ATTENTION ! MANIPULATION D'UN COUTEAU.

Tu veux multiplier une plante ? Rien de plus simple, avec la miniserre à bouturage… et quelques bons conseils !

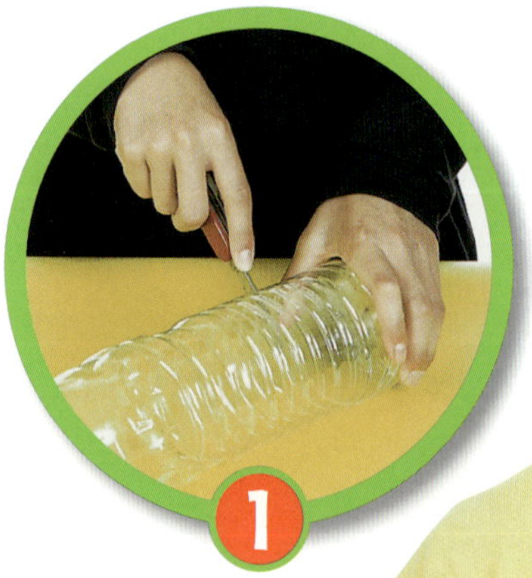

1

À l'aide du couteau, coupe la bouteille de boisson gazeuse à environ 8 cm du bas. Sois prudent !

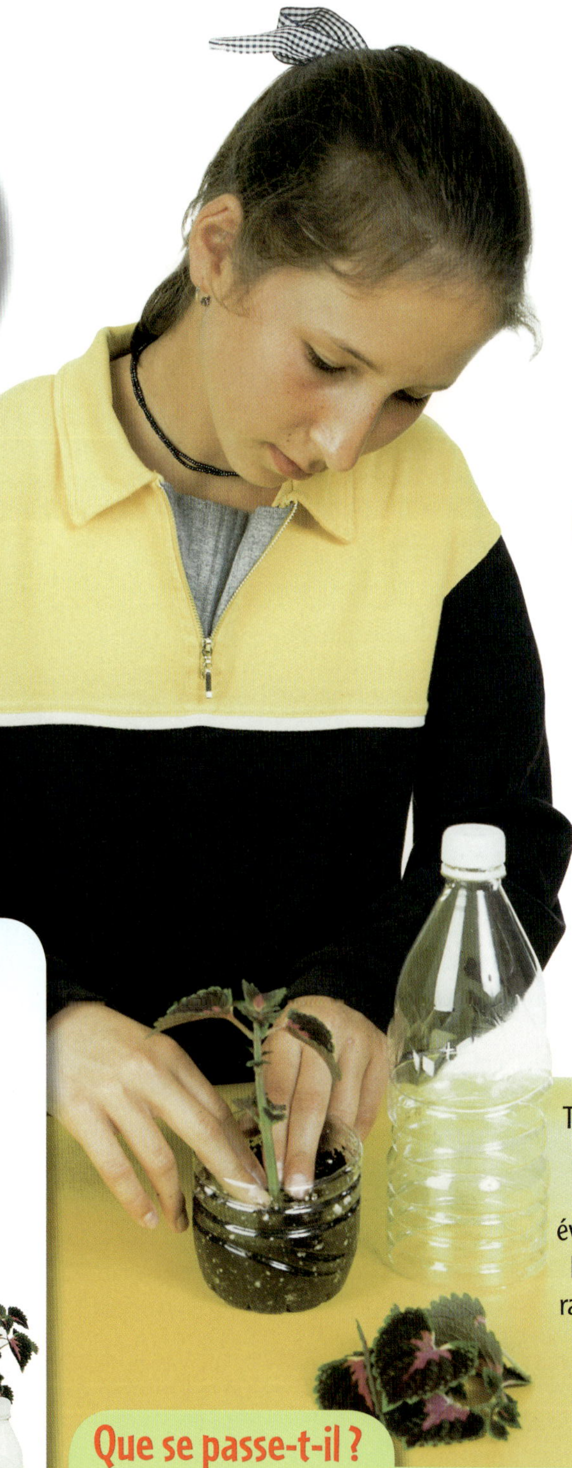

2

Remplis la base avec du terreau à enracinement. Verse ensuite un peu d'eau dans la base. N'en mets pas trop ! Le terreau doit être juste humide.

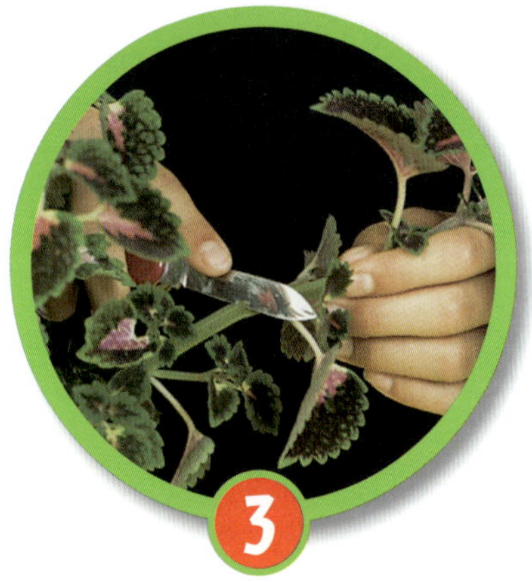

3

Choisis sur ta plante de jeunes tiges en santé et taille-les avec ton couteau. Ce sont tes boutures. Retire les feuilles de la base de tes boutures, puis enfouis-les dans le terreau humide de ta miniserre.

4

Tes boutures sont bien en place ? Insère le haut de la bouteille sur sa base. La vapeur d'eau demeurera prisonnière, évitant ainsi le dessèchement des plantes. Peu à peu, tes boutures formeront des racines. (Tu peux le vérifier en soulevant délicatement chaque bouture. S'il n'y a pas assez de racines, remets-les en place.)

Il te faut :

- une bouteille de boisson gazeuse en plastique clair (1 ou 2 litres)
- du terreau à enracinement
- un couteau tranchant
- une plante d'intérieur facile à bouturer comme un coléus, un pothos ou un piléa (plante aluminium)
- de l'eau
- de la poudre d'enracinement (facultatif)

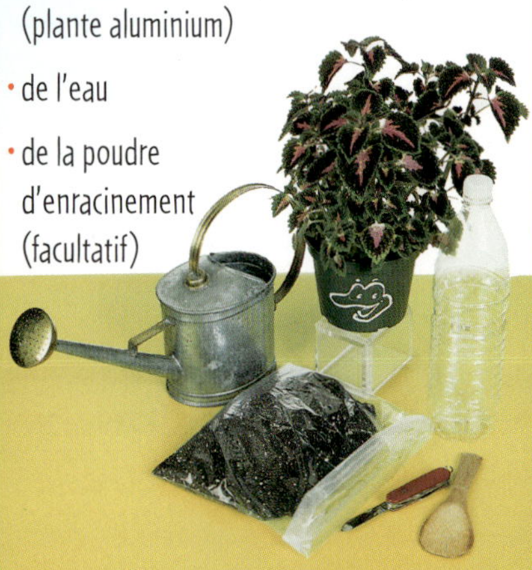

Débrouillarde : Marysol Thibault Photos : Marcel La Haye

Que se passe-t-il ?

Les graines ne sont pas toujours nécessaires à la multiplication des plantes. Certaines techniques, comme le bouturage, produisent des plantes identiques entre elles.

Pour développer des racines qui assureront leur survie, les boutures ont besoin d'eau, de lumière et d'une bonne terre. Cette miniserre permet de maintenir les boutures dans un air humide.

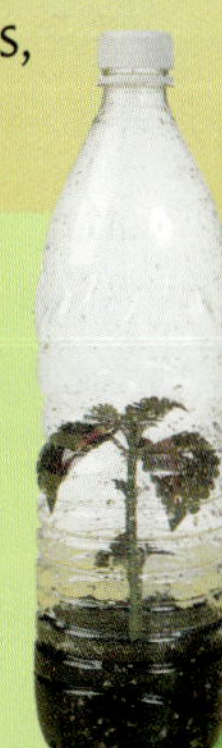

De la mayonnaise maison

Transforme la cuisine en laboratoire scientifique et découvre le secret de la mayonnaise.

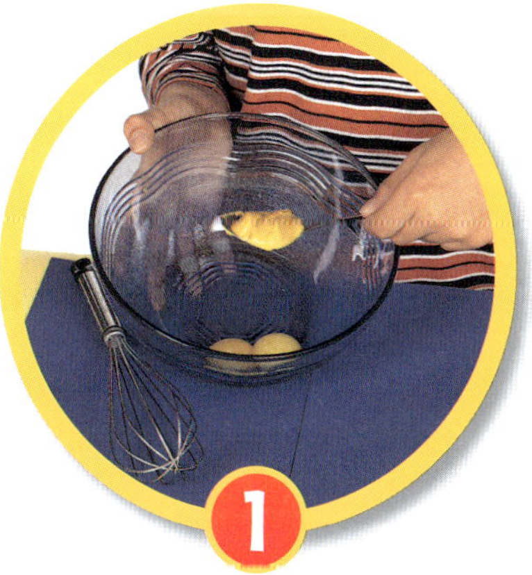

Place la moutarde et les jaunes d'œuf dans le bol, et mélange-les bien à l'aide du fouet.

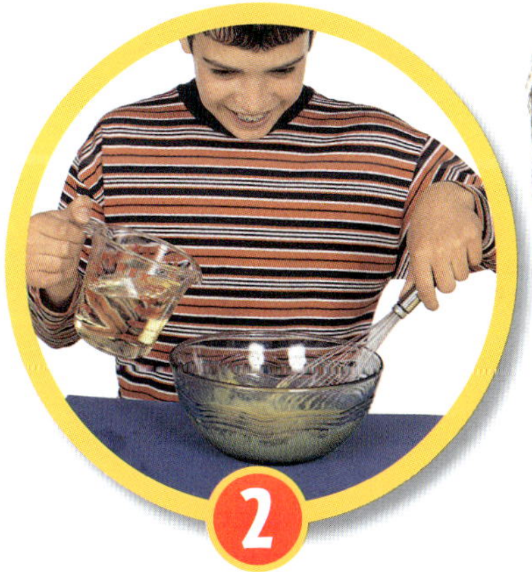

Verse le jus de citron. Continue de fouetter. Ajoute quelques gouttes d'huile. Fouette vigoureusement pour obtenir un mélange uniforme.

3

Verse le reste de l'huile TRÈS lentement, sans arrêter de fouetter. La mayonnaise épaissit au fur et à mesure.

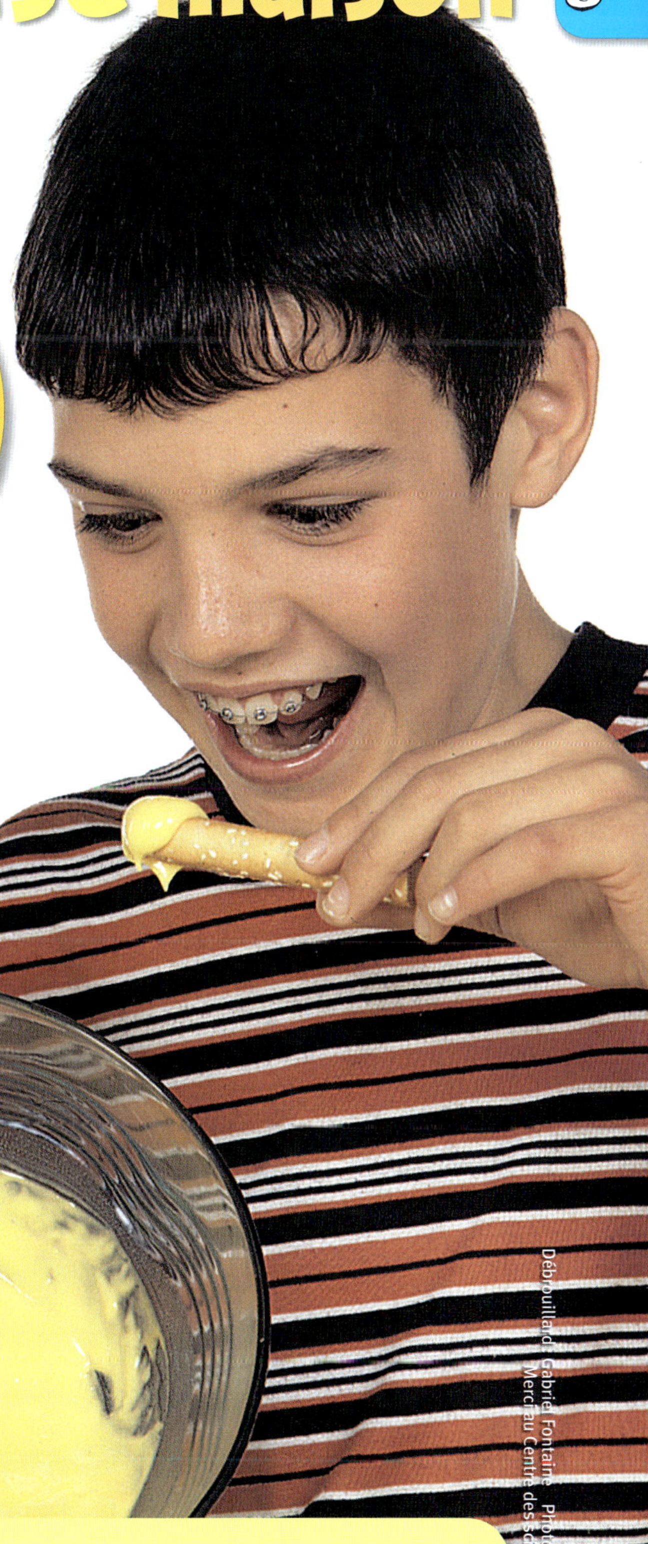

Il te faut :

- deux jaunes d'œuf (à la température de la pièce)
- une cuillerée à table de moutarde
- une cuillerée à table de jus de citron (ou de vinaigre)
- 375 ml (1 1/2 tasse) d'huile végétale
- une tasse à mesurer
- un grand bol
- un fouet

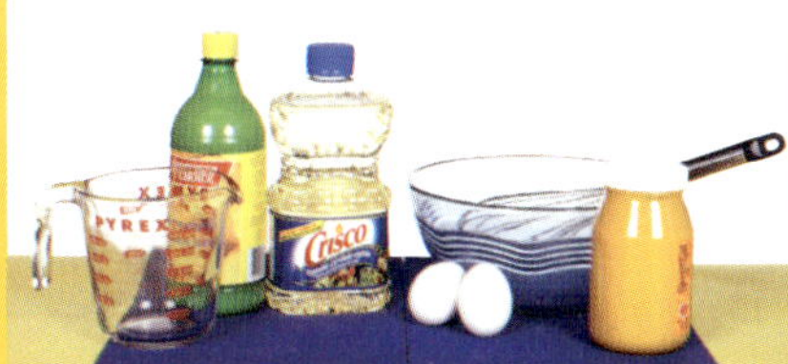

Que se passe-t-il ?

Lorsque tu fouettes le mélange, tu brises l'huile en minuscules gouttelettes et tu libères la lécithine contenue dans le jaune d'œuf. La lécithine est une matière grasse qui possède des affinités avec l'huile. À son contact, la lécithine enrobe chacune des gouttelettes et, du coup, les empêche de se réunir.

L'eau provenant de la moutarde et du jus de citron maintient les gouttelettes d'huile en suspension. Plus tu ajoutes d'huile, plus il y a de gouttelettes. Lorsqu'elles sont très nombreuses, les gouttelettes sont tassées et ont du mal à bouger. Ton mélange est ferme et homogène.

Une dispersion de gouttelettes d'huile dans l'eau est une émulsion. Ta mayonnaise est une émulsion.

Débrouillard: Gabriel Fontaine. Photos: Laurence Labat
Merci au Centre des sciences de Montréal

Brillant comme un clou neuf !

Nettoie de vieilles pièces de monnaie ternies et donne à un clou d'acier l'aspect d'un sou neuf !

RÉSULTATS AU BOUT DE DEUX HEURES.

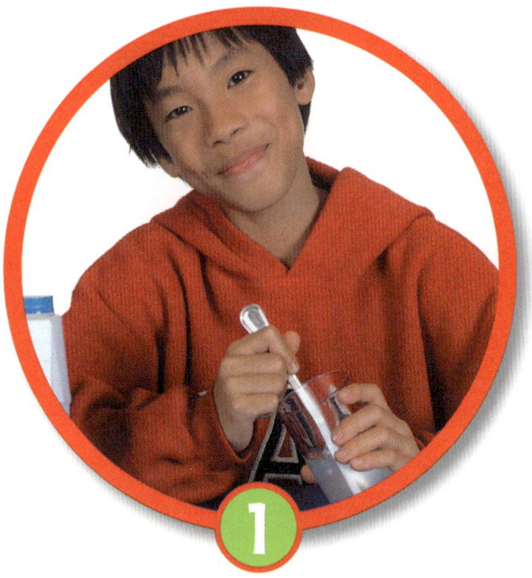

1

Dans le verre (ou le bocal), verse environ 1/2 tasse de vinaigre. Ajoutes-y une cuillerée à table de sel. Brasse avec la cuillère afin de dissoudre le sel.

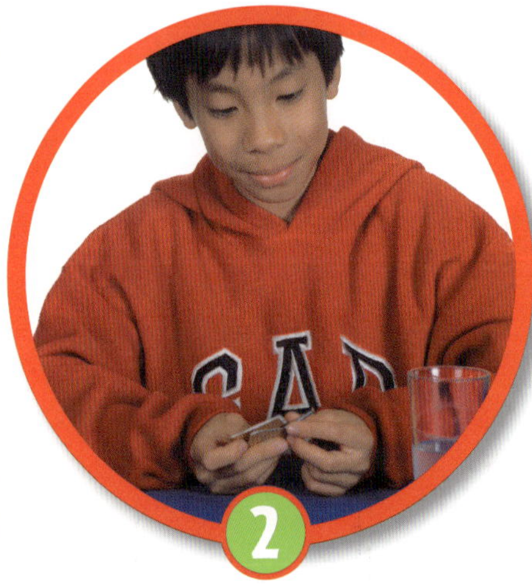

2

Frotte un clou avec le papier d'émeri ou la laine d'acier jusqu'à ce qu'il devienne brillant.

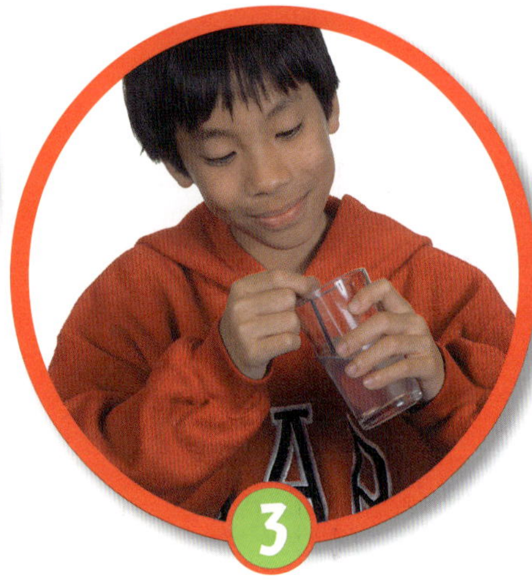

3

Dépose ce clou et les pièces d'un cent dans le verre contenant la solution de vinaigre.

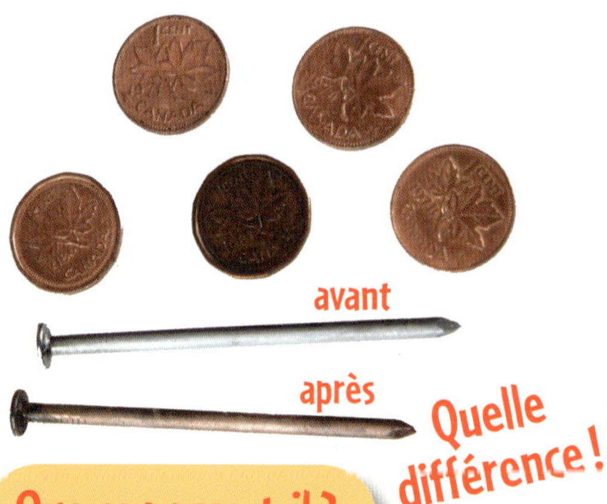

4

Au bout d'environ deux heures, retire le clou et les pièces de monnaie du verre. Compare-les avec des sous et un clou qui n'ont pas trempé dans la solution.

Il te faut :

- un verre transparent (ou un bocal)
- du vinaigre
- du sel de table
- quatre à 10 pièces d'un cent
- deux clous en acier
- du papier d'émeri ou de la laine d'acier
- une cuillère à table

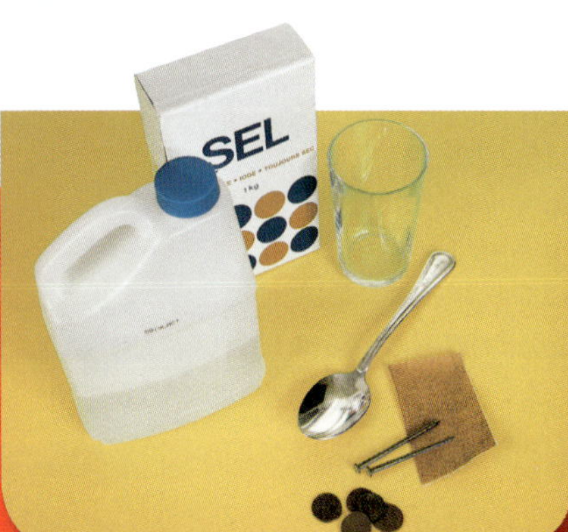

Débrouillard : Alexandre Nguyen Photos : Marcel La Haye

Que se passe-t-il ?

En mélangeant le vinaigre et le sel, il se produit une réaction chimique : le vinaigre et le sel réagissent ensemble et forment un acide, soit l'acide chlorhydrique.

Cet acide attaque les sous noirs, qui sont faits de cuivre. Des particules de cuivre (Cu) se détachent alors de la surface des pièces de monnaie.

Dans la solution de vinaigre, on trouve maintenant du cuivre sous la forme d'ions (Cu+), des particules de cuivre de charge positive.

Les ions de cuivre positifs sont attirés par le clou d'acier car celui-ci a une charge négative. Au contact du clou, ces ions se collent à l'acier, ce qui lui donne un aspect cuivré. La mince couche de cuivre qui recouvre le clou ne peut être enlevée.

Pourquoi les sous deviennent-ils propres ?

Lorsqu'elles sont neuves, les pièces d'un cent sont brillantes. Mais avec le temps, l'oxygène de l'air se combine au cuivre des pièces pour former un oxyde verdâtre, appelé vert-de-gris. En faisant tremper ces pièces usées dans une solution acide, le cuivre terni se détache. Apparaît alors le cuivre brillant qui se trouvait sous cette surface.

Expériences éclair !

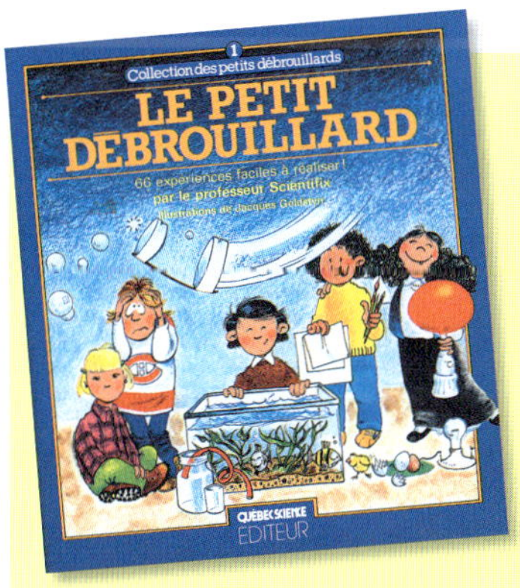

Ces sept expériences sont tirées de mon premier livre. Elles ont fait la joie de bien des Débrouillards ! Elles vont sûrement te plaire toi aussi !

Prof Scientifix

Fabrique une loupe d'urgence

Il te faut :

- un carton rigide
- une agrafeuse
- un carré de papier d'aluminium d'environ 3 x 3 cm
- un crayon à mine bien taillé
- une perforeuse à papier
- un compte-gouttes (facultatif)

Perce le carton avec la perforeuse, puis fixe le papier d'aluminium avec l'agrafeuse. Presse doucement du doigt le papier d'aluminium pour bien lui faire épouser la forme du trou dans le carton. Au centre du creux ainsi obtenu, perce le papier d'aluminium avec la pointe du crayon.

Place maintenant une goutte d'eau juste au-dessus du trou. Et voilà, ta loupe est terminée !

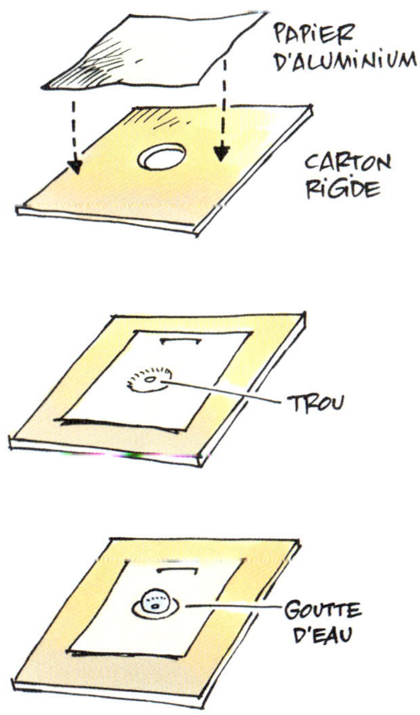

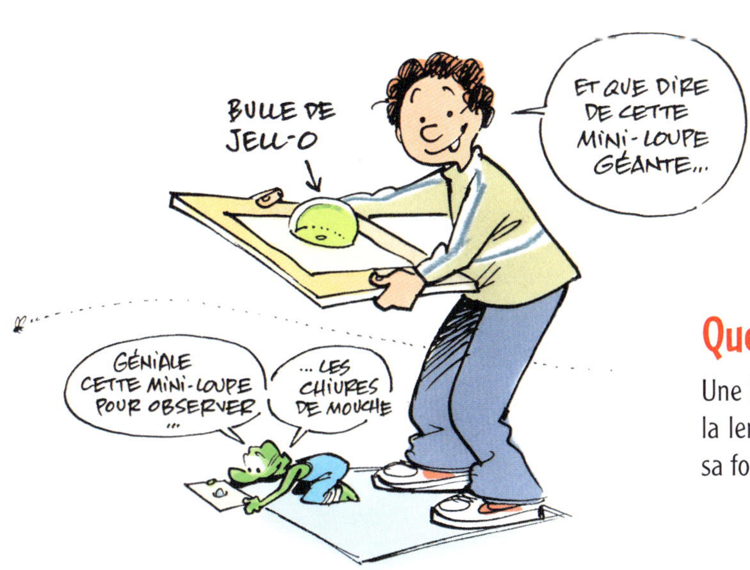

Que se passe-t-il ?

Une loupe grossit une image grâce à la forme bombée de la lentille. La goutte d'eau produit le même effet grâce à sa forme bombée.

Expériences éclair !

Tu es **vraiment fort** !

Il te faut :

- un mouchoir de papier
- une règle
- une grande feuille de papier (une page double d'un journal de petit format fera l'affaire)
- une table

Place la règle sur une table, en laissant dépasser le bout. Place la grande feuille de papier par-dessus la règle, en laissant libre le bout qui dépasse de la table. Assure-toi que le papier est bien à plat. Puis, frappe le bout libre de la règle.

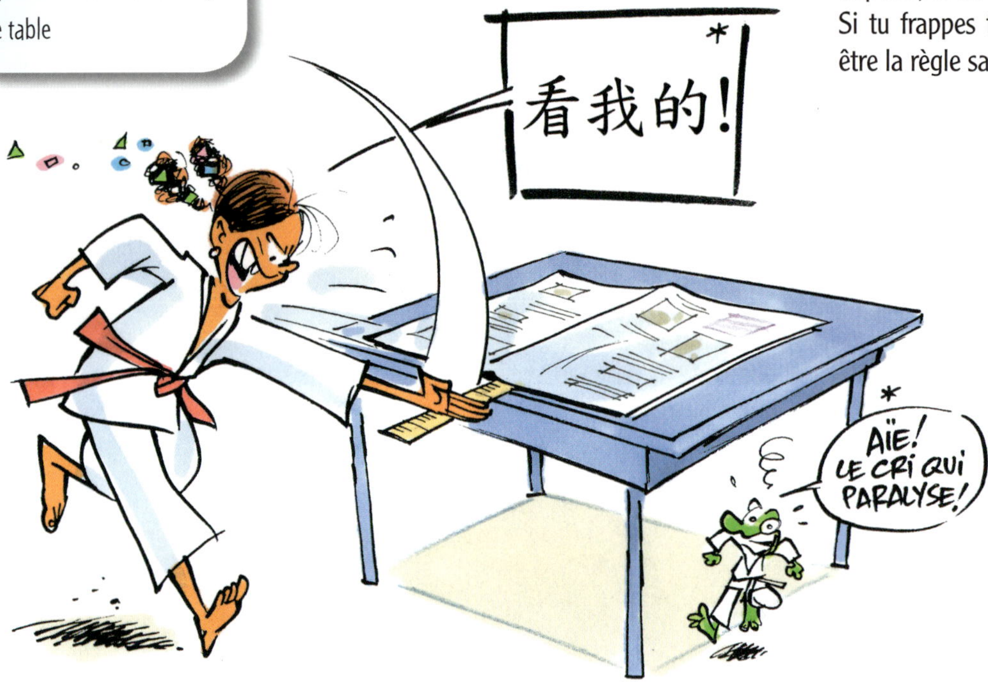

Que se passe-t-il ?

La règle ne se soulève pas car l'air se trouvant au-dessus de la table l'empêche de le faire. La pression de l'air est d'environ 103 kilopascals, soit un peu plus de 2,5 kg/cm^2. Cette pression d'air va résister à la compression soudaine que tu veux lui imposer, et va retenir ta règle sur la table. Si tu frappes très fort, tu casseras peut-être la règle sans déchirer le papier !

Un bon **verre d'air**, s.v.p.

Il te faut :

- un mouchoir de papier
- un verre
- un bol
- de l'eau

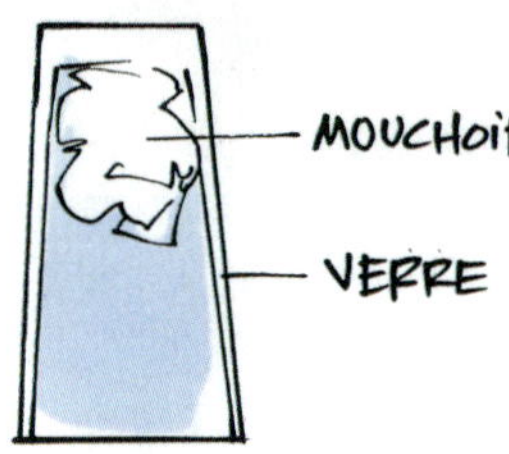

Prends un verre vide et tasse un mouchoir de papier chiffonné au fond. Assure-toi que le mouchoir reste en place quand tu retournes le verre. Remplis ensuite un bol d'eau, et plonge le verre au fond, à l'envers, en le tenant bien droit pendant une minute. Retire maintenant le verre de l'eau, en évitant de le pencher d'un côté ou de l'autre. Surprise ! le papier est parfaitement sec !

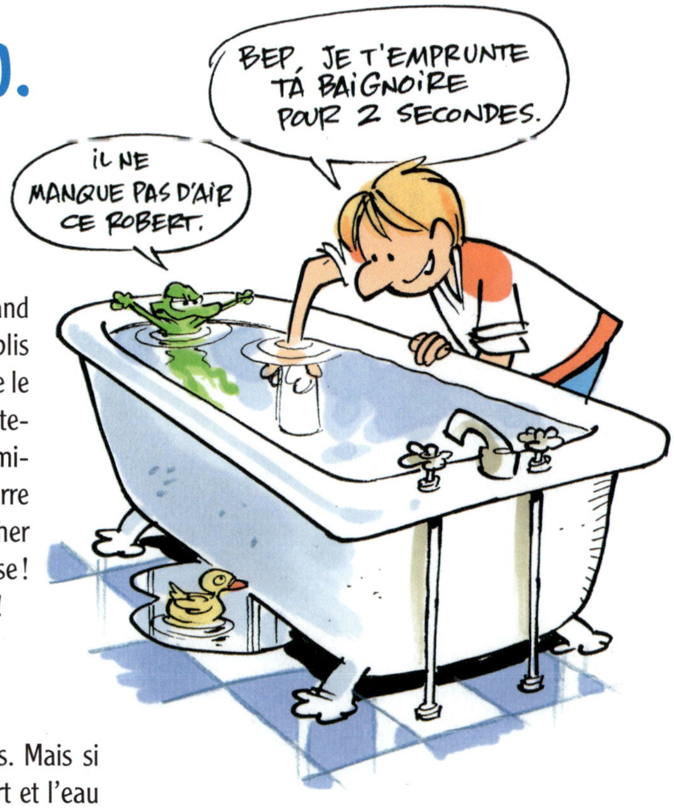

Que se passe-t-il ?

L'eau n'a pas pu pénétrer dans le verre car il était déjà rempli d'air. Puisque l'air est plus léger que l'eau, il n'a pas pu s'échapper par en dessous. Mais si on incline le verre, l'air en sort et l'eau prend la place laissée vide.

Deux yeux valent mieux qu'un

Il te faut :

- une pièce de monnaie
- une tasse ou un verre
- une table
- un ami

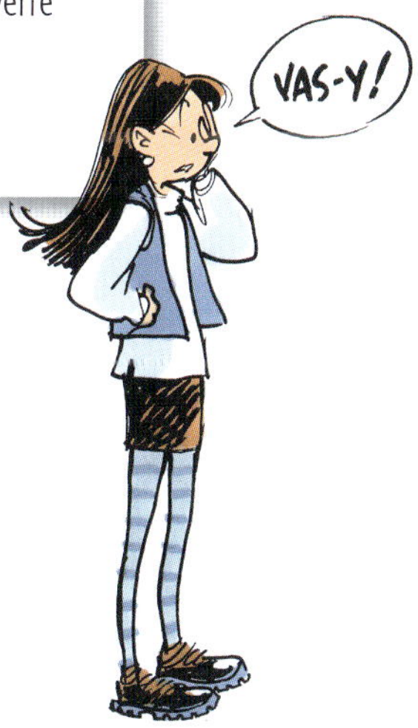

Dépose la tasse sur la table et place-toi à environ trois mètres de celle-ci. Ferme un œil, et demande à ton copain de tenir la pièce de monnaie à bout de bras non loin de la table. Tout en ne regardant que la tasse et la pièce de monnaie, dis à ton ami où diriger son bras pour que la pièce tombe dans la tasse. Une fois qu'il aura laissé tomber la pièce, regarde à quelle distance de la tasse elle se trouve. Tu n'as pas bien évalué la distance ?

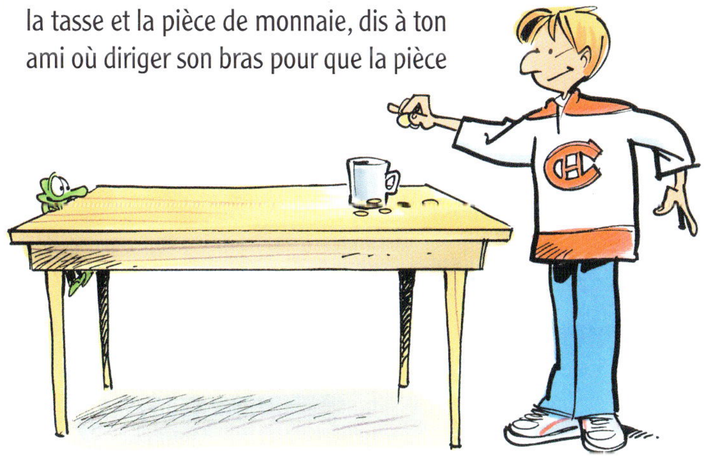

Que se passe-t-il ?

Tes deux yeux étant distants l'un de l'autre, les images que transmet chaque œil à ton cerveau diffèrent légèrement. En comparant les images, ton cerveau reconstitue une image tridimensionnelle t'aidant à évaluer les distances. C'est ce qu'on appelle la vision stéréoscopique. Celle-ci disparaît lorsque tu fermes un œil ; tu obtiens alors une vue à deux dimensions comme sur une photo, rendant ainsi l'évaluation des distances beaucoup plus difficile.

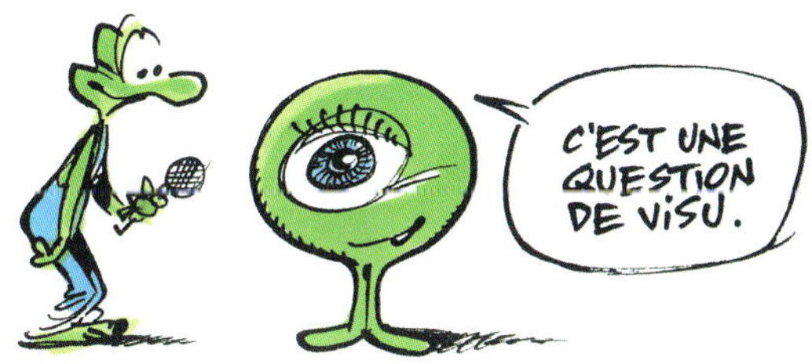

Cette expérience n'est pas sans gravité

Il te faut :

- un marteau
- une règle
- un bout de ficelle
- une table

Après avoir relié les deux extrémités de la ficelle, glisse la règle et le manche du marteau à l'intérieur de la boucle, puis installe le tout comme l'indique l'illustration. Attention : ne place que la tête du marteau sous la table. Seul le bout de la règle repose sur le bord de la table, et l'équilibre est obtenu !

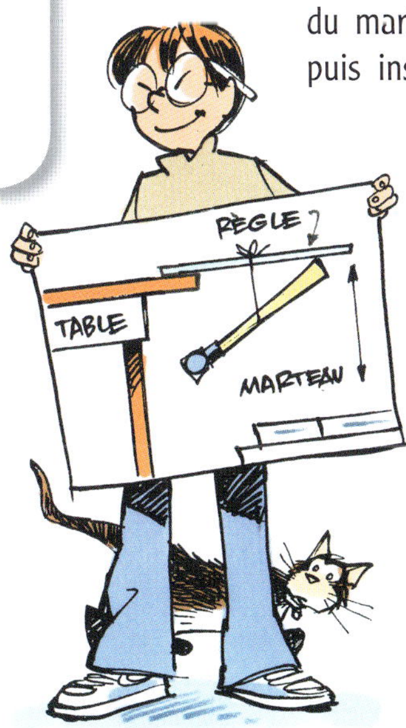

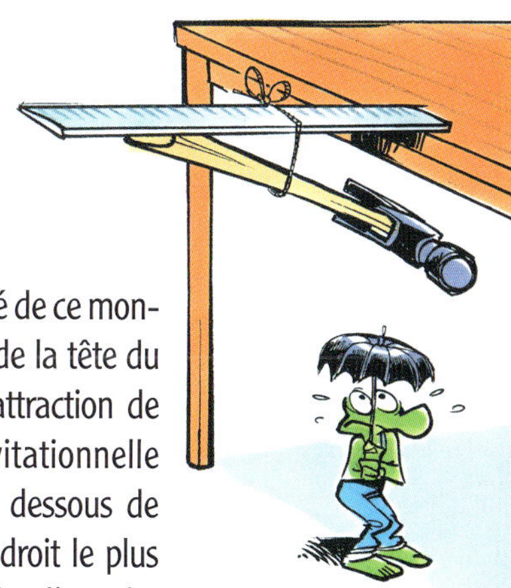

Que se passe-t-il ?

Lorsque tu tiens une règle en équilibre sur le bout d'un doigt, celui-ci se trouve au centre de gravité de la règle. Le centre de gravité d'un objet est un point imaginaire où semble ramassé tout son poids. Le centre de gravité de ce montage se situe près de la tête du marteau. Donc, l'attraction de la force de gravitationnelle vient surtout d'en dessous de la table, sous l'endroit le plus lourd, et non du point d'attache entre le marteau et la règle.

Expériences éclair !

Comment faire une butte d'eau

Il te faut :

- un verre
- de l'eau
- quelques pièces de monnaie
- du colorant alimentaire (facultatif)

Verse de l'eau dans le verre et, si tu le désires, ajoutes-y quelques gouttes de colorant pour mieux voir. Remplis le verre jusqu'au bord puis fais glisser doucement les pièces de monnaie dans l'eau, le long du verre.

Si tu te penches de manière à ce que tes yeux soient vis-à-vis la surface de l'eau, tu verras que celle-ci dépasse le bord du verre, formant ainsi une petite butte (ménisque). Combien penses-tu pouvoir ajouter de sous avant que le verre déborde ?

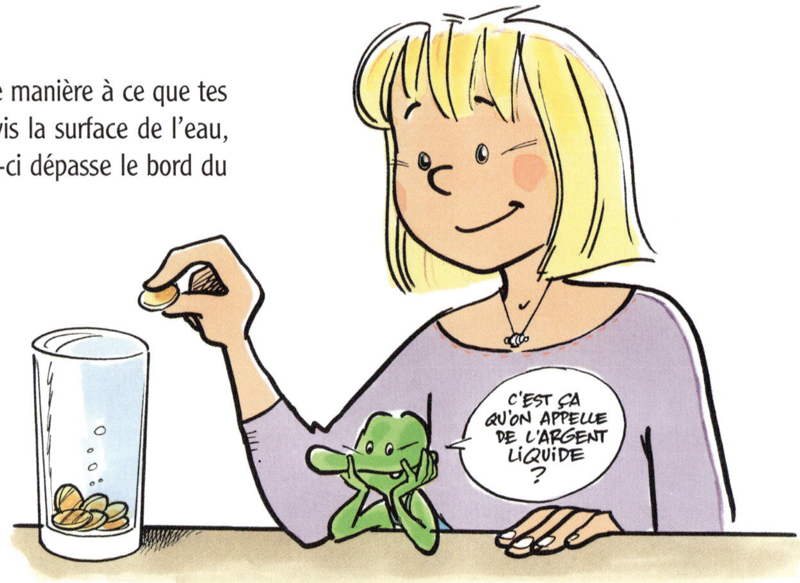

Que se passe-t-il ?

Les molécules d'eau exercent une forte attraction entre elles. Toutefois, à la surface, les molécules non recouvertes d'eau sont fortement attirées par celles qui se trouvent en dessous. C'est la tension superficielle. Cette force est suffisamment forte pour empêcher qu'un verre plein à ras bord, et même davantage, ne déborde… jusqu'à un certain point !

À 500 km de profondeur

Il te faut :

- deux bandes de papier

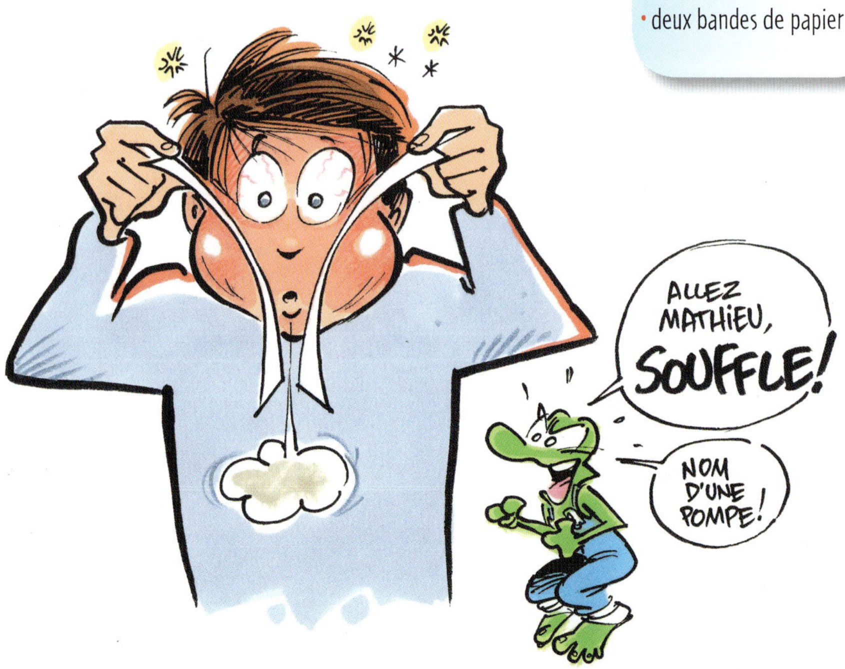

Prends une bande de papier dans chaque main et tiens-les par le bout, à quelques centimètres l'une de l'autre. Souffle de façon continue entre les bandes de papier. S'éloignent-elles l'une de l'autre ? Non, elles se rapprochent !

Que se passe-t-il ?

Nous vivons au fond d'une couche d'air de 500 km d'épaisseur. Tout cet air exerce une pression sur nous et sur ce qui nous entoure. Ici, le déplacement d'air entre les deux bandes de papier entraîne une diminution de la pression de l'air à cet endroit. La pression à l'extérieur des bandes étant plus élevée, celles-ci se rapprochent au lieu de s'éloigner.

Laboratoire du professeur Scientifix

RAPPORT D'EXPÉRIENCE

Nom du Débrouillard ou de la Débrouillarde : Etienne Champagne-Martin

Assistant ou assistante : Johanne Champagne

Lieu et date de réalisation : Montréal, le 7 janvier 2006

Titre de l'expérience : Des objets électrisants

Commentaires sur le déroulement de l'expérience : Au début, aucun grain de poivre n'est venu se coller à la cuillère. Nous avons recommencé avec une autre cuillère de plastique, sans succès. Nous avons ensuite eu l'idée d'utiliser du poivre noir du commerce au lieu du poivre frais moulu. Les grains fins, beaucoup moins lourds, sont venus se coller à la cuillère !

Autres sources d'information sur le sujet (sites Internet, livres, etc.) : Sur Internet, Musée EDF Électricité, dans la section Ben et l'électricité statique www.electropolis.tm.fr/frelectro.html

Etienne Champagne-Martin

(signature du Débrouillard ou de la Débrouillarde)

Commentaires de l'assistant(e) ou des spectateurs : C'est impressionnant de voir les grains de poivre se soulever jusqu'à la cuillère ! Je ne savais pas que l'électricité statique était si puissante !

Laboratoire du professeur Scientifix

RAPPORT D'EXPÉRIENCE

Nom du Débrouillard ou de la Débrouillarde :

Assistant ou assistante :

Lieu et date de réalisation :

Titre de l'expérience :

Commentaires sur le déroulement de l'expérience :

Autres sources d'information sur le sujet (sites Internet, livres, etc.) :

(signature du Débrouillard ou de la Débrouillarde)

Commentaires de l'assistant(e) ou des spectateurs :

Index